The Novel

Praise for *The Novel*

"As a compendious introduction both to the reading of novels themselves and to criticism of the novel as a narrative form, Christoph Bode's book serves a purpose not readily met by other studies, and it will appeal to undergraduates, graduate students, and their instructors alike. Appealingly wide-ranging in his choice of illustrative texts, Bode offers us tools for understanding how the narrative techniques of novels affect their content. While the book's topical arrangement facilitates selective reading, its lively and accessible style, nicely preserved in this translation, amply rewards sequential reading."

Nicholas Halmi,
University College Oxford

The Novel
An Introduction

by Christoph Bode

Translated by James Vigus

(W)WILEY-BLACKWELL

A John Wiley & Sons, Ltd., Publication

This edition first published in English 2011
English translation © 2011 James Vigus
Original German text © 2005 Narr Francke Attempto Verlag GmbH + Co. KG.

Blackwell Publishing was acquired by John Wiley & Sons in February 2007. Blackwell's publishing program has been merged with Wiley's global Scientific, Technical, and Medical business to form Wiley-Blackwell.

Registered Office
John Wiley & Sons Ltd, The Atrium, Southern Gate, Chichester, West Sussex, PO19 8SQ, United Kingdom

Editorial Offices
350 Main Street, Malden, MA 02148-5020, USA
9600 Garsington Road, Oxford, OX4 2DQ, UK
The Atrium, Southern Gate, Chichester, West Sussex, PO19 8SQ, UK

For details of our global editorial offices, for customer services, and for information about how to apply for permission to reuse the copyright material in this book please see our website at www.wiley.com/wiley-blackwell.

The right of Christoph Bode to be identified as the author of this work has been asserted in accordance with the UK Copyright, Designs and Patents Act 1988.

Wiley also publishes its books in a variety of electronic formats. Some content that appears in print may not be available in electronic books.

Designations used by companies to distinguish their products are often claimed as trademarks. All brand names and product names used in this book are trade names, service marks, trademarks or registered trademarks of their respective owners. The publisher is not associated with any product or vendor mentioned in this book. This publication is designed to provide accurate and authoritative information in regard to the subject matter covered. It is sold on the understanding that the publisher is not engaged in rendering professional services. If professional advice or other expert assistance is required, the services of a competent professional should be sought.

Library of Congress Cataloging-in-Publication Data

Bode, Christoph, 1952–
    [Roman. English]
    The novel: an introduction/Christoph Bode; translated [from the German] by James Vigus.
        p.   cm.
    Includes bibliographical references and index.
    ISBN 978-1-4051-9448-8 (hardcover: alk. paper)—ISBN 978-1-4051-9447-1 (pbk.: alk. paper)
    1. Fiction—History and criticism—Theory, etc.   2. Narration (Rhetoric)   I. Vigus, James, 1978–   II. Title.
    PN3331.B64 2011
    809.3—dc22
                                                            2010034987

A catalogue record for this book is available from the British Library.

This book is published in the following electronic formats: ePDFs 978-1-4443-9359-0; Wiley Online Library 978-1-4443-9361-3; ePub 978-1-4443-9360-6

Set in 10/12pt Sabon by SPi Publisher Services, Pondicherry, India.
Printed in Malaysia by Ho Printing (M) Sdn Bhd

1   2011

Contents

Preface

This volume is intended as a general introduction to the critical analysis of novels. One of its main aims is to help the reader to see that an analytical approach to the novel is not an end in itself, but can crucially deepen our understanding of the text and greatly intensify our reading experience.

True, the claim is frequently made that every good literary text can only gain from thorough analysis – yet it seems to me that this is nevertheless experienced all too rarely. And that might have something to do with the fact that readers too seldom grasp the *purpose* of identifying this or that narrative technique. Students perform such analysis because it is required for seminar presentations, essays, and exams: what it's actually good for all too often remains obscure. So they just go through the motions – disposing of it as a matter of form, because it is required. But where the *meaning* of a procedure is not grasped, any new acquisition of knowledge or flash of insight can only occur by accident. So students run into a vicious circle, not knowing why they're doing what they're doing, and for that very reason unlikely ever to find out why.

This book aims to provide a remedy to this problem, in that it constantly foregrounds the consequences that follow when, in a particular novel, this rather than that narrative situation dominates; when the narrative is compressed here but stretched out there; when the traits of one fictional character are brought out using one technique, others differently, and so on. As with so many other kinds of investigation, the guiding question and the alpha and omega of critical analysis is perhaps: *what's the difference?* Or, to put the question more precisely: what *would be* the difference if the narrative structure of this novel were like *that* rather than like *this*? In what way would such a modification effect a change to the other parameters of "the same" text, which would then of course no longer remain "the same" text? To which other position would such a different text ascribe its reader? And what can we therefore say about the novel as it actually lies before us? What is its characteristic feature, what difference does it make and what difference does it realize in the field of possibilities constituted by the whole range of everything that can be said and told?

Seen in this way, we clearly cannot talk at all about the sense and meaning(s) of a novel, or even about its subject – the "what" – without first having talked in detail and repeatedly about the "how," by means of which alone we can achieve an understanding of the "what." "By all means place the 'how' above the 'what',"[1] was the advice of Vladimir Nabokov, one of the most brilliant novelists of the twentieth century, to an imagined "budding literary critic." The present volume radicalizes Nabokov's advice still further and attempts to show repeatedly, on the most diverse levels of analysis and in all conceivable dimensions of fictional texts, that any discussion of the "content" of a novel that disregards how it is actually mediated via narrative techniques is actually meaningless and misses the point. For in a novel, just as in lyric poetry, the "what" *is* nothing other than the "how": the one is not to be had without the other, because they are inextricably involved with each other. In the words of Mario Vargas Llosa:

> In and of itself, no literary theme is good or bad. Any themes can be either, and the verdict depends not on the theme itself but rather on what it becomes when the application of form – narrative style and structure – makes it a novel. [...] the themes of a novel themselves promise nothing, because they'll be judged good or bad, appealing or dull solely in view of what the novelist does to turn them into a reality of words ranged in a certain order. [...] But before we set sail on waters so alluring for those who, like you and me, love and practice the narrative craft, it's worth establishing what you already know very well, though it is not so clear to most readers of novels: the separation of form and content (or theme and style and narrative structure) is artificial, admissible only when we are explaining or analyzing them; it never occurs in reality, since the story a novel tells is inseparable from the way it is told.[2]

Once this is recognized, the question of what the critical analysis of a novel is good for is no longer obscure. It enables us to talk meaningfully about a literary text *as a literary text*, instead of expatiating about the "content" of its action and the traits of its characters as if we were recounting gossip or taking part in a quiz show. Which musical instrument does Oskar Matzerath play? Which animal drives a car in *The Wind in the Willows*? What color is the whale in *Moby-Dick*? Inappropriate questions, and therefore absurd? Yes, of course. For the most that such questions can discover is whether someone has glanced through a summary of the particular novel in an

---

[1]   Vladimir Nabokov, *Strong Opinions*, London, 1974, 66.
[2]   Mario Vargas Llosa, *Letters to a Young Novelist*, trans. Natasha Wimmer, New York, 2002, 23, 25–26.

encyclopedia. Early in 2005 Oxford University Press published a book by the well-known professor and literary critic John Sutherland, entitled *So You Think You Know Jane Austen*? It contains questions such as: what color are Emma Woodhouse's eyes? What does John Knightley do for a living? The answers are: blue; solicitor. This information is not necessarily to be found in every textbook, but it's no less absurd than the question about the color of the whale, because it suggests that novels are *about this kind of thing*.

Against such a view, the present introduction is written in the conviction that the reading of novels is more than that. I maintain optimistically that gaining and describing insights can be pleasurable – for the teacher as well as the student, the writer as well as the reader; that we learn much more easily if we understand the purpose; that a comprehensible series of thoughts leaves a deeper impression than swotted jargon and buzzwords; finally, that everyone who is reading these lines wants to know something. And taken together, these are perhaps not totally outlandish claims.

This volume doesn't claim to be more than a general, accessible introduction. If it does seem to offer something more – so much the better. It's not intended as in any sense a substitute for the fundamental critical works listed in the annotated further reading. Nor does it make an independent contribution to the highly interesting discussions in narratology which have occupied – not to say characterized – critics and scholars of the modern literatures for the past three decades. True to its purpose as an introduction, this book largely forgoes any originality in the matter. I hope, though, to have left my signature clearly in the manner of presentation and train of thought, and that is where the book's *raison d'être* lies: we don't need another impersonal introduction to the novel or to narratology. If I have not always restrained myself from giving my own opinion on certain critical controversies or terminological quarrels, this is only because I happen to have such opinions and did not know where else to put them. But I am not a narratologist in the strict sense of the word, and my only pretension as a guide is that I have made myself familiar with this field. But I am far from having tilled in it. The relationship between narrative theory and the theory of the novel is not, of course, a symmetrical one; nor should we say that the theory of the novel is completely absorbed in narratology as a part within a whole. Narratology is concerned with the traditional literary narrative genres – epic, the novel, the novella, the short story – and also with older, often oral, forms of narrative, such as myth and legend, fairy tale and report, anecdote and joke; but increasingly, too, with narrative in film and television, in video-clips and cartoons, in the fine arts, in historiography and academic discourse. Sometimes you get the impression that narrative is a new foundational paradigm for cultural studies. Almost everything (but not absolutely everything) that narratology has to say is thus in one way or another more or less relevant for the analysis of novels. The converse is also true, that much knowledge that has been gained about the modern novel flows back, in generalized form, into narrative theory. Furthermore, we can try out and see which genre-specific modifications the insights of narrative theory need to assimilate in a literary form as exceptionally varied and prone to development as the novel is, or how selectively and how diversely the genre conventions operate here.

At this point, it's intriguing to note that this genre, which has enjoyed such incomparable success in the past three hundred years, eludes any simple definition precisely because of its exceptional, protean ability to change form and mutate. One good concise dictionary defines "novel" like this:

> an extended work in prose, either fictitious or partly so, dealing with character, action, thought, etc., esp. in the form of a story

The intentional vagueness of "extended" is further increased by the extra modification "fictitious or partly so." The self-assured certainty of "character, action, thought" is magnificently undercut by the addition of "etc." – which, though understandable, leaves everything hanging again. And the concluding point, perhaps delivered with rather a sigh of relief, "especially in the form of a story," appears more fragile the more you look at the word "especially": it implies – correctly – that this is not a *necessary* characteristic of a novel. So we're left with "prose" as the core element. If we reflect, however, that even in the twentieth century some excellent verse novels were written – think of Vikram Seth's *The Golden Gate* (1986), a novel in the form of 590 sonnets – then it's clear that not even prose is absolutely required for a text to qualify as a novel. Please do not misunderstand: I think the above definition is a very good one. In many areas of life and art a certain kind of fuzzy logic is no bad thing. Defining the novel puts us in something like the position of Augustine answering the question, what is time? Of course we know, until someone asks – then we don't know any more.

The first thing most people in our culture think of when they hear the word "novel" (and this is reflected in the above dictionary definition) is a relatively long narration in prose, in which different characters appear. Something exciting or remarkable happens to these characters, who are people with whom we can "somehow" identify (or *would like to* identify, since we obviously aren't like them), because they "somehow" act in a (re)cognizable world. This world is accessible to us without too much effort, since to imagine it and understand it we do not need any particular knowledge of literature or literary history. This is the typical view, crudely modeled on *the* dominant type within the novel genre: the middle-class realist European novel, which began its triumphal progress both in literary and commercial terms around 1700.

We needn't consider the wealth of other forms of the modern novel at this point – we will return to them later. But one element is of interest here, conspicuous by its complete absence from the dictionary definition, but which is really a constitutive part of the popular conception of the novel: *its proximity to reality*. This is the widespread idea that the novel "somehow" reflects reality, or at least constructs a fictional world that, however far removed from the reader's world in time and place, exhibits similarities with that world, relates to it, or forms a continuation of it. Even this aspect of the novel's supposed proximity to reality need not occupy us in this context, except insofar as it clearly could be of importance both for the success story of this modern literary form, and in equal measure for the difficulties of reading these very texts *analytically*. The success of the modern novel, which has achieved a diffusion and popularity unequalled by any other literary genre, is surely in part explicable in terms of its unpretentious non-literariness – i.e., the fact that we can "just read" it, without any special knowledge, literary or otherwise. And that's why, every once in a while, students of literature, on learning that the meaning of a novel lies in *the form in which it is mediated* and not in some sort of paraphrasable "content," ask incredulously: what? Even here? Like in a poem? So is there no escape?

Not so long ago I accepted an invitation to write an introduction to the analysis of lyric poetry. This set me thinking about why – and this is an open secret – school pupils and undergraduates give poetry such a wide berth whenever they can. Part of my answer was that this literary genre is so demonstrably and undeniably *literary* and *self-referential* that anyone who does not actually know how to read in a *literary* way – how, that is, to recognize and describe the *literary* meaning of a *literary* text – will do their best to avoid it. Lyric poetry is considered difficult, because as a rule it's not enough just to recount "the plot" or supposed message: for a recounting of the literal sense of these texts very obviously won't do them justice. Lyric poetry is considered difficult because such literature patently cannot be directly related to something that stands outside it and exists already (i.e., which would be read *referentially*), so that in order to learn its meaning we must refer back to the text itself, to the manner in which it's written, its form, its mediatedness. It's only from this that we can (re-)construct what these linguistic signs, all of them well known in themselves, actually mean *in this configuration*. The *what* is only accessible through the *how* – if indeed we are to fall back on this opposition at all, since such a text "is" basically the *way* in which it is – like this, and not like that.

The idea that novels are different from poetry in this respect is the great error, encouraged no doubt by the seductive impression of greater proximity to reality in this literary genre. Moby-Dick is white: working that out is not rocket science, it's just a fact. Working out what that might *mean* is far more exciting, as is working out why it's the toad who drives the car. To understand *that* is actually to read in a literary way. To investigate and trace *how* this kind of meaning is actually produced is one task (among others) of literary criticism.

We readily assume that literary texts are texts which can be read in a non-referential way, since they do not relate directly to an extra-textual, preexistent reality, but to something that they themselves create in the imagination of their readers. Robinson Crusoe's island lies only there, nowhere else. It's obvious that this must become extremely exciting in *the* literary genre that typically (though hardly exclusively) pretends to relate itself "somehow" to the reality in which the reader lives. That's why this genre always thematizes our relation to "reality," whether explicitly or not (and in novels where this question remains only implicit, it's arguably all the more pressing). In other words, it is through *illusion* that the *constructed* nature of any supposedly given "reality" is exposed – that we readily take for substance what is only appearance. How does a novel do this? There is only one way to find out. Observe as closely as you can. What could be more straightforward? And on top of that – there is no other way.

A skeptical reader of these pages might raise an objection here. However necessary it may be to analyze the different levels and aspects of the text of a novel, the concluding synthesis of all these analytical finds is equally indispensable – the integration, that is, of the particular results of the enquiry, which goes beyond a modest "this fits together with that." That objection is completely justified. When in the following chapters I discuss, say, narrative time and narrated time, story and discourse, narrative situations, symbolism, etc. separately, this is only for heuristic reasons: I will make a *general* sketch of the possibilities of narrative technique that are available to the novel as a genre, and then use *concrete* examples to illustrate how these devices function in practice.

One last thing: this introduction to the critical analysis of novels is intended for students of modern literature in all languages. Examples are taken from English, German, French, Italian, Spanish, Russian, and Scandinavian literature. If these examples are more often drawn from the various Anglophone literatures, that is not only because these constitute quantitatively – and perhaps qualitatively too – a very important part of all the novels produced around the world. I am by training a specialist in English and American literature, and cannot deny that I tend to think first of examples from my field. I comfort myself and reassure others with the empirical wisdom that an apposite example remains an apposite example regardless of which national literature it might come from. In the mid-nineteenth century, the British cultural critic Matthew Arnold vehemently castigated the narrow-minded nationalism of his countrymen in cultural matters and urgently called on them to dare to look beyond their own insular noses. To the definition of his reforming plan "to learn and propagate the best that is known and thought in the world" he added the harsh warning: "By the very nature of things, as England is not all the world, much of the best that is known and thought in the world cannot be of English growth, must be foreign[.]"[3] – a sobering admonition which has hardly lost its legitimacy for any national readership. The majority of all literature is foreign, always and everywhere.

A note on citations: for ease of reference, since the texts of the novels quoted are often available in various different paperback editions, I cite primary texts (where appropriate) by explaining the location (e.g., "at the beginning of chapter 7").

I should like to thank, first of all, my student assistants Anna Auguscik, Ann-Christin Focke, Angelika Rehschütz, Ina Schneider and Martina Taubenberger for having compiled thousands of pages of relevant secondary sources for the writing of the original German version of this book. In preparing this edition, the help of Lilian Loke has been invaluable.

As always, my secretary, Doris Haseidl, has proved an inexhaustible source of serenity and equanimity. I cannot thank her enough.

My colleagues, Professors Katharina Rennhak and Sebastian Domsch, of Wuppertal University and LMU Munich, respectively, were kind enough to carefully and critically read a first version of the book, and I am deeply obliged to them for their highly welcome and invariably constructive feedback. All remaining errors and infelicities are, of course, my own.

I should also like to thank the anonymous readers who suggested that Wiley-Blackwell publish an English edition of *Der Roman*. The support of these polyglot colleagues has been a privilege and an encouragement that I can barely hope to ever pay back.

The same is true of Emma Bennett, Senior Editor at Wiley-Blackwell in Oxford, whose support, from the very beginning, has been enthusiastic and unswerving. I am immensely grateful to her for a collaboration that has been highly professional and a personal delight at the same time.

Because of other, pressing obligations, I could not provide the translation myself. Dr. James Vigus kindly stepped in, and he has taken extraordinary pains to render the original German into an English version that is both accessible and accurate, and retains the nuances of the source language. Our long hours of discussion bespeak his high standards and his incorruptible determination to get it "right." They were a singularly impressive experience for both of us, and I must thank him for both his endeavor and the result. Without James Vigus, this book simply would not exist. What more can you say?

[3] Matthew Arnold, "The Function of Criticism at the Present Time," in *The Norton Anthology of English Literature: Fifth Edition*, ed. M. H. Abrams, New York, 1986, 1: 1408–1424, here 1422.

It would not exist either if it hadn't been for the innumerable students I have taught, in the course of more than three decades, at the universities of Kiel, Giessen, Bamberg, Los Angeles (UCLA), and at LMU Munich and with whom I fortunately could share my enthusiasm for and my curiosity about literature. From the unique enthusiasm they returned and from their exceptional dedication I have profited far, far more than any of them may have realized at the time. It was a privilege to have met with them.

The greatest gratitude, however, I owe to my wife Helga and our children Jennifer, Andreas, and Benjamin. This book is dedicated to them. They have enriched my life to a degree that cannot be put into words.

Christoph Bode
LMU Munich
July 2009

Translator's Note

Works first published in languages other than English are quoted, wherever appropriate, from extant translations, with occasional adjustments signaled in the notes.

The present book uses and elucidates a number of key technical terms in narrative theory. One of these in particular, the German *Erzählinstanz*, lacks an established equivalent in English. I translate this word as "narrative authority" or "narrating authority" – an expression that reflects the fact that *Erzählinstanz* was introduced in the first place to avoid the misleading impression that an "authorial narrator" is a *human person*, while at the same time "narrating/narrative authority" retains the idea that this particular mode of narration is, after all, the most authoritative one (this translation also conveys the judicial implication of the German *Instanz*). The combined effect should be to suggest that a narrative authority is more substantial than a mere voice, yet less personal, more "super-human," than a narrator.

Third-person pronouns – he, she, one – present challenges to translators no less than to authors. Chapter 7 section 3 directly discusses whether traditional narratology is involved in perpetuating gender inequalities and gender bias, and on the basis of this discussion I have settled on a pragmatically flexible rather than strictly uniform policy. For authorial narrators and narrative authorities, who are as a rule conceived as non-gendered, "s/he" seemed most appropriate; in most other cases, purely to avoid cluttering the text, I use masculine pronouns as the default position – but also plural or passive constructions where stylistically appropriate.

My translation has benefited immeasurably from extensive collaboration with the author himself: I thank Christoph Bode for all that I have learned from him in the process of this work. I am also very grateful to those friends and colleagues who assisted with suggestions and advice. I would like in particular to thank Stefan Blechschmidt, Christian Deuling, Josephine von Zitzewitz, and – above all – my wife, Cecilia Muratori.

Acknowledgments

The author and publisher gratefully acknowledge the permission granted to reproduce the copyright material in this book:

Mario Vargas Llosa, *Letters to a Young Novelist*, translated by Natasha Wimmer (New York: Picador, 2002), 52–53.

B. S. Johnson, "Aren't You Rather Young to be Writing Your Memoirs?" in *The Novel Today: Contemporary Writers on Fiction*, edited by Malcolm Bradbury (Glasgow, 1977), 151–168. Reproduced by kind permission of the Estate of B. S. Johnson c/o MBA Literary Agency.

Theodor W. Adorno, "The Position of the Narrator in the Contemporary Novel," in *Notes to Literature*, edited by Rolf Tiedemann, translated by Sherry Weber Nicholson (New York: Columbia University Press, 1991), 30–36. German text: "Form und Gehalt des zeitgenössischen Romans," *Akzente* 1 (1954), 410–416. Reprinted with permission of Columbia University Press.

Julian Barnes, *Flaubert's Parrot*, copyright © 1985 by Julian Barnes. Used by permission of Alfred A. Knopf, a division of Random House, Inc., and the Random House Group UK.

Short extracts translated from *Romantheorie: Texte vom Barock bis zur Gegenwart*, edited by Hartmut Steinecke (Stuttgart, 1999). Used with kind permission of Philipp Reclam jun. Verlag GmbH.

E. M. Forster, *Aspects of the Novel* (Penguin, 1977) and *A Passage to India* (1924). Reprinted with permission of the Provost and Scholars of King's College, Cambridge and the Society of Authors as the Literary Representative of the Estate of E. M. Forster.

Dieter Wellershoff, *Von der Moral erwischt: Aufsätze zur Trivialliteratur* (Frankfurt am Main, 1983). In *Werke 4. Essays, Aufsätze, Marginalien* by Dieter Wellershoff © 1997 by Verlag Kiepenheuer & Witsch GmbH & Co. KG Cologne.

Salman Rushdie, "Is Nothing Sacred?" from *Imaginary Homelands: The Herbert Read Memorial Lecture for 1990.* © 1981, 1982, 1983, 1984, 1985, 1986, 1987, 1988, 1989, 1990, 1991 by Salman Rushdie. Reprinted with permission of Wylie Agency and Viking Penguin, a division of Penguin Group (USA) Inc. All rights reserved.

Denis Diderot, *Jacques the Fatalist and his Master*, translated by Michael Henry, introduction and notes by Martin Hall (Penguin Classics, 1986). © Michael Henry 1986. Introduction © Martin Hall. Reprinted with permission of Penguin UK.

Malcolm Bradbury, "A Jaundiced View," from *"Who Do You Think You Are?" Stories and Parodies* (London: Secker & Warburg 1976, 1986). Reprinted with permission of Curtis Brown Group Ltd.

Thomas Mann, *The Magic Mountain*, translated by H. T. Lowe-Porter, 1927. Translation copyright © 1927 and renewed 1955 by Alfred A Knopf. Copyright © 1952 by Thomas Mann. Also published in the UK by Secker & Warburg. Reprinted with permission of Random House Group Ltd. UK and Alfred A. Knopf, a division of Random House, Inc.

Franz K. Stanzel, *A Theory of Narrative*, translated by Charlotte Goedsche with a preface by Paul Hernadi (Cambridge: Cambridge University Press, 1984, 1986). Reprinted with permission of Vandenhoeck & Ruprecht GmbH & Co. KG, Göttingen.

Gérard Genette, *Narrative Discourse Revisited*, translated from the French by Jane E. Lewin. Translation copyright © 1988 by Cornell University. Used by permission of the publisher Cornell University Press.

Franz Kafka, *The Castle, Definitive Edition*, translated by Willa and Edwin Muir, copyright © 1930, 1941, 1954 by Alfred A. Knopf. Copyright renewed 1958 by Alfred A. Knopf, Inc. Used by permission of Schocken Books, a division of Random House, Inc., and the Random House Group UK.

Jurij Lotman, *The Structure of the Artistic Text*, translated by Gail Lenhoff and Ronald Vroon (Ann Arbor, 1977). Reprinted with permission of Michigan Slavic Publications.

Walter Benjamin, "The Storyteller: Reflections on the Works of Nikolai Leskov," translated by Harry Zorn. In *Narrative Theory: Critical Concepts in Literary and Cultural Studies*, Volume 3: *Political Narratology*, edited by Mieke Bal, 88–106. This translation was first published in *Illuminations*, edited by Hannah Arendt (New York: Harvard University Press and Harcourt, 1968), 83–107.

Virginia Woolf, *To The Lighthouse*, 1927. Reprinted with permission of the Society of Authors as the Literary Representative of the Estate of Virginia Woolf.

Every effort has been made to trace copyright holders and to obtain their permission for the use of copyright material. The publisher apologizes for any errors or omissions in the above list and would be grateful if notified of any corrections that should be incorporated in future reprints or editions of this book.

1

Beginnings
What Do You Expect?

1   Beginning

In the beginning was the word. Or, according to Goethe's *Faust*, the deed. Or, putting both together, the word-deed – the speech act. Someone turning to someone else and saying: "Let me tell you about how …"

… how it came about that there is something, rather than nothing – myths of creation and origin: how being came out of nothing, how it divided itself into living and non-living, into people and animals, into man and woman (one notes the order: how every segmentation seems to imply a hierarchy).

Such myths try to "make sense," in that they divide, order, rank, but even so never get round the problems surrounding the very beginning: what was, before there was anything? How can we speak about it? What was God doing all through eternity before he created the world? Didn't he get bored? So was he, the Idea of perfection – heresy! – incomplete, imperfect, before he created the world? Did he need us? These are questions the Church Fathers raised. Luther's answer to the question about God's pastimes: God went into the wood and cut himself a cane to thrash people who ask questions like that. Every beginning is a *positing*. Period.

In Mallarmé's notes about his *Livre* we read: "Un livre ne commence ni ne finit: tout au plus fait-il semblant."[1] That is true of narratives in general: they only *pretend* to begin with the beginning, they *fake* a beginning, necessarily. This fabricated beginning is an initial rupture, an initial differentiation

---

[1]   "A book neither begins nor ends: it does all that seemingly." The French text is quoted from Norbert Miller (ed.), *Romananfänge: Versuch zu einer Poetik des Romans*, Berlin, 1965, 7.

The Novel: An Introduction. By Christoph Bode. Translated by James Vigus. English translation © 2011 James Vigus. Published by John Wiley & Sons, Ltd.
Original German text © 2005 Narr Francke Attempto Verlag GmbH + Co. KG.

into this and that. It's always possible to question this initial differentiation, but not to get to the bottom of it, for every time we attempt to get to the bottom of it we just fall into an infinite regress. What does the world rest on? The back of a giant elephant, says the wise Brahmin. And what is the elephant standing on? The back of a turtle. And the turtle? On the back of another turtle. And the other turtle? The Brahmin, like Luther: "You can't fool me. It's turtles all the way down!"

It comes down to this: you have to start somewhere. And "you can't begin before the beginning" (Ludwig Wittgenstein). That, however, is a *pragmatic* reason, one not grounded in ontology or epistemology. In his *Poetics*, Aristotle offers this definition:

> By "beginning" I mean that which does not have a necessary connection with a preceding event, but which can itself give rise naturally to some further fact or occurrence. An "end," by contrast, is something which naturally occurs after a preceding event, whether by necessity or as a general rule, but need not be followed by anything else. The "middle" involves causal connections with both what precedes and what ensues.[2]

Aristotle's first sentence pulls the carpet from under every narrative attempt to invest what *is* with an aura of necessity: for every beginning is the exact opposite of necessary – it is completely contingent. And for that very reason it's so incredibly important and fraught with consequences. It could have begun completely differently, but in fact it started like this … Much depends on the beginning – in narrative, everything depends on it.

2   Sense and Meaning

… now I'll tell you what happened to me, or to someone – departure and return home; in between, war, adventures, peril – which only one man, full of cunning, escaped; how someone who has been away for years and gone through all that must change: no one knows him any more.

While Penelope just *is*, waiting, the man needs three things to prove his identity:

- the childhood scar, which his wet-nurse recognizes (i.e., sheer *physical continuity*);
- the unique ability to string the bow of Odysseus (i.e., a *capacity* that he – and only he – has);
- lastly: being able to tell the secret of the marriage bed (i.e., what he alone *knows*).

[2]   *The "Poetics" of Aristotle*, trans. and ed. Stephen Halliwell, London, 1987, 39.

He is the man he was. And at the same time, of course, he is not at all the man he was. It's his history that has made him who he is, the man people know him for. He is Odysseus – the one who was away, who wanted to come home (yeah, really?) and was again and again hindered from doing so. He is who he is "now," *after* all that: only this makes him worthy of report at all – that he "has" a history. And the fact that he has a history suggests in turn that what happened to him *makes sense* – or at least could have made sense.

The *Odyssey* is, of course, no *Bildungsroman*.[3] It raises the question of the meaning of life not on the level of the fulfillment of the individual ("I am the person I became ..."), but in a much more general and fundamental way – against the background of the *death of everyone else*. What is special about *this* life? Odysseus is the only survivor – and thus, although plenty will still be told *about* him (but within this narrative he is allowed to tell his own story), he is the first ancestor of every other lone survivor who, by some compulsion, so it seems, must tell their stories. They alone are still alive, they alone can relate how it was – and their stories are perforce about how it came to be that they alone are still alive, about how that can be explained, what rhyme or reason that might have.

Robinson Crusoe, shipwrecked on an island on which he has spent 28 years, comes to conceive his fate as God's punishment for his rebellious disobedience to his father, who had firmly advised him to remain in the country and make a decent living. At the end, Robinson reaps with full awareness the reward of his disobedience – his immense wealth. Every narrative works out its own sense and meaning, and the best allow us to recognize as well that something is being worked out – and so, mercifully, leave plenty left over for the reader.

Samuel Taylor Coleridge's "Ancient Mariner," not the hero of a novel, admittedly, but an epic hero nonetheless, is an anachronistic figure even in his own time. He believes himself guilty, by a thoughtless transgression, of the death of all his mates: not in the causal sense, but, far more uncannily, in a supernatural sense. He alone survives, for the purpose (so he believes) of being able to preach this moral to others – of *having* to do so – and he hypnotizes his audience, who actually had other plans, through the power of his own obsession. He now lives only to tell (the inverse of Scheherazade, who tells in order to survive) – his very existence a warning.

---

[3]   A message in a bottle to that future reviewer who might think it necessary to make the shrewd remark that the *Odyssey* is not a novel at all, and therefore should not be brought up as an example here: granted. Cf. by the way, Gérard Genette, *Narrative Discourse Revisited*, trans. Jane E. Lewin, Ithaca, NY, 1988, first published in French as *Nouveau discours du récit* (1983). In this sequel to the earlier *Narrative Discourse*, Genette self-critically qualifies some of his earlier assessments, and specifically regarding the *Odyssey* writes (94): "It cannot [...] be said that the *Odyssey* exhibits 'the origins of epic narrating'; I see it, rather, and I have said so elsewhere, as the beginning of a transition, both formal and thematic, from the epic to the novel. The mists of time are a little more remote."

Finally, there's "Ishmael," the narrator of *Moby-Dick* – he's another in this line. "And I only am escaped alone to tell thee" – this quotation from the Book of Job is placed as the motto to his epilogue. Since the catastrophe, he has obsessively collected everything written about the whale – and he lays it all out in front of us. And the more we read about the whale, the stronger our impression becomes that the narrative is about everything other than whales. In *Studies in Classic American Literature*, D. H. Lawrence wrote these clear-sighted words about the great white sperm whale:

> Of course he is a symbol.
> Of what?
> I doubt if even Melville knew exactly. That's the best of it.[4]

But the point here is not whether Melville, as the author, knew what he wanted to tell us with this symbol. The point is that even here – precisely here – something particular is expressed, "without thinking or referring to a universal. Whoever grasps this particular in a vital way at the same time receives the universal, without becoming aware of the fact, or only becoming aware of it later."[5] That is Goethe's definition of the "nature of poesy" – but we'll return later to discuss symbolism in more detail. In the present context only this seems important: as a matter of course in the novel and in any narrative, something is said concretely and something else is implied at the same time.

At the beginning of his existentialist novel *La Peste* (1947), Albert Camus quotes as follows from, of all writers, that progenitor of middle-class realism, Daniel Defoe: "It is as reasonable to represent one kind of imprisonment by another, as it is to represent something that really exists by that which exists not." In *both* cases mentioned by Defoe, narrative works with *replacement*. In other words: in *both* instances the subject of narrative is "actually" not what it directly says, but always what it *points to*, what it promises (in this sense, narrative is also non-literal speech). And what does every narrative make? Sense, hopefully. What does the reader expect to find? Meaning(s).

When a narrative tells how somebody acted and was acted upon, it first of all assumes their identity. At the same time, however, it assumes that something fundamental occurs with respect to them, or has changed them – that's what makes the story worth relating at all. Every narrative of this kind thus unfolds differences – thematizes the unity of continuity and discontinuity (and that's only possible in *time*) – and claims *through its mere*

---

[4]   D. H. Lawrence, *Studies in Classic American Literature*, Harmondsworth, 1978 [1923], 153.
[5]   Johann Wolfgang von Goethe, "Maximen und Reflexionen," *Werke* (*Hamburger Ausgabe*), Munich, 1982, 12: 365–547, here 471.

existence that it *makes sense*. Otherwise, why tell it? That is what the reader, fairly enough, expects: sense and meaning.

Yet the idea that something *makes sense* is only conceivable against the backdrop that, theoretically, it could have been meaningless. To narrate is to claim that something makes sense – and it's this sense that the narration is to bring out. Narration is the endowment of sense against the possibility of the absurd. This is of course also – and especially – the case when a narration addresses this possibility, where this boundary, the failure of the attempt, is taken into account. That's true even if the attempt to make sense proves senseless and fails, since that can itself only be perceived against a horizon of meaningfulness.

Narration is the self-pledged obligation of one who is (still) alive towards the others. Even if the narrative is not that of an "only survivor." The listener or reader fairly enough expects sense and meaning from narratives – not because there *is* any meaning in the first place, but because narratives are there to *produce* it.

3   Rules of the Game

"Have you heard the one about ...?" Or: "Once upon a time ..." As members of a common culture we're able to differentiate different types of narrative, even before the first "real" sentence is completed, and to decode them accordingly. We anticipate what's coming, because without needing to reflect too much we've already identified the type of narrative, and bring to it a prior knowledge of the rules that apply. We know the rules of the game, both general and particular.

In a fairy tale, for instance, we are not surprised to encounter giants and elves, wizards and witches, animals who speak, dragons and unicorns – they belong to the customary inventory for texts of this kind; we almost include them in our conception of what a fairy tale is. And because we know that, we have no problem in believing in the existence of such beings *within* a narrative of this type, even if we naturally know that "there are no such things."

That is a phenomenon of framing, and the rules that apply within a frame, but not outside it. The chessboard has only 64 squares, and the pieces may only be moved there, and only there do their moves make sense. That isn't actually a problem, because everyone spontaneously (though of course this spontaneity is – does it have to be said? – socioculturally learnt) practices what the English Romantic writer Coleridge (in only a slightly different context) called "the willing suspension of disbelief for the moment."[6] *For*

---

[6]   Samuel Taylor Coleridge, "Biographia Literaria," *Norton Anthology of English Literature*, Vol. 2, ed. M. H. Abrams, New York, 1986, 386–547, here 398.

the duration of our reading we put aside our disbelief, and we do so with complete willingness. For we know that a fundamental skepticism, while fully appropriate with regard to extra-textual reality, i.e., in the case of a *referential* text, would be absolutely out of place and counterproductive here, in the present case of a non-referential, fictional text. We'd spoil the game and the fun for ourselves. Indeed, to insist on the supposed referentiality of a statement and its evident falsity ("but there's no such thing as a unicorn!") would only show that this know-all had completely misunderstood and missed the point. They'd be committing a category mistake, falling foul of a very fundamental misreading.

To be sure, that happens only very rarely with fairy tales; more often, though, with realistic novels, and probably more often than one imagines with texts that serve our fantasies or play on our fears or needs – romances, horror stories, pornographic or erotic literature. An equally serious mistake is made by readers who mistake what they read for true (or just probable) and by those who criticize these texts for their lack of realism, considering that the very *raison d'être* of these texts consists precisely in their distance from reality.

The conventions of the different types of narrative are socioculturally prescribed (albeit always liable to change). This means that, in practice, logical problems about propositions hardly ever arise in the form in which philosophy has tended to construct them – has *had* to construct them, since they're almost never to be met with in the wild: "Sherlock Holmes lived at 221b Baker Street." Is this statement true or false? Well, it all depends. Within the fictional world that Sir Arthur Conan Doyle drew up, this statement is accurate – that is the address specified in the tales about the master detective. So: true. Outside this fictional world the statement is false or, to put it more precisely, meaningless, since Sherlock Holmes is a fictional character who cannot possibly have lived in Baker Street, which really exists in the West End of London.[7] So: false. The truth-content of the proposition thus varies, and depends completely on the frame of reference – relating to which set of facts is it true or not?

Not that such distinctions are unimportant. Quite the contrary: if someone tells us "their side of the story," the truth-criteria are completely different from those that would operate if they were telling us a fantastic tale. And we'd be justifiably put out if they told us a tall story when we'd expected the truth. I'm just saying that, as a rule, we get on with these distinctions smoothly and unproblematically in daily life. (Just as, by the way, the vast majority of adults can get on with the "framing" of a dramatic scene on the

---

[7]   And that's not due to the fact that at the time the Sherlock Holmes stories are set, there was no such house number in Baker Street (it was introduced later to keep curious tourists happy). Even if this house number had existed at that time, Sherlock Holmes wouldn't have lived there.

stage: what happens is "real" within the frame of the play, although obviously if you think of the frame at the same time, it's only "acted.") This kind of double perspective doesn't cause us any problems at all: it's part of our basic cultural equipment.

However, if the conventions of the various types of narrative text are socially and culturally prescribed, then from the word go there is always the possibility of playing with them. A text can play around with fundamental distinctions, cover them up, teasingly leave readers or listeners in the dark, or lead them astray. In an illusion-based art, the art of illusion can't be something questionable. Many realistic novels pretend to be relations of fact rather than fiction, and that is true not just for the first modern novels (which will be considered in detail later), but continues into the present. In 1981 Wolfgang Hildesheimer's *Marbot: Eine Biographie* came out. The book's blurb begins like this:

> Sir Andrew Marbot, the hero of this biography, is as good as woven into the cultural history of the early nineteenth century. He had contact with Goethe, Schopenhauer, Platen, Byron, Baron von Rumohr, Leopardi and others, kept track of their writings and liberally expressed his approval, reservations and criticism. His principal field of research, however, was painting, which he undertook to analyze from the perspective of the artist's spiritual condition. Thus he became the first exponent of a psychoanalytically based aesthetic in the fine arts, making essential contributions to this field. He was the first to recognize that an overflow of creativity is a deviation from "normal" psychological mechanisms, that genius can never "conform." To be sure, he was eminently adapted – not to say predestined – to recognize such phenomena, for his own private life was anomalous in a truly unique respect.

It is thus suggested – and is maintained throughout the whole book – that there really was such a person as Sir Andrew Marbot, as a historical figure (which isn't true), and so that we are reading a work of scholarship rather than a "mere invention." Hildesheimer began *Marbot* after completing his great biography of Mozart: working on the latter had made it clear to him how much imagination was needed to make a life story out of the "facts" of a life. *Marbot*, then, was the logical consequence of this experience: a completely imaginary biography, the novel as complete mimicry.

Wolfgang Hildesheimer wasn't the first to have had this idea (which is no disparagement of his work). In 1958 the fictional biography *Jusep Torres Campalans*, by Max Aub, was published in Mexico:

> Max Aub's voluminous monograph about "a forgotten companion of Picasso" was, as a book, designed fully in the serious style of the world-famous art monographs of the Swiss publisher Skira. It looked similar enough to be confused with one of them; and for the book launch a gallery in Mexico City

displayed the originals of some of the pictures of Jusep Torres Campalan reproduced in the book (as was also done later in New York).[8]

There were plenty of connivers at this fake: Octavio Paz and Carlos Fuentes, the painter Siqueiros, the director of the Museum of Modern Art in Paris, and the life partner of the anarchist Victor Serge. That Picasso himself was deliciously amused by the farce, though, is (probably) apocryphal.

When *Marbot* was published, I witnessed (but in this context, can I expect to be believed without evidence?) a customer in a bookshop asking, incredulous and unsure of herself, whether it was true that – as she had heard – *Marbot* wasn't a "real" biography, but an "invented" one, in other words, a novel. The question seemed to me sensible: the lady wanted to know *how to read the book*, whether "Marbot" has or had a referent in extra-linguistic, historical reality or not. For if not, the *topic* of the book would have been (as indeed it was) a completely different one, albeit not so easy to pin down. She wanted to know – her entitlement as a customer – what to expect, but also what was expected *from her* as a reader. That is a question about how to "file" a text, not about its "substance," its "essence," its "character," or whatever. The joke is that the text itself doesn't disclose this. It's disclosed by "settings" that are given beforehand. We produce the text by approaching it in a certain way.

This is familiar from other literary genres. Peter Handke's "The line-up of FC Nürnberg on 27 January 1968" in *The Innerworld of the Outerworld of the Innerworld* (1969) should be read differently in the context of his book than, say, in the context of the sports pages (another phenomenon of framing); except that in Handke's case the context itself discloses the displacement, whereas in *Marbot* the whole artefact – i.e., the book as a physical object – participated in the illusion.

When authors do not want to create a witty illusion *à la* Hildesheimer, but rather to make sure that their text is appropriately or "correctly" received, they too can, of course, have the content spelt out on the cover (even if the same isn't true the other way round, that only when the word "novel" is on the cover must the book be a novel). When Bruce Chatwin's *The Songlines* (1987) appeared in German under the title *Traumzeit*, the genre specification "novel" was prominently displayed on the dust jacket. This was done to comply with the author's wish. The original English edition did not have this feature, and Chatwin found the consequent confusion and uncertainty unpleasant:

> Within Jonathan Cape [his English publisher], there had been confusion over how to market the book. Bruce was adamant: he did not wish to be regarded

[8]   Wolfram Schütte, "Die Geburt des Kubismus aus dem Geiste der Anarchie," *Frankfurter Rundschau*, December 9, 1997.

as a travel-writer. If *The Songlines* was marketed as a travel book, it would be slotted in the travel-section beside "the Cyclades on $5 a day." On the other hand, "in literature it would be beside Chaucer."[9]

This reasoning might sound coquettish, but Chatwin certainly took the differentiation seriously. When *The Songlines* was nominated for the Thomas Cook Travel Award, the renowned prize for travel literature, the author gave the following statement: "The journey it [the book] describes is an invented journey, it is not a travel book in the generally accepted sense. To avoid any possible confusion, I must ask to withdraw it from the shortlist."[10] Correctly categorizing the book as *fiction* was more important to him than the almost certain distinction of book of the year in the wrong category. *The Songlines* should be regarded and read *like this*, as a novel. The specification of the genre functions like a musical clef, regulating both the reader's expectations and the process of decoding. That's after all what codes are there for.

Other texts appeal to the privileged status that follows from the basic human right of the freedom of the arts: we're only fiction, they say ("The characters and action in this book are invented. Any similarity to persons living or dead is purely coincidental."), and at the same time they count on not being read as fiction in certain parts: a *roman à clef*. The *roman à clef* puts the person it portrays in an almost helpless no-win situation. If they don't speak up, the novel's presentations and claims remain uncontradicted out in the world; if they protest, or if the trustees of their estate do so – as the actor and producer Gustav Gründgens did about Klaus Mann's novel *Mephisto* (1935), the publication of which in West Germany was successfully hindered for years – they paradoxically "out" themselves, by saying: "That's not me, but it could be. Although this and that isn't true, it's obviously me who's *meant* – and I protest, *because* this or that isn't true or disparages and insults me."

Thus the duplicity of the *roman à clef* crosses the *Marbot*-line from the other side: it deliberately provokes scandal, using a (time-honored) camouflage of categories (that the *roman à clef* has a great deal more to offer is shown for instance by Martin Walser's *Tod eines Kritikers* [*Death of a Critic*], 2002). The *roman à clef* lures with promises that, at the same time, ascribe a stooped position to its readers – peering, as they must, through the keyhole. It performs a transgression of the rules, hoping on the quiet that the victim will keep to the rules – and so lose; or not keep to the rules – and so lose anyway.

[9] Nicholas Shakespeare, *Bruce Chatwin*, London, 1999, 486.
[10] Shakespeare, *Chatwin*, 487.

4   Links and Connections

We can speak of "narration" when at least two events are linked together by language. One single reported event (e.g., "It was raining") does not yet constitute a narrative; nor do two unconnected events ("It was raining. Krakatowa erupted in 1883"). Narrative *is* the linguistic and mental linking of events.

That's the case not just with everyday accounts and novels, comic strips and films, but also in the writing of history. One isolated fact *per se* has no meaning at all. It attains meaning only through narrative embedding, through the narrative connection with other facts,[11] as Benedetto Croce remarked: "Where there is no narrative, there is no history."[12]

However, since it is possible for a narrative to link events and facts in substantially different ways, we're no longer talking about one (hi)story, but a whole collection of (hi)stories. That doesn't have to mean that we doubt or even deny the "reality" of the facts themselves (although some would make this radical claim). As a disconnected fact, the event can remain uncontroversial and constant. Its meaning, however, varies according to the narrative in which it is embedded. But just a moment: what is a fact without meaning? Meaningless?

The next question might be whether merely putting two events in a temporal relationship ("first this, then that" or "and then and then and then") counts as making a connection, or whether a stronger emphasis of the "actual" relation is required, in terms of sequential logic ("first this, and then, therefore, that"). In his informal – and so too easily underestimated – little book *Aspects of the Novel*, E. M. Forster is convinced that he can give a clear account of the difference between *story* and *plot* based on these two types of connection. (Chapter 3 in the present volume is dedicated to this fundamental differentiation in narrative theory, which also offers us small but significant, fine-tuned distinctions between *fabula* and *sjuzet*, *histoire* and *discours*, *history* and *narrative*.) Forster:

> Let us define a plot. We have defined a story as a narrative of events arranged in their time-sequence. A plot is also a narrative of events, the emphasis falling on causality. "The king died and then the queen died" is a story. "The king died, and then the queen died of grief" is a plot. The time-sequence is preserved,

---

[11]   Cf. Hayden White, *Metahistory: The Historical Imagination in Nineteenth-Century Europe*, Baltimore, 1973; White, *Tropics of Discourse: Essays in Cultural Criticism*, Baltimore, 1978; and White, *The Content of the Form: Narrative Discourse and Historical Representation*, Baltimore, 1987.

[12]   Quoted in White, *The Content of the Form*, 28.

but the sense of causality overshadows it. [...] Consider the death of the queen. If it is in a story we say: "And then?" If it is in a plot we ask: "Why?"[13]

The more you think about it, the clearer it becomes that Forster's distinction between merely temporal connection on the one hand, and causal connection on the other can't really be sustained so easily. (And not just because, at least since David Hume, we have known that "causality" is anyway an idea based only on the association of representations. The idea of causality arises when we observe one event following upon another with sufficient frequency: it's basically an imaginative reinforcement of purely temporal connections, with no compelling claim to be considered as a law.)

In the example chosen by Forster, even a minimal alteration could produce a decisive change: "The king died, and just a few days later the queen died too." Although "just a few days later" is a purely temporal modification, attentive readers may not need any further explanation to understand it as a causal motivation as well – as discreetly implying that she died of grief at the death of her husband.

That means, however, that the causal connections between the events need not be *explicitly* stated at all: it's enough for them to be implicit and plausible, simply possible. That is extremely important, since it suggests that a large part of the essential narrative work of connecting can be carried out by the reader, who will clearly respond even to the smallest signal. (The lifeblood of a whole genre of short prose, the joke, consists in using such signals to send readers or listeners off in the wrong direction, in order to demonstrate at the end that the information they'd been given could have been construed differently: as a rule, the playful frustration of our expectations triggers a more or less powerful release of tension through laughter.)

So strong, in fact, is the impulse of the reader or listener to create coherence through connections that it was far from easy for me just now to think of an example of two events described in successive sentences that, apart from this chance juxtaposition, don't have any further linguistic connection with each other. "It was raining. The *Titanic* sank with thousands on board." Doesn't that suppose a colossal amount of precipitation? "It was raining. FC Bayern lost the game." So it was all to do with the turf? The wrong studs? As we are conditioned to do, we seek possible links, patterns – meaning.

This means that gifted readers can read even mere lists or chronicles of events as narratives: they themselves make the essential connections, provided the list gives them sufficient occasion. Julian Barnes' novel *Flaubert's Parrot* (1984) is about the widowed country doctor Geoffrey Braithwaite. After the death of his unfaithful wife, he develops an obsessive interest in Gustave Flaubert, the author of *Madame Bovary* (1857), that novel about the unfaithful wife of a

---

[13]   E. M. Forster, *Aspects of the Novel*, Harmondsworth, 1977 [1927], 87.

country doctor, which ends in her suicide. Barnes' book, which presents Geoffrey Braithwaite as the writer of the text, contains a whole collection of curious chapters. One, for instance, is called "Flaubert's Bestiary" (an annotated catalogue of all the animals of any significance in Flaubert's life and work); another takes the form of an exam paper; another is modeled on Flaubert's *Dictionnaire des idées reçues* (published posthumously in 1881). The second chapter of *Flaubert's Parrot* is entitled "Chronologies" and offers three chronological tables of Flaubert's life. Here is the beginning of the first one:

1821   Birth of Gustave Flaubert, second son of Achille-Cléophas Flaubert, head surgeon at the Hôtel-Dieu, Rouen, and of Anne-Justine-Caroline Flaubert, née Fleuriot. The family belongs to the successful professional middle class, and owns several properties in the vicinity of Rouen. A stable, enlightened, encouraging and normally ambitious background.

1825   Entry into service with the Flaubert family of Julie, Gustave's nurse, who remains with them until the writer's death fifty-five years later. Few servant problems will trouble his life.

c.1830   Meets Ernest Chevalier, his first close friend. A succession of intense, loyal and fertile friendships will sustain Flaubert throughout his life: of particular note are those with Alfred le Poittevin, Maxime du Camp, Louis Bouilhet and George Sand. Gustave inspires friendship easily, and fosters it with a teasing affectionate manner.

And here is the beginning of the second chronology:

1817   Death of Caroline Flaubert (aged twenty months), the second child of Achille-Cléophas Flaubert and Anne-Justine-Caroline Flaubert.

1819   Death of Emile-Cléophas Flaubert (aged eight months), their third child.

1821   Birth of Gustave Flaubert, their fifth child.

1822   Death of Jules Alfred Flaubert (aged three years and five months), their fourth child. His brother Gustave, born *entre deux morts*, is delicate and not expected to live long. Dr. Flaubert buys a family plot at the Cimetière Monumental and has a small grave dug in preparation for Gustave. Surprisingly, he survives. He proves a slow child, content to sit for hours with his finger in his mouth and an "almost stupid" expression on his face. For Sartre, he is "the family idiot."

There's no need to quote both tables right up until Flaubert's death in 1880; perhaps just the two entries for the year of his death:

1880   Full of honour, widely loved, and still working hard to the end, Gustave Flaubert dies at Croisset.

1880   Impoverished, lonely and exhausted, Gustave Flaubert dies. Zola, in his obituary notice, comments that he was unknown to four-fifths of Rouen, and detested by the other fifth. He leaves *Bouvard et Pécuchet* unfinished. Some say the labour of the novel killed him; Turgenev told him before he started that it would be better as a short story. After the funeral a group of mourners, including the poets François Coppée and Théodore de Banville, have dinner in Rouen to honour the departed writer. They discover, on sitting down to table, that they are thirteen. The superstitious Banville insists that another guest be found, and Gautier's son-in-law Émile Bergerat is sent to scour the streets. After several rebuffs he returns with a private on leave. The soldier has never heard of Flaubert, but is longing to meet Coppée.

It's easy to recognize that the first case tells a story of unequalled success; the second, a depressing story of permanent failure. The thing is: all the biographical facts are, as far as one can see, true. So on that level we can't accuse the compiler of error or deception.

Rather, the decisive point is the *selection* from all the available facts, which follows a *preexistent* type of narrative (success story or failure). This pattern is so clearly present in the arrangement which the reader soon – perhaps after roughly the third entry? – recognizes as the mode of connection and uses to understand or to produce the tale of the chronology. This happens without, to repeat, the list itself explicitly spelling out these connections. Hayden White writes about the way form thus supports meaning in historiography:

> When the reader recognizes the story being told in a historical narrative as a specific kind of story – for example, as an epic, romance, tragedy, comedy, or farce – he can be said to have comprehended the meaning produced by the discourse. This comprehension is nothing other than the recognition of the form of the narrative.
>
> The production of meaning in this case can be regarded as a performance, because any given set of real events can be emplotted in a number of ways, can bear the weight of being told as any number of different kinds of stories. Since no given set or sequence of real events is intrinsically tragic, comic, farcical, and so on, but can be constructed as such only by the imposition of the structure of a given story type on the events, it is the choice of the story type and its imposition upon the events that endow them with meaning.[14]

However, it is through such mediated invitations to meaning that the historian (and not only the historian) constantly works: *we ask for something like that to be there* – at the slightest opportunity we help to provide connections and to interpret patterns that we ourselves have collaborated to create.

---

[14] White, *The Content of the Form*, 43–44.

By the way, the most interesting chronology in *Flaubert's Parrot* is the third one. It consists without exception of quotations from Flaubert, arranged by year. The selection discloses no obvious pattern, no narration, at least not at first glance. Perhaps that's why this chronology, after the transparent arrangements of chronological tables 1 and 2, strikes us as the most attractive. It stimulates the reader more strongly than the first two; and precisely because of its shapelessness, it has the appearance of being closer to reality – assuming we don't believe that life is something that has an order from the beginning, and that sense and meaning are something "given."

That brings us to a paradox. Narrative should produce meaning (that's what we'd like), but not in such a way as to give us the impression of strain and coercion. We clearly prefer to receive it carefully prepared and laid out as a buffet, from which we can freely choose. To change the metaphors: the statue which, according to Michelangelo, is always concealed in the block of marble, needs – and this takes effort – to be freed from everything it is encumbered with: only then will it become visible. That is of course – in the case of sculpture we appreciate this more easily – a fabrication. Or true only insofar as the master "sees" what can be made out of a material, which may be the material of one's own life.

5 I

The hermeneutist and theoretical founder of the *Geisteswissenschaften*, Wilhelm Dilthey, wrote that in autobiography "a life-course stands as an external phenomenon from which understanding seeks to discover what produced it within a particular environment." He considered it the highest and most instructive form of the understanding of life, for "the person who understands it is the same as the one who created it. This results in a particular intimacy of understanding."[15]

What exactly does "understanding" mean here?

> When we look back through memory, we see the nexus of the past parts of a life-course in terms of the category of meaning. When we live in the present, the positive or negative value of the realities that fill it are experienced through feeling. And when we face the future, the category of purpose arises through a projective attitude. We interpret life as the actualization of some overriding

[15] Wilhelm Dilthey, "Drafts for a Critique of Historical Reason," *Selected Works, Vol. 3, The Formation of the Historical World in the Human Sciences*, ed. and trans. Rudolf A. Makkreel and Frithjof Rodi, Princeton, NJ, 2002, 221. German text: Wilhelm Dilthey, "Entwürfe zur Kritik der historischen Vernunft," *Seminar: Philosophische Hermeneutik*, ed. Hans-Georg Gadamer and Gottfried Boehm, Frankfurt am Main, 1979 [1976], 189–220, here 199.

purpose to which all particular purposes are subordinated, that is, as the realization of a highest good.[16]

We can thus speak of a sense of the whole only if each part can be integrated purposefully through a *network of meaning*:

> The sense of life lies in giving shape to things and in development; on its basis the meaning of the moments of life is determined in a distinctive way; it is both the experienced, intrinsic, value of the moment and its productive force.
>
> Each life has its own sense. It consists in a meaning-context in which every remembered present possesses an intrinsic value, and yet, through the nexus of memory, it is also related to the sense of the whole.[17]

Therefore, according to Dilthey, meaning is not just the basic category of human understanding, but of the understanding of all objects of *historical* (as opposed to scientific) knowledge as such:

> The category of purpose, or of the good, which considers life as it is directed toward the future, presupposes that of value. But this category too cannot bring out the connectedness of the life-nexus, for the relations of purpose to each other are only those of possibility, choice, and subordination. Only the category of meaning overcomes the mere juxtaposition or subordination of the parts of life to each other. As history is memory and as the category of meaning belongs to memory, this is the most distinctive category of historical thought.[18]

Now, Lichtenberg once caustically remarked that some people have begun to lie as soon as they say "I." But that only underlines how right Dilthey was: autobiography is the attempt to demonstrate that we are justified in saying "I" – that we have our own history. The "I" should be able to say at the end: I have grasped how it was that I became who I am now. I have understood myself and have therefore arrived at my end, my goal, my purpose. To some extent every autobiography follows the pattern of Hegel's *Phenomenology of Spirit*: when the world-spirit (*Weltgeist*) has apprehended itself in terms of concepts, it has come to itself, and dialectic and development have a (putative) end.

That also explains why the category of purpose, which in actual life belongs to the future, is displaced, as it were, onto the dimension of the past: in narrating the past, the autobiographer is no longer working towards a future, but begins at the sources and follows the course of the

---

[16]   Dilthey, "Drafts," 222–223.
[17]   Dilthey, "Drafts," 221.
[18]   Dilthey, "Drafts," 223.

brook, then of the river, until the present moment – the rest is twilight, oceanic feelings, the great beyond.

The end and purpose of narration must, however, be developed consistently from its beginning, otherwise it won't look coherent. It must be possible to make the end plausible as the fulfillment of a purpose.

> In my beginning is my end.
>
> (T. S. Eliot, "East Coker," first line)
>
> In my end is my beginning.
>
> (T. S. Eliot, "East Coker," last line)

But such a plausibility does not arise on its own, and every narrative of a life labors under a suspicion: it may have submitted the past to "the violence of a retrospective interpretation,"[19] it may have used it for a purpose, namely to fabricate a telos for its life. Every autobiography makes a final plea for the coherence of the life it describes. Every fictional first-person narration does the same thing (or thematizes this attempt, or fails), and also finds itself faced with the task of creating meaning by making connections. It must be possible for everything to follow from the beginning – at least retrospectively it must make sense, including – and especially – when one hadn't grasped it at the time.

It is essential for the production of sense and the generation of meaning that there must actually be no coincidences, seen from the end of the day. Of course, it is generally recognized that there is such a thing as coincidence, but in narrative coincidences are retrospectively transformed into a chain of causes and effects, giving rise to the illusion of fate and predestination. "It *had* to happen, because …'; or "If I hadn't missed the bus, we'd never have run into each other." The basic model for this kind of narrative of meaningfulness and fated inevitability (born from coincidences) with regard to one's own story is the love story ("Do you remember …?"). Lovers, reassuring each other, tell this story back and forth, again and again – converting contingency into necessity ("only because I'd forgotten my mobile phone and had to go back again …") in order to convince themselves that their being together now was inevitable. *This* love *had* to be – nobody else could lie here beside me.

The basis of such narratives, which follow causal threads backwards in order to present the present as the logically necessary consequence of everything that went before, is of course the principle of causality (no effect without a cause, no cause without an effect), in its exaggerated form: determinism. Characteristic of determinism, however, is that its effects can only be

---

[19]   Jürgen Habermas, *Erkenntnis und Interesse*, Frankfurt am Main, 1979 [1968], 192.

identified retrospectively, after something has occurred, but never in advance – otherwise everyone would be able to predict the future. Tristram Shandy emphasizes repeatedly how convenient he finds it that none of his readers could ever guess, let alone know, what's going to happen next. The continuation of the story has to be unpredictable: that's what makes it interesting and exciting. Looking forwards, narrative faces *contingency*. In this very quality of unpredictability, narratives – even unrealistic ones – imitate life. As soon as a possibility has crystallized in the present, however, it can be passed off as the consequence of the *one* previous event or encounter (or of a causal chain) that has proved decisive, the prime factor among the abundance of prior conditions. Realistic novels tend to hide this retrospective choice by relating an abundance of details and circumstances whose relevance to the narrative is not always equally evident, but which in their very accumulation can produce a sense of proximity to reality. In other words, while selection intimates necessary connection, a "surplus" of circumstances gives the impression of reality. The relation of both these constituent factors to each other varies.

Gottfried Keller, for example, begins *Green Henry* (written 1846–1859, published 1854/55, considerably revised much later [1879/80]) with a chapter entitled "In Praise of my Origin," which begins like this (trans. A. M. Holt, 1960):

> My father belonged to the peasantry of an ancient Alemannic village which derived its name from the man who, when the land was divided up, stuck his spear in the ground and built a house there. When, in the passing of the centuries, the race that had given its name to the village died out, a feudal lord adopted the name as his title and built a castle. Nobody knows now where it stood, nor when the last scion of that race died. But the village stands there still, populous and more alive than ever.

We can't do much with that – yet. We can't recognize any organization of the elements of the circumstantial situation that might produce meaning, except for a certain accumulation of incidents of disappearance and forgetting. In contrast, the following beginning (Josef von Eichendorff, *From the Life of a Good-for-Nothing*, 1826; trans. J. G. Nichols, 2002) is larded with parallels and oppositions, which splendidly generate meanings:

> My father's mill-wheel was once more rumbling and splashing away, the snow was dripping industriously from the roof, and the sparrows were twittering and playing about. And I was sitting on the doorstep and rubbing the sleep out of my eyes, feeling very comfortable in the warm sunshine. Then my father, who had been bustling about in the mill since daybreak, came out of doors with his nightcap on askew and said to me, "You good for nothing! There you are sunning yourself again and stretching your weary limbs and leaving me to

do all the work by myself. I can't go on feeding you any longer. Spring is coming. So out into the wide world with you and earn your own living for once."

The *rumbling* wheel, the *playing* birds – the sitting boy; the *industriously* dripping *snow* – the warm *sunshine*; day*break* – *spring*; *house* – *world*; *the busy father* – *the idle son*; *sleep* in the eyes – the father's displaced *night*cap; further: the *threshold* – that's perhaps even a bit *too* closely organized.

The beginning of *Robinson Crusoe* (1790) – from which so much can be drawn that it will serve as an example many times over – achieves a happy medium:

> I was born in the year 1632, in the city of York, of a good family, tho' not of that country, my father being a foreigner of Bremen, who settled first at Hull. He got a good estate by merchandise, and leaving off his trade lived afterward at York, form whence he had married my mother, whose relations were named Robinson, a very good family in that country, and from whom I was called Robinson Kreutznaer; but by the usual corruption of words in England, we are now called, nay, we call our selves and write our name, Crusoe, and so my companions always called me.
>
> I had two elder brothers, one of which was lieutenant collonel to an English regiment of foot in Flanders, formerly commanded by the famous Coll. Lockhart, and was killed at the battle near Dunkirk against the Spaniards. What became of my second brother I never knew any more than my father or mother did know what was become of me.

The "I" – the first word of this paradigmatically modern novel – is here situated firmly in the historical and geographical reality of seventeenth-century England. Everything is historical, no longer consigned romance-like to a never-never land. Even his name has a history (Kreutznaer > Crusoe). Both brothers – the first deceased, the second lost without trace – are merely named, never to be mentioned again, for the sake of completeness. Further, the death of one brother in a historical battle anchors the fictional story, which presents itself as a factual account and not as a novel, in the real world of the reader.

But as even the first paragraph makes clear, every narration that sets great store on causality and necessary connection has a tendency to infinite regression: the cause of the effect is effect of another cause, and that came about like this, etc., etc. … That is carried out to excess in Laurence Sterne's *Tristram Shandy* (1759–67): for the formalist Viktor Shklovsky the archetypal novel of world literature,[20] because it so intelligently and playfully lays

---

[20]   Victor Shklovsky, "A Parodying Novel: Sterne's *Tristram Shandy*" (originally published in *O Teorii Prozy*, Moscow, 1929), trans. W. George Isaak, in *Laurence Sterne: A Collection of Critical Essays*, ed. John Traugott, Englewood Cliffs, NJ, 1968, 66–89. For a different translation, see Viktor Shklovskii, "The Parody Novel: Sterne's *Tristram Shandy*," trans. Richard Sheldon, in *Review of Contemporary Fiction* 1 (1981): 190–211.

bare the *devices* of the novel, with its conspicuous foregrounding. Tristram, who sets out to narrate his life, is famously only born in the third of nine books – really not just because of the distractedness to which he is fated, but because he wants to present his story nicely and fully and with unbroken causality, a task that constantly forces him to go further back in the narrative, in order to explain how it happened in turn that …

In this world of coincidences and accidents there will be, retrospectively considered and when the work of narrative is done, no coincidences left, but only chains of causes and effects, and this means one can't be too careful. What you do or don't do has incalculable consequences. Really incalculable? In that case human beings, though equipped with reason, would be released from responsibility – released, at the same time, into a world of chaos. Here is Tristram's first sentence in his struggle for order:

> I wish either my father or my mother, or indeed both of them, as they were in duty both equally bound to it, had minded what they were about when they begot me; had they duly considered how much depended upon what they were then doing;—that not only the production of a rational Being was concerned in it, but that possibly the happy formation and temperature of his body, perhaps his genius and the very cast of his mind;—and, for aught they knew to the contrary, even the fortunes of his whole house might take their turn from the humours and dispositions which were then uppermost:——Had they duly weighed and considered all this, and proceeded accordingly,——I am verily persuaded I should have made a quite different figure in the world, from that, in which the reader is likely to see me.—

It *could* all have turned out differently. Since it turned out as it has, it can now be demonstrated why it *had* to turn out thus. The narrator suspends himself between these two poles, so that by the end he emerges as the hero, if not of his life (in which he was mostly passive), then at least of his narrative: as one who simultaneously witnessed and produced himself in narrative.

> Whether I shall turn out to be the hero of my own life, or whether that station will be held by anybody else, these pages must show.

So begins *David Copperfield* (1849/50) by Charles Dickens, and since "life" can also mean "biography," the distinction introduced just now by *Tristram Shandy* is cleverly blurred by ambiguity. Whether the first-person narrator finally emerges as the hero of his own life story must in fact be shown by the narrative he has presented, his text. That the person who is writing, however, is by no means still identical with the person whose life he is describing, would be clear even if Dickens' first chapter were not entitled (as it is) "Chapter I: I am born."

Writing one's own story, whether as autobiography or fiction, always involves an awareness of previous models and some way of relating to them (think of Augustine's *Confessions* [ca. 400 AD] – Rousseau's *Confessions* [written 1765–70, published 1782–89] – Wordsworth's *The Prelude* [begun in 1798, published 1850] – through to William Boyd's *The New Confessions* [1987]). Or, equally likely, there can occur a *rejection* of a model: this should be *my own* story that doesn't follow any pattern, that cannot possibly be derivative if it is to be both authentic and worth telling:

> If you really want to hear about it, the first thing you'll probably want to know is where I was born, and what my lousy childhood was like, and how my parents were occupied and all before they had me, and all that David Copperfield kind of crap, but I don't feel like going into it. (J. D. Salinger, *The Catcher in the Rye*, 1951)

The next step would be the rejection of an identity that others ascribe to the narrator, but with which he doesn't want to be "identified": "I am not Stiller." (Max Frisch, *Stiller*, 1954) – so begin the memoirs of one Jim Larking White. He is sitting in custody because he is suspected of being the sculptor Stiller, who has vanished. "White" ultimately finds himself forced to accept the "Stiller" identity, although he believes himself – with justification, in his view – to be someone else. The novel offers a (specious) answer, in that in the brief second part, the "public prosecutor's epilogue," it introduces a second viewpoint, that of an observer of the first observer Stiller/White.

"Call me Ishmael." So begins Herman Melville's *Moby-Dick* (1851). And this is not by way of throwing his arm around the reader's shoulders and getting on first-name terms, but rather hides what is most deeply his – his name – behind a cipher. The cipher can be read, with the aid of an encyclopedia of Judaeo-Christian culture, or a learned footnote explaining the significant connection.[21]

The name functions as a mask; the mask reveals a type: the loner. As the only survivor, he will tell how it came about that he alone is still alive. He will see the world only *sub specie cetacearum* – and since he links *everything* with whales, he makes both the whales and his own history into an allegory of everything: an allegory in the form of a life story in the form of a whale-encyclopedia – it's all a question of how the connections are made.

That is why conjunctions are so important:

> Granted: I am an inmate of a mental hospital; my keeper is watching me, he never lets me out of his sight; there's a peephole in the door, *and* my keeper's eye is the

---

[21] Ishmael is Abraham's oldest son. His mother Hagar, an Egyptian, had to flee into the desert, where an angel revealed to her that she was pregnant – she was to call the child Ishmael. He will be "a wild man" whose "hand will be against every man, and every man's hand against him" (Genesis 16.12).

shade of brown that can never see through a blue-eyed type like me. (Günther Grass, *The Tin Drum*, 1959; trans. Ralph Mannheim, 1999; emphasis added)

The reader might be irritated: the narrator's presentation of himself as possibly unreliable ("Granted") might still be welcomed as a sign of his sincerity. But the italicized *and* brings us up short: leaving aside the fact that the connection between eye-color and the ability to see through someone whose eyes are a different color seems to need some explanation, you'd surely expect the conjunction *but* – wouldn't you? And so we read on, hoping to be enlightened. That just goes to prove that the universal maxim of an experienced novelist – write the first sentence in such a way that the reader can't resist reading the second – can even be fulfilled like that. But that's another story.

6   First Sentences: Enticements

"It was a dark and stormy night; the rain fell in torrents ..." – undeterred, the ambitious young author Snoopy (from *Peanuts*), sitting on the roof of his kennel, hammers out on the keys of his typewriter this novel-opening from Edward Bulwer-Lytton (*Paul Clifford*, 1830). Snoopy is either an unoriginal epigone (or even plagiarist), or a cunning, craftily postmodern disciple of Borges's "Pierre Menard, Author of the *Quixote*." Bulwer-Lytton was much acclaimed in his time. Nowadays this novel-opening serves as a motto on the homepage of the Bulwer-Lytton Fiction Contest, which identifies the most pathetic novelists. How could it have come to this? Was it unavoidable? Is a cliché a cliché at birth? Or does it become a cliché in time?

Successful novel-openings don't necessarily shy away from the lurid; these for instance:

> It might be most dramatically effective to begin the tale at the moment when Arnold Baffin rang me up and said, "Bradley, could you come round here please, I think that I have just killed my wife." (Iris Murdoch, *The Black Prince*, 1973)[22]

---

[22]   Granted: this is, unfortunately, not a real novel-opening, but to some extent a fake one: two forewords are inserted previously, which form part of the fiction. Unfortunately, in this sense one of the greatest openings of all doesn't count as an opening either:

> Lolita, light of my life, fire of my loins. My sin, my soul. Lo-lee-ta: the tip of the tongue taking a trip of three steps down the palate to tap, at three, on the teeth. Lo. Lee. Ta.
>   She was Lo, plain Lo, in the morning, standing four feet ten in one sock. She was Lola in slacks. She was Dolly at school. She was Dolores on the dotted line. But in my arms she was always Lolita. (Vladimir Nabokov, *Lolita*, 1955)

These captivating sentences (best read aloud) are prefaced by a foreword from one Dr. John Ray. This is not the only respect in which *The Black Prince* imitates *Lolita*.

> It was the afternoon of my eighty-first birthday, and I was in bed with my catamite when Ali announced that the archbishop had come to see me. (Anthony Burgess, *Earthly Powers*, 1980)

But they don't have to be like this. The reader can be drawn in (not to say captivated) just as well by an apparently paradoxical contrast:

> For forty-two years, Lewis and Benjamin Jones slept side by side, in their parents' bed, at their farm which was known as "The Vision." (Bruce Chatwin, *On the Black Hill*, 1982)

Or it can be done with a value judgment, to which the reader can (or must) react in this or that way. William Golding recalls the first sentence of his first novel, which he wrote at the age of twelve (and unfortunately didn't publish): "I was born in the Duchy of Cornwall on the eleventh of October, 1792, of rich but honest parents."[23] Golding had, he said, tried all through his life to keep up this level. "Rich but honest" – what a searing insight that gives into the precocious boy's whole worldview and open-eyed critique of society ... that's the stuff future Nobel prizewinners are made of.

The implicating of the reader in an *evaluative* perspective is perhaps rarely more economically achieved than in Jane Austen's ironic opening of *Pride and Prejudice* (1813) –

> It is a truth universally acknowledged, that a single man of good fortune must be in want of a wife.

– where it is obvious that this can only be the view of families who have nubile daughters and know precisely what a rich young bachelor really needs, regardless of whether he is himself conscious of these necessities or not.

Compare that winking beginning, which works through silent complicity – and successfully! – with the apodictic opening of Leo Tolstoy's *Anna Karenina* (1875/76):

> All happy families are alike; each unhappy family is unhappy in its own way.

I always thought this sentence would make no less sense in reverse (an opinion I found perfectly confirmed by the beginning of Vladimir Nabokov's *Ada or Ardor: A Family Chronicle*, 1969), despite my admiration for the author. I could still save Tolstoy for myself by reflecting that in fiction, *every* sentence is to be read not as a referential statement, but as a semi-proposition

---

[23]   Bernard Oldsey, "William Golding," *Dictionary of Literary Biography*, Vol. 15: 1, Detroit, 1983, 119–134, here 121.

with no more truth claim than is required to contribute to the characterization of the narrator. The continuation, though –

> All was confusion in the Oblonskys' house. The wife had found out that the husband was having an affair with their former French governess, and had announced to the husband that she could not live in the same house with him. This situation had continued for three days now, and was painfully felt by the couple themselves, as well as by all the members of the family and household. (Leo Tolstoy, *Anna Karenina*, trans. Richard Pevear and Larissa Volokhonsky, 2003)

– informs us that the narrator of *Anna Karenina* might have meant something different: unhappiness is much easier to tell – indeed, is more interesting than happiness. And that is easy to understand.

But whether a narrative opens with a portrayal of a harmonious status quo or with the disturbance of this situation, the beginning must be a "disturbance," an interruption ("Tom!") of normalcy. The more radically this intrudes on everyday life, the more ominous the effect:

> Someone must have traduced Joseph K., for without having done anything wrong he was arrested one fine morning. (Franz Kafka, *The Trial*, 1925; trans. Willa and Edwin Muir, 1937)

Here, conjecture about the reason for the outrage is given precedence over the onset of the horror, which right until the end never loses its mysteriousness, since the minute tracing of the "what" – the trial itself – can never be a substitute for the missing answer to the question "why?"

If the conjecture about the meaning of an incident, an action, or the whole plot is shifted onto the protagonist, then the latter feels constantly compelled to explain and interpret, and only an observer of his observations can determine possible misinterpretations:

> The construction worker Josef Bloch, who had previously been a famous goalkeeper, was told when he went to work in the morning that his services were no longer required. At least, Bloch interpreted the fact that when he appeared at the door of the site hut where the workers were hanging around, only the foreman glanced up from his snack, as being such a message, and left the construction site. (Peter Handke, *The Goalkeeper's Fear at the Penalty Kick*, 1970)

An interpretation like this is also always a speculation about others' expectations. As goalkeeper I know that the penalty-taker usually shoots into the left-hand corner – so I'll throw myself that way. But since the penalty-taker also knows that I know that he always shoots left, he'll now choose the right-hand corner. But since I know … If we orient ourselves according to others' expectations, we fall into insoluble problems.

Thus the presence of a third, who merely observes events and interpretations (as events), seems to guarantee a higher level of truth to reality:

> The journey of Mercier and Camier is one I can tell, if I will, for I was with them all the time. (Samuel Beckett, *Mercier and Camier*, 1970/74)

When it subsequently comes to light, however, that most of the time the two protagonists Mercier and Camier were alone, we recognize that we have fallen for a metafictional ploy on the narrator's part: he was there the whole time, not because he shared a world and a life with them – no, but because they are *fictional* figures. The narrator can pledge himself for the truth of the narrative because it's entirely his: a fictional narrative – nothing more. He wasn't stretching the truth in his first sentence: we are the ones who have once again confused life and literature.

Beckett's debased tramps, with their dreams, projects, and endless preparations, recall something of Flaubert's *Bouvard et Pécuchet* (1881). The real ancestor, though, is Diderot's *Jacques le fataliste et son maître* (1796). This, too, is a largely dialogic novel, which right at the beginning grumpily overturns the reader's expectation of a realistic narrative situation:

> How did they meet? By chance like everybody else. What were their names? What's that got to do with you? Where were they coming from? From the nearest place. Where were they going to? Does anyone ever really know where they are going to? What were they saying? The master wasn't saying anything and Jacques was saying that his Captain used to say that everything which happens to us here below, both good and bad, is written up above. (Denis Diderot, *Jacques the Fatalist and his Master*, 1796; trans. Michael Henry, 1986)

We see the usual suspects: how did it happen? By chance – and so we already have a fundamental opposition to the worldview of Jacques, the fatalist and determinist, according to which *everything* is preordained (Diderot greatly admired Laurence Sterne for his *Tristram Shandy*, and knew exactly why). But this worldview, according to which the modern novel *must* function, is the machine that transforms coincidence into necessity, chaos into meaning. Further: the names? What's it to you? Yes, indeed, what's in a name? And sure, you always come from wherever you just were and want to go on – but *ultimately* where? – that's a metaphysical question. Whatever (hi)story lies there is entirely up to the conversation of this unequal pair. The self-enlightenment of pre-revolutionary society has to occur in conversation, in discourse, since after the Enlightenment no truth can any longer be imagined as lying outside discourse; even if, admittedly, distinctions will be introduced into discursively produced truth:

There was a depression over the Atlantic. It was travelling eastwards, towards an area of high pressure over Russia, and still showed no tendency to move northwards around it. The isotherms and isotheres were fulfilling their functions. The atmospheric temperature was in proper relation to the average annual temperature, the temperature of the coldest as well as of the hottest month, and the a-periodic monthly variation in temperature. The rising and setting of the sun and of the moon, the phases of the moon, Venus and Saturn's rings, and many other important phenomena, were in accordance with the forecasts in the astronomical yearbooks. The vapour in the air was at its highest tension, and the moisture in the air was at its lowest. In short, to use an expression that describes the facts pretty satisfactorily, even though it is somewhat old-fashioned: it was a fine August day in the year 1913. (Robert Musil, *The Man Without Qualities*, 1930–1952; trans. Eithne Wilkins and Ernst Kaiser, 1980)

Not a bad beginning for a novel which, however ironically, stands up for humanity, which has become marginal, against the superior strength of what humankind produced in the first place but has now become dominant (something "beautiful" is by definition not measurable), and at last tries to find salvation in a "different state."

Appropriation of previous beginnings always seems to imply diminution (compare Dickens–Salinger, above). The sun on Musil's pleasant August day continues to shine in Beckett's *Murphy* (1938) on what is proverbially (i.e., since long before the start of the modern novel) beneath it: nothing new. "The sun shone, having no alternative, on the nothing new." Yet nevertheless – there's no thwarting narrative tradition – even that happens necessarily, without alternative.

When Helmut Heißenbüttel intertextually weaves in a quotation from Goethe's *Elective Affinities* –

Eduard – let that be the name we give to a radio journalist in the best years of his life – Eduard had spent the loveliest hours of a July afternoon in the fast train from Munich to Hamburg (arrival time at the main station 21.19) and surveyed the scenery between Lüneburg and Hamburg with pleasure. (Helmut Heißenbüttel, *Projekt Nr. 1. D'Alemberts Ende*, 1970)

Eduard – let that be the name we give to a wealthy baron in the best years of his life – Eduard had spent the loveliest hours of an April afternoon in his nursery grafting young trees with shoots newly arrived for him. (Johann Wolfgang von Goethe, *Elective Affinities*, 1809; trans. David Constantine, 1999) –

– it is nevertheless hard to determine whether the irony cuts the earlier, classical text or the object of the recent narrative. One fears – both (the time is stretched out [*hours* instead of *hour*] and specified with two sets of numbers; the tempo is faster, but only technically – the man himself is no longer responsible for his movement, but rather *is* moved).

Every beginning, however, presupposes a world about which we can ask – regardless of "willing suspension of disbelief" – whether it can still be taken for granted in this way. Attacking the Surrealist André Breton, the Christian-conservative Paul Valéry once stated that he personally would refuse to begin a novel with the sentence "La marquise sortit à cinq heures." [The Marquise went out at five o'clock.][24] – that kind of thing just wasn't done any more. And when Claude Mauriac did exactly that, in order to refute Valéry and show him that you could indeed still do that kind of thing, he did not, of course, succeed in his refutation at all. For what Valéry meant was not that it *can't* be done, but that it no longer should be done by a writer who wanted to be taken seriously – as someone in the philosophical and artistic vanguard of the time, and on top of their material. None of the elements in the sentence "La marquise sortit à cinq heures" can any longer be uttered, because all its decisive parameters have come into question. Something like this can no longer be narrated.

Valéry's admonition is well worth reflecting on (and the fact that others just continue to write as if nothing had happened makes no difference to his point). The modern novel is, in common with other literary genres, a historical phenomenon through and through – with a beginning, a middle, and indeed an end, too. It is unique among the major literary genres only in this respect: that it arose *after* the invention of printing and contemporaneously with the advent of the book *trade*.[25] It's a profitable genre. It is the youngest and most successful literary genre in human history. Part of its success certainly stems from the fact that it narrates. It took over this role from epic poetry, which has since persisted only very sporadically – a successful displacement. The novel's takeover of the role or function of narrative was so eminently successful because to read a narration in a (somehow) realistic novel you don't need any particular cultural or literary background knowledge – you just read it.

But could it be that the function of narrative has meanwhile migrated not just to another genre, but even to a completely different medium? B. S. Johnson, the great experimenter among English novelists of the 1960s, argued in this way when he wrote:

> It is a fact of crucial significance in the history of the novel this century that James Joyce opened the first cinema in Dublin in 1909. Joyce saw very early on that film must usurp some of the prerogatives which until then had belonged almost exclusively to the novelist. Film could tell a story more directly, in less time and with more concrete detail than a novel; certain aspects of character could be more easily delineated and kept constantly before the audience (for example, physical characteristics like a limp, a scar, particular ugliness or

---

[24]   André Breton, "Erstes Manifest des Surrealismus," *Surrealismus in Paris 1919–1939: Ein Lesebuch*, ed. Karlheinz Barck, Leipzig, 1990, 82–120, here 88.

[25]   Cf. Mikhail M. Bakhtin, "Epic and Novel," *The Dialogic Imagination*, ed. Michael Holquist, trans. Caryl Emerson and Michael Holquist, Austin, 1981, 3–40.

beauty); no novelist's description of a battle squadron at sea in a gale could really hope to compete with that in a well-shot film; and why should anyone who simply wanted to be told a story spend all his spare time for a week or weeks reading a book when he could experience the same thing in a version in some ways superior at his local cinema in only one evening?

It was not the first time that storytelling had passed from one medium to another. Originally it had been the chief concern of poetry, and long narrative poems were bestsellers right up to the works of Walter Scott and Byron. The latter supplanted the former in the favours of the public, and Scott adroitly turned from narrative poems to narrative novels and continued to be a bestseller. You will agree it would be perversely anachronistic to write a long narrative poem today? People still do, of course; but such works are rarely published, and, if they are, the writer is thought of as a literary flat-earther.

[...] In some ways the history of the novel in the twentieth century has seen large areas of the old territory of the novelist increasingly taken over by other media, until the only thing the novelist can with any certainty call exclusively his own is the inside of his own skull: and that is what he should be exploring, rather than anachronistically fighting a battle he is bound to lose. [...] What happens is nothing like as important as how it is written.[26]

That corresponds to the view of those who believe that twentieth-century painting entered the realm of abstraction because its natural territory, mimetic depiction, was so efficiently usurped by the new invention of photography: when such a thing happens, you get out of the core business and do something else. The question is whether mimetic depiction ever was the core business of painting. Or whether the portrayal of observable things ever was the core business of the novel. If not, there must be other reasons for the development of the modernist and postmodern novel apart from the technological one proposed by Johnson: reasons that could also explain the incontestable (and enormously successful) continued existence of types of novel which, according to Valéry and B. S. Johnson, should have long since historically and aesthetically worn themselves out. How about if the function of the novel was instead to do something like this: to produce exemplary meaning by transforming contingency into (narratively charged) necessity? Or: literally to make sense – to show forms of sense-making and meaning-production in process? Or: to say one thing and mean another, while letting the reader participate in this translation – inviting us, in fact, to undertake it ourselves using what is given, i.e., the data.

The function of the modern novel can only be ascertained historically. So we must go back to the beginning – to which all we have just discussed applies, for the history of the novel itself is nothing other than a narrative.

[26] B. S. Johnson, "Aren't You Rather Young to be Writing Your Memoirs?" In *The Novel Today: Contemporary Writers on Fiction*, ed. Malcolm Bradbury, Glasgow, 1977, 151–168, here 151, 152.

2

The Modern European Novel
Predecessors, Origins, Conventions, Sub-Genres

1   Dangers and Allurements of Novel-Reading: What's Novel about the Novel?

The first modern European novel is a novel about the dangers of novel-reading: for Miguel Cervantes Saavedra's *Don Quixote de la Mancha* (first part 1605, second part 1615) famously tells the story of the down-at-heel squire (*hidalgo* – only in the second part is he promoted to *caballero*) Quijada or Quesada or Quijana – "this, however, is of but little importance to our tale; it will be enough not to stray a hair's breadth from the truth in the telling of it," the first page informs us – who indulges excessively in the reading of chivalric novels to the neglect of daily life, finally subsiding into madness. "Don Quixote" (for this is the name he now takes on) exchanges a gray, unmeaning present for a glorious past. The gaunt fifty-year-old himself turns into a character from one of his beloved chivalric romances, a knight-errant, "the knight of the sad countenance." Mounted on his nag Rosinante, armed with a lance and accompanied by the rotund, down-to-earth Sancho Pansa as his squire, he engages in all kinds of adventures – fighting with giants, wizards, and hostile armies – for the fame and honor of his idolized lady Dulcinea, who is actually just a farmhand from the next village.

That can only work, of course, if reality is permanently subordinated to a radically new interpretation, totally different from the way the rest of humankind understands it: windmills are giants, a flock of sheep is an army, and the barber's shaving bowl turns into Mambrino's priceless helmet. Don Quixote possesses an unusually lively poetic–metaphoric imagination, but he is completely unconscious of his translation of images. Always confronted with

The Novel: An Introduction. By Christoph Bode. Translated by James Vigus. English translation © 2011 James Vigus. Published by John Wiley & Sons, Ltd.
Original German text © 2005 Narr Francke Attempto Verlag GmbH + Co. KG.

only the *results* of his transformations, he lives in a world of metamorphoses, whose "real" constituents have been faded out. That is his delusion: that he can no longer differentiate the mere productions of his fantasy from what is "really" out there. Don Quixote doesn't know how much he projects – how much of what he encounters is of his own making. Don Quixote is, it must be said, in more than one respect the archetype of a bad reader. For Don Quixote is not just, as everyone knows, a bad reader of chivalric romances, because he can't separate literature from life, mixes the two up and so – as we readers see – (mis-)takes the one for the other. He also becomes by virtue of this trait a bad reader *of his own life*, because he no longer recognizes his fictions and fantasies as such. *Don Quixote* shows what awful consequences being a bad novel reader can have *for one's own life*.

This kind of novel reader, who confuses reality with the novelistic world and so falls into absurd or tragic misinterpretations, comes up again and again in the history of the modern novel. We encounter this reader in Catherine Morland in Jane Austen's *Northanger Abbey* (1818), who has read a surfeit of Gothic novels. Another is Gustave Flaubert's Madame Bovary (in the eponymous novel), whose weakness for love stories together with her suffering of the emptiness of provincial life with a loveless, boring husband leads her to seek romances in life. She casts herself in roles taken from her novels (hence the name *Bovaryism* for this kind of role-playing) – a self-deception which, unlike in the witty Jane Austen's work, ends in the protagonist's suicide. Excessive, over-involved novel-reading may damage your health and could result in death. Yet also, paradoxically: for information about possible risks and side-effects please consult – your novelist.

Don Quixote can without further ado be read as a satirical reckoning with chivalric romances, which were still popular in Cervantes' time. In the sixteenth century, numerous derivative, epigonal texts were written on the model of the *Amadís novel* (the origin of the subject matter is unclear; the first written version was Garcí Rodríguez de Montalvo's *Amadís de Gaula* – the fourth book of the *Amadís* in particular was used as a guide to polite conduct and conversation). These works mixed love and adventure, the noble and the fantastic, in an easily predictable way: they were entertaining, undemanding light fiction – and Don Quixote's favorite reading matter.

If *Don Quixote* was about nothing more than this straightforward opposition between the fantasy of the chivalric novel and the realism of *Don Quixote*, we could swiftly dismiss Cervantes' work as a practical manifesto for a new kind of novel. That would be no mean feat: the modern novel's self-creation by bracketing itself off from the traditional genre of fantastic chivalric romance. But the situation is more complicated and therefore much more interesting: *Don Quixote* itself obscures its relationship to the genre it parodies. It does so not so much by exempting *Amadís* alone from the bonfire of books in chapter 6 (though later, on his deathbed, Don Quixote curses *Amadís*!), as by systematically stirring up doubts about its own "reality," its own "truth" and reliability. At the end of chapter 8 (first part) the description of the fight between Don Quixote and the Biscayan breaks off and we read:

> But it spoils all, that at this point and crisis the author of the history leaves this battle impending, giving as excuse that he could find nothing more written about these achievements of Don Quixote than what has been already set forth. It is true the second author of this work was unwilling to believe that a history so curious could have been allowed to fall under the sentence of oblivion, or that the wits of La Mancha could have been so undiscerning as not to preserve in their archives or registries some documents referring to this famous knight; and this being his persuasion, he did not despair of finding the conclusion of this pleasant history, which, heaven favouring him, he did find in a way that shall be related in the Second Part. (Miguel de Cervantes Saavedra, *The Ingenious Gentleman Don Quixote of La Mancha*, trans. John Ormsby, 1885)

Then in chapter 9 the "second author," who had already in the preface confusingly referred both to the story as his "brainchild" and to himself as only the "stepfather" of *Don Quixote*, recounts how he had by chance stumbled across the original manuscript of the *History of Don Quixote of La Mancha, written by Cide Hamete Benengeli, an Arab historian* in Toledo. He pays a Morisco (a Moor who has undergone forced baptism) in kind to translate the whole thing from Arabic into Castilian, "without omitting or adding anything" – and then he can continue the interrupted description of the fight.

Of course, that raises a series of questions: for instance, what actually was the textual basis of the narrative up to this point? Why, if the whole thing is the Morisco's translation of Cide Hamete Benengeli's narrative, did the description of the fight have to be interrupted on the ground that the manuscript broke off, when the latter is after all complete and enables the continuation? The textual situation is "impossible."

Anyway, from now on (if not before) the text has three fathers: first, Cide Hamete Benengeli (and Salman Rushdie never tires of mentioning, with a wink, that the actual author of the first modern European novel was confessedly an Oriental – as in *The Moor's Last Sigh*, 1995); second, the translator into Castilian; and third, the "second author." This auctorial triple star doesn't promise a particularly high level of authenticity. On the contrary, such a constellation throws up huge problems of credibility. First, we are not (we learn) reading an original text at all, but a translation, whose quality and faithfulness we can't judge. Then, the "second author" says that Arabs are notorious liars and that we can anyway assume that since "they are our bitterest enemies," "there were omissions rather than additions made" in Cide Hamete Benengeli's story (really? Does that follow?). When the "second author" now simply appropriates the text (claiming it has all one could wish for, blaming any deficiencies on his predecessor, that "hound of an author"), the confusion is perfect: from now on at least three voices intertwine and fabricate the "reality" of this novel text – an evident construct, a conglomerate.

This is not the place to go into the ideological and cultural implications of this constellation "Christianity–Islam–Interpreter" (with slight variations, Salman Rushdie resumes the motif of the threefold origin in *Midnight's Children*, 1981). The key point is: from now on, the reality of *Don Quixote* is *basically no better attested* than that of the chivalric romances. *Don Quixote* is ostentatiously *fiction*, and the passages of auto-referential self-commentary are among the most interesting in the book. That this apparently "realistic" construction of fiction, the *fabrication* of reality, is in fact a *theme* of the novel becomes fully clear at the end of the first part, when "the author" takes his leave:

> The author asks of those that shall read it nothing [...] save that they give him the same credit that people of sense give to the books of chivalry that pervade the world and are so popular; for with this he will consider himself amply paid and fully satisfied, and will be encouraged to seek out and produce other histories, if not as truthful, at least equal in invention and not less entertaining.

The difference between this novel and chivalric romance is thus effaced. If the "other histories" mentioned are not as truthful as this one, yet equal in invention, the question arises how much invention there actually is in this "truthful history."

The second part of *Don Quixote* (published as mentioned in 1615, a year after the forged continuation by Avellaneda) takes this game even further. Owing to the success of the first part, Don Quixote is now a famous man – known and courted – who lives in present-day Spain and for instance came across Avellaneda's forgery in 1614 – one of many devices Cervantes thinks up to punish Avellaneda, for Don Quixote's judgment of the fake continuation is, of course, withering. But curiously the first, "genuine" part of "his" novel is not spared either: when Don Quixote finds out that it was not written by, say, an (authorial?) wizard, who managed to record dialogues between himself and Sancho Pansa word for word, but originally by an Arab, the *caballero* falls into cursing the general mendacity of Moors. A fictional character openly doubts the trustworthiness of "his" inventor. And that is only the beginning of the modern European novel – by no means its postmodern end.

To what sort of situation is *Don Quixote* – this novel about the way "reality" can be fabricated *and at the same time* about the danger of failing to keep fiction and reality properly apart – an answer? Horst Weich sketches the terrain:

> The period around 1600 is an epoch of manifold crises. Crisis hits the fundamental world-picture. Whereas the medieval cosmos was held together

at the deepest level by an all-powerful God, and there was only one truth, the new experiences of the early moderns broke up the picture of the unity of the world into the liberating, but also disturbing plurality of worlds. Such experiences included the "discovery" of America; the questioning of Catholicism via reforming counter-currents; and not least the demise of the Ptolemaic world-picture, according to which the earth was at the centre of the universe, and its replacement by the heliocentric world-picture, which places the sun at the centre at least of our solar system.

And crisis hits signs and meanings as well. Whereas in the Middle Ages – as in chivalric romance – all signs always referred ultimately to their secret source – God – and their meanings were thus always guaranteed independently of their respective situation, signs have now become deceptive: their meanings fluctuate, and the previously guaranteed single meaning fragments into a fullness of possible significations.[1]

This also helps to frame Heinrich Heine's classic evaluation of *Don Quixote*: "Cervantes founded the modern novel [...]. He blends the ideal with the mean, the one serves the other for shading or illumination, and the element relating to the nobility is just as powerful as the popular."[2] The novel contains everything within itself – high and low, ideal and mundane, true and fictitious – and as an *omnium gatherum* it ushers in the dissolution of the old order of community and world. A hierarchical order based on deference to the next level is finally shattered. Now meaning is produced by a play of signs, the fictitiousness of which can be revealed in a fiction. But the play of signs also produces a reality: meaning emerges from the movement of elements that cannot be held in their customary place by a supposedly external force-field. Something has started to move and is now in flux.

About a hundred years before the novel *Don Quixote*, a literary work had already waved goodbye to knights, courtly love, and fantastic adventures – but one that in terms of genre still belonged to the other, "old" school: Ariosto's magnificent epic *Orlando Furioso* (i.e., *The Mad Roland*: written 1505–1515, published 1532) – a disorderly, unconnected poetic work of prodigious length and overflowing digressions. This parodic epic too can display the once glorious Christian knight only in *madness*, in the madness of his individual desire, no longer within an objectively valid order – and the incoherent form of the epic reflects this. Across the genre boundary, the novel *Don Quixote* salutes the epic *Orlando Furioso* as its predecessor, and begins something new: now it *constructively* thematizes the feasibility of meaning-making, which can be liberating, but also disquieting. In the modern age, we are well

[1]   Horst Weich, *Cervantes' "Don Quijote,"* Munich, 2001, 35.
[2]   Heinrich Heine, "Einleitung zur Prachtausgabe des *Don Quijote* (1837)," *Sämtliche Werke in sieben Bänden*, Stuttgart, n.d., 5: 128–142, here 135.

practiced in self-interpretation and self-fashioning and indeed depend upon them – that always includes the possibility, too, of getting it "wrong," which, however, can only be observed from yet another point.

When the "second author" of *Don Quixote* takes his farewell at the end –

> and so doing shalt thou discharge thy Christian calling, giving good counsel to one that bears ill-will to thee. And I shall remain satisfied, and proud to have been the first who has ever enjoyed the fruit of his writings as fully as he could desire; for my desire has been no other than to deliver over to the detestation of mankind the false and foolish tales of the books of chivalry, which, thanks to that of my true Don Quixote, are even now tottering, and doubtless doomed to fall for ever. Farewell.

– he ushers one world out and opens the door to another, new one: his hero is "true" – as attentive readers, we have observed how such truth is generated through artistic illusion, and therefore how fragile, questionable, and fictitious it is.

Don Quixote's madness also thrives on the fact that others play along – to forestall worse things (Sancho Pansa); to enjoy mischief at the expense of the noble lunatic (the Duke and Duchess); but also to free him from his madness, to draw him out of it playfully (the pastor, the barber, and the "Knight of the Mirrors," Sansón Carrasco). The fiction of his madness is thus "infectious," reality-bending – for those *who get involved with it* for whatever reason. Probably that, too, is an allegory of reading, an allegory of how the modern novel works. But you don't have to go crazy in the process.

2   Fact and Fiction: No Man is an Island

Readers can see for themselves that *Don Quixote* is fiction – it virtually parades the fact. That, however, is by no means a necessary attribute of a novel, as chapter 1 of the present book discussed. In the case of what is arguably the first modern English novel, Daniel Defoe's *Robinson Crusoe*, it wouldn't be so easy to make this judgment plausible on the basis of the text alone: for this novel makes every possible effort to appear not as fiction, but as fact, not as a novel, but as an account of real events.

The title page of the first edition (1719) can be seen in figure 2.1.[3] It is striking that the name of the author, Daniel Defoe, never appears; rather, the text is presented as an autobiographical account by Robinson Crusoe. Not only are all conceivable hallmarks of fiction omitted, but the "editor" even expressly dismisses any suspicion that it might after all be an invented

---

[3]   From Daniel Defoe, *The Life and Adventures of Robinson Crusoe*, Harmondsworth, 1982, 23.

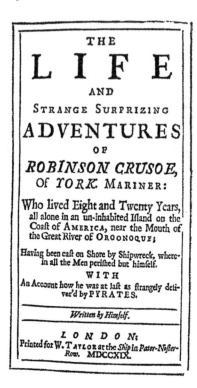

THE

L I F E

AND

Strange Surprizing

ADVENTURES

OF

ROBINSON CRUSOE,

Of *YORK* Mariner:

Who lived Eight and Twenty Years,
all alone in an un-inhabited Ifland on the
Coaft of America, near the Mouth of
the Great River of Oroonoque;

Having been caft on Shore by Shipwreck, where-
in all the Men perifhed but himfelf.

WITH

An Account how he was at laft as ftrangely deliver'd by PYRATES.

Written by Himfelf.

L O N D O N:
Printed for W. Taylor at the *Ship* in *Pater-Nofter-
Row.* MDCCXIX.

Figure 2.1

story: "The editor believes the thing to be a just history of fact; neither is there any appearance of fiction in it [...]." And the narrative that follows truthfully follows the advertised program. What we read is impossible to differentiate from an account of a real shipwreck (such as that of Alexander Selkirk) and lonely survival on a tropical island. The fake is perfect: fiction is camouflaged as fact.

This literary mimicry can, of course, only succeed if all the parameters of longer narratives are aligned with potential readers' perception of reality, so that readers don't stumble over any "literary" difference from their usual world and thus become suspicious. *Robinson Crusoe* achieves that with such ideal perfection that Ian Watt, in his classic study of the beginnings of the bourgeois-realist novel, *The Rise of the Novel* (1958), uses it (along with *Moll Flanders* [1722], and the novels of Samuel Richardson [*Pamela*, 1740/41, *Clarissa*, 1747/48] and Henry Fielding [*Joseph Andrews*, 1742, *Tom Jones*, 1749]) to develop the ideal type of his concept of "formal realism." So what defines "formal realism," as opposed to non-realistic forms of narrative such as romances, chivalric tales, fables, myths, and so on?

1. *Original plots*. That's obvious: I won't be able to sell anyone my story as "true" if its content has clearly been known for centuries and only been worked over in my telling. The content of the story must be *new*. Although the term "novel" first became established at the end of the eighteenth century, this aspect of novelty continues to be stressed more in the Anglo-American literary tradition than in continental histories of literature. The latter, after all, derive their terms for this genre from the old French "roman" or later "romance": an etymology that tends to foreground the everyday language of this form of prose, its popular accessibility. This rejection of traditional, universally valid content and stories (I'm deliberately keeping the terminology vague) coincides with setting tremendously high store on *individual, new, one-off experience*. The specific is the order of the day, the interesting exception. "For telling a story means having something *special* to say" is Theodor W. Adorno's generalization (he then goes on to complain that from the perspective of the supposed end of the traditional novel, the modern, bureaucratic world increasingly hinders that possibility).[4] At least three points follow from the increased value of the special and the specific.

2. The characters in the "formal realist" novel are *special people*. Not in the sense that they have to be outstanding personalities – on the contrary, such novels' inventory of characters is often notably ordinary by comparison to the narrative forms that had dominated earlier periods. Rather, they should be recognizable individuals, not allegorical figures like the medieval "Everyman" or like Christian in John Bunyan's *The Pilgrim's Progress* (1678/1684) and all those he encounters (Faithful, Hopeful, Hategood, the Giant Despair, Mr. Worldly Wise-man, Ignorance, Talkative, etc.), not stereotypes as in the *Commedia dell'arte* or popular burlesque narratives, not white knights and noble ladies guarded by dragons. The new heroes are called Robinson Crusoe and Moll Flanders, Clarissa Harlowe, Tom Jones and Pamela or Joseph Andrews – they have commonplace names. That of the three novelists discussed by Watt only Henry Fielding still plays with speaking names – Heartfree, Allworthy, and Square unrealistically denote *types*, as if in reality everybody carried the names they deserve and names were not arbitrary signs – demonstrates his closeness (and not only in this respect) to Cervantes: for the latter's choice of names sparks a galaxy of "unrealistic" allusions.[5]

3. If a story is about individual, unique experience, then *when* it took place is important. In contrast to its predecessors, the realistic novel *historicizes* its content. Fairy tales, fables, and myths establish themselves in a timeless

---

[4]   Theodor W. Adorno, "The Position of the Narrator in the Contemporary Novel," in *Notes to Literature*, trans. Sherry Weber Nicholson, ed. Rolf Tiedemann, New York, 1991, 30–36, here 31.

[5]   Cf. Dominique Reyre, *Dictionnaire des noms des personnages du Don Quijote de Cervantès*, Paris, 1980, available in very useful extracts in Weich, *Cervantes' Don Quijote*.

space, because what they want to say is not bound to concrete circumstances. Chivalric tales and romances, too, are "frozen" in a medieval era that lacks any historical dimension, undergoes no development, and is the vehicle for communicating (supposedly) universal or eternal truths about human existence. That necessarily presupposes ahistoricity: the specific, singular case is not essential to such narratives. But Robinson Crusoe was born in 1632, and Clarissa Harlowe dies at 6.40 p.m. on Thursday, September 7th – it's easy enough to work out the year. Once the particulars have been set out like this, it doesn't matter whether the events of the novel take place in the reader's present, the immediate past, or the historical past – the characters inhabit *one and the same time-continuum* as the reader. The events of ahistorical narrative texts, on the other hand, take place in a kind of time warp, without connection to our time.

4. What is true about time is equally true about *place*. The place of action in non-realist texts can't be found in an atlas, and doesn't need to be. When these narratives do borrow from reality, they needn't be faithful, just as in non-realist drama: Bohemia is allowed to have a coast, and we shouldn't scratch our heads too much over the exact geographical location of Prospero's island. "Formal realism," on the other hand, places its characters in *our* three-dimensional world – "I was born in the year 1632, in the city of York," begins *Robinson Crusoe* – and unfolds in *this* space. No matter if the plot occurs in a place distant from our own – we nevertheless share *the same space-continuum*.

To these four parameters noted by Watt – original plot, individual characters, historical time, concrete place – we could add a fifth: the principle of causality. For in the realist novel everything that happens must of course be explicable in realistic terms – there's no place for miracles, acts of God, or suchlike supernatural interventions. The laws of our world must also be the laws of the fictional world, if the latter is to appear as a part or continuation of the former. That's so obvious as to seem tautological – yet it raises at least two basic questions. First, what is actually to be gained by discarding a literature of universal validity in favor of a literature that celebrates the specific and particular? And second, why should an author, as in *Robinson Crusoe*, make such an effort to write a fiction that pretends not to be fictional? Or to put the question more circumspectly: how is it that "realism" suddenly (historically speaking the change happened very quickly) became a serious artistic–literary aim?

These two questions can be answered together, since they both relate to the same phenomenon. To take the emphasis on the specific and particular first: a literature of universal validity assumes static, unchangeable relationships. The more dynamically human relationships change, the more frequently are people confronted by questions and problems that *couldn't* have arisen previously. They then recognize themselves less and less in a literature that does not contain precisely what they are now buffeted by: radical change, revolution, new and uncertain experiences. It's not just conceivable, but really the case in cultural history that other elements of the reading public seek security in a literature that is exactly innocent of all that, or which steadfastly ignores change: such readers turn to escapist romances and chivalric tales (or their modern equivalents). *Don Quixote* thematizes precisely this dialectic of the flight from reality resulting from its excessive demands: human beings cannot bear very much reality.

However, the novelty of the modern European novel is precisely that it picks people up where they are: in the midst of this radical change for which there are still no prescriptions (and never will be, apart from transcendent ones), because it is historically (always) singular. There are no further rehearsals – we're already in the premiere, the first and last performance simultaneously, as in life, so in the story. And indeed this is what the modern novel in this historically specific situation offers us among other things: look what happened to one of you under these particular, concrete conditions and what came of it. It is therefore not coincidental that we speak of the European novel of the *modern* age. The novel is a part and a reflex of this enormous, unique social, economic, cultural *unleashing*, the unforeseeable freedoms and possibilities of which it reflects as much as the risks and pitfalls. But it can't possibly pretend that nothing has changed, that it's a matter of indifference where and when something happened to someone, as if there were nothing new under the sun. The modern novel filled a gap and found a great *need*, a great *demand* – more than any other literary genre the novel is also an economic phenomenon.

Ian Watt's judgments have been much disputed.[6] Is *Robinson Crusoe* really the first modern English novel, rather than Aphra Behn's *Oroonoko* (ca. 1678)? Or even *The Adventures of Master F.J.* by George Gascoigne (in two versions, 1573 and 1575), if not John Lyly's *Euphues* (?1578) or Thomas Nashe's *The Unfortunate Traveller* (1594)? And are there not at least scattered realistic scenes, passages, and episodes in Bunyan, Chaucer, and Boccaccio, in Apuleius' *Golden Ass* (written after 175, published 1469), in Petronius' *Satyricon* (written 66, published 1482), in the ancient Greek novel – not to mention Homer? (The *prose* factor is brushed under the carpet in vague genealogies like this, as if it were irrelevant – like, incidentally, the question of length, and whether the whole text presents itself in a novelistic way.)

---

[6]   See, for example, Michael McKeon, *The Origins of the English Novel 1600–1740*, Baltimore, 1987; J. Paul Hunter, *Before Novels: The Cultural Contexts of Eighteenth-Century English Fiction*, New York, 1990.

It's noteworthy that those who make objections of the first kind continue to apply Watt's criteria in answering the question whether "their" text is "still only" a prose romance or Chaucerian novella, or in fact "already" a fully grown novel. So there's no dispute about the main point, and these debates recall somewhat the debates about paleobiology or paleoanthropology: is that "only" a dinosaur or "already" a bird, a hominid or "only" a primate? The analogy with biological evolution can illustrate quite vividly the continued existence of other forms of narrative after "the rise of the novel": the modern European novel of the dominantly realist type (and we'll come to the other types presently) does not replace the older forms without leaving any trace of them – it merely emerges as something new, drives some rivals out and is extraordinary successful, assertive, powerful, and protean, and without doubt capable of prodigiously reinventing itself. But other forms continue as before, and in no small measure. When Samuel Taylor Coleridge praises "the marvellous independence and true imaginative *absence* of all particular space or time"[7] in Edmund Spenser's *Faerie Queen* (1590), we see how attractive the non-specific and the non-particular can be: so it too fulfills a function, and persists.

Those who make objections of the second kind perhaps overlook the outstanding dynamism and flexibility with which the early modern novel reacted to the revolutionary turmoil of its epoch. They overlook that this new genre envisions and realizes an exceptionally strong linkage between literature and reality, a sustained linkage that is unlike isolated approximations in former periods – not to mention the fact that *then* reality wasn't changing at such a breakneck speed. The realism of past eras may be like a glove, which fits a hand grown to a particular size. Modern realism is like a skin that grows too, but in time with the plastic growth of the body, or like the body's shadow, which keeps up with all the unforeseeable movements of that body (and this metaphor would not even intimate the *anticipatory* dimension of realism). If you read the narratives in Chaucer's *Canterbury Tales* (from 1387) or Boccaccio's *Decameron* (1470) side-by-side with the first thirty pages of *Robinson Crusoe*, you register the difference straight away.

This sketch of the "advantages" of an up-to-date literature of specifics, a literature of this world, does not, however, banish the second question – about the sense and meaning of a fiction that pretends not to be fiction. Perhaps it even brings up this question more urgently: for what does a narrative literature have to offer which apparently levels off the constitutive difference between fiction and reality?

In eighteenth-century England a fortunate coincidence of various factors brought about something approaching a mass literary market, where

---

[7]   Quoted by Ian Watt, *The Rise of the Novel: Studies in Defoe, Richardson and Fielding*, Harmondsworth, 1974 [1957], 25. Italics mine.

literature was actually bought and sold like other commodities, thus bringing it into a closer, unprecedented connection with its readership. There was nevertheless one factor that, at least at first glance, didn't seem so propitious for the modern novel: the opposition to art and fiction raised by a Protestant, especially Puritan public, whose influence was disproportionately great in precisely those sections of society which could in later periods be identified as "carriers" of this new literary genre (the "*middle class* modern novel"). It was not only extreme, fundamentalist-oriented circles which found art and fiction despicable, or at least suspicious; for both were considered capable of diverting people from their central care in life: saving their souls.

The truth, the *one* truth, was to be found in *one* book: the Bible. If need be, that was – had to be – sufficient. A literature of edification was permissible in addition, such as tracts which portrayed exemplary spiritual awakenings and conversions – true stories narrated to promote the Christian message. Spiritual autobiographies, too, in which the protagonist himself configures his life story as a spiritual pilgrimage to the kingdom of God – and of course Bunyan's allegorical transposition of this model. Unlike the tracts and spiritual autobiographies, *The Pilgrim's Progress* does not attribute symbolic meaning to concrete people or objects and generalize them on a spiritual level, but – the reverse process – illuminates the universal through concrete personifications.

The literary and everyday basis of all this Protestant edificatory literature is, however, the *diary*, in which each individual renders their account before God regarding the *spiritual* meaning of what has befallen them day by day. The Puritan hostility to art and fiction thus has its counterpart in a marked inclination to exegesis and interpretation, the strongest possible compulsion to read signs, which in extreme cases refuses to leave any detail of life untranslated: *everything* is (potentially) significant, everything is a sign, everything is not just itself, but at the same time it *means* something else.

Bible interpretation in church and parish instructed people in this permanent hermeneutic of their own lives. Not that the *fourfold* sense of the text always had to be in play, but the idea that a text means more than it literally says – that its *real* meaning is discovered only through interpretation and translation, was by no means eccentric for the general English public at the beginning of the eighteenth century: it was understood as a matter of course. Texts – provided they are not balance books – are to be read like that: as at least *doubly* coded. Reading is exegesis.

We can thus clearly understand these texts of edificatory literature as a reflection of the way a life was read: one's own life becomes a text that demands interpretation and whose correct interpretation doesn't easily come to light. The realities of life – the vicissitudes and incidents, encounters and developments – are like the literal sense of a text, behind which the actual message is to be found. One runs the course of one's life as though it were a text, reading and interpreting. In European cultural history there has seldom been such a markedly book- and text-centered culture; it had its counterpart, if at all, on the other side of the Atlantic, in Puritan *New England*. Paradoxically, Protestants are, for all their hostility to literature, the best literary readers imaginable: they're quick to spot double-coding, and indeed bring this attitude to the text, since it seems to them normal and the only sensible procedure. They bring what is essential for literary reading: a highly developed consciousness of signs.[8]

It is only against this backdrop that we can realize what a brilliant coup the 59-year-old Defoe's first novel was. Himself a Dissenter (i.e., a radical Protestant), he smuggled his fiction onto the market as a relation of fact, and could thus rely on the likelihood that one part of the reading public would simply devour *Robinson Crusoe* as an exciting adventure novel and would see through the fictitiousness of the "editor," while others would read the same text as a conversion story, in which the 28 years of loneliness (despite Friday) on the island may be understood as God's method of bringing the rebellious prodigal son back to the straight and narrow. Robinson makes this interpretation himself when – having much time on his hands – he attempts to fathom the *meaning* of his fate, reading the novel of his life as a succession of errors followed by a fateful transcendent reprimand. The Protestant reader encounters his double in the protagonist of this "realistic" novel: "this" means "that," x is *really* to be understood as y.

Yet contemporary readers should also have been able to spot that, as briefly sketched in chapter 1 of this book, Robinson's self-interpretation isn't as unequivocal as all that. When he prospers as a result of his rebelliousness, then *no* connection is established between his initial disobedience and his current state. But things aren't going so well for him, that will be interpreted as a *consequence* of his departure from home. That means, however, that Robinson interprets highly selectively and has to understand his happiness and eventual wealth as the result of his insight, conversion, and penitence – rather than, as would certainly be possible, as the ultimate result of his offense against his father's advice. The novel is capacious enough to leave the conflicting remainder of his interpretative work open for all to see.

Back to fact and fiction. As we have seen, that's one of the secrets of those fictions that disguise themselves as factual report (whether or not via a fictitious editor): completely regardless of whether the reader sees through the trickery or not, the text enters a (literary) culture that treats even factual reports as though their true meaning lay behind their literal meaning. Thus the question about the value of a narrative literature that apparently levels out the constitutive difference between fiction and reality in fact rests on a

---

[8]   In German, a particularly outstanding reading of literature in the light of Protestantism is Heinz Schlaffer, *Die kurze Geschichte der deutschen Literatur*, Munich, 2002, esp. 54ff.

false assumption: when life and reality are already read as an interpretable text, the entry of a text that pretends not to be fiction does not lead to a meaningless duplication of what exists already, but rather the practised play of interpretation and the search for meaning is simply continued using the new material. That is of course just as true of novels that, unlike *Robinson Crusoe*, do not seek to hide their fictitiousness at all, such as *Tom Jones*. From the outset such novels are understood as fiction and naturally submitted to such an interpretative procedure, too.

That's how the success of the realist modern European novel works: the novel offers the public a "novel" specificity and proximity to reality, unprecedented in literature, trusting confidently – whether or not the fiction is obvious or disguised as fact – in readers' facility for decoding. While this facility is the product of an era that is about to disappear, it remains active, notwithstanding the increasing obsolescence of the aim of establishing the *one* truth and the *one* meaning in the twilight of the gods of the early modern period. Novels now dramatize in miniature the processes by which the search for meaning takes place: these processes are widely varied for an increasingly diverse public, and convey *content* much less than *processes and possibilities* of orientation. Above all, they *reveal and demonstrate themselves* at work.

In a literary culture for which anyway "this" never means just "this," but also "that" or "the other," realism is a literary program that makes sense. For on the one hand it relates to the topicality and specificity of a new kind of situation, but on the other hand it by no means claims: it is what it is. You *can* have it both ways. A public that understands John Donne's lines, "No man is an island, entire of itself; every man is a piece of the continent, a part of the maine," does not need a lengthy explanation of the meaning of Robinson Crusoe's enforced confinement to an island. At least, there is no doubt that the story doesn't mean just *that* and nothing more.

3   Fiction, Illusion, Realism

In an exam, a law student has a fictitious case to work on. He knows that this case didn't really occur, but was constructed to enable him to give a model solution to a problem of precedent. We can deal with fictitiousness: it fulfils a useful role in reality.[9]

It's no different with fictionality. Normal novel readers do not need to be told (barring extreme or borderline cases) that what they are reading is

---

[9]   Cf. Dieter Henrich and Wolfgang Iser (eds.), *Funktionen des Fiktiven* (*Poetik und Hermeneutik X*), Munich, 1983; "Fiktion im Recht," *Zeitschrift für Semiotik* 12/3 (1990): 175–242.

fiction, not reality, any more than visitors to an exhibition are likely to confuse a magnificent Italian still-life with the buffet laid out in the next room. Even in the case of a realist novel, readers just *know* it's fiction: that's cultural knowledge.

The illusion constructed by fictional texts (but also other artworks) of the realist type is exactly that: *illusion*, and not *delusion*.[10] To encounter an artwork that operates through illusion is to interact with a fabrication which is recognized as such and which we allow to impinge on us "for the moment." We're not trapped in total self-deception, or a delusion and madness that does not know itself.

Thus every art that strives to produce illusion always – and indispensably – has this double-aspect: it fabricates something, and it shows *that* it fabricates something, and as recipients we are aware of *both* aspects, otherwise we wouldn't perceive the object as an art object. In the case of fictional literature in particular we know that the signs in the text don't relate referentially to something external that preceded the text. It is only in reading that an imaginary world emerges to which the text then refers. But since this fiction can only emerge in imaginative and interpretative negotiation with the text itself, the reader's attention must be directed *towards the text* and not, as with referential, non-fictional texts, *away from it* towards an extra-textual reality. Since fictional texts are in this sense non-referential and context-free, we refer to them (like poetic texts) as self- or auto-referential.

And although the basic material of these texts is nothing other than our language, what happens with these linguistic signs is exactly (but more extremely) what happens to all other signs when they are freed from context and thus released into self-referentiality: they become ambiguous.[11] In order to find out what they could all mean there is only one thing to do: to read them in their concrete configurations. Fictional texts only set something free, whose potential is severely constricted – textually and situationally filtered out, so to speak – in the context of pragmatic, everyday communication: the enormous ambiguity of human language (a proof of the economy of natural language). In pragmatic contexts we attend above all to the "what" – the "how" isn't allowed to push itself into the foreground, otherwise communication would be endangered or become communication about communication. In fictional texts, however, the "what" can only be established *through the "how."* Indeed, since literary texts construct meaning in their special way, one could say that in literary texts the *how* is the *what*, their "content" *is* their special "form." Language

---

[10]   Cf. Frederick Burwick, *Illusion and the Drama: Critical Theory of the Enlightenment and Romantic Era*, University Park, PA, 1991, esp. 7, 16, 267–303.
[11]   Cf. Christoph Bode, *Ästhetik der Ambiguität: Zu Funktion und Bedeutung von Mehrdeutigkeit in der Literatur der Moderne*, Tübingen, 1988, 25–170.

as language is in the limelight, similarly to the case of lyric poetry. *From the word go we read these texts differently.*

The question whether fictionality is thus a necessary or even a sufficient condition for literariness may – nay, must – be answered with elegant pragmatism: in the absence of any sort of distinguishing *textual* characteristics that would reliably reveal in each and every case the presence of fictionality or literariness, it makes sense to look for the ground of these texts' particular mode of being *outside them* – in the way we handle them, the way we process them.[12] Our special way of reading them calls forth all the phenomena which we then see "in them." "Literature" is an open, pragmatically defined category of texts – it includes all texts which a given culture conventionally deals with in a particular way (such as by reading them non-referentially). We *could* in theory do that with every text – but in practice we don't.[13] In terms of literary study, anyway, only the collective cultural practice is of interest. Individual idiosyncrasies are the province of other disciplines.

If we accept, then, that every illusionary art fabricates a (fictive) reality, which simultaneously declares itself as fabrication,[14] it's perfectly possible to investigate historically by what means these arts have sought to realize such a reality-effect at different times, but also, by what methods they might have "reminded" their recipients that this reality-effect is ultimately illusion, only *fiction*. To repeat: with illusionary art we're dealing with both *simultaneously, always and indispensably*. But the two elements can be differently accentuated – and indeed the change in the accentuation is a significant source of aesthetic stimuli.

Investigations of the first element (and there's no shortage of them) lead us in the broadest sense to the so-called problem of realism. Investigations of the other side of the illusion, however – its fictionality and the foregrounding of its fictionality, i.e., the disclosed mechanism of the fabrication – lead us to

---

[12]   Cf. Bode, *Ambiguität*, 340–378; Stanley Fish, *Is There a Text in This Class? The Authority of Interpretive Communities*, Cambridge, MA, 1995.

[13]   It's well known that a considerable number of texts are from the very beginning equipped with *markers*, which in a given culture at a given time function as signals of fictionality. But this is irrelevant: the decisive point is that texts can in practice belong to this open category even when no "fiction signals" are evident. Cf. also Harald Weinrich, "Fiktionssignale," *Positionen der Negativität (Poetik und Hermeneutik VI)*, ed. Harald Weinrich, Munich, 1975, 525–526. Contrast Dorrit Cohn, "Signposts of Fictionality: A Narratological Perspective," *Poetics Today* 11/4 (1990): 775–804; in Cohn, *The Distinction of Fiction*, Baltimore, 1999, 109–131.

[14]   The word "simultaneously" is important: in my view the expressions "creating an illusion" and "breaking an illusion" encourage the misunderstanding that something is *subsequently* broken which was *first* built up. Artistic illusion is, however, right from the start *always already* fabrication and not *delusion* from which the reader or spectator must then be freed. Cf. Werner Wolf, *Ästhetische Illusion und Illusionsdurchbrechung in der Erzählkunst. Theorie und Geschichte mit Schwerpunkt auf englischem illusionsstörenden Erzählen*, Tübingen, 1993.

the functioning of the text, to the way it is made. The latter investigations are as a rule formalist or structuralist. If what we have just said about fiction is roughly right, the relation between these two elements can hardly be symmetrical: rather, it is only possible to get at the "what" of an artistic illusion by determining the "how" (and prior to that: of the possible "why"). And that wouldn't be a detour, but the only possible way.

Resentment against fiction was not peculiar just to the Puritans and their continental counterparts (according to the reformed Swiss theologian Gotthard Heidegger writing in 1698, "only the reading of histories guarantees practical and intellectual utility, as well as genuine insights into the workings of providence").[15] It is also famously present in Plato, who proposed to banish all poets from his ideal republic. Yet the opposite opinion found at least equally vigorous support. Thus in chapter 9 of his *Poetics* Aristotle even ranks the art of poetry above the writing of history, on the ground that, whereas the historian only narrates what has occurred, the poet describes what "probably or necessarily" *could* occur: "It is for this reason that poetry is both more philosophical and more serious than history, since poetry speaks more of universals, history of particulars."[16] And responding to the stolid accusation that "poets are liars," Sir Philip Sidney could point to the special prepositional logic of claims in fictional and poetic texts: "I truly think, that of all writers under the sun the poet is the least liar [...]. [...] for the poet, he nothing affirms, and therefore never lieth."[17] Indeed, literary texts are non-referential texts.

If the main objection to this new genre, the novel, was that it spread immorality[18] – and it surely did not help matters that the first French treatise on the theory of the novel, the *Traité de l'origine des romans* (1670) by the bishop (!) Pierre-Daniel Huet, defined these modern texts as "des fictions d'aventures amoureuses"[19] – its affective power was nevertheless not in doubt, and it was possible to counter: why not use the tremendously popular new form to *promote* morality? Defoe himself argued this when he explained in the continuation of the above-quoted passage from the preface

---

[15]   Hartmut Steinecke and Fritz Wahrenburg (eds.), *Romantheorie: Texte vom Barock bis zur Gegenwart*, Stuttgart, 1999, 87; cf. generally Eberhard Lämmert et al. (eds.), *Romantheorie 1620–1880: Dokumentation ihrer Geschichte in Deutschland*, Cologne, 1971; Lämmert et al. (eds.), *Romantheorie: Dokumentation ihrer Geschichte in Deutschland seit 1880*, Cologne, 1975; Matthias Bauer, *Romantheorie*, Stuttgart, 1997.

[16]   *The "Poetics" of Aristotle*, trans. and ed. Stephen Halliwell, London, 1987, 41.

[17]   In *The Norton Anthology of English Literature: Fifth Edition*, Vol. 1, ed. M. H. Abrams, New York, 1986, 518, 519.

[18]   "Nowadays many novels are translated from the French and Italian which in truth are not worth the effort, for the content of many of them is positively dissolute and worthless." Johann Rist, "Gespräch über Romane" (1668), *Romantheorie*, ed. Steinecke and Wahrenburg, 54–57, here 56.

[19]   *Romantheorie*, ed. Steinecke and Wahrenburg, 77.

of *Robinson Crusoe* that, regardless of whether it's fact or fiction, "[t]he editor [...] thinks [...] that the improvement of it, as well to the diversion as to the instruction of the reader, will be the same[.]" In other words, the *prodesse et delectare* of Horace is equally well fulfilled whether the work is fiction or a factual report. Defoe's German imitator Johann Gottfried Schnabel took the same line when he asked: "so why should a well-written fiction [...] be contemptible and reprehensible?"[20] The end justifies the means. Over twenty years previously the Lutheran pastor Erdmann Neumeister had already promoted one conceivable end as no less than the main aim of the new genre: "to teach gallant conduct."[21] Of course, novels make suitable conduct books or conversation books only when they approach reality as closely as possible – and in this respect they still left something to be desired:

> But in my view the execution of this kind of novel requires a considerable level of understanding – indeed a fully developed philosopher, who can achieve a precise science of human nature and temperament, such that he knows how to make all the circumstances properly reasonable and believable – in which two points most novels fall fairly short.[22]

The demand that novels be realistic is thus *also* ethically–morally based: this work of education can only succeed if the novel observes and depicts circumstances and people *precisely* – otherwise it has no purpose.

The English word "verisimilitude," like the French "vraisemblance," denotes the effect intended by the realist novel better than the German "Wahrscheinlichkeit" – for in modern usage the latter suggests "probability" rather than the more appropriate "having the appearance of the true and real." The double aspect of the illusion is well preserved both in veri*similitude* and vrai*semblance*; probability is only a subordinate feature, albeit one that's necessarily implied. Gérard Genette has recently shown how strongly the concept of verisimilitude in the novel was itself linked, right from the beginning, to moral notions of propriety and decorum.[23] Genette notes the extent to which contemporary critics of the first French psychological novel, *The Princess of Clève* (1678) by Marie-Madeleine La Fayette, complained of its lack of *vraisemblance*, because the princess's confession to her husband that she is passionately in love with the Duke of Nemours was considered indecorous – in other words, the concept of verisimilitude is here still thoroughly prescriptive in the sense of a corporate doctrine of virtue.

---

[20]   *Romantheorie*, ed. Steinecke and Wahrenburg, 107.
[21]   *Romantheorie*, ed. Steinecke and Wahrenburg, 97.
[22]   *Romantheorie*, ed. Steinecke and Wahrenburg, 98.
[23]   Gérard Genette, "Vraisemblance and Motivation," *Narrative* 9/3 (October 2001): 239–258.

The requirement of realism or probability is generally fulfilled when a narrative text's forms of presentation coincide to a large extent with the conventional forms of perception of its readership. But since notions of "reality" have changed quite fundamentally in the course of the last 300 years, as have the possibilities and forms of the novel, the problem of realism is the problem of a correlation between two variables.[24] It is not the approximation of literature to a supposedly changeless reality that stands in question – realism is not a characteristic of some kind of "content" of a text – but the relative proximity or distance, difference from or congruence with prevalent *apprehensions* of reality.

For that reason, too, the often fundamentally different ways in which "reality" has been constructed philosophically and scientifically in the last 300 years – whether in the empirical sense of John Locke, the critical idealism of Immanuel Kant, the dialectical materialism of Karl Marx, or in radical constructivism – have had relatively little impact on the literary debate about realism. Contrary to other claims, we don't need to know the "ultimate essence" or "reality of reality" and can confidently believe in the reality of fiction just as much as in the fiction of reality, in order to be able to say: yes, this seems more realistic than that. Even a concept of reality dissolved in fiction still admits that. The dialectical play of two variables does not leave any problems in its wake that could be solved by some kind of triad;[25] just as in order to make judgments like "bigger than," "smaller than," "of equal size," we don't need to know the absolute values involved.

When a culture's ideas of reality undergo change in time, however, one can see why new modes of presentation crop up in a genre whose rallying cry is proximity to reality –and that always in the name of an even greater realism in contrast to the established modes of presentation, which themselves had nevertheless appealed to precisely that same principle. Realism as a programmatic *concept* is informed by a rhetoric of overreaching; as artistic *practice* it is a highly variable phenomenon – the trace of an endeavor. Did the Victorians really cry as much, and did they burst into tears as easily as Victorian social and sentimental novels suggest? Was it that they weren't as advanced in the "process of civilization" (Norbert Elias) and so didn't have their emotions under control as we do? Or was that just a literary convention that had little to do with the reality of the time? Hard to say. The fact that this nowadays strikes us as unrealistic,

---

[24]   Cf. Eckhard Lobsien, *Theorie literarischer Illusionsbildung*, Stuttgart, 1975; Bode, *Ambiguität*, 148ff.
[25]   This is certainly out of the question if these variables are defined in Wolfgang Iser's terms as "the real," "the fictive," and "the imaginary": *The Fictive and the Imaginary: Charting Literary Anthropology*, Baltimore, 1993, 2ff.

whereas 150 years ago no one seems to have been bothered by it, does at least suggest that *something* has changed. Either people's behavior, or what they consider "realistic" …

When Henry Fielding published *Joseph Andrews* in 1742 (the title-page proclaimed: "Written in Imitation of The Manner of CERVANTES, Author of *Don Quixote*") he attempted in the preface to construct a theoretical foundation for this new type of literature, "which I do not remember to have seen hitherto in our language." He defined the new genre, with classificatory precision, as "comic epic poem in prose" – exactly what Johann Adolf Schlegel echoed only ten years later in Germany, when he declared this "particular prose genre" to be a "prosaic art of poetry, a poetry without rhyme or meter."[26]

It was obvious that the novel was an epic, i.e., narrative, form; that it in effect *replaced* epic first became a critical commonplace in the second half of the eighteenth century. Friedrich von Blanckenburg put it like this in his 1774 "Essay on the Novel": "I regard the novel – the *good* novel – as what the epopee was for the Greeks at the dawn of Greek culture; I believe, at least, that the *good novel* could take up that mantle for us."[27] Georg Friedrich Meier offered the following reflections on the heroines of Samuel Richardson's novels as early as 1750: "If Telemachus teaches us the heroic virtues, Pamela displays the middle-class virtues in situations in which anyone might find themselves. The story of Clarissa, also penned by the famous author of *Pamela*, is designed in the same way."[28] (With postmodern irony, Italo Calvino's *The Baron on the Trees* [1957], set in the eighteenth century, plays with the conceivable consequences of this education in middle-class virtue through novel-reading: the leader of a band of robbers borrows books from Cosimo and so becomes "middle class" – *Clarissa* is especially effective – but the consequence is just that he neglects his trade as a robber, and easily – it wouldn't have happened before – gets caught and eventually hanged.)

However, it was Johann Karl Wezel who, in 1780, first located the sociocultural place of the novel as "the true middle-class epic,"[29] so that Hegel's rather terse comments on the novel in his *Lectures on Aesthetics* take up an established discourse: Hegel famously calls the novel the "modern *middle-class* epic."[30] It's interesting to see how Hegel defines the historical position and function of the modern novel (whose *cognitive gain and cognitive*

[26] *Romantheorie*, ed. Steinecke and Wahrenburg, 142, 143.
[27] *Romantheorie*, ed. Steinecke and Wahrenburg, 181.
[28] *Romantheorie*, ed. Steinecke and Wahrenburg, 132.
[29] *Romantheorie*, ed. Steinecke and Wahrenburg, 203.
[30] Georg Wilhelm Friedrich Hegel, *Vorlesungen über die Ästhetik, Dritter Teil: Die Poesie*, ed. Rüdiger Bubner, Stuttgart, 1977, 177.

stimulus he obviously has to deny completely – art can only make *sensuously palpable* the kind of knowledge that philosophy has gained first):

> A novel in the modern sense of the word presupposes a world already prosaically ordered; then, on this ground and within its own sphere whether in connection with the liveliness of events or with individuals and their fate, it regains for poetry the right it had lost, so far as this is possible in view of that presupposition. Consequently one of the commonest, and, for the novel, most appropriate, collisions is the conflict between the poetry of the heart and the opposing prose of circumstances and the accidents of external situation; this is a conflict resolved whether comically or tragically, or alternatively it is settled either (i) when the characters originally opposed to the usual order of things learn to recognize in it what is substantive and really genuine, when they are reconciled with their circumstances and effective in them, or (ii) when the prosaic shape of what they do and achieve is stripped away, and therefore what they had before them as prose has its place taken by a reality akin and friendly to beauty and art. So far as presentation goes, the novel proper, like the epic, requires the entirety of an outlook on the world and life, the manifold materials and contents of which come into appearance within the individual event that is the centre of the whole.[31]

The starting point is the fact that the world has become prosaic – the genre's objective, however, is to fabricate a totality. There are two sides to this project – and that's why Hegel's example is so excellently chosen. The one is external and aims to make available in a broad social panorama a totality of social experience that is no longer available to us in reality – a point made perhaps better than anywhere else in Christian Garve's "Consideration of some differences between the works of ancient and modern writers, especially poets" (1770):

> Why have our plays, our novels, suddenly become so attractive, not to say so necessary? Partly because they return us to the human community from which we are to a certain extent excluded; because they show us people of all classes, acting and talking in far more important scenes of their lives than we ourselves have the opportunity of seeing; because they lead us back into the houses of the great, to which we no longer have access, and flatter us with the notion that these great ones are more similar to us, and less elevated above us, than they seem when we merely look at the walls of their palaces; because they show, in the lowest classes to whom out of prejudice, pride and habitual revulsion we do not wish to condescend, the manifestations of nature that we like in ourselves. In a word, because they recreate in fiction what we have lost in reality, the pleasure of being among people – people of all kinds; and because

---

[31] *Hegel's Aesthetics: Lectures on Fine Art*, trans. T. M. Knox, 2 vols., Oxford, 1975, 2: 1092–1093. *Translator's note:* Knox translates the German "Roman" as "romance"; I have changed this in each case to "the novel." For the German text, see Hegel, *Vorlesungen über die Ästhetik*, 177–178.

at the same time they supplement that part of our knowledge that we can no longer collect through experience.[32]

The other side, in linking the principle of causality and the postulate of probability, aims to explain an individual's behavior as the outcome of their *thoughts and feelings*. The basis for this is the law of causality:

> If the vaunted principle of imitation has any meaning at all, it must be this: proceed in the connection, in the arrangement of your work just as nature proceeds in producing hers.
>
> It is the poet's work to arrange characters and events in an order and to link them. They must be interconnected, given what we have assumed above, in such a way that they are reciprocally causes and effects, thus forming a whole in which all these parts are interlinked with each other and with the whole, so that the end or result of the work is a necessary effect of all that went before. The poet's work must constitute a small world, as similar to the big world as it *can* be.

If the subject matter of the novel is "people's actions and feelings," however, i.e., how the inner and outer are causally connected, no pardon can be granted to a novelist who fails to achieve this: "It would be disgraceful for a poet to exculpate himself by arguing that he does not know what passes inside his characters. He is their creator: they have received all their characteristics, their whole being, from him; they live in a world that he has ordered."[33]

So it makes sense that so many novels of the late seventeenth and the whole eighteenth century play on exactly that faultline that Hegel indicated. In the above-mentioned *Princess of Clèves*, for instance, the confession of passionate love results in the renunciation demanded by society – a demand also self-imposed, however, by the individual; *Manon Lescaut* (1731) by the Abbé Prévost openly dramatizes the ironic alternative of living out a relationship not tolerated by society, which, however, as a relationship of *dependency* could only have brought the protagonist to ruin anyway; *Clarissa* (1747/48), Goethe's *Sufferings of Young Werther* (1774), through to Thomas Hardy's *Tess of the d'Urbervilles* (1891) – the list is endless.

---

[32] *Romantheorie*, ed. Steinecke and Wahrenburg, 167.

[33] All quotations from von Blanckenburg (1774), in *Romantheorie*, ed. Steinecke and Wahrenburg, 193–194, 186, 190. Also cf. the early anonymous text from 1744, "Some thoughts and rules respecting German novels," though this brings the presentation of inner and outer into chronological order: "For a novel should have verisimilitude [...]; the actions of the people described only have verisimilitude, however, when they are appropriate to their characters. [...] It is therefore necessary that the main characters be presented prior to the narration of their story, so that we know their inclinations, and can refer to the latter as a touchstone of their actions. This presentation of the inner qualities of the novel's characters is more necessary than most novelists' habitual care in painstakingly depicting the bodies of their fictitious people." In *Romantheorie*, ed. Steinecke and Wahrenburg, 121.

But the German novel displays its greatest power when, rather than taking on the role Hegel assigns to it, it simply imitates the logic of his *Phenomenology of Spirit*. I'm referring, of course, to the *Bildungsroman*. From the *History of Agathon* (1766/67) by Christoph Martin Wieland ("the German Fielding," according to von Blanckenburg) to Goethe's *Wilhelm Meister's Apprenticeship* (1795/96),[34] the middle-class subject unfolds itself through endless vicissitudes, but teleologically: it has an end, and sketches out as meaningful *for itself* what must never be purely contingent, but not necessary either (in the sense of predetermined): *one's own life* – and it is only in *narration* that the possibility of this negotiation of contingency and necessity is presented as even possible.[35]

It is no coincidence that Goethe himself, in his *Maxims and Reflections*, had rather archly drawn attention to the question of how writers are meant to realize the totality of a community in their work, and had spoken of the *subjective epic* rather than the *middle-class* epic – an instructive difference: "The novel is a subjective epic, in which the author requests permission to treat the world in his own way. The question is then simply whether he has a 'way'; the rest will take care of itself."[36]

This "way" that the writer must have brings us back to the method of creating an effect of reality,[37] to fulfill the requirement of ver*isimilitude*. In his *Eloge de Richardson* (1762), Denis Diderot – though himself inclined rather to slim dialogue-novels – celebrated the accumulation of lifelike detail.[38] *In itself*, however, this (together with the other parameters noted above in the discussion of Ian Watt) only supplies something which must then prove to be a model for the production of meaning. In his *Aesthetik* of 1856, Friedrich Theodor Vischer can still claim that the middle-class novel, especially in the hands of the English and above all Richardson, succeeded in a meaningful integration:

---

[34]   Schelling considered only two novels worthy of the name: *Don Quixote* and Goethe's *Wilhelm Meister*. Schopenhauer, on the other hand, always more cosmopolitan, added Rousseau's *Nouvelle Héloïse* and Laurence Sterne's *Tristram Shandy*, and so accepted at least four. Cf. *Romantheorie*, ed. Steinecke and Wahrenburg, 272, 374.

[35]   In Britain it was none other than George Eliot (Marian Evans) who defended *Wilhelm Meister* against accusations of supposed immorality, in the name of an unreserved sincerity – exactly what she, as a literary realist, was calling for from the "social novelist" of her time and country. Cf. George Eliot, "The Morality of *Wilhelm Meister*" and "The Natural History of German Life," *Selected Critical Writings*, Oxford, 1992, 129–132, 260–295.

[36]   Johann Wolfgang von Goethe, *Werke* (*Hamburger Ausgabe*), Munich, 1982, Vol. 12, 498 (Nr. 938).

[37]   Cf. Roland Barthes, "L'effet de réel," *Communications* 11 (1968): 84–89.

[38]   Cf. Hans Robert Jauß, "Nachahmungsprinzip und Wirklichkeitsbegriff in der Theorie des Romans von Diderot bis Stendhal," in Jauß (ed.), *Nachahmung und Illusion (Poetik und Hermeneutik I)*, Munich, 1969 [1963], 157–178; J.-J. Mayoux, "Diderot and the Technique of Modern Literature," *Modern Language Review* 31 (1936), 518–531; Marie-Louise Roy, *Die Poetik Diderots*, Munich, 1966, 51–65.

1. [...] The *middle-class* novel [...] is the really normal species. It combines what is true in the aristocratic and the popular novel, for it brings us into the middling sections of society, which combines the treasure of the people's heart of gold with the solid property of humanity, combines the truth of life with the elegant semblance, and the elegant surface, the deeper life of the soul enriched through education, to the truth of life. The family hearth is the true focal point of the novel's world picture, and it first attains its meaning when characters unite around it who balance out the tougher truths of life with the softer aspects of an enlarged spiritual world. It is in these circles only that the true picture of morals and manners, far from extremes, is first experienced and unfolds. The English, who have given the new literature its most meaningful impulses in all its forms, were also in the vanguard of this genre. Its originator, Richardson, is a pedant in description, a painstaking anatomist in psychological analysis, an abstract moralist; and yet in accordance with the requirements of his chosen art-form he originated the realistic style with its sharp depictions, and pointed to the true goal of unfolding a portrait of souls in this style, giving that portrait as a focal point the pure ethical content of our educated, middle-class orders.[39]

Yet he had just previously suggested – following Solger[40] – that the hero of a novel "really now deserves the name only in an ironic sense, since he doesn't actually act, but is essentially the more dependent center that only processes, a center in which the conditions of mundane life, the leading forces of the sum total of a period's culture, the maxims of society, the effects of its relationships, converge"[41] – more acted upon than acting, in other words.

This, then, was an early recognition of what Robinson Crusoe still understood as predestination, what later writers would explain as fate or chance, and what Adorno would much later pick out as the difference between the early and concluding phases of the novel:

The novel was the literary form specific to the bourgeois age. At its origins stands the experience of the disenchanted world in *Don Quixote*, and the artistic treatment of mere existence has remained the novel's sphere. Realism was inherent in the novel; even those that are novels of fantasy as far as their subject matter is concerned attempt to present their content in such a way that the suggestion of reality emanates from them.[42]

---

[39] *Romantheorie*, ed. Steinecke and Wahrenburg, 368.
[40] Karl Wilhelm Ferdinand Solger, *Vorlesung über Ästhetik*: "Irony is linked with particularity, which must come to the fore especially in the novel, in which character appears as more essential, and yet at the same time as empty." *Romantheorie*, ed. Steinecke and Wahrenburg, 300.
[41] Quoted in *Romantheorie*, ed. Steinecke and Wahrenburg, 366.
[42] Adorno, "The Position of the Narrator in the Contemporary Novel," *Notes to Literature*, ed. Rolf Tiedemann, trans. Sherry Weber Nicholson, New York, 1991, 30–36, here 30. German original: "Form und Gehalt des zeitgenössischen Romans," *Akzente* 1 (1954): 410–416.

Now, however:

> The identity of experience in the form of a life that is articulated and possesses internal continuity – and that life was the only thing that made the narrator's stance possible – has disintegrated. One need only note how impossible it would be for someone who has participated in the war to tell stories about it the way people used to tell stories about their adventures. A narrative that presented itself as though the narrator had mastered this kind of experience would rightly meet with impatience and skepticism on the part of its audience.[43]

Adorno thus assigns to a much later date (and furthermore attributes it to a change in reality) a paradox that could well be regarded as *constitutive* for the middle-class realist novel: the great realistic social panoramas of Fielding, Dickens, Thackeray, Balzac, and Tolstoy, though they evidently still attempt to fulfill what seems to be their task in cultural history, i.e., to show the meaningful place of the individual within the whole, cannot do this under the remit of realism. For they fall between the two stools of verisimilitude and the production of meaning, and cannot deliver something that the "reality" to which they are ultimately obliged does not supply. Hence, too, the increasingly pessimistic tone of naturalistic novels (among others by Emile Zola, Frank Norris, Stephen Crane, Theodore Dreiser), which in consistently pursuing the realist program can only establish that it's no longer possible to construct a meaningful totality from the perspective of the individual, and that from the godlike perspective of the authorial narrator this can only be claimed at best arbitrarily or even ironically.

Exactly at this point, however, just as old and venerable a basic tendency of the modern European novel increasingly takes over and realizes – also in pursuit of the aim of ever greater proximity to reality – the intention that has always been present in realism: to offer and demonstrate not meaning itself, but *possibilities* of the production and construction of meaning. But then this tendency no longer necessarily required a literary realism.

---

[43]   Adorno, "The Position of the Narrator in the Contemporary Novel," 31. Adorno thus takes up over twenty years later a thought that Walter Benjamin had formulated in his essay "Experience and Poverty" (1933) with regard to the experience of the *First* World War: "No, this much is clear: the stocks of experience have fallen, and that in a generation which in 1914–18 had one of the most monstrous experiences in world history. Perhaps that is not as strange as it seems. Wasn't it possible at that time to assert: people returned from the trenches utterly transformed and out of tune […] Not richer, but poorer in communicable experience." Walter Benjamin, *Sprache und Geschichte: Philosophische Essays*, Stuttgart, 1992, 134–140, here 134. One might add: today, peace is the emergency. The concluding chapter (9) of the present book offers a fuller discussion of Adorno and Benjamin's views of the end of narrative and the traditional novel.

4 Variety of Types: Triumph of Polyphony

How so? The self-referentiality that, as we noted above, is generally constitutive for signs in art – a phenomenon that manifests itself *pragmatically* and is not an ontological characteristic – hits certain problems in the case of literary material. In contrast to the basic material of musical composition or of the fine arts, literature comprises elements that always already mean something – the words of a language. The basic material of language is far from semantically neutral; indeed, it is strongly loaded. Now, that helps the building up of linguistic–aesthetic structures in the sense that a self-referential coding or decoding always presents at least two meanings: the literal and the literary (the latter being of course the "real" meaning of the text – a paraphrase of the literal sense of a literary text cannot pass for a reconstruction of the meaning[s] of the text). But "sticking to the primary reference" in the realm of the linguistic arts also has a considerable disadvantage when the requirement is to realize ever higher levels of self-referentiality and artistic complexity. In human language, the centrifugal force of semiotic dispersion is always counteracted by the centripetal force of the primary reference: arising from their material, the linguistic arts have far more problems than music or painting in stepping into pure self-referentiality, even though this general development stands out as one of the main tendencies of the modern period. In the course of this development, around 1900, the obligation to depict something (which is hardly the only possible aesthetic program) is increasingly conceived as a *shackle* – Ezra Pound, for instance, writes in 1912: "In every art I can think of we are dammed and clogged by the mimetic"[44] – and experiments were tried to burst free of conventions that in the course of time had become oppressive and constricting.

Interestingly, this decisive paradigm shift did not take place in a unified way in literary history; rather, it differed in highly instructive fashion from genre to genre. It was lyric poetry (in the first instance in French Symbolism) that dared to leap into the non-mimetic and aspired to become *poésie pure*, while narrative prose in all national literatures lagged clearly behind.[45] Why, then, was lyric poetry in the vanguard and why did epic cling much longer to a practice that, just as before, gave priority to reality? The answer is clear: in ("somehow") realistic narrative all such parameters are built in – person, time, place, action, causality, etc. – as, acting as crash barriers for the understanding, conjure up an illusion of a reality similar in its vital aspects to reality outside the text. Poetry, on the other hand, doesn't replicate such parameters in *that* way (and that's why all non-literary readers find poetry generally "harder" than novels). These are persistent conventions that must

---

[44] Quoted in Bode, *Ästhetik*, 154.
[45] Cf. the sections "Lyrik als Einfallstor der Ambiguität" und "Ambiguisierung – Widerstände der Prosa" in Bode, *Ästhetik*, 161ff. and 146ff.

first be dismantled before radically post-mimetic texts can emerge – texts which evade the expectation that they should narrate something. "The story of this novel," comments Robert Musil about his *The Man without Qualities*, "comes down to this: that the story that it should tell is not told."[46]

That may be new, but it's not really surprising. It has after all been clear since *Don Quixote* that, rather than providing a prepackaged meaning to be unwrapped, the modern novel relies on thematizing *possibilities* for the production of sense and meaning. Since the actual "literary" meaning of a reasonably complex narrative text, even one written according to a realist program, can hardly ever be pinned down unambiguously, the realistically oriented European novel could live with that fairly easily – the fetters only make themselves felt when someone tries to move. Excitingly, the anti- or post-mimetic modern novel grew (how else?) out of the realistic–naturalistic paradigm. The demand for ever closer adherence to reality led on the one hand to a descent into the ramifications and dark recesses of the human psyche (stream of consciousness novel), and on the other to attempts at progressively more minute depictions of "outside" reality. So that one day, in pursuit of this "realistically" defined objective, the presented "what" turned into a conspicuous foregrounding of the "how" – just as if you look ever more closely at a photo in a newspaper, you suddenly can't make out the pictured object any more, but only the component dots. The radically realized program of realism tips over into radically self-referential language art.

This "tipping over" or "toppling over" into another literary–aesthetic program is well exemplified by the novel that is often considered – with good reason – the paradigmatic novel of the twentieth century: James Joyce's *Ulysses*. Joyce bragged that if Dublin were ever destroyed, it could be rebuilt using the description in *Ulysses* exactly as it appeared on June 16, 1904, and he enquired from abroad whether a particular fence was high (or low) enough to climb over. But at the same time he uses so many narrative methods in this novel of the century, while semiotically charging his text with extremely dense and "thick" references and connotations, both intra- and intertextual, that in fact it's impossible to feel even for a moment that mimesis is still the basic operative principle here. (Or else the concept of mimesis would have to be stretched so far that it would be hard to say what wouldn't qualify as mimesis.) *Ulysses* sounds the death-knell of naturalism, according to the early judgment of Richard Aldington;[47] or perhaps better, it's both the high point of naturalism *and* the point at which naturalism obviously turns into something else.

---

[46]   Quoted in *Romantheorie*, ed. Steinecke and Wahrenburg, 431.
[47]   Cf. Bode, *Ästhetik*, 159.

Yet despite the logic of this development into literary modernism (and postmodern narrative is still concerned with entertainingly playing through and testing out the possibilities of this new level), the response of many readers and some critics persists: more than a hundred years after the breakthrough to post-mimesis, they still want to base their reception on the old parameters – although non-objective painting and all kinds of absolute music have long since become familiar. What Alain Robbe-Grillet saw as the defining feature of avant-garde films and books of the 1950s –

> Not only do they claim no other reality than that of the reading, or of the performance, but further they always seem to be in the process of jeopardizing themselves in proportion as they create themselves. Here space destroys time, and time sabotages space. Description makes no headway, contradicts itself, turns in circles. Moment denies continuity.[48]

– tends to be suppressed or ignored in the reception, as Nathalie Sarraute pointed out in connection with the radically self-referential *nouveaux romans* of Robbe-Grillet, Michel Butor, Claude Simon, and others:

> And so, no matter what the novelist may do, he cannot distract the reader's attention from all sorts of objects that just any novel, whether good or bad, can furnish him.
>
> Many critics encourage this absent-mindedness and frivolity in readers by giving in to it themselves, thus fostering confusion.
>
> Indeed, it is astonishing to see with what complacency they dwell upon anecdotal features, relate the "story" and discuss the "characters," appraising their verisimilitude and examining their morality.[49]

So it quite often seems as though these texts encounter a certain stubborn, stalling *resistance* from the reader – as if, say, someone still tried diligently to narrate the action of Samuel Beckett's trilogy of novels (*Molloy/Malone Meurt/L'Innommable*) (1951/1951/1953), to describe their characters, etc. (a procedure comparable to searching for the object that "must somehow exist" in an abstract painting). But that's okay. Possibly these texts are constructed so as to offer a reader some rudiments of mimetic straws to clutch, but then pit themselves against this conventionalized reading and aim precisely to break it up. *Actio* and *reactio* would be equally strong. To be sure, the text's resistance must be registered by readers and understood as an index of their own mental inflexibility, if the relationship between the two is to be converted into a *productive* one.

---

48 Alain Robbe-Grillet, *For a New Novel: Essays on Fiction*, trans. Richard Howard, Evanston, IL, 1989, 155.
49 Nathalie Sarraute, *Tropisms, and The Age of Suspicion*, London, 1963, 132–133.

What we've just said applies only to a quantitatively small proportion of twentieth-century and present-day novels, however. In fact what's always astonishing, if you think of the whole contemporary scene as well as retrospectively of developments since the early seventeenth century, is the plenitude and variety of species and sub-genres within this genre. In a certain way, like once upon a time with the dinosaurs, there seems to be a connection between the completely indisputable dominance of this species and its *internal* variety of forms. As Herder put it as early as the eighteenth century, the novel integrates everything,[50] but precisely by virtue of being *omnivorous* it's also able to serve all possible needs and fulfill all possible functions. It offers something for everyone and caters for every taste. But that also means it's anything but a coincidence that this *most successful* of all literary genres is practically *impossible to define* in a satisfactory way ("*the* novel"), since every definition that can cover *all* "novels" is so general as to say almost nothing at all. Its combined power lies exactly in this distinctive *capacity to be everything*: in sum, the novel covers the largest imaginable spectrum; this protean genre fills every conceivable ecological niche.

Adventure novels, maritime stories, horror stories, fantasy, science fiction, thrillers, romances, erotic and pornographic novels, the historical novel and the sensation novel (a Victorian mixture of mystery and crime), the above-mentioned *Bildungsroman*, epistolary novels, psychological novels, stream of consciousness novels, the *nouveau roman*, magical realist novels, hospital novels, German *Heimatromane*, westerns, etc. – there's actually no end either to the enumeration or to the more finely differentiated subdivisions. For it's not as though these sub-genres of the novel existed as Platonic ideas, as a philosophical realism would have us believe: common sense tells us these are only conventional groupings that one can either use or do without.

Subdividing the mammoth genre of the novel does have two advantages. First, it offers the potential reader a rough guide as to what to expect. Publishers' lists, the layout of bookshops, the arrangement of offers from Internet mail-order companies, reflect (or help create) this order – that's simply helpful. Just as the musical clef sets the key in which the coming piece of music (good or bad, it doesn't matter) is to be played, so this classification of a given novel signals how the reader is expected to deal with the text.

Second, certain conventions with regard to form and content can be introduced into each of these sub-categories (otherwise a book purchaser would be none the wiser for the information "this is a western"), which new texts can in turn make use of or play around with. It may be that the new text overstates and underlines the established pattern, or it may be a matter of

---

[50]   Cf. *Romantheorie*, ed. Steinecke and Wahrenburg, 236.

varying, circumventing, crossing it, or whatever. Almost every original refusal to follow an established genre has at least one quality: it is *new*. In many cases it's even attractive, since it evokes the relevant model in the informed reader's mind. So it's by no means a disadvantage to know the conventions of the sub-genres (which needn't be enumerated here), just as our enjoyment can increase when we already know many examples of a group. In other cases, though, it reduces the pleasure, because we're not so easily impressed and see through the "new" as a derivative concoction.

A number of the novel genres just mentioned flourished in a particular historical period (e.g., the Gothic novel in the Romantic age, or science fiction in the twentieth century), while others seem to have an immutable permanency (like the social novel or romances), and yet others are historically specific, disappear, then return after a long break in a new guise, though still clearly recognizable. The picaresque novel, for instance, originated in sixteenth-century Spain (*Lazarillo de Tormes* [anonymous], 1554, soon afterwards proscribed by the Catholic Inquisition). The basic ingredients are always the same: the protagonist of humble stock goes through a series of episodes in various social spheres and situations, part exciting and part grotesque. He's a plaything, not master of his fate, and – unlike the hero of the *Bildungsroman* – he doesn't change much. The first German novel, Hans Jacob Christoph von Grimmelshausen's *Der abenteuerliche Simplicissimus Teutsch* [*The Adventurous Mr. Simplicissimus*] (1669) can be seen as such a picaresque novel, as can Alain René Lesage's *Gil Blas* (1715–1735). In the latter it becomes especially clear that the picaresque novel primarily criticizes society and the morals of the day from the underdog's perspective, and has nothing to do with the personal development of a middle-class subject. In the second half of the twentieth century novels emerge again that can in this sense be described as "neo-picaresque" (John Wain, *Hurry on Down*, 1953; Saul Bellow, *The Adventures of Augie March*, 1953; Kingsley Amis, *Lucky Jim*, 1954 – and Günter Grass's *The Tin Drum* counts as one of these) – an interesting phenomenon whose social origins deserve investigation.

But if Grimmelshausen's *Simplicissimus* is the first German novel, why isn't *Lazarillo de Tormes* the first Spanish novel – and not *Don Quixote*? The question is reasonable and not easily answered, and it brings others in its wake. Couldn't Rabelais's *Gargantua et Pantagruel* (1532–1564) be regarded as the first modern novel? According to the established view, *Gargantua et Pantagruel* does indeed comprise isolated episodes which wildly mix together the satirical and the grotesque, folk tales and chivalric romances, social criticism and bawdy, but these aren't integrated into a whole – and the protagonists still include lumbering giants! It would make sense, then, as in the case of Jonathan Swift's *Gulliver's Travels*, to speak simply of an extended tradition of prose satire. Yet this proves once again that even in the narrative of the history of the modern European novel every beginning is obviously a *positing*, which just masquerades as the only possible beginning.

It's perhaps noticeable from the above (far from exhaustive) list of sub-genres that many are defined by their subject matter (horror story, western), but only a considerably smaller number by their form of mediation (e.g., the epistolary novel or the magic realist novel). No lesser writer than E. M. Forster dismissed "classification by subject matter": he thought it "silly" to talk of "the literature of Inns" or "the literature of Sussex."[51] The English novelist and professor of English Malcolm Bradbury, himself one of the leading writers of campus novels after 1945, protested against being categorized in that way: he pointed out that if locality was the important thing, we could also devise a group of "castle novels," which would include both Kafka's *The Castle* (1926) and P. G. Wodehouse's comic "Jeeves and Wooster" novels of the 1920s – a palpable absurdity, or so it would seem.

Forster's and Bradbury's examples are witty and well chosen – yet they prove nothing at all. The fact that no one has introduced "castle novel" as a sub-genre that would cover both Franz Kafka, P. G. Wodehouse, and also Kurt Tucholsky (*Schloß Gripsholm*, 1931), proves only that this designation is for the time being not a meaningful common denominator – whereas "western" is a perfectly sensible sub-group, since that term (like "romance') immediately calls up or brings into play a cluster of interconnected features. Even in introducing sub-genres, the golden rule applies: if it works, it's good.

On the other hand it's incontestable – and after all that we've said this should hardly come as a surprise – that a *more essential* difference within the mass of novels is the one between texts that proffer themselves for consumption, i.e., that meet the reader's expectations so perfectly that we can no longer register any discrepancy between what we expected and what we were offered (because it was tailor-made), and those other texts that come over as more or less unfamiliar or strange. The difference amounts to confirmation and reinforcement in the first case and subversive questioning in the second: the question is whether in the course of reading the reader becomes (however slightly) a different person, or returns from the encounter with the text entirely unchanged, exit level = entry level. It's the old difference between formulaic, stereotyped light fiction, and "demanding" highbrow literature – though one needn't necessarily think of this in the sense of an ideological opposition in the struggle for cultural hegemony or supremacy, but purely pragmatically as an observable difference between very dissimilar kinds of encoding and decoding.

---

[51]   E. M. Forster, *Aspects of the Novel*, Harmondsworth, 1977 [1927], 29.

In 1969 Dieter Wellershoff presented a highly amusing and apt analysis of a medical novel, *Lockende Gefahr für Dr. Bruhn* [*A Dangerous Temptation for Dr. Bruhn*]:

> Who is Dr. Stefan Bruhn? I was ready for anything – but the fact that he's a gigantic, broad-shouldered, blond, young, enormously talented assistant doctor with steel-blue eyes set in a chiseled, suntanned face, and walks with an elastic spring in his step, surprised me nevertheless. He's presented in a few lines with laconic ease. Then we learn that he's highly susceptible to female beauty, also very ambitious, but without any great inclination to scientific work, which he regards only as a means of getting on. These are character traits that, together with his perfection, make him a person at risk, someone who has got to have an experience.
>
> A temptress awaits him, the beautiful, spoiled woman of luxury Sibylle Termeulen. She'd had her appendix removed by the famous Professor Fahrenkamp at the university clinic and makes use of a few days of convalescence to lure the professor's assistant from the right path. She goes out with him to a gourmet restaurant, tells him that she is the owner of a private clinic for cosmetic surgery, and impresses him so much that he goes to visit her when he has a free weekend. There, in her luxurious place, Sibylle becomes his lover, and to secure the relationship offers him a well-paid job as a surgeon in her clinic. Still hesitating, he goes back to the university town, but when his boss reprimands him roughly for being late, that proves the decisive turning point.
>
> Meanwhile a subplot has been developing. The medical student Martina Feldmann is called home by a telegram. Her father, who works as a country doctor in the small town of Brackwede on the Heath, has died of a heart attack while on the way to visit an elderly patient. The family doesn't know what will become of them. For a short period it's possible to get a replacement for the practice; Martina, the eldest daughter, decides to give up her studies for the time being and earn some money. A job ad leads her to Sibylle Termeulen's private clinic "Woodland Quiet" at about the same time as Dr. Bruhn. He only notices her, however, as a pleasant peripheral presence, since he's entirely engrossed with Sibylle Termeulen, the life of luxury, and his less pleasurable new professional experiences. The senior consultant, Dr. Georg Bitner, a horrible mephisphelean man, apparently not just Sibylle's business partner but also her former lover, is making life difficult for him. Worse, however, he gradually discovers Sibylle's unscrupulous attitude. Ageing screen goddesses and ghastly *nouveaux riches* are treated in the clinic, but a young woman who lost her beauty in an accident is not to be operated on because it is not certain whether her husband will still pay for the operation. Yet that would be a restorative operation to rescue a marriage, whereas the rich clients want a pretty face just for the sake of a frivolous life. Dr. Bruhn's eyes are fully opened when the clinic owner and her shady chief consultant agree to give an American gangster a new face for twenty thousand dollars. Despair brings him to Martina, who understands him immediately, and at Christmas he pops up in

her father's former house and offers himself to the happy family as the replacement doctor. Having lost his parents as a young man, he feels at home in the Feldmann family: with Martina's support, he learns what is to be done in the practice. They've been in love with each other for a while before they profess it to each other and he asks her to become his wife.[52]

Even without having read *A Dangerous Temptation for Dr. Bruhn*, doesn't that all strike you as strangely familiar? Wellershoff gets to the heart of the starkly dichotomized arrangement of signs (blond versus red-haired, outside versus inside) when he sums up: "These are firm orientations to stabilize a compulsive moral, and the novel, as the demonstrative reflection of the moral, shows itself to be an over-integrated system that allows contradictions only in the form of deception."[53] The medical novel sketches an *unambiguous* world, which is designed to speak directly to those readers who *are looking for exactly that* and during the time of their identificatory reading live vicariously – an experience for which an aesthetically stimulating foregrounding of the form, of the way in which it is written (which always implies a reflective distance from the "content'), would be truly fatal. Such novels offer meaning, direction, and instruction, all prepackaged:

> This, then, is a novel that really constructs or confirms norms, above all because it communicates not just value judgments, but also exemplary behavior. What does the family do in the event of bereavement? First, like Martina Feldmann, one displays grief; then practical reflections follow. What does the faithful employee do when her employers hit problems? Like Anna, she says that the salary isn't so important for the time being, and makes sure that everything stays as it was. What do the employers do? They pay her salary nevertheless. How does a potential boss behave? Occasionally he rants and raves, like Professor Fahrenkamp, then returns to paternal joviality. What does a jilted lover do? Like Pit Engel, Martina's fellow student, he remains a good friend and also gets on marvelously with the bridegroom. And how does a bride look? Pale and serious, her eyes radiate happiness. But what happened to Dr. Bruhn? He appears "no longer as radiant and carefree as he was a year ago." He is more mature, more humane, but why doesn't he have that cheeky, daring look any more, or that elastic spring in his step? What's happened to him? Dr. Bruhn has been caught by morality.[54]

If we compare that, however, with the beginnings of the modern European novel, and in particular with what continental readers said about Richardson's

---

[52]   Dieter Wellershoff, *Von der Moral erwischt: Aufsätze zur Trivialliteratur*, Frankfurt am Main, 1983, 9–11.
[53]   Wellershoff, *Moral*, 10.
[54]   Wellershoff, *Moral*, 14–15.

work, it's clear that these ingredients have always been part of the recipe. Even the "hypergamy" (Anthony Burgess), i.e., the upstart "marriage above one's station" (chambermaid–young nobleman) is retained in twentieth-century light fiction (nurse–young senior doctor), with barely any attenuation. (This also helps to explain the identificatory or compensatory charm this literature has for its predominantly female readership – "she's corrupted with princes," goes a song by the German songwriter Konstantin Wecker; to complete the picture it's worth mentioning that the situation is no different with the male role models offered by westerns or space fiction.)

The alternative scenario, however, is that rather than offer prepackaged sense and meaning, the novel thematizes *possibilities* of meaning-construction and so offers readers the chance to do this for themselves. This is still in the twenty-first century what it was at the very outset – a question of the authenticity and seriousness of an art which can no longer confine itself to the reproduction and redoubling of "reality" (whatever that may be) without producing an anachronistic effect: "If the novel wants to remain true to its realistic heritage and tell things how they really are, it must abandon a realism that only aids the façade in its work of camouflage by reproducing it."[55]

To be sure, all these are novels, just as all sorts of things can be categorized as "food." It is only in the first group of novels, the ones that invite identificatory readings, that we can fall into the trap of Don Quixote, of Catherine Morland, or Emma Bovary; within the other group of novels, the text itself prevents us from making this mistake. What is common to *all* these texts, however, is that they relate to our perception of reality, whether by way of confirming or undermining it. *That* is ultimately the relation to reality that *all* novels can indisputably claim: *what they trigger off in our minds.*

In his brilliant apologia, the essay "Is Nothing Sacred?," Salman Rushdie quotes the Mexican writer Carlos Fuentes:

> Carlos Fuentes has called the novel "a privileged *arena*." By this he does not mean that it is the kind of holy space which one must put off one's shoes to enter; it is not an arena to revere; it claims no special rights *except the right to be the stage upon which the great debates of society can be conducted.* "The novel," Fuentes writes, "is born from the very fact that we do not understand one another, because unitary, orthodox language has broken down. Quixote and Sancho, the Shandy brothers, Mr. and Mrs. Karenin: their novels are the comedy (or the drama) of their misunderstandings. Impose a unitary language: you kill the novel, but you also kill the society."[56]

---

[55] Adorno, "The Position of the Narrator in the Contemporary Novel," 32.
[56] Salman Rushdie, "Is Nothing Sacred?" *Granta* 31 (Spring 1990): 97–111, here 103.

Since there's no such thing as the One (any more), seeking and *recherche* is required: "The elevation of the quest for the Grail over the Grail itself, the acceptance that all that is solid *has* melted into air, that reality and morality are not givens but imperfect human constructs, is the point from which fiction begins."[57]

That is the one *difficult* freedom that the youngest of all genres entrusts us and demands that we exercise. The novel tends rather to pose questions than give answers:

> [W]hile the novel answers our need for wonderment and understanding, it brings us harsh and unpalatable news as well.
>
> It tells us there are no rules. It hands down no commandments. We have to make up our own rules as best we can, make them up as we go along.
>
> And it tells us there are no answers; or, rather, it tells us that answers are easier to come by, and less reliable, than questions. If religion is an answer, if political ideology is an answer, then literature is an inquiry; great literature, by asking extraordinary questions, opens new doors in our minds.[58]

This hugely diffused literature is at the same time the most private medium, since it provides a cinema of the mind, which cannot be closed down (except in worlds like George Orwell's *Nineteen Eighty-Four* [1949], Aldous Huxley's *Brave New World* [1932], or Ray Bradbury's *Fahrenheit 451* [1953] – and that's also why passionate readers experience these as the ultimate horror-utopias).

> And this, finally, is why I elevate the novel above other forms, why it has always been, and remains, my first love: not only is it the art involving least compromises, but it is also the only one that takes the "privileged arena" of conflicting discourses *right inside our heads*. The interior space of our imagination is a theatre that can never be closed down; the images created there make up a movie that can never be destroyed.[59]

Yet since no man is an island, this literature, received entirely privately by individuals, is of course *socially, politically,* and culturally *irreducibly subversive*, through and through: *for it makes distinctions and promotes diversity*:

> Literature is the one place in any society where, within the secrecy of our own heads, we can hear *voices talking about everything in every possible way*. The reason for ensuring that that privileged arena is preserved is not that writers want the absolute freedom to say and do whatever they please. It is that we, all of us, readers and writers and citizens and generals and godmen, need that

---

[57]   Rushdie, "Sacred," 105.
[58]   Rushdie, "Sacred," 106.
[59]   Rushdie, "Sacred," 109.

little, unimportant-looking room. We do not need to call it sacred, but we do need to remember that it is necessary.[60]

This is necessary if only because those who do not wish to recognize the provisionality and constructedness of their views, the contingency of their persuasions, considering themselves rather spokespersons or preachers of the *one* truth that (saving others against their will) must be spread and enforced, ruthlessly so since they are above the law that is valid only *for others*, and in the name of a higher power to which nevertheless no one else may lay claim *for themselves* – because, I say, these people are so dangerously *opposed to civilization: for on such principles, human society is unimaginable, unliveable.*

---

[60]   Rushdie, "Sacred," 111.

3

The Object of Every Analysis
The How *of the* What
(Discourse and Story)

Everyone will admit that even in daily conversation it's not entirely irrelevant how a story is actually told. Some people know how to draw in those listening and grip them, others bore them with a story perhaps not so uninteresting in itself, but whose interest somehow doesn't come across. The one type are born joke-tellers, who have everyone creased up and rolling on the floor well before the end of the story; with the other type, it goes down like a lead balloon. The great difference is in the *how*. Perhaps many of us have had the experience of retelling a story that had seemed so hilarious when we heard it, doing our best with it, but even so not getting much response.

To repeat our claim for literary narratives (and that obviously includes the novel): not only does the how of the story make a decisive difference, but the actual meaning of a literary narrative is inseparable from this how. We can't talk meaningfully about the narrative, without having grasped the concrete manner of its mediation, since ultimately the meaning (a word we might well always think of in the plural: meanings) of a literary narration is realized in this specific mediatedness. Were the latter different, the former couldn't be the same either.

If that's correct – and this way of seeing it brings fiction closer to poetry, but also closer to other arts such as painting, graphic art, sculpture, and music, than is generally acknowledged – then every analysis of a novel must begin from a very precise identification of its form, of the way it functions as a narrative; and not from what at first glance appears to be its paraphrasable "content." Paraphrase – of narrative texts just like any other literary texts – is heresy.

The Novel: An Introduction. By Christoph Bode. Translated by James Vigus. English translation © 2011 James Vigus. Published by John Wiley & Sons, Ltd.
Original German text © 2005 Narr Francke Attempto Verlag GmbH + Co. KG.

To put it more concretely: we must look at *this specific* narrative text, at how it "gets its story across." And since we have at our disposal a whole series of useful parameters, which we know provide rich information about the "mechanics" of a narrative text, and whose identification helps to pinpoint the narrative, this analytical inspection certainly doesn't have to proceed in a rambling or arbitrary way. We can work through the list of techniques relevant to narrative – like the handling of time, portrayal of the characters, the narrative situations, etc. – step by step. That's possible, although we don't have to work so schematically.

In a sense this insight, that the key must be the concrete narrative mediatedness, is banal to the point of being self-evident. If we're going to analyze a novel, what is the object of the investigation if not this very text, open in front of us? On the other hand, this project of directing our cognitive interest to the *how* of the narrative *more than* (to put it modestly) to *what* is narrated throws up a number of problems that must not be underestimated. Some of these problems are of a logical or conceptual kind (and indeed unavoidable), others are terminological (and in my view not inevitable). Although not everyone relishes the work of clearing terminological thickets, and I too find the first set of problems much more interesting, it may be wise to begin with a few conceptual explanations.

One pair of concepts traditionally used to grasp the relationship of the how to the what of a narrative has already been discussed above: story and plot. *Story*, according to E. M. Forster, is the narration of events in a purely temporal sequence, whereas *plot* emphasizes the causal connections between the narrated events; we could also say that the plot performs this causal connection. (It's already been noted how difficult it is to draw the line between purely chronological sequence and causal connection.)

Forster's distinction can be pressed further, by defining story as roughly equivalent to the *relaying of content*, as guides to the novel or literary handbooks often do, but plot as the actual literary shaping or presentation of this story in a particular, given text, i.e., that which lies before the reader. Or in David Lodge's words: "the representation of that story in an aesthetically motivated discourse, with all the gaps, elisions, rearrangements, repetitions, and emphases which invest the story with meaning."[1]

Story and plot thus correspond roughly to the pair of concepts used by the Russian formalists, *fabula* and *sjuzet* (indeed, the definition by Lodge which I just quoted is admittedly a definition of *sjuzet*), for *fabula* is the basic stuff of the narration, "the material of the narrative construction,"[2] while *sjuzet*, to give a slight variation of Lodge's characterization, signifies (in Umberto

---

[1] David Lodge, "Milan Kundera, and the Idea of the Author in Modern Criticism," *Critical Quarterly* 26 (1984): 105–121, here 111.
[2] Victor Erlich, *Russian Formalism*, 3rd edn, New Haven, CT, 1981, 240.

Eco's words) "the story as actually told, along with all its deviations, digressions, flashbacks and the whole of the verbal devices."[3]

But confusion could arise because some narratologists have simply inverted the meanings of plot and story just outlined, or even attributed such an inversion to Forster himself.[4] However inexcusable the latter mistake may be, the former is understandable, since when we ask someone about the basic action of a drama, we ask about its *plot*; and as H. Porter Abbott rightly observes,[5] children who want to hear their favorite *story* expect it word for word, not in the form of a summary of content. In this sense the choice of words for this intended distinction may have been a bit unfortunate.

That, then, was possibly one of the reasons why British and American critics of the 1970s turned to a new terminology, clearly modeled on the concepts of French structuralism. The terms *histoire* and *discours*, even if their theoretical baggage and finer nuances weren't always imported along with them, could readily be taken up as *story* and *(narrative) discourse*, and this at least got rid of the unhappy word "plot."[6]

Of course, such a binary segmentation of a field isn't somehow naturally determined. It is we who do this, it is not in the "order of things," and that is why it's immediately possible to think up threefold or even fourfold divisions: it all depends which additional aspects of the field "narrative" (in French, *récit*) strike us as important enough to be conceptually separated out – such as the fact that we're (often) dealing with a *printed* text, or that the narrative is indeed a performative *act* (unfolding in time).

The field "narrative" can, however, be segmented completely differently, for instance if someone (surely with good reason) denies that the causal connection of events in a narrative already presented an artistic arrangement, arguing instead that the former is the prerequisite of the latter, i.e., that it must be assigned rather to *histoire*/story, not in the first place to *discours*/discourse.

Monika Fludernik has constructed a diagram to show how the conceptual schemes of selected narratologists relate to each other (see table 3.1).[7] Without wanting to dispute particular attributions, one thing seems to

[3]   Umberto Eco, *The Role of the Reader: Explorations in the Semiotics of Texts*, Bloomington, 1979, 27. Cf., on Tomashevsky's classic definition of *fabula* and *sjuzet*, Jurij Lotman, *The Structure of the Artistic Text*, trans. Gail Lenhoff and Ronald Vroon, Ann Arbor, 1977, 232.

[4]   Cf. the entry "Narratology" in the *Encyclopedia of Contemporary Literary Theory: Approaches, Scholars, Terms*, ed. Irena R. Makaryk, Toronto, 1993.

[5]   Cf. H. Porter Abbott, *The Cambridge Introduction to Narrative*, Cambridge, 2002, 16.

[6]   Cf. esp. Seymour Chatman, *Story and Discourse: Narrative Structure in Fiction and Film*, Ithaca, NY, 1993 [1978].

[7]   Monika Fludernik, *The Fictions of Language and the Languages of Fiction: The Linguistic Representation of Speech and Consciousness*, London, 1993, 62.

Table 3.1   *narratologists*

	Events in chronological order	Events causally connected	Events ordered artistically	Text on page	Narration as enunciation
Genette	*histoire*		*discours* *(récit)*		narration (voice + focalization)
Chatman	story		discourse		
Bal	*fabula*		story and focalization		narration (plus language, plus voice)
Rimmon-Kenan	story			text	narration
Prince	narrated			narrating	
Stanzel	–	story			mediation by teller or reflector + enunciation if teller figure

emerge beyond all doubt from this table: any beginner could be excused for finding the terminological terrain rather impenetrable, and would probably soon be overwhelmed if a further distinction were made between, say, early and late Genette.

But it's also true that all analysis of narrative operates – *grosso modo* – with a model in which the concretely applied narrative techniques, as they appear in narrated discourse (the *how*), are brought out differentially against the background of a story "as such" (the *what*). And precisely this assumption presents a logical–conceptual problem of the first order, which exists to a large extent independently of the specific terminological questions just sketched (incidentally, for a deeper understanding of the latter, a good reference book will help).[8] The gist of this tricky, absolutely fundamental logical–conceptual problem is as follows: whereas the narrative discourse is always available and at hand, the *story isn't* immediately available, but must first be abstracted from the discourse. The story is something to be gleaned from the narrative discourse by a particular interpretative and logical procedure – it is the *result* of particular efforts from the reader.

[8] Cf., for example, *The Routledge Encyclopedia of Narrative Theory*, ed. David Herman, Manfred Jahn, and Marie-Laure Ryan, London, 2005.

This fact, which has serious implications, was brushed under the carpet in the first few decades of the twentieth century because formalist and early structuralist narratologists[9] were above all interested in discerning basic patterns in a wide range of narratives (especially fairy tales, myths, and legends). They then presented these basic patterns as "deep structures," from which numerous different individual narratives (with different "surface structures") were generated. The abstract idea of a story, then, seemed to generate diverse manifestations or variations of itself.[10]

It was thus forgotten that, as a rule, readers are confronted with only one such concrete manifestation, and generally do not consider it a goal of their reading – whether they're pursuing professional analysis or lay distraction – to make a generalizing identification of the text at hand (or elements of it) with this or that basic prototype. On the contrary, the reader's desire is usually to appreciate the *specific qualities* of the particular text – and that's perfectly okay.[11]

Jonathan Culler gets to the heart of the matter: "What readers actually encounter […] is the discourse of a text: the plot is something readers *infer* from the text."[12] Or in H. Porter Abbott's words:

> One important point that the distinction between story and discourse brings out is that we never see a story directly, but instead always pick it up *through* the narrative discourse. The story is always mediated – by a voice, a style of writing, camera angles, actors' interpretations – so that what we call the story is really something that we construct. We put it together from what we read or see, often by inference.[13]

---

[9]   See, for example, Vladimir Propp, *Morphology of the Folktale*, 2nd edn, Austin, 1968; Claude Lévi-Strauss, *Mythologiques: Introduction to a Science of Mythology*, 4 vols., trans. John Weightman and Doreen Weightman, London, 1970–1981.

[10]   This past is not yet so past: Gerald Prince's *A Grammar of Stories: An Introduction* (The Hague, 1973) begins with the classic sentence: "In this study I attempt to show that a finite number of explicit rules could account for the structure of all the sets and only the sets which are generally and intuitively recognized as stories." After thirty years' work, Christopher Booker came to the realization that there are essentially only seven types of story: "Overcoming the Monster, Rags to Riches, Quest, Voyage and Return, Tragedy, Comedy and Rebirth," to which after further consideration he added "Rebellion against the One" and "the detective story." Christopher Booker, *The Seven Basic Plots: Why We Tell Stories*, London, 2005 – quoted from a review in the *Times Literary Supplement*, February 21, 2005. Remembering Borges, we should perhaps add as a tenth possibility "stories written with a very fine brush."

[11]   "The concrete organization of characters and functions, in which historical, cultural and aesthetic differences are expressed, disappear in Propp's analysis – the escape of the hero of a Russian fairytale and James Bond's flight in the red stunt car result in an identical function." Jochen Vogt, "Grundlagen narrativer Texte," in *Grundzüge der Literaturwissenschaft*, ed. Heinz-Ludwig Arnold and Heinrich Detering, Munich, 1997, 287–307, here 292.

[12]   Jonathan Culler, *Literary Theory: A Very Short Introduction*, Oxford, 1997, 85

[13]   Abbott, *Narrative*, 17.

Of course, it's possible to object to this. Does not the simple fact that a certain story – such as that of Cinderella, for example – can be transposed into various media (from oral transmission to a fairy tale fixed in print, and from there to a ballet, a comic and a film), show clearly that there really is such a thing as *the* story of Cinderella, something like the invariable core of all these different narratives?[14]

But I don't think this objection is really valid. The argument, after all, was not that there are absolutely no such things as stories, but rather that they come to light by *abstraction*. And obviously script writers must establish what the essential elements of the action are, what the *story* is, before writing a script for the film version of a literary work – otherwise the film would not be recognized or accepted as the film adaptation of this particular novel. Moreover, screenplay authors who are interested in more than just "copying" the novel onto the screen, and attempt an artistic transformation into their medium, can't avoid reflecting on the special way in which the content is mediated. They can then find corresponding creative equivalents in the medium of film. The important point, therefore, is this: transpositions into a different medium are themselves a convincing example of how stories always have to be *constructed* first, as an intermediate step of abstraction on the way towards a genuine filmic rendition.

And what about the possible objection that there is no need for a grand construction of a story, story being the natural consequence of the events before the narrator (or author) muddles them up for the sake of particular effects? A good example would be any novel about a secret or a crime. Charles Dickens' *Great Expectations* (1860/61) for instance, in which Pip learns (and also informs his readers at a late stage, although at the time of narration he himself obviously knows) that the generous financial support which enables him to live as a gentleman in fact came from the prisoner Magwitch, whom he once helped. Or take another Dickens novel, *Oliver Twist* (1837–1839). The eponymous hero was – although he doesn't know it – the illegitimate child of Edwin Leeford and Agnes Fleming, and a large part of the injustices he suffers are thanks to his legitimate half-brother Edward, alias "Monks." But we learn all this only towards the end of the novel – and with good reason, too. A four-part film version of 1999, however, changed that:

> The first episode of the four-part series consists of a detailed narration of the love affair between Oliver's parents, Edwin and Agnes. This narrative not only moves the facts of their story to the beginning, unlike Dickens' novel which leaves them at the end, but it also depicts the affair "firsthand," with the

---

[14]   Cf. Chatman, *Story and Discourse*, 20: "This transposability of the story is the strongest reason for arguing that narratives are indeed structures independent of any medium."

characters speaking their own dialogues and acting out the events, rather than having them retold by "Monks" and Leeford's friend, Brownlow.[15]

Couldn't we say that this TV adaptation has simply restored the story's natural sequence of events (perhaps because viewers, unlike readers, can't be trusted to wait so long for the solution to the mystery of Oliver's origins, even though this may basically eliminate the suspense and point of the story)? A story that doesn't await some sort of ingenious "construction" from the reader, but which is merely withheld intentionally until just before the end, and then presented with all the clarity we could wish for? The *real* story was *like that*, before it was defamiliarized through literary and narrative techniques.

This common-sense objection once again makes clear why it is absolutely necessary to insist that the *histoire* of a novel is a *construct*, which the reader produces during and after the reading. For in fiction there is no such thing as the "real" story, which is *then* somehow manipulated. There is only *this here*: the narrative discourse. *And* there is the possibility of abstracting and rearranging, reconfiguring – but that process does not *restore* an "original version": the reader simply produces, constructs. This operation is as normal and obvious as it is necessary, but: it is an operation.

Precisely because narratology also legitimately deals with non-fictional narratives, i.e., with narratives which order *real* events into the sequential form of a narrative, it's essential to keep insisting on this difference, this distinction of categories. A real event takes place outside a narrative (even if it can only be preserved in a narrative or in narratives) – whereas a fictional event takes place exclusively within a narrative discourse, and nowhere else.

For that very reason, it's rather dangerous, because misleading, to say when discussing fiction: "A plot can make a wedding the happy ending of the story or the beginning of a story – or can make it a turn in the middle."[16] This comment makes sense in relation to a wedding that actually took place – this event can really function differently in different stories. But a wedding in a fictional narrative is always already the one or the other, or a third thing, or interestingly none or all of these together – *without*, though, being "made into" this or that. No one has put this more clearly than Jonathan Culler himself, when he wrote: "[...] I am interested in more restricted analyses which explicitly identify *fabula* not as the reality reported

---

[15]   Paul Cobley, *Narrative*, London, 2001, 5.

[16]   Culler, *Literary Theory*, 85. In this section of his book, Culler uses the words *plot*, *story*, and *discourse* in a way that departs somewhat from the standard usage introduced above (repeatedly, Culler says "plot or story"). This is, however, irrelevant to the question we're discussing here.

by discourse but *as its product*"[17] – although here too it's worth noting that he should have taken Vladimir Nabokov's warning to heart that "reality" is one of the few words that is meaningless without quotation marks.[18]

Strictly speaking we should also avoid saying that particular events or actions are "represented" in fictional narratives – they are, rather, *presented*, because previously they did not exist anywhere. It's always instructive to observe how some shy away from such a radical consequence and try to get round it. Thus, for instance, the author of *The Cambridge Introduction to Narrative*, H. Porter Abbott, rejects the position just sketched:

> Where is this story before it is realized in words or on stage? The answer, so the argument goes, is: Nowhere. If that is the case, then all renderings of stories, on the stage or on the page, are *presentations* not representations. The extent to which stories are at the mercy of the way they are rendered is an important issue, and I will return to it in this chapter and later in this book. But for my definition, I will stick to the term "representation." I do this in part because the word is so commonly used in the way I am using it and in part because it describes at least the feeling that we often have that the story somehow pre-exists the narrative, even though this may be an illusion.[19]

What seems to me noteworthy is not just the way this quotation expresses a politically correct consternation about stories taken, as it were, as hostages – a problem that at some point had to be acknowledged – but also the way everyday language and that "somehow" feeling ("the feeling [...] that [...]

---

[17]   Jonathan Culler, "Fabula and Sjuzhet in the Analysis of Narrative: Some American Discussions," in *Narratology: An Introduction*, ed. Susana Onega and José Angel García Landa, London, 1996, 93–102, here 95, italics added. This reprinted essay was first published in 1980. Only a short time afterwards, in chapter 9 ("Story and Discourse in the Analysis of Narrative") of his book *The Pursuit of Signs: Semiotics, Literature, Deconstruction* (London, 1981), Culler expressed the paradoxical dilemma of (what seemed to him) a narratologically necessary, yet nevertheless unsustainable presumption: "I am not, of course, suggesting that narratologists believe that the events of a Balzac story actually took place or that Balzac conceived the events first and then embodied them in narrative discourse. I am claiming that narratological analysis of a text *requires one* to treat the discourse as a representation of events which are conceived of as independent of any particular narrative perspective or presentation and which *are thought of* as having the properties of real events. [...] the analyst *must assume* that there is a real or proper temporal order [...]. The analyst *must assume* that the events reported have a true order, for only then can he or she describe the narrative presentation as a modification or effacement of the order of events" (171, all italics added). Then, however, he continues: "Positing the priority of events to the discourse which reports or presents them, narratology establishes a hierarchy which the functioning of narratives often subverts by presenting events not as givens but as the products of discursive forces or requirements" (172). The deeper sense of this "double logic of narrative" was considered in chapter 1, above.
[18]   Vladimir Nabokov, "On a Book Entitled *Lolita*," *Lolita*, Harmondsworth, 1989 [1980], 309–315, here 310.
[19]   Abbott, *Narrative*, 14.

somehow") are invoked in order to decide a rather important question in literary criticism.

Finally, it might be objected that at least the literary treatment of traditional fictional material (*not* its adaptation in a different medium) must necessarily begin from a preexistent story. To take a few examples, the Romeo and Juliet story in Bandello's version, in Shakespeare's drama, in *West Side Story* by Leonard Bernstein, in *Romeo und Julia auf dem Dorf* [*Romeo and Juliet in the Village*] (1856) by Gottfried Keller, etc. Or the Faust story that in some way forms the basis of the plays of Christopher Marlowe and Johann Wolfgang von Goethe, perhaps also of Lord Byron's *Manfred*, and certainly of Thomas Mann's great novel *Doktor Faustus* (1947). Or the story of Don Juan told by Tirso de Molina, E. T. A. Hoffmann, Byron, and finally Max Frisch (*Don Juan oder die Liebe zur Geometrie* [*Don Juan or the Love of Geometry*, 1953]).

The better our knowledge of these texts, however, the more obvious it is that there's no such thing as *the* invariable core over which the various authors lay more or less decorative drapings. Quite on the contrary: essentials are often removed or turned upside down – such as when Byron's Don Juan is constantly beset by women. The supposed "core story" persisting through *all* realizations of the material would presumably have to be remarkably small, especially in the case of stories that are often retold. And yet everybody talks about the XY-story, the XY-material – quite rightly. Yet that's not because *the* story exists, but rather because there is a network or rhizome of elements that holds together a concrete number of narratives as a group, in the sense of Wittgenstein's often-quoted *family resemblances*.[20] It makes sense to then designate the group of such narratives with a pragmatically motivated shorthand: "Romeo and Juliet," "Faust," "Don Juan."

If it thus makes sense to claim that story (or in Mieke Bal's terminology, *fabula*)[21] is "the most abstract of all narrative levels,"[22] and if it makes sense to refer to story, *fabula*, *histoire* as "that abstract *object* of observation,"[23] yet doesn't make sense (because it's disorienting) to claim, "plot, story-as-discoursed, exists at a more general level than any particular objectification, any given movie, novel or whatever,"[24] then a basic problem remains, as a continuing challenge, as it were: how are we to tell the difference between a narrative text in front of us and something abstracted from it?

---

[20]   Ludwig Wittgenstein, *Philosophische Untersuchungen*, in *Werkausgabe, Vol. 1, Tractatus logico-philosophicus, Tagebücher 1914–1916, Philosophische Untersuchungen*, 11th edn, Frankfurt am Main, 1997 [1984], sections 65–67.
[21]   Mieke Bal, *Narratology: Introduction to the Theory of Narrative*, Toronto, 1985.
[22]   *Narratology*, ed. Onega and Landa, 93.
[23]   Ruth Ronen, "Paradigm Shift in Plot Models: An Outline of the History of Narratology," *Poetics Today* 11/4 (1990): 817–842, here 824, italics added.
[24]   Chatman, *Story and Discourse*, 43.

The simple answer is: by reading.

For the very reason that the story isn't already there beforehand, but is made by the reader in the act of reading (on the basis of the text, of course), a space opens in which the reader's interpretative activity amounts to the construction of a story (or multiple stories). However, that the meaning of a literary text can't be identical with this story is clear from the fact that "plot summaries" of novels of any narrative complexity always seem grotesquely to miss the point – the point being the concrete reading experience. Reading plot summaries of *A la recherche du temps perdu* or *Ulysses* or the Beckett trilogy makes you want to groan "okay, sure, but that's not the essential point ..." – just as it's not enough for us to know about (say) a Cubist still life that it depicts a guitar and a bottle of wine. Not that that's wrong, but we can't accept it as essential, precisely in view of all the countless other still lives our culture has produced. It misses the point in an absurd way, it's trivial.

The counter-argument can be made, however, that by no means all novels push their action into the background with such sophisticated artistry that a summary of their content will seem to us trivial or somehow mistaken. That's certainly true. With a modicum of polemical exaggeration Anthony Burgess, himself both a gifted novelist and a sharp and witty critic, once claimed a basic distinction between two types of novel-writers:

> Novelists, like poets, work in the medium of language, but some may be said to work in it more than others. There is a kind of novelist (conveniently designated as Class 1), usually popular, sometimes wealthy, in whose work language is a zero quantity, transparent, unseductive, the overtones of connotation and ambiguity totally damped [...] Such work is closer to film than to poetry, and it invariably films better than it reads. The aim of the class 1 novel can only properly be fulfilled when the narrated action is transformed into represented action: content being more important than style, the referents ache to be free of their words and to be presented directly as sense-data.[25]

Compare Burgess' so-called "Class 2 novelist":

> To the other kind of novelist [...] it is important that the opacity of language be exploited, so that ambiguities, puns and centrifugal connotations are to be enjoyed rather than regretted, and whose books, made out of words as much as characters and incidents, lose a great deal when adapted to the visual medium. [...] The beginning of literary wisdom, at least in the field of the novel, lies in the realization that Class 1 and Class 2 novelists have somewhat different aims.[26]

---

[25]   Anthony Burgess, *Joysprick: An Introduction to the Language of James Joyce*, London, 1973, 15.
[26]   Burgess, *Joysprick*, 15, 16.

That may be so, but the difference is perhaps not as categorical as Burgess (albeit with fair reason) wants to suggest. There are certainly many novels that we can simply devour because they hardly set up any resistance to our reading. They can be read so fast since the way they present "reality" is so close to our daily perception of reality (transmitted through language) as practically to coincide with it, and so their difference doesn't stand out.[27] They're designed especially so that readers can consume them quickly. Even so, readers of these novels must still construct a reality for the story. That's admittedly very easy to do – but it must be done. Thus we could say that novels written by "Class 2 novelists" only make us conscious of a process that in principle also operates when we decode other, deliberately simple novels. And they make us conscious of this by making something more difficult (often much more difficult) which in other cases ("Class 1 novelists") just happens unnoticed, because these eliminate in advance almost everything that might have directed attention to the *how*. Even the least challenging of literary narrative texts confirm *ex negativo* that the production of the story is ultimately the reader's work, since that story does not exist "before" or "outside" the narrative discourse. Only that sometimes this work is ludicrously easy, sometimes harder.

The meaning of a literary text, then, lies in the extent to which it instigates us to try out different configurations of sense and meaning. If it does this only to a small extent, there isn't much to get out of it: if everything's clear, we don't have a great deal to do. As we are encouraged to fabricate "real stories" – for *we* are the ones who do so, no one else – we aren't simply *shown* how meaning is produced through narration on the basis of something pre-given, which doesn't *contain* it yet (though all the ingredients are there apart from the last one: the reader), but we are allowed to *do it ourselves*. This is what essentially differentiates the versions of a story made by the reader and indeed continually revised during the reading from the retrievable content summaries in York Notes, literary encyclopedias, guides, and handbooks, etc.: *our consciousness of the experience of the process by which we configure them* (or the memory of this experience).[28]

And if we observe ourselves during this process, such as when we construct Henry James' novella *The Turn of the Screw* (1898) first as a ghost story, then as a "neurotic nanny terrorizes little ones" story, then it becomes clear that excellent fiction always provides, as a matter of course, that little extra, a certain problematization: it problematizes not just the construction of fictional realities, but the very *possibility* of their construction, and their

---

[27] Cf. Christoph Bode, *Ästhetik der Ambiguität: Zu Funktion und Bedeutung von Mehrdeutigkeit in der Literatur der Moderne*, Tübingen, 1988, 146ff.
[28] On this, see (among others) Wolfgang Iser, *The Act of Reading: A Theory of Aesthetic Response*, Baltimore, 1978.

contingency. Without assumptions about meaning and sense none of this is possible, but they are just that: *assumptions*, neither conclusions based on evidence, nor beliefs. For these fall into the domain of other faculties.

It can therefore be said that the meaning of a novel consists in the ensemble of the narrative techniques it uses and in the devices it employs to stimulate thought and imagination. To grasp and understand what's there in front of us means to recognize *what difference* this or that technique, this or that device makes in the wide range of possibilities, but thereby also in the wide field of effects and responses.

Now it's time to present the individual members of the ensemble.

4

Time

1 Narrative Time and Narrated Time

One of the most important narrative devices in the novel – perhaps the most important of all – is the manipulation of time. The analysis of the handling of time is both relatively easy and extremely informative: so one wonders why it doesn't receive more attention and why many critics present it as a rather annoying compulsory exercise, not noticing the opportunity it offers. Perhaps nowhere else in the analysis of the novel is the relation between input and output as favorable as when we analyze the temporal dimension of narrative.

To tell a story you need time. This time is called *narrative time*, even if we no longer listen to orally narrated stories, but read them in printed form. Narrative time thus corresponds to the time we need for reading. It doesn't matter whether we read fast or slowly – readers anyway vary the speed of their reading each time they pick up a book anew, and even throughout any one stretch. The main thing is rather the order of magnitude of the time spent reading; individual statistical anomalies aren't significant. The narrative time of novels usually ranges between a few and many hours, depending on the work's extent. Someone once suggested that narrative time could be measured by the number of pages in a book. I don't quite see what we'd actually gain from that (not to mention the fact that we'd then have to go further and work out the average word-count per page), since it would still be necessary to convert that space into time. So why not just say straightaway, without beating about the bush: this novel takes about five hours to read?

The Novel: An Introduction. By Christoph Bode. Translated by James Vigus. English translation © 2011 James Vigus. Published by John Wiley & Sons, Ltd.
Original German text © 2005 Narr Francke Attempto Verlag GmbH + Co. KG.

The antithesis of narrative time is narrated time: or it might be neater to talk about discourse time versus story time. Narrated time is the period of time a narration covers, for example, several decades in the case of *Robinson Crusoe*, several years in the majority of other novels, down to less than 24 hours in James Joyce's *Ulysses*.

Both quantities – narrative time and narrated time, or discourse time and story time – can be worked out quite quickly, but, isolated from each other, they aren't really that exciting. It is rather the *relation* between these two quantities that is significant, because it is a narratological indicator of the first rank. Three basic situations are conceivable. First, the narrative time a may be less than the narrated time b, i.e., $a < b$. That's the norm in the modern novel: the duration of the story is many times greater than its reading time, which is usually measured in hours. That is possible because narrators have at their disposal a whole arsenal of techniques of compressing, contracting, shortening, omitting, etc. (of which more below), and because it's true of most actions that they are quicker to tell than to perform.

The second possible relation between narrative time and narrated time is that of equivalence, i.e., $a = b$: we need roughly the same amount of time to read as the narrated action itself requires. The prime example of this is dialogue. Here is a passage from Denis Diderot's *Jacques le fataliste et son maître*, a novel written for a great part in dialogue form:

JACQUES: My Captain used to add that every shot fired from a gun had some-one's name on it.

MASTER: And he was right …

(After a short pause Jacques cried out:) May the devil take that innkeeper and his inn!

MASTER: Why consign one's neighbour to the devil? That's not Christian.

JACQUES: Because while I was getting drunk on his bad wine I forgot to water our horses. My father noticed and got angry. I shook my head at him and he took a stick and hit me rather hard across the shoulders. There was a regiment passing through on its way to camp at Fontenoy, and so out of pique I joined up. We arrived. The battle started …

MASTER: And you stopped the bullet with your name on it?

JACQUES: You've guessed it. Shot in the knee. And God knows the good and bad fortunes that were brought about by that shot. They are linked together exactly like the links of a fob-chain. Were it not for that shot, for example, I don't think I would ever have fallen in love, or had a limp.

MASTER: So you've been in love then?

JACQUES: Have I been in love!

MASTER: And all because of a shot?

JACQUES: Because of a shot.

MASTER: You never said a word of this to me before.

JACQUES: Very likely.
MASTER: Why is that?
JACQUES: That is because it is something that could not be told a moment
             sooner or a moment later.
MASTER: And has the moment come for hearing about these loves?
JACQUES: Who knows?
MASTER: Well, on the off-chance, begin anyway ... [1]

I've chosen this passage (which is from the beginning of the novel) since it displays clearly the two relationships just noted between narrative time and narrated time ($a < b$ and $a = b$) *simultaneously*. For up until the temporal contraction "After a short pause Jacques cried out," the relationship of the two times is 1 : 1 – to read the dialogue requires about as much time as to speak it (at this point we needn't worry about the fact that most people can read considerably faster than they can talk). If it did not encourage misunderstandings (see the previous chapter), we could say that the dialogue is "represented" exactly as it occurred.

Jacques's narration in this dialogue is also, however, a fine example of $a < b$ or *summary narration* (or *compression*). For Jacques very rapidly puts together the links in the causal chain "drunkenness – neglect of duty – fine – running away – joining the army – battle – shot in the knee," and also gives a small glimpse into the future, into what is obviously *of greater importance to him*: namely, his love story. It's given away here that he will take far *more time* to narrate that.

And this already raises the most important point that can be made about the aspect of "duration" in narrative texts. The variable relationship $a : b$ is the measure of *narrative speed* (v), and <u>narrative speed in its turn is a fairly reliable indicator of the *importance* of what is narrated</u>. $a < b$ signals a narrative speed of "normal" proportions; if it approaches $a = b$, the narrative slows down, and the third possible situation occurs when discourse time is greater than story time, i.e., when the description of an action or event lasts longer than the event itself ($a > b$).

It's easy to imagine in what kind of situation this latter technique crops up: when, say, something decisive occurs in a matter of seconds, but is related minutely – almost in slow motion – because it's meant to appear significant. This stretching out of time – in fact an extreme reduction of speed – is of course always necessary in (for instance) such narratives of conversation between two or more characters as "reproduce" not just what was actually spoken, but also everything that was going on within the characters during the conversation: inarticulate feelings, things not said, nuances

---

[1]   Denis Diderot, *Jacques the Fatalist and his Master*, trans. Michael Henry, Harmondsworth, 1986, 21–22.

of silent response, the motivations behind what was actually said. The presentation of events within consciousness is thus the main province of this kind of time-relation.

For illustration, here's a passage from the middle of Henry James' *The Golden Bowl* (1904). One of the main characters, Charlotte, speaks two sentences – and then attention focuses on Amerigo, the other main character:

> "It's awfully sweet of you, darling – our going together would be charming. But you mustn't mind us – you must suit yourselves: we've settled, Amerigo and I, to stay over till after luncheon."
>
> Amerigo, with the chink of this gold in his ear, turned straight away, so as not to be instantly appealed to; and for the very emotion of the wonder, furthermore, of what divination may achieve when winged by a community of passion. Charlotte had uttered the exact plea that he had been keeping ready for the same foreseen necessity, and had uttered it simply as a consequence of their deepening unexpressed need of each other and without the passing between them of a word. He hadn't, God knew, to take it from her – he was too conscious of what he wanted; but the lesson for him was in the straight clear tone that Charlotte could thus distil, in the perfect felicity of her adding no explanation, no touch for plausibility, that she wasn't strictly obliged to add, and in the truly superior way in which women so situated express and distinguish themselves. She had answered Mrs. Assingham quite adequately; she hadn't spoiled it by a reason a scrap larger than the smallest that would serve, and she had, above all, thrown off, for his stretched but covered attention, an image that flashed like a mirror played at the face of the sun. The measure of *everything*, to all his sense at these moments, was in it – the measure especially of the thought that had been growing with him a positive obsession and that began to throb as never yet under this brush of her having, by perfect parity of imagination, the match for it. His whole consciousness had by this time begun almost to ache with a truth of an exquisite order, at the glow of which she too had so unmistakeably then been warming herself – the truth that the occasion constituted by the last few days couldn't possibly, save by some poverty of their own, refuse them some still other and still greater beauty. It had already told them, with an hourly voice, that it had a meaning – a meaning that their associated sense was to drain even as thirsty lips, after the plough through the sands and the sight, afar, of the palm-cluster, might drink in at last the promised well in the desert. There had been beauty day after day, and there had been for the spiritual lips something of the pervasive taste of it; yet it was all nevertheless as if their response had remained below their fortune. How to bring it by some brave free lift up to the same height was the idea with which, behind and beneath everything, he was restlessly occupied, and in the exploration of which, as in that of the sun-chequered greenwood of romance, his spirit thus, at the opening of a vista, met hers.

When the narrative's actual aim is to present the inner world of its characters, the narrative speed becomes very low: $v = a > b$.

To repeat: the variable relation $a : b$ is the measure of *narrative speed* (v), and narrative speed in turn is a fairly reliable indicator of the *importance* of what is being narrated. This only makes full sense, however, when we realize what the term "variable relation" actually means: not just that $a < b$, $a = b$, and $a > b$ are all possible (that's trivial), but that all these relations can appear one after the other in the same novel (and indeed they do so, as a rule, in constant alternation), but that *within* any one time "situation" the speed can be reduced or accelerated (the case $a = b$ excepted). So it's not just in the *alteration between* $a < b$, $a = b$, and $a > b$ that accelerations and decelerations occur, but – and this in fact more frequent – accelerations and decelerations *within* $a < b$ and $a > b$. And precisely this *change* of speed deserves our special attention.

Isn't that all rather abstract? The relation between narrative time a and narrated time b is the narrative speed v – and are we really supposed to note its *alteration*, which would require a rather complicated mathematical equation? No: it isn't abstract at all. Exactly as we feel the pressure of extreme acceleration in the seat of a car, train, or airplane, and when the brakes are applied we're thrown forward and don't need to look at the speedometer to know whether the speed is increasing or decreasing (*absolute* measurements aren't necessary for this: acceleration and deceleration are *relative* quantities, precisely *changes* in speed), so in reading we don't need a speedometer or a stopwatch. We register automatically – albeit not physically, as in the examples of traveling – whether the speed is increasing or decreasing. And since *changes* of speed are the norm in novels, the above formulation should be adjusted: *changes* in narrative speed are a fairly reliable indicator of the *importance* of what is being narrated.

By way of illustration, let's return to the $a = b$ situation. There are novels, so-called dialogue novels, consisting mainly of such scenic presentations, which sometimes constitute 80–85 percent (Henry Green, *Nothing*, 1950) or even 90–95 percent (Ivy Compton-Burnett, *Mother and Son*, 1955) of the text.[2] There are also novels consisting of almost 100 percent dialogue. Here's the opening of Gabriel Josipovici's *Now* (1998):

> –I'm tired, Licia says.
> –Nobody's tired at your age, Sam says.
> –I'm tired.
> –At my age you've got a right to be tired, Sam Says. Not at your age.
> –What has right to do with it?
> –It's not natural.
> –Leave her alone Dad, Freddy says.
> –Nobody's tired at her age, Sam says. Are you tired?

[2] Cf. F. K. Stanzel, *A Theory of Narrative* [1979], trans. Charlotte Goedsche, Cambridge, 1986, 67.

–Sure.

–All the time?

–Most of the time.

–That's because you work too hard.

–No I don't, Freddy says.

–But what does she do? Sam says. I'll tell you what she does. She does nothing. That's why she's tired. That's why she thinks she's tired. If she got a job like everyone else she wouldn't have time to feel tired.

–Let it go Dad, Freddy says.

–The laburnum's in flower, Nina says.

–If you've got something to do you don't have time to feel tired, Sam says.

–I can see it from my window, Nina says. Quite suddenly, it's all in flower.

–If she hadn't given up her job she wouldn't feel so tired, Sam says.

–Let it go Dad, Freddy says.

–You can't see it from here, Nina says. But you can from my window.

–You've got a lovely view from your window, Julie says.

–I look right down on it, Nina says. If my arms were just a bit longer I could lean out and touch it.

–At least if you got up at a normal time you wouldn't feel so tired, Sam says to his daughter.

–I'm too tired to get up at a normal time, Licia says.

You may have noticed that even this isn't 100 percent pure dialogue, because "Licia says," "Sam says" is strictly speaking *outside* the dialogue. But it gives you an idea. Now, this carries on for another 150 pages or so, and in fact provides an absolutely fascinating, moving portrait of a family. There are a number of aesthetic motivations supporting this radical experiment. Perhaps the most important is that readers here have to supply, deduce, imagine the whole surround of the dialogue – in contrast to texts that are *mediated* by a narrator, i.e., in which the dialogue is *embedded*, but also in contrast to a dramatic performance, which would usually give us considerably more information than the mere dialogue. Naturally the author wrote the text *like that*, but *within* this fictional world there is no authority that has "processed" the material, separating the important parts from the less important, selecting and assessing their relevance. And, of course, adding "Licia says" or "Sam says" hardly amounts to "processing" the dialogue. Precisely this absence can provide an alluring challenge for the reader. But there is no instance whatsoever of a change in speed in this novel. In this respect the text doesn't give the reader any assistance in discerning "important" passages.

The situation is completely different with all those innumerable novels that are not dialogue novels, but only contain dialogue strewn throughout, alternating with passages of narrative report. In these cases the exact *distribution* of these dialogues within the text of the novel produces widely different profiles: is it even or uneven? If it's uneven, where does the frequency of dialogue increase? Is it at the beginning, in the middle, or at the end?[3] (It should be clear that we're interested here not in dialogue as dialogue, but in dialogue as an especially pertinent example of *narrative slowed down* – "slowed down" only, of course, if we begin from the "normal" case $a < b$; in the extract from Henry James given above the "spoken" word is on the contrary an example of *accelerated* narration, since we take $a > b$ as the point of departure). It's evident that whenever a narrative text takes time to present a dialogue word for word, instead of just summarizing it or mentioning it in passing, greater importance is clearly attributed to that dialogue. Or – to get away from any suppositions about the intention of the text or the author and to make a liberating change in perspective – *we* suppose that something presented more extensively is also more important than something the text quite quickly passes over. And we don't register that only retrospectively ("Look, I think I've really just read a dialogue that stretched over five-and-a-half pages – wow, that must be *so* important!"); rather, we register the slowing of the pace, the change in speed, at the very moment when it occurs, and then we read *sensitively*, with increased attention, because we can expect that something's now "about to happen." Slowing the pace is therefore also a tried and tested method for generating *suspense*. The word "suspense" itself vividly conveys the aspect of delay, deceleration, leaving things hanging. What was the bestselling Victorian author Wilkie Collins' advice to his colleagues? "Make 'em laugh, make 'em cry, make 'em wait!"

It's fair to say that changing the narrative pace or speed is just about the most efficient means of manipulating the reader. And therefore just about the most efficient starting point for an analysis of a narrative text is the analysis of time manipulation, or the handling of the temporal dimension: seeing through what the text does with us in this respect, often subliminally. For instance, a simple analysis of the time relations in John Fowles' *The Enigma* (1974) can rapidly establish that the actual topic of this long short story (or novella) is not the mysterious disappearance of the Conservative MP John Marcus Fielding, but the questions discussed in the long dialogue between the investigating Sergeant Michael Jennings and the artistically and philosophically inquisitive Isobel Dodgson. These are questions about the relationship between reality and fiction, between roles and authenticity; questions for which the disappearance of the MP is just the peg. The dialogue between these two characters (1 : 1 in time, as opposed to the weeks of investigation compressed into a short narrative) takes up almost half the text.

I have repeatedly said that narrative speed, especially a *change* in narrative pace, is a "fairly reliable indicator" of the importance of what is then

---

[3]   Cf. Stanzel, *A Theory of Narrative*, 65–66.

being narrated. The modesty of this formulation is not due to over-caution: whole sub-genres of the novel (like mysteries or thrillers) deliberately exploit the fact that we are conditioned to the idea that "slow, detailed" = "important," and "compressed, summarized" = "not so important." These works hide vital clues and important information in apparently innocent passages, which are *not* flagged up specially. And E. M. Forster is even famous for having his characters die in lapidary and abrupt sentences, so that the contemporary critic Lionel Trilling spoke of Forster's "addiction to sudden death":[4] apt evidence for the argument that we're not dealing with laws of nature here, but with literary and aesthetic rules of thumb, which can readily be contravened for the sake of a particular effect. After all, it's not as though a text is obliged to fulfill the reader's expectations.

In general it remains true, however, that a slowing of the pace implies importance, acceleration a reduction in relevance. When, for instance, we read the following information about the individual books of Fielding's *Tom Jones* (1749) –

Book I.   Containing as much of the birth of the foundling as is necessary or proper to acquaint the reader with the beginning of this story
Book II.   Containing scenes of matrimonial felicity in different degrees of life, and various other transactions during *the first two years* after the marriage between Captain Blifill and Miss Bridget Allworthy
Book III.   Containing the most memorable transactions which passed in the family of Mr. Allworthy, from the time when Tommy Jones arrived at *the age of fourteen till* he attained *the age of nineteen* […]
Book IV.   Containing the time of *a year*
Book V.   Containing a portion of time *somewhat longer than half a year*
Book VI.   Containing *about three weeks*
Book VII.   Containing *three days*
Book VIII. Containing *above two days*
Book IX.   Containing *twelve hours*
Book X.   In which the history goes forward *about twelve hours*
Book XI.   Containing *about three days*[5]

– we can reasonably assume that through such compression and stretching of story time, respectively, the relative importance of each chapter will remain roughly constant: not exactly a bad strategy if we want the reader to stick at it.

The three basic modes of narrative speed are compression, stretching, and scenic presentation ($a = b$). They are at the same time the basic modes of presentation of *duration*. Gérard Genette has added two further modes

---

4   Lionel Trilling, *E. M. Forster: A Study*, London, 1944, 10.
5   Italics added to the times for clarity.

(though to make way for them he has removed one of those just mentioned, in conflating equal time [$a = b$] and stretched time [$a > b$] under *scène*).[6] It must be said that technically the two additional types of duration proposed by Genette are borderline cases – not because they're very unusual (they are not!), but because here in the relationship between narrative time *a* and narrated time *b*, or discourse time and story time, one of the two quantities must always be zero. One case is the pause, the other the ellipsis.

In a pause, the narrator takes (so to speak) a time-out from relating the action, in order to add descriptions or reflections. The narrated time is zero, and the relationship *b* : *a* for the narrative speed *v* is therefore also zero. That's like a tire-change or – to underline its normality – like a refueling stop on the narrative journey, before we then carry on. It is not only impatient readers who tend to skip over such pauses, pages of prolix landscape description, and the like. Yet such narrative pauses can also be exceptionally stimulating and they are often underestimated. Take *Moby-Dick*, that colossus of American literature: it doesn't begin, as most people think (see above), with "Call me Ishmael," but in fact with material about (you guessed it) whales ("Etymology," "Extracts"), that make up more than ten pages of text, before the novel's narration gets underway. Authors who characteristically incline to extensive pauses are of course fair targets for parody. Here is the beginning of a typical Iris Murdoch novel, which Malcolm Bradbury wrote for her:[7]

"Flavia says that Hugo tells her that Augustina is in love with Fred."
Sir Alex Mountaubon stood with his wife Lavinia in one of the deeply recessed mullion windows of the long gallery at Bishop's Breeches, looking out at the topiary peacocks on the terrace beyond. In front of them the fountain, topped with statuary in which a naked Mars played joyously with a willing Venus, gently coruscated, its tinkle audible through the open windows. The scene before them was of order and peace. They could look down the park at the mile-long drive of lindens, the colour of jaundice; to one side, away from its necessary order, stood one dark and contingent cedar tree. Beneath it their older daughter, Flavia, could be seen from the window, sitting on a white wooden seat, in her unutterable otherness, her pet marmoset on her shoulder, her cap of auburn hair shining like burnished gold on her head. Nearer to the house, in the rose-garden, their younger daughter, seven-year-old Perdita, strange, mysterious and self-absorbed as usual, was beheading a litter of puppies with unexpectedly

[6] Gérard Genette, *Narrative Discourse: An Essay in Method*, Ithaca, NY, 1980, reprinted 1994.
[7] Malcolm Bradbury, "A Jaundiced View," *Who Do You Think You Are? Stories and Parodies*, London, 1986 [1976], 165–171, here 167.

muscular and adult twists of her slender arm. Her cap of golden hair shone like burnished auburn on her head.

Alex turned, catching sight of himself in the big, gilt, rather battered cupid-encrusted mirror that soared over the mantel. Mortality was there in the darkened eyes, but most of what he saw there, the solid, round face of a man of principle, pleased him exceedingly. His book, a philosophical study of Niceness, was almost complete; in its writing Lavinia, his second wife, had proved the perfect helpmeet and companion. No one lay dying upstairs. He looked around at the familiar objects, the Titians and Tintorettos, glowing in their serried ranks with jewelled beneficence, the twined, golden forms of bodies twisted together suggesting a radiant vision of another world. In cases stood the Sung cups, the Ting plates, the Tang vases, the Ming statuettes, the Ching saucers; these last must, almost certainly, go.

"Who says whom tells her that who is in love with whom?"

Lavinia, her arms full of lilies, did not turn. "Flavia," she said.

"And are they?"

"They think so. I don't think they quite know."

So pressing the narrative pause button immensely facilitates the incorporation of essential material, without running the risk of having to catch up with what happens "meanwhile": the action is just temporarily arrested.

In the other case, the ellipsis, the time relations are exactly reversed: on the level of story time something must already have occurred, but in the discourse it's not considered worthy of relating or mentioning. *b* evidently has a value (x), but since a = zero, the narrative speed passes into infinite acceleration.[8] Most ellipses in narrative texts tend to be of the *implicit* type, "that is, those whose very presence is not announced in the text and which the reader can infer only from some chronological lacuna or gap in narrative continuity."[9] However, when the text itself draws attention to its omissions – *explicit* ellipses – then these omissions are often justified by the limited importance of what is left out. The narrator of Henry Fielding's

---

[8] "Theoretically, indeed, there exists a continuous gradation from the infinite speed of ellipsis, where a non-existent section of narrative corresponds to some duration of story, on up to the absolute slowness of descriptive pause, where some section of narrative discourse corresponds to a non-existent diegetic duration." Genette, *Narrative Discourse*, 93–94.

[9] Genette, *Narrative Discourse*, 108. Cf. Italo Calvino, *Six Memos for the Next Millennium: The Charles Eliot Norton Lectures [Harvard] 1985–6*, Cambridge, MA, 1988, 35: "In any case, a story is an operation carried out on the length of time involved, an enchantment that acts on the passing of time, either contracting or dilating it. Sicilian storytellers use the formula 'lu cuntu nun mette tempu' (time takes no time in a story) when they want to leave out links or indicate gaps of months or even years. The technique of oral narration in the popular tradition follows functional criteria. It leaves out unnecessary details but stresses repetition: for example, when the tale consists of a series of the same obstacles to be overcome by different people. A child's pleasure in listening to stories lies partly in waiting for things he expects to be repeated: situations, phrases, formulas." See also the following section, "Order."

Tom Jones reminds the reader of this narrative principle at the start of the third book:

> The reader will be pleased to remember that at the beginning of the second book of this history we gave him a hint of our intention to pass over several large periods of time in which nothing happened worthy of being recorded in a chronicle of this kind. In so doing, we do not only consult our own dignity and ease but the good and advantage of the reader; for besides that by these means we prevent him from throwing away his time, in reading without either pleasure or emolument, we give him at all such seasons an opportunity of employing that wonderful sagacity of which he is master by filling up these vacant spaces of time with his own conjectures; for which purpose we have taken care to qualify him in the preceding pages.

Obviously, to what extent and in what detail we actually do want to fill up these omitted periods of time is entirely up to us. Also, not every omission automatically and necessarily has a temporal dimension. Laurence Sterne's *A Sentimental Journey* (1768) ends with one of the most famous ellipses in English literature:

> So that when I stretched out my hand, I caught hold of the fille de chambre's ——

Presumably only one single word has been left out here, but no "time." Unless the reader continues the yarn and imagines elaborate continuations – then, of course, "a great deal" has been left out, an *infinite* amount, in fact. After all, the book has *finished*, and *everything* that has not yet been narrated has been irretrievably omitted! With a wink and tacitly understanding Sterne, the old wag and master of the omission and the crossing-out, and we know: *actually* it *never* happens in fiction that *something or other* is "omitted," only that that impression is given, and it's exactly in this alternating play of leaving out and naming, of telling and pausing, of compressing, stretching and 1 : 1 reporting that the specific *narrative rhythm* of a novel consists: *dance the Moby-Dick, dance the Magic Mountain, dance In Search of...*

For the sake of completeness Genette also mentions the case of *hypothetical* ellipses, i.e., those we can only assume. I'm also mentioning them only for the sake of completeness, so that no one has to speculate about their omission.

We can now see: Genette's useful addition of the phenomena "pause" and "ellipsis" to the aspect of presenting *duration* does not change the basic truth sketched out above. Not just that – it even underlines that basic truth: reduction in speed (up until complete standstill) signals importance, increase in speed (up until omission of whole stretches of story time) irrelevance.

However, the relation of narrative time to narrated time, or discourse time and story time, can also be seen from a different perspective than that of duration: namely from the viewpoint of (in Genette's terminology) *order* and *frequency*. That, though, needs a separate section.

2 Order

Order refers to the succession of narrated events in the discourse, seen against the foil or the norm of a "natural," presumed sequence of the story. When these two sequences don't coincide, we speak of *anachrony*. Basically, two forms of *anachrony* are conceivable. Either an event is narrated "earlier" than it occurs in the "actual" sequence – in which case we're dealing with a *foreshadowing*, or in Genette's terminology a *prolepsis*. Or an event is narrated "later" than it occurs in the "actual" sequence – in which case we have a *reversion*, or in Genette's terminology an *analepsis*, although I prefer the expression *flashback*, drawn from film. The established English terms are *foreshadowing* and *flashback* (sometimes the word *flashforward* is also used for prolepsis, but that seems to me rather artificial).

The classic work *Bauformen des Erzählens* [*Types of Narrative Construction*] by the German narratologist Eberhard Lämmert has perhaps pressed terminological differentiation with regard to "order" farthest of all, differentiating flashbacks and forshadowings into innumerable types and sub-types. I'll spare you the details.

Genette is a bit more restrained in assigning terms to such cases; but less so in recording the different levels of time in Proust's *A la recherche du temps perdu* (1913–1927), which, after all, is the "specific subject" of his investigation.[10] Thus after an analysis of the relationship between time and order in a 29-line extract from Proust's several thousand page work, he can present the following complete formula:

$$A4[B3]C5-D6(E3)F6(G3)(H1)(I7 < J3 > < K8(L2 < M9 >) > 9N6]O4^{11}$$

Even Genette, though, sometimes has to lay down his arms:

> In fact, the very frequency of interpolations and their reciprocal entanglement often embroil matters in such a way as to leave the "simple" reader, and even the most determined analyst, sometimes with no way out. [...] Retrospective advance notices? Anticipatory recalls? When later is earlier, and earlier later, defining the direction of movement becomes a delicate task.[12]

[10] Genette, *Narrative Discourse*, 21.
[11] Genette, *Narrative Discourse*, 43. It's not clear whether a square bracket, [, isn't missing near the end.
[12] Genette, *Narrative Discourse*, 79, 83.

Yet in novels that are not quite as complex in their organization of time as Proust's *magnum opus*,[13] we can rest assured that flashbacks and foreshadowings are as straightforward to recognize as their function is easy to specify. For example, it's a time-honored technique of such narratives as begin *in medias res* – albeit *pace* Genette's initial opinion, not so conspicuously evident in the *Iliad* as it is in the *Odyssey* (generally a rich source for the narrative manipulation of time!) – to relate the pre-history by flashback after the main narrative has got underway. This flashback can be more or less full and detailed – that varies. The same analepsis often happens when new characters are introduced or new strands added to the plot. *How* extensive the flashback is – and why it is like this and not like that – is once again a question that comes under the rubric of "duration." Other instances of flashback, of course, include complete retrospective solutions of mysteries, criminal cases, and so on and so forth.

Flashbacks and foreshadowings thus play games with the allocation of information to the reader: they are late dispatches from the past, or a special delivery of information from the narrative future. Flashbacks can take the form of a particularly reader-friendly narrative service ("I'll just quickly bring you up to speed on that") or, in contrast, the consequence of an author's arbitrary wielding of power ("you didn't need to know that before"). Foreshadowings, on the other hand, depending on how specific they are, either create an ominous, suspense-building effect (the narrator of the *Rocky Horror Picture Show*: "It was a night they were going to remember for a long, long time …"), or they evoke a sense that everything is already preordained, they suggest a certain (narrative) determinism. Muriel Spark's *The Driver's Seat* (1970) interrupts the detailed description of a woman named Lise, a description of her face and her strikingly eccentric behavior, with this foreshadowing: "She is neither good-looking nor bad-looking. Her nose is short and wider than it will look in the likeness constructed partly by the method of identikit, partly by actual photography, soon to be published in the newspapers of four languages." Then, even more explicitly: "She will be found tomorrow morning dead from multiple stab-wounds, her wrists bound with a silk scarf and her ankles bound with a man's necktie, in the grounds of an empty villa, in a park of the foreign city to which she is travelling on the flight now boarding at Gate 14." So she's going to be the victim of a macabre murder. By means of a foreshadowing the reader is allowed a

[13]   Genette (*Narrative Discourse*) also never tires of noting how singular and unusual the *Recherche* is – whether because the work contains hardly any cases of certain phenomena that do exist according to some logical deduction, or because it contains many phenomena that are hardly to be found in any other narrative literature. All this raises the question to what extent Genette's narrative theory was really developed on the *Recherche* (which anyway would be methodologically somewhat problematic), or whether he didn't first draft it in an *abstract*, *systematic* (*taxonomic*) form and only then *illustrated* it with Proust.

more or less informative glimpse into the "future." From this point on the reader is above all interested in finding out what will be the exact sequence of events leading up to that known outcome. Foreshadowing always presupposes that what is going to occur has already occurred – which from the standpoint of a non-present narrative is clearly true. But if the grammar starkly reminds us of this obvious point – a nice example to quote is Tristram Shandy's "a cow broke in (to-morrow morning) to my Uncle Toby's fortifications" (Vol. 3, chapter 38)[14] – then we're taken aback: tomorrow a cow *broke* in? Exactly why this isn't so unusual after all we'll investigate below, in the section "Tense and Narrative."

Both forms of anachrony, flashback and foreshadowing, can also be distinguished according to how extensively these insertions intrude on the narrative (that's once again a phenomenon to be filed under "duration"); and then according to how far "the anachrony's reach"[15] extends – which is a phenomenon of *distance*.

This seems to me the important point: precisely because a narrative, rather than being bound to a "natural" sequence of events, is subject only to its own logic, it has complete freedom to do this and "leave out" that. The only caveat is that this must serve a purpose – but then again the narrative alone defines this purpose for itself. Incidentally, it's necessary to know how to handle this freedom, to prevent the narrative order that's supposed to be set up from sinking into chaos – which more than once confronts the notoriously distracted and disorganized Tristram Shandy:

> You must know, my uncle Toby mistook the bridge as widely as my father mistook the mortars;——but to understand how my uncle could mistake the bridge,—I fear I must give you an exact account of the road which led to it;——or to drop my metaphor, (for there is nothing more dishonest in an historian, than the use of one,)——in order to conceive the probability of this error in my uncle Toby aright, I must give you some account of an adventure of Trim's, though much against my will. I say much against my will, only because the story, in one sense, is certainly out of its place here; for by right it should come in, either amongst the anecdotes of my uncle Toby's amours with widow Wadman, in which Corporal Trim was no mean actor,—or else in the middle of his and my uncle Toby's campaigns on the bowling-green, – for it will do very well in either place;——but then if I preserve it for either of those parts of my story,—I ruin the story I'm upon,—and if I tell it here—I anticipate matters, and ruin it there.
>
> —What would your worship have me to do in this case?
>
> —Tell it, Mr Shandy, by all means.——You are a fool, Tristram, if you do. (Vol. 3, chapter 23)

---

[14] Additionally, this is a rare example of a text's iconicity, since "into" is split into "in" and "to."
[15] Genette, *Narrative Discourse*, 48.

Since the narrative's temporal order is a construction through and through, and not something given, it can also collapse at any time, or if various claims of narrative logic come into conflict, its establishment can be totally blocked until in a decisionist move the narrative is continued. In any case, however, we can't ignore the fact that we have been witness to a fabrication.

Finally, an unusual temporal order (which Genette doesn't consider at all) occurs when time in a narrative text flows backwards. This has become easier to imagine since films and other visual recording media, for these enable recorded material to be played through in reverse order. The basic idea is present as early as a passage in Kurt Vonnegut's *Slaughterhouse Five* (1969); and while it's been transposed into short fiction by Ilse Aichinger ('Spiegelgeschichte" ["Mirror Story"]) and Alejo Carpentier ("Journey to the Origin"), to my knowledge the only novel that consistently and continuously maintains time in reverse gear is Martin Amis's (appropriately titled) *Time's Arrow* (1991).

At first sight, life in this kind of topsy-turvy world seems quite funny: for instance, you bring goods to the supermarket, get a handout of money from the checkout, and then put the items back on the shelf. You take the morning newspaper out of the waste-paper bin, read the articles from end to beginning, ending with the captions, and then put it in the front garden (we're in America), where a paper boy will later collect it and return it to the printing house, where the pages of the newspaper are run together by a complex process onto a huge roll of paper and big rollers finally take the black ink from the paper. It's only logical that reading in this world is a process of forgetting, of annihilating information. Reading from back to front eliminates what we knew before. The whole of life is a process of forgetting. Here, relationships begin at the end: sometime a partner runs backwards into the flat yelling, but after that it actually gets progressively better. Unlike Martin Amis, I will spare you a more detailed description of the processes of nutrition and excretion in this world – suffice it to say that everything happens the other way round.

Amis's novel turns on the fact that the purely technical reversal of time's arrow is not neutral from a moral or ethical perspective. Here, for instance, hospitals are institutions in which people are dreadfully messed in return for immense amounts of money. If you have a black eye and several broken ribs you're better off bumping into a street gang, who'll look after you until you've completely recovered – then, remembering nothing, everyone will go about their business again. This moral inversion was exactly Amis's point. For the beginning towards which the narrative's main character, a certain Tod T. Friendly, is heading, is the concentration camp Auschwitz, where he once eagerly helped the Nazis with the "final solution of the Jewish question" (he then "later" flees to the USA and continues to live there under his assumed name). For a long time, though, the reader doesn't know that. That's because the narrator of the story of the Nazi doctor, perceived and told in reversed sequence, is not the character himself, but a narrative authority that functions as a kind of "soul": and this "soul" (a point that might be criticized for being inconsistent) has no idea about the future (= past) awaiting the person it's assigned to.

If we see this reversal of time's arrow in Martin Amis's novel as just a narrative gag, no doubt this way of thematizing the Holocaust could strike us as tasteless. On the other hand, this way of setting out the order of time forces the reader to translate (so to speak) each action in the novel back again. That defamiliarizing process can eventually make us see in no uncertain terms the monstrosity of what happened in the Holocaust – something that other depictions of the same events which, however, rely on more conventional, stereotyped methods of narrative, unfortunately don't always manage to achieve any more. The chimneys of the crematorium suck smoke in, and inside the Nazis create the Jewish people. They put clothes on them, give them all a little suitcase, and then off they go into the world, to their home towns, where they can live happily ever after … Millions of people receive the gift of life … The enormity strikes you once you have deduced the positive from that negative.

I said above that the temporal order of a narrative is every inch a construction, not something given beforehand. We can now add and emphasize: the sequence of the narrative always expresses a particular relationship to the world, to life – whether fatalism, determinism, contingency, being cast and thrown abruptly into existence, freedom and openness as to the shaping and formation of one's own fate, character, whatever. It is here in particular that the individual signature of a narrative text appears: precisely because it can do absolutely anything it wants to, it's highly informative to see in which way it has made use of that freedom, whether it has done this and not that. It doesn't *have* to do anything. That's why it's so significant that the narrative text has ordered things exactly like *this*.

3   Frequency

Genette notes somewhat regretfully that the third category (alongside duration and order) of the investigation of temporal relationships between *discours* and *histoire*, i.e., *narrative frequency*, "has been very little studied."[16] Perhaps that's because there isn't much to get out of it?

Working with the fact that something can occur once or multiple times, and that something can also be narrated once or multiple times, Genette combines these possibilities to produce four conceivable cases:

> Schematically, we can say that a narrative, whatever it is, may tell once what happened once [*singulative* narrative], *n* times what happened *n* times [*anaphoristic*

[16]   Genette, *Narrative Discourse*, 113.

narrative], *n* times what happened once [*repetitive* narrative], *once* what happened *n* times [*iterative* narrative].[17]

How often do each of these cases crop up? And what is their identification good for? One common case, to be sure, is the iterative narrative ("Last summer we met up every Friday evening, went to the cinema and after that for a meal"). That's the standard instance of a compressed *summary*. Even more common are singulative narratives ("Yesterday was Friday, and in the evening she actually came to the cinema with me and afterwards for a meal!"). Repetitive narratives are rarer – they mainly occur when an event is described from different perspectives (e.g., William Faulkner, *The Sound and the Fury*, 1929, and *As I Lay Dying*, 1930; Graham Swift, *Last Orders*, 1996) or when a consciousness obsessively returns again and again to one event (Alain Robbe-Grillet, *La Jalousie*, 1957). The final case – narrating *n* times what happened *n* times – is a logical postulate to fill the fourth quadrant, but in fact is identical with a sequence of singulative narratives, and we should perhaps just leave it at that. It may be satisfying for a mind that is keen on comprehensiveness and systematics to deduce the existence of a phenomenon just as scientists deduce chemical elements in the periodic table that have yet to be discovered – but this example shows that not everything that can be defined conceptually is also of great relevance for the analysis of narrative.

Looking back over what we've just considered, we might notice three points. First, the analysis of the relationship of narrative time to narrated time is most fruitful when it works with the aspect of *duration*, because even the mere recording of narrative pace and its changes directs us to different levels of importance of the narrative. Second, the *anachronies* of a text present rearrangements of blocks of time, whose actual composition provides rich information about the drift of the discourse. It is true that discourse time and story time are already separated when we look at narrative speed (except in scenic presentation, of course) – but the complete "rearrangement" of a sequence is at least as radical, and with this latter operation we can – indeed must – always ask ourselves what the effect would have been if the "natural" sequence (such as we can infer it) had been "maintained." And *in contrast to that*, what is the effect *now*? Third, identifying the *frequency* of a narrative helps illuminate its relationship to the narrated past. Iterative narratives of the type "and on Fridays, after our bath, mother would always give us warm milk, into which we would dunk cookies" certainly have a different (perhaps nostalgic) relation to the past – and also a different *flavor* – from singulative narratives of the type "then lightning

---

[17]   Genette, *Narrative Discourse*, 114. The additions in square brackets are mine, as is the italicization of *once*, which has been left out in the English edition.

struck and the whole place burnt down." Whether the analysis of frequency tells us much more than we already knew, however, seems to me less certain than with the investigations of the other two aspects.[18]

4   Tense and Narrative

Normally, novels and other narratives employ the grammatical tense known as the imperfect (or preterite): this seems the "most natural" tense. But this need not be so, and other tenses are increasingly chosen, such as the present or even the subjunctive – though these perhaps suggest themselves only for shorter texts.

The peculiar thing about the imperfect tense in narrative texts is that the reader doesn't actually experience it as past, but as a fictitious present. In other words, while reading we automatically, and as a rule unconsciously, translate the imperfect into a present – and so dive into the world whose presence we have conjured up.

In *The Logic of Poetry*, Käte Hamburger explains this special effectiveness of the epic preterite as follows: "the change in meaning consists in the fact that the imperfect tense [in fictional narrative] loses its grammatical function of denoting what is past."[19] Furthermore, she claims that this process is specific to fiction. (Hamburger also emphasizes that only in fiction is it possible for verbs of thinking and feeling to relate to events within the consciousness of a third person; and she wants to count only (s)he-narratives, not I-narratives, as fiction.[20] These claims need not concern us here – neither of them are matters of tense.)

Her standard example sentence "Tomorrow was Christmas," however, is by no means completely impossible (i.e., possible only in fiction). On the contrary, it's perfectly feasible even in narratives that are anything but fictional. The combination of the imperfect with adjectives like "here,"

---

[18]   Admittedly, that goes against Genette's findings: "[...] no novelistic work, apparently, has ever put the iterative to a use comparable – in textual scope, in thematic importance, in degree of technical elaboration – to Proust's use of it in the *Recherche du temps perdu*. [...] It is as though Proustian narrative substituted for summary, which is the synthetic form, the iterative: a synthesis not by acceleration, but by assimilation and abstraction. Thus the rhythm of the narrative in the *Recherche* is essentially based not, like that of the classical novel, on the alternation of summary and scene, but on another alteration, that of iterative and singulative" (*Narrative Discourse*, 117, 143). But that would assume that summary and iterative lie on the same level of analysis, which they clearly don't: the one is an aspect of duration, the other an aspect of frequency. It seems evident that, on the contrary, iterative narration can perfectly well be considered a *form* of summary. Yet who'd want to pick a fight with Gérard Genette? And above all about the *Recherche*?
[19]   Käte Hamburger, *Die Logik der Dichtung*, Stuttgart, 1980 [1957], 65.
[20]   Hamburger, *Logik*, 78ff.; cf. 60.

"today," or "now" isn't suitable as an objective textual criterion, as a *differentia specifica* of fictional texts ("only there, nowhere else"). There is no grammatical criterion for fictionality. Instead, our *predisposition* – which is spontaneous and can't be traced back to individual reflection – *not* to read a given text's grammatical past tense in a temporal–functional way, seems in fact to be the *consequence* of our recognition that we're dealing here with narrative fiction. This decisive predisposition is, of course, also the result of particular cultural pragmatics.[21]

We can also understand expressions like "Tomorrow was Christmas" as a superimposition of one temporal standpoint on another, i.e., the narrator's ("was") on that of a character ("tomorrow"): recall Sterne's "the cow broke in (to-morrow morning)." On this view it would be the phenomenon of a specific narrative situation. This was a further serious objection to Hamburger's theory, especially since such expressions actually do seem to occur frequently in texts that rely on free indirect speech or are defined by what some call a figural narrative situation – but we'll come back to this later.

Other theoretical attempts to stipulate the relationship between tense and narrative include, for example, the ambitious work of Harald Weinrich,[22] who distinguishes clearly between "discussing" and "narrating" tenses and from there deduces varying attitudes of speech ("relaxed" and "tense"). Such attempts have not yet found many followers either.[23]

Regardless of how one explains it, however, it's uncontroversial that when reading fiction we mentally process the past tense in a different way. We translate it automatically and enter imaginatively into a present, which is conducive both to identification and to the increase of suspense.

Nevertheless, present-tense narration is certainly not a phenomenon peculiar only to modernity. In the form of the *historic present* it's always been deliberately used to reduce distance, in other words, to create the impression that we are seeing especially "close up" – but only in isolated passages. The historic present always appeared in a more or less clearly preterite framework, the change of tense having a dramatizing function. If it accompanies a considerable reduction in pace, we're coming close to the *scenic present*; but if it's linked to acceleration, it merely supports the dramatic shortening. A good example is Jacques's relation, given above, of how he went from getting drunk to being shot in the knee – all in the present tense!

[21] Cf. Christoph Bode, *Ästhetik der Ambiguität: Zu Funktion und Bedeutung von Mehrdeutigkeit in der Literatur der Moderne*, Tübingen, 1988, 342ff.

[22] Harald Weinrich, *Tempus: Besprochene und erzählte Welt*, 6th rev. edn, Munich, 2001.

[23] Nor, perhaps, are they likely to in the future; cf. Monika Fludernik, "Tempus und Zeitbewußtsein: Erzähltheoretische Überlegungen zur englischen Literatur," in *Zeit und Roman: Zeiterfahrung im historischen Wandel und ästhetischer Paradigmenwechsel vom sechzehnten Jahrhundert bis zur Postmoderne*, ed. Martin Middeke, Würzburg, 2002, 21–32.

In the foreword to *The Magic Mountain* (1924, trans. H. T. Lowe-Porter, 1927), Thomas Mann says:

> [...] this story, we say, belongs to the long ago; is already, so to speak, covered with historic mould, and unquestionably to be presented in the tense best suited to a narrative out of the depth of the past.
>
> That should be no drawback to a story, but rather the reverse. Since histories must be in the past, then the more past the better, it would seem, for them in their character as histories, and for him, the teller of them, rounding wizard of times gone by.

If that is correct, what is to become of (and what is happening in) novels written entirely in the present tense?[24] We've already seen examples, such as Josipovici's *Now* or Muriel Spark's *The Driver's Seat*. J. M. Coetzee's *Waiting for the Barbarians* (1980) or Walker Percy's *The Moviegoer* (1961) could be mentioned here too. But here is yet another example of "making present": ironically, Malcolm Bradbury's *The History Man* (1975) belies its title by keeping the narration in the present tense throughout ("throughout" in the sense that the grammatical present is the *basic time*, from which there can of course be departures in the form of grammatically highlighted flashbacks and foreshadowings). It reads like this:

> He walks along the terrace, with its cracked pavement stones, its scatter of broken glass; the rain soaks his hair, and begins to stipple the leather of his coat. The terrace curves around him; once an exact and elegant half-circle, the curious dentistry of demolition has attacked it, pulling out house after house from the curve as they have become empty. Most of those that still stand are unoccupied, with broken roofs and vacant, part-boarded windows, plastered with posters for political parties, pop groups, transcendental meditators, or rather surreptitiously occupied, for they are visited by a strange, secret, drifting population of transients. But, though there are few residents, the terrace has been metered for parking; the Kirks have to keep their minivan some streets away, in a square up the hill. A police car heehaws on the urban motorway being sliced through the demolition; buses grind below him, on the promenade. An air-force jet flies in off the sea, its line of flight an upward curve that brings it into sudden visibility over the jagged tops of the houses across the terrace from the Kirks' tall, thin house. He turns the corner; he walks up the hill. The long latticed metal of a construction crane swings into his eyeline, dangling a concrete beam.

The events are presented without differentiation. There's clearly no selection and no weighing up. That also means that essential work in the process of

[24]   Cf. Dorrit Cohn, *The Distinction of Fiction*, Baltimore, 1999, ch. 6; Monika Fludernik, *Towards a "Natural" Narratology*, London, 1996, 249–260.

mediation is not done: the filtering and sorting, accentuating and shaping, are left to the reader. There are only sporadic aids to orientation, which depart from the present ("once an exact and elegant half-circle") or provide abstract generalizations that don't emerge from any immediacy of sense-perception ("they are visited by a strange, secret, drifting population of transients").

Small authorial interventions like that, however, only strengthen the otherwise dominant effect of an unfiltered present – this story can't have accrued any "historical patina" at all, because it's happening "right now" – a present in which the relevance or irrelevance of particular details can't be determined yet. Every single detail might be (or *become*) extremely important or totally irrelevant: we don't know (yet), since no authority from a temporal distance could have taken on this work of sorting out. Just like in real life, in fact. It seems that everything is *shown* – and that, at least in this novel, is thematic: here is history in the making. History (a story, too) is *made* when someone selects particular events, embeds them in a long narrative and then claims they are important for this or that reason. History in the making, as they say. ATk S

Narratives in the present tense pretend to show their raw material – but of course they only pretend. And more often than not they highlight the difficulty, if not the impossibility, of coping with the present that flows into and assails the self (see, for example, Ingeborg Bachmann's *Malina* [1971], "Time: today").

And in contrast to this "novelty" of the present-tense novel (whose unexpectedness in Spark's *The Driver's Seat* is superbly balanced by foreshadowings, which, in a counter-movement, intimate determinism), it suddenly becomes clear what one likes so much about the epic preterite: it gives the impression of immediacy, and yet everything is at the same time so nicely prepared and laid out. So completely different from the present tense of life, in fact. Lean back and enjoy.

5

Characters

1 Character Conception

In book 6, chapter 38 of his life and opinions, Tristram Shandy wants to give a persuasive explanation of the stunning attractions of Widow Wadman, with whom Uncle Toby is hopelessly in love. With this aim he invites the (male) reader to do the following:

> To conceive this right,—call for pen and ink—here's paper ready to your hand.—Sit down, Sir, paint her to your own mind—as like your mistress as you can—as unlike your wife as your conscience will let you—'tis all one to me—please but your own fancy in it.

What follows is reproduced here almost as in the original book:

– a blank page in the original, only part of a blank page here for reasons of cost. And then:

The Novel: An Introduction. By Christoph Bode. Translated by James Vigus. English translation © 2011 James Vigus. Published by John Wiley & Sons, Ltd.
Original German text © 2005 Narr Francke Attempto Verlag GmbH + Co. KG.

– Was ever any thing in Nature so sweet!—so exquisite!
– Then, dear Sir, how could my Uncle Toby resist it?

As usual in *Tristram Shandy*, this folly is a perfectly logical one: all novel readers will come up with a picture of this or that character on the basis of the information the text puts at their disposal, and fill up the inevitable "gaps of indeterminacy" or blank spaces[1] in the text on the basis of their own experience of life and reading. These blank spaces are inevitable not because, as Forster supposed,[2] the author knows his characters inside out yet prefers not to confide everything to us, but rather because literary characters are always composed of a *finite* number of elements. There is always something that such a composition does *not* say, as opposed to "leaves out" – for after all, fictional characters exist only in fiction and what is not said about them isn't "there."

So when Tristram gives the reader a free hand with regard to "the most desirable female being imaginable" (and of course what readers come up with will vary enormously – *chacun à son goût* – but nevertheless it would be identical in one respect: *all* will show the most desirable female being that the respective reader can possibly imagine), he just illuminates a process that has served fiction since time immemorial. In evoking "his" characters, the author can rely pretty heavily on the reader completing his work. These blank spaces or gaps, then, are (like other blank spaces and gaps) a necessary condition of the effect of the literary text.[3] Only because *not everything* is there can the reader "supplement" or "complete" it. You imagine a character on the basis of particular techniques of characterization deployed by the text; but you imagine that character *yourself* (for everyone the most desirable [fe]male being that [s]he can imagine).

For that reason I'd like to stick with a pair of concepts introduced in the analysis of drama and tried and tested there: *character conception* and *characterization* (sometimes referred to as *character portrayal*).[4] The way I use these terms, however, involves a vital shift in perspective: character conception in a novel is not the author's plan, not an "anthropological model" on which the character is based[5] and which the author realizes through particular techniques for imparting information (i.e., the techniques of characterization and portrayal). Rather, character conception is an idea

---

[1]   Cf. Wolfgang Iser, *The Act of Reading: A Theory of Aesthetic Response*, Baltimore, 1978.
[2]   E. M. Forster, *Aspects of the Novel*, Harmondsworth, 1977 [1927], 69.
[3]   Cf. Wolfgang Iser, "Die Appellstruktur der Texte: Unbestimmtheit als Wirkungsbedingung literarischer Prosa," in *Rezeptionsästhetik: Theorie und Praxis*, 2nd edn, ed. Rainer Warning, Munich, 1979, 228–252.
[4]   Cf. Manfred Pfister, *The Theory and Analysis of Drama*, trans. John Halliday, Cambridge, 1991, first published as *Das Drama: Theorie und Analyse*, Munich, 1977, 176–195.
[5]   Pfister, *Drama*, 176.

that *readers come up* with for themselves – on the basis of the discourse, of the text, of course.

Attentive readers will have noticed that I'm suggesting "character conception" and "character portrayal" as analogues to "story" and "discourse." Just as the story isn't something that preexists, but something that we *abstract* from the concrete narrative, so the conception of a character isn't there beforehand, but is rather the idea that we *build up* in the course of our reading.

But the example of Widow Wadman I used to open this chapter takes only the *external, physical* features of a character into account – and it seems to me no coincidence that the external features in question are those of a *female* character. To get a picture of the character's personality, however, we have to find out other things, too: above all, of course, how they *behave* in particular situations. Therefore, the *action* of a novel is an essential medium for the portrayal and unfolding of character; and conversely action can only take place if there are characters as *agents*.

There was a lengthy debate in European literary theory about whether characters are subordinate to action, or whether action serves the gradual unfolding and development of character. The former was Aristotle's contention:

> The most important [element] is the structure of events, because tragedy is a representation not of people as such but of actions and life, and both happiness and unhappiness rest on action. The goal is a certain activity, not a qualitative state; and while men do have certain qualities by virtue of their character, it is in their actions that they achieve, or fail to achieve, happiness. It is not, therefore, the function of the agents' actions to allow the portrayal of their characters; it is, rather, for the sake of their actions that characterization is included. So, the events and the plot-structure are the goal of tragedy, and the goal is what matters most of all.[6]

The contrary opinion was maintained – explicitly or implicitly – by all *Bildungsroman* authors and generally by those who wrote about personal development, by authors of psychological novels anyway. It's no coincidence that so many novels of, say, the nineteenth century take the name of their hero(ine) as their title (*Madame Bovary, Emma, Huckleberry Finn* [1884/85], *Père Goriot* [1835], *Oliver Twist, David Copperfield, Tess of the d'Urbervilles, Anna Karenina, Adam Bede* [1859], *Daniel Deronda* [1876], etc.).

The dispute, however, like the chicken-and-egg debate in some progressive circles about whether society or the individual must change first, is obviously moot. Character and action are mutually dependent, and obviously there are some novels that at first sight seem to emphasize the former, and others that

---

[6] *The "Poetics" of Aristotle*, trans. and ed. Stephen Halliwell, London, 1987, 37.

seem to foreground the latter. Probably they have different intentions. But perhaps the two aren't so different either, as segments of a continuum of possibilities. The neatest of all final words (but notoriously some debates just carry on regardless after the final word) was once spoken by Henry James in his classic essay "The Art of Fiction" (1884):

> There is an old-fashioned distinction between the novel of character and the novel of incident which must have cost many a smile to the intending fabulist who was keen about his work. It appears to me as little to the point as the equally celebrated distinction between the novel and the romance – to answer as little to any reality. There are bad novels and good novels, as there are bad pictures and good pictures; but that is the only distinction in which I see any meaning, and I can as little imagine speaking of a novel of character as I can imagine speaking of a picture of character. When one says picture one says of character, when one says novel one says of incident, and the terms may be transposed at will. What is character but the determination of incident? What is incident but the illustration of character? What is either a picture or a novel that is *not* of character? What else do we seek in it and find in it?[7]

How important action is for a character's development (not in any psychological sense, but from the point of view of narrative technique) can be seen for example in the characterization at the opening of Jane Austen's novel *Emma* (1816):

> Emma Woodhouse, handsome, clever, and rich, with a comfortable home and happy disposition seemed to unite some of the best blessings of existence; and had lived nearly twenty-one years in the world with very little to distress or vex her.

If that were to *remain* the case, there'd be no apparent reason why we should read on. The word "seemed" in "seemed to unite," however, already signals a possible tension between reality and appearance; the all too smooth surface of this first sentence almost cries out for a disturbance; and the rest of the novel also serves (subordination of action to character) to present the eponymous heroine in her arrogant self-absorption and her incapacity for empathy – but moreover it serves to suggest a way out of this egocentricity. Emma Woodhouse is indeed a *main character* to whom we grant development (this time in the psychological sense), not one of those static figures who crop up as *marginal characters*. Even so, a novel can perfectly thematize what is static about a main character – think of Ivan Alexandrovich Goncharov's novel *Oblomov* (1859).

---

[7]   Henry James, "The Art of Fiction," *The Art of Criticism: Henry James on the Theory and Practice of Fiction*, ed. William Veeder and Susan M. Griffin, Chicago, 1986, 165–196, here 174. "Picture" here obviously means "portrait"; if "painting" in general were meant, the argument wouldn't make much sense.

Character conceptions can be distinguished according to the degree of their complexity, the degree of their dynamism. (Since a novel can only impart information in a gradual and linear way, dynamism is nothing other than the temporal imprint of complexity.) The least complex characters are those whom we can understand as embodiments of an idea – and nothing else. Such *personifications* occur not just in allegorical literature (e.g., in John Bunyan's *The Pilgrim's Progress*, 1678, 1684), but also frequently in the realistic novel (certainly in fantasy and mass fiction), and they don't necessarily work just with speaking names. Charles Dickens' novelistic world, for instance, is peopled to a remarkable extent by (very impressive) characters who can quite easily be seen to represent a concept. Take Mr. Micawber (from *David Copperfield*), the embodiment of an unbroken optimism, who doesn't let things get him down and even in the most difficult circumstances still sees something saving and hopeful "on the horizon"; or Uriah Heep (from the same novel), the embodiment of thoroughgoing hypocrisy, who behind the mask of his obsequiousness goes about his criminal machinations. To be sure, the reader learns this afterwards – but we're not really surprised: that's what Uriah Heep "is," we could have worked that out for ourselves.

Only a little more complex than these are *types* or *stock figures*, which are defined not by one idea, but by a *cluster* or complex of features. These include particular social types (e.g., the factory boss, the worker), gender-specific types (the *femme fatale*, the confirmed bachelor), religious types (the Catholic, the Puritan), and also age-types (the greenhorn, the spinster – which is also a gender type, just as the confirmed bachelor is also an age-type), etc., etc. The key thing is that such figures function as representatives of their respective group and so are *de-individualized* to the point of being interchangeable. They are meant to represent a certain universal quality, and that's how we understand them. A text might portray a miserly Jew or a Pole who steals cars – and in response to protest it could be argued that somewhere in the world there's surely a Jew who is a miser and Pole who pinches the odd car. But the point is that a type doesn't represent any individual at all, but a group. Thus, of all literary characters, this is the one most suitable for exploring social, sexual, national, religious (etc.) *stereotypes*. As a rule, such types are sketched with broad strokes and much is left to the recipient's knowledge of relevant prejudices. It's undeniable that stereotyping can also be a source of comedy, a method of social criticism, even a form of self-irony. But most often, the victims of such a presentation are those who have no power to (re)present themselves; but perhaps those who develop a sense of identity only through assigning stereotypes to others are victims as well…

The opposite of the de-individualized type is ultimately the distinctive *individual* – complex, liable to change, and, due to this developmental dynamic, also potentially *open*. The fact that this openness of a character can be arrested, especially at the end of a novel, and that a clearly individualized character's *lack* of openness, or significant stasis, can be thematized (e.g., in Kazuo Ishiguro's *The Remains of the Day*, 1989, or in *When We Were Orphans*, 2000) is of course no objection to this scale of increasing complexity: no personification, no type can be an *open* character – by definition these are *closed* characters.

It was no lesser writer than Jacob Burckhardt who pointed out in his great study *The Civilization of the Renaissance in Italy* the culturally and historically significant circumstance that in European modernity, the "discovery of the outside world" coincided with the discovery of the individual, the discovery of each person's inner world and the recognition of the intrinsic value of the distinctive and irreducible individual.[8] It also makes sense to regard the history of the modern European novel – that "historically and philosophically outstanding, privileged form of modern consciousness"[9] – as the sequence of forms in which the individuality of literary figures is fabricated, and in which moreover literature explores the *possibilities* of the consciousness and actions of the "single human being."[10] This enables us to see why a large segment of the European novel keeps on playing through the following aporia: that a character must on the one hand appear plausibly determined and defined (as the concrete, individual, one-off point of intersection of so many determinants, with *these* specific characteristics), but on the other hand must be presented in such a way that we can imagine him or her as *free*. This aporia of the individual as a character is concretely resolved if and when a character's behavior can *surprise us in a convincing way*.

But that is nothing other than E. M. Forster's brilliant definition of a *round character* as opposed to a *flat character*:

> We may divide characters into flat and round.
>
> Flat characters were called "humours" in the seventeenth century, and are sometimes called types, and sometimes caricatures. In their purest form, they are constructed round a single idea or quality; when there is more than one factor in them, we get the beginning of the curve towards the round. The really flat character can be expressed in one sentence such as "I will never desert Mr. Micawber." There is Mrs. Micawber – she says she won't desert Mr. Micawber; she doesn't, and there she is. [...]
>
> The test of a round character is whether it is capable of surprising in a convincing way. If it never surprises, it is flat. If it does not convince, it is flat pretending to be round. It has the incalculability of life about it – life within the pages of a book.[11]

---

[8]   Jacob Burckhardt, *The Civilization of the Renaissance in Italy*, trans. S. G. Middlemore, London, 1990 (first published in German in 1859), 185ff.

[9]   Heinz Schlaffer in Clemens Lugowski, *Die Form der Individualität im Roman*, Frankfurt am Main, 1976 [1932], xviii.

[10]   Lugowski, *Form der Individualität*, 14ff.

[11]   Forster, *Aspects*, 73, 81.

Decades later, the structuralist Jurij Lotman offered a somewhat more complicated definition of the essential point:

> The image, which is unified on one sufficiently abstract level, but which on lower levels is divided up onto a number of substructures – perhaps not even mutually opposed, but simply independent and varied – creates the possibility on the level of the text for actions which are simultaneously regular and unexpected, that is, it creates conditions for maintaining the informativeness and reducing the redundancy of the system.[12]

In other words the character's actions are unexpected, but we nevertheless perceive them as the actions of *one* character.

Both the descriptions just quoted contain – even if partly concealed – a temporal element: round or *multidimensional characters* surprise us with behavior that we *retrospectively* recognize as coherent ("Sure, I hadn't expected that, but now I can see that [s]he was capable of it"). Such characters compel us, that is, to modify our conceptions of them, to refine our idea of them. Multidimensional, dynamic figures keep the reader on the go.

What forms the basis of this refined modification on the reader's part are assumptions about the probability of a given piece of human behavior in real life, allowing for certain literary conventions (the super-agent James Bond has unusual abilities, but no supernatural ones). This evaluation of the behavior of fictional characters through assumptions about probability in real life (which themselves are obviously historically and culturally contingent) inevitably leads to problems if the novel changes its aesthetic program and no longer considers itself bound to the (re)presentation of "reality."

In Robert Musil's *The Man Without Qualities* we see described the ultimate point of that parable whose beginning was sketched by Jacob Burckhardt: viz. the coincidence of the individual's lack of qualities with his impotence against the totality of the outside world that has become incomprehensible. " 'One can do what one likes,' said the man without qualities to himself with a shrug, 'in this tangle of forces it doesn't make any difference.' " But with the increased foregrounding of those techniques with which fiction creates the *effect* of reality, the novel disclosed the conventionality of its apparently "natural" parameters (character, action, space, time). It revealed the *constructedness* of these parameters, and thus thematized (once again) *possibilities* of the construction of sense and meaning. The idea of a "unified character" had to be abandoned in the process of the novel's increase in self-referentiality,[13] for it was precisely the de-composition of the constructs that

---

[12] Jurij Lotman, *The Structure of the Artistic Text*, trans. Gail Lenhoff and Ronald Vroon, Ann Arbor, 1977 [1971], 255.

[13] Cf. Thomas Docherty, *Reading (Absent) Character: Towards a Theory of Characterization in Fiction*, New York, 1983; Baruch Hochman, *Character in Literature*, Ithaca, NY, 1985; James Phelan, *Reading People, Reading Plots: Character, Progression, and the Interpretation of Narrative*, Chicago, 1989.

then became thematic, together with a focus on *process* rather than on *product*. Insofar as narratology increasingly sees characters as constructs, "only marks on a page,"[14] it's only catching up with a fact that was already evident before: that we should attend less to stories than to discourse, less to what is abstracted (which then too easily attains independence as supposedly "preexistent" and "primary") and more to the given data (a pleonasm, for sure) that enable this or that abstraction (or which systematically undermine them – a possibility we must always bear in mind).

For once, the present chapter is proceeding "top down" – for historical reasons. As in chapter 3, the direction of the analysis is "actually" *bottom up*: from processes to ideas, from *character portrayal* to *character conception* – from given data to result (however provisional the latter may be).

2   Character Portrayal

In literary and aesthetic terms, the most effective way to endow literary figures with character is undoubtedly to *show them in action*, to present them (as if) unmediated, so that as recipients we get to know them *directly* and form a picture of them for ourselves. It can, though, be more efficient from the standpoint of time economy simply *to say, to claim* by way of summary that the character XY is such and such or regularly behaves in a certain way. These two techniques of characterization are thus not neutral with regard to the aspect of time manipulation: the former approaches scenic presentation ($a = b$), the latter makes use of extreme narrative compression ($a < b$). Further, what we said above about how the handling of time relations signals "importance" applies to both techniques: we attribute greater importance to something that the text lingers on for a longer time than to something that it passes over more or less briskly and hurriedly.

As far as characterization is concerned, that assertion is supported by the fact that something we have to work out for ourselves obviously stimulates our imagination more strongly, sticks with us longer and leaves a more lasting impression than something presented to us as a finished, unambiguous given. There's already a considerable difference between our reaching the conclusion on the basis of a sequence of reported actions that Mr. Scrooge is a complete skinflint, or receiving "the same" evaluation of this character ready served. That's why just now I emphasized this difference: that although the one technique might be more efficient, the other frequently produces a more enduring and impressive effect.

[14]   H. Porter Abbott, *The Cambridge Introduction to Narrative*, Cambridge, 2002, 127; cf. Shlomith Rimmon-Kenan, *Narrative Fiction: Contemporary Poetics*, London, 1986 [1983], 29ff.

These two techniques, which in most narrative texts are of course mixed together and used alternately, I have presented here in an ideal form, i.e., as purely opposed to each other. Traditionally, this opposition has been linked to a distinction that Plato makes in Book III of the *Republic*: namely between the narrative mode in which "the poet himself speaks in his own person and never even tries to distract us by assuming another character" – Plato calls that *haplê diêgêsis*, i.e., "simple narration" – and the contrary mode in which the poet tries to create the impression that it's not he who is speaking, but this or that other character. Plato names the latter *mimesis* or imitation, so that "if the poet were at no time to disguise himself, the imitation would be dropped."[15] Plato himself then gives an example from the *Odyssey*: Plato transposes one of Homer's dialogue scenes into indirect speech, works it up poetically, and thus makes diegesis out of mimesis. Diegesis doesn't *show* immediately, but it supplies a *narrative mediation*.

The opposition that Plato designated by *mimesis* and *diegesis* later attained huge significance in American and British narrative theory in the terminological guise of *showing* and *telling*. That was certainly justified to some extent: for it does seem that there are really two basically different modes of narrative (regardless of the fact that there are competing claims about whether simple narrative or immediate showing – Henry James: "Dramatize it! Dramatize it!"[16] – should be the *real* goal of narrative fiction:[17] such normative controversies actually only tend to cement a binary conceptualization). And to be sure, the terms "showing" and "telling," like "round" and "flat character," are persuasively concise and elegant.

But in this conceptualization there is a problem with quite serious consequences: in a narrative, unlike in drama, something like an *immediate, direct presentation* of an action is strictly speaking completely impossible. The action is always *mediated* – by the narrative. Here's Gérard Genette:

> From our own strictly analytic point of view it must be added [...] that the very idea of *showing*, like that of imitation or narrative representation (and even more so, because of its naively visual character), is completely illusory: in contrast to dramatic representation, no narrative can "show" or "imitate" the story it tells. All it can do is tell it in a manner which is detailed, precise, "alive," and in that way give more or less the *illusion of mimesis* – which is the only

<hr>

[15] Plato, *The Republic*, section 393ff. Quoted from *The Dialogues of Plato translated into English with Analyses and Introductions by B. Jowett, M.A. in Five Volumes*, 3rd rev. edn, Oxford, 1892, Vol. 3, 77ff.

[16] Henry James, "Preface," *The Altar of the Dead/The Beast in the Jungle/The Birthplace/And Other Tales* (New York Edition 17), New York, 1909, xii–xiii.

[17] Cf. Percy Lubbock, *The Craft of Fiction*, London, 1921; Wayne C. Booth, *The Rhetoric of Fiction*, 2nd edn, Chicago, 1983.

narrative mimesis, for this single and sufficient reason: that narration, oral or written, is a fact of language, and language signifies without imitating.[18]

The written "reproduction" of a spoken dialogue in a novel is indeed a different kind of reproduction from the performance of a dialogue on the stage. The latter *performs* what it is – a dialogue *is* a dialogue; the former only *describes a dialogue, stands for* a dialogue. To be sure, it could be argued, against Genette, that there are in fact forms of *oral* narrative that offer mimesis, e.g., when in "reproducing" a dialogue between two characters the narrator imitates them using different voices. The *linguistic* nature of narrative by itself doesn't exclude the possibility of mimesis in narration – Genette somewhat overshoots the mark here. But *writing* does exclude that possibility.

However, if in a narrative *everything becomes narrative*, then the following is true: "All that a narrative can do is create an illusion, an effect, a semblance of mimesis, but it does so through diegesis (in the Platonic sense). The crucial distinction, therefore, is not between telling and showing, but between different degrees and kinds of telling."[19] This would complete an extreme extension of the concept of diegesis – just as, mirror-like, Aristotle instigated an extreme extension of his concept of mimesis: for according to Aristotle, narrative and direct presentation are only two types of mimesis (or, imitation).[20] Simplifying very crudely we could therefore say: for Aristotle, mimesis is an end, whereas for Plato it is a means (alongside diegesis); for Plato, diegesis is an end, for Aristotle it is only a means (alongside mimesis). Is it not interesting that in *both* theoretical configurations the concept that is regarded as the *end* reappears as a privileged *means* to reach that very end? This is a peculiarity we'll encounter again in certain theory designs.

For our purposes here, *showing* and *telling* (to stick with this attractive pair of twins) are *two types of diegesis*, two ways of designing and constructing a world in narrative.

If we want to work out how in any particular novel "people are made out of sentences,"[21] we have to investigate who says what about whom. It's not only in undergraduate seminars that a question about character portrayal is sometimes answered with information about the character conception ("Charlotte Haze," to take an example from Vladimir Nabokov's novel *Lolita* of 1955, "is a frustrated single woman who hits on her lodger Humbert Humbert because she's in some kind of panic about her biological clock ticking. This means she gets more and more jealous towards her

---

[18]   Gérard Genette, *Narrative Discourse: An Essay in Method*, trans. Jane E. Lewin, Ithaca, NY, 1980, 163–164.

[19]   Rimmon-Kenan, *Narrative Fiction*, 108.

[20]   Cf. *The "Poetics" of Aristotle*, trans. Halliwell, ch. 25, 61–63.

[21]   Cf. Herbert Grabes, "Wie aus Sätzen Personen werden," *Poetica* 10 (1978): 405–428.

teenage daughter Lolita") – i.e., with emphasis laid less on the *how*, the technique of portraying (*how* is that *done?*) than on the result, the *what*. But surely it is of no small importance that we owe this disparaging picture of the widow Haze exclusively to a highly partisan narrator, the nympholept Humbert Humbert, who longs for the death of the "old cow" Charlotte and indirectly brings it about, in order to make his sexual assault on Lolita undisturbed. If that's neither here nor there…

We can best make an analytical approach to the question "who tells what about whom?" by keeping in mind the abstract possibilities open to a narrative text. For the genre of drama, Manfred Pfister has drawn up with unsurpassed clarity a system of classification that enables us to specify the conceivable techniques of characterization. Beginning from the idea that a piece of "characterizing information" either stems from a character ("figural") or from the author ("authorial"), and that furthermore it can be delivered either *explicitly* or *implicitly*, Pfister deduced four classes of characterization techniques: explicit–figural, implicit–figural, explicit–authorial, and implicit–authorial.[22]

To what extent can that scheme be transferred to narrative literature, where everything is diegetically narrated rather than shown, as in the drama? It is easiest to find correspondences for Pfister's two authorial techniques, namely when there is an authorial narrator, a narrating authority who stands outside the world of the narration and is ontologically different from it, like a puppet master from his puppets. What the authorial narrator tells *is* the case – that's the rule of the game. However, whereas in drama the explicit–authorial characterization techniques are predominantly to be found in the secondary text (such as stage directions, prefaces) and perhaps also in speaking names, these characterization techniques play a much more important role in the novel. Every *telling* in an authorially narrated novel contains explicit–authorial characterizations. And every *showing* contains implicit–authorial characterizations, i.e., the sort (unlike the explicit) that the reader must configure into a character conception.

So to a certain extent that works out, but there's nevertheless a big snag, since authorial characterizations (whether explicit or implicit) occur on an ontologically different plane in narrative as opposed to drama. Notwithstanding the fact that Pfister defines "authorial" as "associated with the position of the implied author as its expressive subject,"[23] the author of a dramatic secondary text is actually the real author of the play, a dramatist, a flesh-and-blood human being, whereas the authorial narrator is an aspect of a *text*, planted there in a narrative text by an author. The forewords to the plays of

[22] Cf. Pfister, *Drama*, 184.
[23] Pfister, *Drama*, 136. On the problem of the concept of the "implied author," cf. the remarks on Wayne C. Booth in chapter 7, this volume.

George Bernard Shaw are by George Bernard Shaw, whereas the explicit characterizations in *Tess of the d'Urbervilles* or *Middlemarch* (1871–1872) come from the authorial narrator.

And what about Pfister's "figural" techniques of characterization, that is, when a dramatic character comments explicitly on himself or others (in a soliloquy or dialogically, in the presence or absence of other characters), or when a character implicitly characterizes himself through action and speech?[24] How would that work in narratives, such as the novel? Now, this case certainly arises when the narrator himself is part of the world in which his narration takes place – and as a rule those are the more exciting situations. For just as everything the authorial narrator tells is not open to doubt and must be unquestioningly accepted ("It is so"), so everything that a non-authorial narrator regales us with – *as a player in the game talking about other players in the same game* – must be taken with a pinch of salt. Commentaries and narrations by characters about characters always follow this rule of the game (also, of course, in authorially narrated novels). But here the narrator hasn't removed himself from the game altogether, but mixed himself with the others – what he says is therefore no longer privileged, but is subject to the same doubt, the same relativity as all (human) utterance. That can be a great gain, as far as the stimulation and challenge of realizing a character conception is concerned – or indeed the task of coming up with a general picture of the story. About character X it says here … yes, but that's what Y says, and what does it say about Y, that Y says that about X? Every explicit statement about another character becomes an implicit self-characterization (and just as with every explicit self-characterization it's especially amusing when self-perception and perception by others are at odds). And how much more amusing (or disturbing) if a narrator is palpably at a loss, not quite up to the story (e.g., Lockwood in Emily Brontë's *Wuthering Heights*, 1847). As with the three-body problem in physics, it's impossible to determine the value or worth of particular statements with complete precision, because we have to allow for a certain level of relativity (roughly analogous to what Pfister calls the distortion of perspective with regard to a character's self-presentation).[25] But that level of relativity can, in turn, only be calculated if we treat the statements of other characters with a

---

[24] Since Pfister also lists "clothing, properties, interiors" under this point (*Drama*, 190), it's not totally clear where he draws the boundary line between figural and authorial techniques of characterization. If choices can be made with regard to "clothing, properties, interiors," they're made by the director and actors, not by the characters; and if these things are prescribed, aren't we then dealing with an implicit–authorial characterization, even though Pfister's only example of the latter is "emphasis on the contrasts and correspondences that exist between one figure and the others" (*Drama*, 195)?

[25] Cf. Pfister, *Drama*, 124.

similar caution. *Approximations* at best are possible here – what's fascinating is the *process* of investigation, especially since not every piece of information is simultaneously available, but is inevitably always emerging in time.

When investigating the portrayal and function of a character it's clearly very useful heuristically to look at that character as the concrete intersection of various relationships of opposition and equivalence concerning "characteristics" and "actions" (in the style of a semantic analysis of components – Humbert Humbert is male, around forty, educated, European; Lolita female, a teenager, uneducated, American).[26] It also makes sense to think of a character as "the sum of the contrasts and correspondences linking it with the other figures in the text."[27] The web of characters in novels – in contrast to shorter forms of fiction – is often put together in a rather complex way, more like a mobile that is suspended in the air than a static pattern chart for knitting. However, we should never make these topological observations without situating them, without evaluating "what's behind them." It's not only information in secret dossiers that demands to be analyzed and *evaluated* before it can form the basis of any action (even if with fiction the consequences of inadequate evaluations shouldn't be quite so existential).

A terminological awkwardness needs to be noted at this point. It has become standard practice to refer to explicit characterizations as "direct" (which is perfectly justifiable), but also to implicit characterizations as "indirect," which is at least counter-intuitive, if not completely absurd. Because that entails – does it not? – that a characterization that operates via a scenic-style "showing" and displays a character with a certain *immediacy* (albeit an immediacy fabricated by the narrative – mimesis in Plato's sense) is classified as "*indirect* characterization," whereas the purely diegetic and *mediated* characterization of the explicit type ("Isabel Archer was a young person of many theories": Henry James, *The Portrait of a Lady*, 1881) is curiously designated "*direct* characterization."[28] That amounts, it seems to me, to an absurd terminological topsyturvydom. Rimmon-Kenan even writes: "A presentation is *indirect* when rather than mentioning a trait, it *displays* and exemplifies it in various ways."[29] To call the immediate presentation of a character trait "indirect" but the *mention* of it by a narrator (that is, the mediated presentation) "direct" can really only lead to confusion. The use of the unpretentious terms *showing* and *telling* seems less prone to misunderstanding, even if it admittedly doesn't sound as scholarly as "direct definition" and "indirect presentation."[30]

---

[26] Cf. Lotman, *Structure*, 239ff.

[27] Pfister, *Drama*, 163.

[28] Cf. Hans-Werner Ludwig (ed.), *Arbeitsbuch Romananalyse*, 6th edn, Tübingen, 1998, 143–144.

[29] Rimmon-Kenan, *Narrative Fiction*, 61, emphasis added.

[30] Rimmon-Kenan, *Narrative Fiction*, 60–61.

Herman Melville's narrative *Bartleby, the Scrivener* (1853) is about the absurd life of a copyist who one day refuses to copy any more documents, but nevertheless goes into the office every day as before and at last no longer leaves at all until he's dragged out and eventually dies in prison. Interestingly enough, it is Bartelby's employer, however, who narrates the story, a lawyer who declares of himself, "Imprimis: I am a man who, from his youth upwards, has been filled with a profound conviction that the easiest way of life is the best." The text is (among other things) a document of radical incomprehension, but also the record of the continual provocation of what cannot be understood – which, however, ultimately gives way to a deep (self-)comprehension on the narrator's part.

In Virginia Woolf's *Mrs. Dalloway* (1925) the eponymous heroine leaves the house to buy flowers for her party. We're inside her consciousness, her memories. Then she has to wait at the kerb to let a delivery van pass:

> She stiffened a little on the kerb, waiting for Durtnall's van to pass. A charming woman, Scrope Purvis thought her (knowing her as one does know people who live next door to one in Westminster); a touch of the bird about her, of the jay, blue-green, light, vivacious, though she was over fifty, and grown very white since her illness. There she perched, never seeing him, waiting to cross, very upright.

We've seen her from outside for the first time, through the eyes and thoughts of another character, who is of no further significance in the novel. But in this way she has already become, in part, another person for us.

In *Aspects of the Novel*, E. M. Forster writes about the extent to which we can understand fictional characters:

> [P]eople in a novel can be understood completely by the reader, if the novelist wishes; their inner as well as their outer life can be exposed. And this is why they often seem more definite than characters in history, or even our own friends; we have been told all about them that can be told [...] we can know more about [Homo Fictus] than we can know about any of our fellow creatures, because his creator and narrator are one.[31]

Similarly to Forster, Geoffrey Braithwaite – the widowed country doctor in Julian Barnes' *Flaubert's Parrot* – believes: "Books say: she did this because. Life says: she did this. Books are where things are explained to you; life is where things aren't. I'm not surprised some people prefer books. Books make sense of life. The only problem is that the lives they make sense of are other people's lives, never your own." But Geoffrey Braithwaite is only a *character*, not an authorial narrator, a survivor with a sad fate. And the

---

[31]   Forster, *Aspects*, 57, 63.

longer you read *Flaubert's Parrot*, the more you ask yourself whether Geoffrey Braithwaite has really and truly understood why there is such a thing as literature at all (a question that can so easily and devastatingly be turned against the questioner).

One last, longer example of the unavoidable but also extremely variable *mediatedness* of character portrayal in the novel comes from the third chapter of Thomas Mann's *The Magic Mountain*, from the section "Of course, a female!":

> There were two incidents during the course of the meal of which Hans Castorp took note, so far as his condition permitted. One was the banging of the glass door, which occurred while they were having the fish course. Hans Castorp gave an exasperated shrug and angrily resolved that this time he really must find out who did it. "I must find out," he whispered with exaggerated earnestness. Miss Robinson and the schoolmistress both looked at him in surprise. He turned the whole upper half of his body to the left and opened wide his bloodshot blue eyes.
>
> It was a lady who was passing through the room; a woman, or rather girl, of middle height, in a white sweater and coloured skirt, her reddish-blond hair wound in braids about her head. Hans Castorp had only a glimpse of her profile. She moved, in singular contrast to the noise of her entrance, almost without sound, passing with a peculiarly gliding step, her head a little thrust forward, to her place at the furthest table on the left, at right angles to the verandah door: the "good" Russian table, in fact. As she walked, she held one hand deep in the pocket of her close-fitting jacket; the other she lifted to the back of her head and arranged the plaits of her hair. Hans Castorp looked at the hand. He was habitually observant and critical of this feature, and accustomed when he made a new acquaintance to direct his attention first upon it. It was not particularly ladylike, this hand that was putting the braids to rights; not so refined and well kept as the hands of ladies in Hans Castorp's own social sphere. Rather broad, with stumpy fingers, it had about it something primitive and childish, something indeed of the schoolgirl. The nails, it was plain, knew nothing of the manicurist's art; they were cut in rough-and-ready schoolgirl fashion, and the skin at the side looked almost as though someone were subject to the childish vice of finger biting. But Hans Castorp sensed rather than saw this, owing to the distance. The laggard greeted her table-mates with a nod, and took her place on the inner side of the table with her back to the room, next to Dr. Krokowski, who was sitting at the top. As she did so, she turned her head, with the hand still raised to it, toward the dining room and surveyed the public; Hans Castorp had opportunity for the fleeting observation that her cheek-bones were broad and her eyes narrow. – A vague memory of something, of somebody, stirred him slightly and fleetingly as he looked.
>
> "Of course, a female!" he thought, or rather he actually uttered, in a murmur, yet so that the schoolmistress, Fräulein Engelhardt, understood. The poor old spinster smiled in sympathy.

"That is Madame Chauchat," she said. "She is so heedless. A charming creature." And the downy flush on her cheek grew a shade darker – as it did whenever she spoke.

"A Frenchwoman?" Hans Castorp asked, with severity.

"No, she is a Russian," was the answer. "Her husband is very likely French or of French descent, I am not sure."

Hans Castorp asked, still irritated, if that was he – pointing to a gentleman with drooping shoulders who sat at the "good" Russian table.

"Oh, no," the schoolmistress answered, "he isn't here; he has never been here, no one knows him."

"She ought to learn how to shut a door," Hans Castorp said. "She always lets it slam. It is a piece of ill breeding."

And on the schoolmistress's meekly accepting this reproof as though she herself had been the guilty party, there was no more talk of Madame Chauchat.

What a treasure trove of characterization techniques! These range from proleptically significant, speaking names – Mme. Chauchat really turns out to be a cat on heat – to the response which is, reversing the "normal" order, put in front of her entry (Hans Castorp is already infuriated before he's even set eyes on her), to a view from outside ("It was a lady who was…"), whose limitation is explicitly asserted ("Hans Castorp had only a glimpse of her profile"); after the notably detailed description of her hands ("Hans Castorp looked at the hand") comes the authorial narrator's clarification that what is apparently being observed is but a *projection* of the still angry Hans Castorp ("But Hans Castorp sensed rather than saw this, owing to the distance"), then a switch over to Hans Castorp's inner world ("a vague memory"), before the scene changes to dialogue and we now have a double view of Chauchat – but also of Castorp in his relationship to Engelhardt, and Engelhardt in her relationship to Castorp, and of both in their relationships to Chauchat.

All these examples – Melville, Woolf, Barnes, Mann – show conclusively that no halfway satisfying analysis of the characters in a novel is possible unless we first ascertain the *narrative situation*. "Who tells what about whom?" But that doesn't just define the individual characters; rather, it defines the *whole type* of the novel as well. The heart of every analysis of a novel is therefore the discriminating identification of the narrative situation, and that's what we come to now.

6

Teutonic Rosette or Gallic Taxonomy?
Identifying the Narrative Situation

1 Prologue

We can identify the narrative situation of a novel in different ways. On the European continent, the most widely invoked approaches are probably those of the Austrian Anglicist Franz K. Stanzel and the French literary critic Gérard Genette. In recent years it has sometimes seemed as though the debate between the supporters of Stanzel's "typological circle of narrative situations" and his Francophile critics was degenerating into a veritable religious dispute. At least it had the traits of squabbles like that between PC and Mac-users, even if many departments and many students didn't have to make the choice: for higher authorities had already decided which approach was the only admissible one. *Cuius regio, eius religio.*

What's more, it actually doesn't matter which model one uses, which terminology one prefers. Narrative situations don't "exist" – at least not in the sense in which the book you're holding in your hand exists. Narrative situations are concepts that we build through a process of abstraction on the basis of particular experiences and data – with the aim of applying them in turn as analytical instruments to narrative texts. As with any other instrument, its suitability is to be measured by its specific performance: how well can I work with it? How handy is it? How much information does it yield beyond what I already know? How great is its resolution, its depth of field, what does it depict, and what can't it show at all, for systematic reasons? Perhaps most importantly: how well does it serve my concrete interests in gaining a particular kind of knowledge?

The Novel: An Introduction. By Christoph Bode. Translated by James Vigus. English translation © 2011 James Vigus. Published by John Wiley & Sons, Ltd.
Original German text © 2005 Narr Francke Attempto Verlag GmbH + Co. KG.

And seen in that way – as a tool for a specific purpose – it certainly *does* matter which approach you follow. All models simplify – that's ultimately what they're there for, like a good map, which, if it's to be serviceable, *mustn't* show everything, but nevertheless should put essential, detailed information at our disposal, otherwise it wouldn't be any good at all. Also, no system of terminology is possible without idiosyncrasies and neologisms – there's always a first time for the usage of every term as a concept, rather than as a mere expression. But with regard to *how exactly* one or the other narrative–theoretical approach conceives a situation or problem, *how exactly* it tries to get a grip on that situation, to present it and describe its function – there are at times considerable differences, differences we need to know about.

That's why there's possibly nothing more harmful than following one particular approach *blindly* – whether because that's the done thing, because it is demanded or expected from us, or through not knowing better – without being clear about the strengths and weaknesses of the chosen instrument, about which phenomena it puts in a nutshell with special elegance and economy, and which ones it ultimately doesn't show, for systematic reasons *can't* show. It is only such knowledge about the connection between the method of investigation and its object – in other words, how my method actually *constitutes* and devises the object under scrutiny – that allows self-reflexivity on the part of the investigator: and it's only there that scholarship, good academic practice, and science begin. Clarity, scope, and practicability: these are some of the criteria that a narratological model should meet, and surely a conceptual apparatus that raises more problems than it answers is hardly the most user-friendly.

In the following discussion of how to identify narrative situations I introduce you to both Stanzel and Genette. This is not due to an anxiety to grant equal airtime and avoid commitment: I do this, rather, because it's through contrast, through reciprocal illumination, that the profile of both conceptual schemes can be brought out in a particularly clear-cut way. The final decision anyway lies with the customer or user: at any rate this vendor doesn't get a percentage cut on the sale of one brand or the other.

2 Stanzel's Typological Circle: A Preliminary Overview

According to Stanzel, there are three different narrative situations, which differ from each other in a fundamental way. These are the *first-person narrative situation*, the *authorial narrative situation*, and the so-called *figural narrative situation*. Stanzel arranges these three narrative situations on his "typological circle" such that each narrative situation controls one third of the circle. (Stanzel borrowed the circular arrangement from Goethe, who in his "Notes and Essays towards a better understanding of the West–East Divan" wanted to visually illustrate the relationship between the three basic literary genres – epic, lyric, and drama.)[1] The typological circle is as brilliant as it is simple, elegant, and efficient (without going into whether those three qualities actually make up the definition of brilliance). At one fell swoop it achieves three things:

1. It illustrates that each of the three narrative situations defines itself against the two others, since each displays a particular characteristic that the other two lack (of which more in a moment).

2. At the same time it illustrates that despite this polar opposition between the three narrative situations there are also areas of transition between them (i.e., you can move around the circle clockwise or anti-clockwise – and back again). Indeed, it's the proportion of mixed ingredients in the transition zones that is, in a way, the most fascinating to analyze and that requires special attention – these mixed phenomena have a systematic place in this model.

3. The circular arrangement offers the possibility not just of establishing the narrative situation ahistorically, i.e., in a purely systematic way, but also of placing the results of this analysis in terms of literary history. It works like this: we write on the outer part of the circle the titles of the novels, chapters of novels, novellas, short stories, etc. whose respective narrative situations we have identified. We do this in such a way that each title roughly stands in the section of the circle that best fits it (taking account of whether it is pure or mixed, and if mixed, mixed in which way; as is clear from point (2), a work rarely belongs to one single position on the chart, but often covers a certain range, i.e., an arc). Once this is done, we can see that the three big sectors of the circle are not equivalent in terms of historical period: rather, the upper half of the circle fills up rapidly after 1700, while the figural narrative situation appears later, but assumes a dominant role in the era of classical modernism (early twentieth century).

The typological circle thus reflects a *development*. It highlights clear differences but at the same time gives transitions the attention they deserve – a bit like a hi-tech automatic gearbox with infinite levels (hopefully, the sporty gear-shifting driver will not immediately use this analogy against Stanzel).

And how do we make use of this typological circle? Experience suggests that for many readers, the least problematic narrative situations to identify are the first-person narrative situation and the authorial narrative situation (not surprisingly – we're more familiar with texts that use these narrative situations), and for that reason I begin with these here. First, I'll roughly sketch the terrain, and only later come to the variations, nuances, and specific aporias of the three basic situations.

---

[1] Johann Wolfgang von Goethe, *Werke (Hamburger Ausgabe)*, Munich, 1982, 2: 187–189.

Looking at the helpful diagram of the typological circle in figure 6.1, we see a dotted boundary line that runs (without going all the way through) from the top right down to the bottom left, the "first-person/third-person" boundary. On one side of the first-person/third-person boundary is the first-person narrative situation, on the other side are the two other narrative situations. That's straightforward. The first-person narrative situation is defined by the fact that an "I" presents a narrative about himself/herself or about others who share this fictional world – something that doesn't occur in the two other narrative situations. The first-person narrator belongs to the fictional reality s/he narrates, being an "embodied 'I,'"[2] a character alongside other characters. That's why Stanzel has also put "identity of the realms of existence" in the inner circle of the category "first-person narrative situation" – referring to the identity of the narrator's and the characters' realms of existence. The "I" of the first-person narrative situation signals the identity of the realms of existence: the narrator, too, appears (as it were) on the stage.

This is completely different in an authorial narrative situation. An authorial narrator stands outside the world s/he's narrating. The introduction to William Thackeray's *Vanity Fair* (1847/48), "Before the Curtain," makes that clear through an apt metaphor: the authorial narrator is the puppet-master who lets the puppets dance, has full control over them, and never gets involved with them (as puppet among puppets). For that would break the illusion: the puppet-master standing over the stage isn't just "somehow" divided from the puppets in space, but s/he is *ontologically* different from them. The puppeteer's existence is of a different order (s/he's made out of flesh and blood, they of wood and fabric) – not least because as far as the stage-world is concerned, s/he sees everything and knows everything (and causes everything). The authorial narrator is, as has often been observed, the god almighty of narrative authorities.

The typological circle illustrates this fact by means of the "internal perspective/external perspective" boundary line running from top left to bottom right. On one side of this boundary is the authorial narrative situation only, while on the other side are the other two narrative situations. Thus only in the authorial narrative situation does the narrator have a godlike view of the whole of the narrated world; that's why in the inner circle Stanzel notes "external perspective (omniscience)." In the other two narrative situations, the narrated world has an inside perspective, i.e., the point of view is always *inside* this reality, and therefore *necessarily limited* (if you're inside, you can't see everything. To see everything is to be as God, and is that a human possibility or conceivable in any way?).

Even though the authorial narrative situation is so easy to identify, beginners often fall into a couple of unnecessary misunderstandings, which it's

---

[2]   Franz K. Stanzel, *A Theory of Narrative*, trans. Charlotte Goedsche, Cambridge, 1986 [1984], 92.

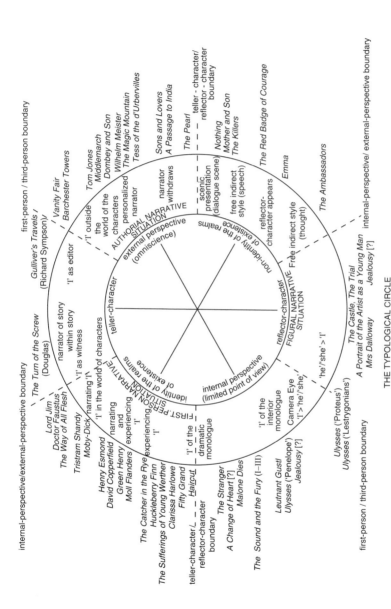

internal-perspective/external-perspective boundary

first-person / third-person boundary

Figure 6.1

THE TYPOLOGICAL CIRCLE

first-person / third-person boundary

internal-perspective/ external-perspective boundary

Gulliver's Travels /
(Richard Sympson)/

Vanity Fair
Barchester Towers

'I' as editor

'I' outside
the
world of the
characters

Tom Jones
Middlemarch
Dombey and Son
Wilhelm Meister
The Magic Mountain
Tess of the d'Urbervilles

Sons and Lovers
A Passage to India

The Pearl

teller - character/
reflector - character
boundary

Nothing
Mother and Son
The Killers

The Red Badge of Courage

Emma

The Ambassadors

internal-perspective/ external-perspective boundary

AUTHORIAL NARRATIVE
SITUATION

narrator
personalized
narrator

narrator
withdraws

scenic
presentation
(dialogue scene)

free indirect
style (speech)

external perspective
(omniscience)

non-identity of the realms
of existence

reflector-
character appears

Free indirect style
(thought)

FIGURAL NARRATIVE
SITUATION

teller-character

reflector-character

The Castle, The Trial
A Portrait of the Artist as a Young Man
Mrs Dalloway   Jealousy [?]

'he'/'she' > 'I'

identity of the realms
of existence

internal perspective
(limited point of view)

FIRST-PERSON NARRATIVE
SITUATION

'I' of the
dramatic
monologue

'I'
narrating
and
experiencing
'I'

narrator of story
within story

'I' as witness

'I' in the world of characters

'I' of the
interior
monologue

Camera Eye
'I'>'he'/'she'

'I'>'he'/'she'

Ulysses ('Proteus')
Ulysses ('Lestrygonians')

Leutnant Gustl
Ulysses ('Penelope')
Jealousy [?]

The Sound and the Fury (I–III)

A Change of Heart [?]
Malone Dies

The Stranger

teller-character/
reflector-character
boundary

The Catcher in the Rye
Huckleberry Finn
The Sufferings of Young Werther
Clarissa Harlowe
Fifty Grand   Haircut

Henry Esmond
David Copperfield
Green Henry
Moll Flanders

Tristram Shandy
Moby-Dick narrating 'I'

Lord Jim
Doctor Faustus
The Way of All Flesh

The Turn of the Screw
(Douglas)

worth clearing up at once. The first misunderstanding is the idea that an authorial narrator can't possibly say "I" – a narrator who does that must, they think, be a first-person narrator. This, though, is not the sense in which the boundary between I and s/he is intended: it isn't a *grammatical* line of demarcation, but an *ontological* one – a line that divides realms of existence from each other. Thus Doris Lessing's "To Room Nineteen" (1963) begins with the sentence: "This is a story, *I suppose*, about a failure in intelligence: the Rawlings' marriage was grounded in intelligence" (emphasis added). But in what follows it becomes clear that the narrator is not an acquaintance of the Rawlings, nor has s/he got his or her extensive knowledge of their marriage from others' gossip or any sort of written records – s/he doesn't have *any* "contact" with the people involved, but *knows everything, right from the outset*. In other words, s/he is an omniscient authorial narrator.

The second avoidable misunderstanding relates to the expression "internal perspective/external perspective." The mistaken idea is that the inner life of a character cannot be presented through an authorial narrative situation, because the latter "only" allows for a view of the characters "from the outside." Clearly, that's absurd. The authorial narrative situation allows *everything* – really everything, full stop. "External perspective" means precisely that standpoint *outside the world* that enables the narrator to tell and present everything: the outer *and* inner lives of the characters, their past, present, and future. There is nothing that an authorial narrator cannot narrate. There may well be disadvantages to this narrative situation (we'll come shortly to the advantages and disadvantages, possibilities and limitations of all three narrative situations), but these do not lie in a supposed "restriction" to a "view of the exterior."

That leaves the third narrative situation, the figural. This is the most unusual of the three, and the one that experience suggests is the most difficult to identify: and it may be some consolation that we can at least always say to ourselves, "If it's neither a first-person narrative situation nor an authorial narrative situation, it has to be a figural narrative situation." But the figural narrative situation should not be something that just gets "left over" – it's much too important for that. Although Stanzel identifies "mediacy" (i.e., the fact that what is told is *mediated*) as a defining characteristic of the genre of narrative,[3] he does of course realize (like Plato) that within mediated narrative there can also be an *illusion of immediacy*, and that this always occurs if the mediating narrator retreats from view or disappears completely.[4] We're already familiar with that from Plato's concept of

---

[3] Cf. Stanzel, *Theory*, 4ff.

[4] Cf. Stanzel, *Theory*, 66: "The novel is not a homogeneous genre but a mixture of diegetic–narrative and mimetic–dramatic parts. In the narrative parts, however, a gradual progression from the pronounced diegetic–narrative to the mimetic–dramatic can be noted. Free indirect style, indirect speech, speech report and largely dramatic scene are more closely related to the mimetic–dramatic than are a narrator's very compressed report of action and authorial commentary."

mimesis, from "showing," and from the notion of scenic presentation. Stanzel, however, doesn't define the latter, drama-like phenomenon as the core area of figural narration, but rather those situations in which as a reader you find yourself inside the consciousness of "a character in the novel who thinks, feels and perceives,"[5] though without this actually being narrated, i.e., "processed" or mediated. That indeed is the source of the (illusionary) impression that the presentation is direct: "the distinguishing characteristic of the figural narrative situation is that the illusion of immediacy is super-imposed over mediacy."[6] So a character whose consciousness we (so to speak) inhabit is not a narrator, nor – according to Stanzel at least – is what that character thinks, feels, and perceives narrated by anyone else; rather, this is a *reflector* character, in whose consciousness we see the world reflected: a world to which we have no direct access. (This is a bit like Tennyson's Lady of Shalott in the poem of that name: she had to weave an image of the world copied from what she saw reflected in a mirror, but on pain of death wasn't allowed to look *directly* at the object of presentation. I'll refrain here from a discussion of the consequences for every reflection theory, the implied portrait of the artist, or the connection to the myth of Medusa.)

In purely logical terms, that's very elegant: the illusion of directness is bought by renunciation of immediate access to (fictional) reality. What's offered directly is the *medium* in which reality is reflected: human conscious-ness. It seems hard to get the world's mediacy out of the world. (Admittedly, this view departs from Stanzel's definition: "*presentation*, i.e., the reflection of the fictional reality in the consciousness of a character, which creates in the reader the illusion of immediacy of perception of the fictional world.")[7]

The typological circle displays the opposition between narration and presentation such that beneath the "teller-character/reflector-character" boundary line, narration no longer happens at all – that is the defining qual-ity of the figural narrative situation when the reflector-mode is dominant – whereas above this boundary line a "processing" narrator (whether authorial or first-person) is at work.

Each of the three above-mentioned boundary lines thus illustrates an opposition of the following kind: in each case *one* characteristic (e.g., the iden-tity of the realms of existence) applies to *one* narrative situation (in this case, the first-person narrative situation), while the opposite characteristic (non-identity of the narrator's and characters' realms of existence) applies to the other two narrative situations. It only remains to add that Stanzel has terms for these dichotomies too ("perspective" for the opposition "internal perspective/

[5] Stanzel, *Theory*, 5.
[6] Stanzel, *Theory*, 5.
[7] Cf. Stanzel, *Theory*, 48. *Translator's note:* I have translated this quotation, however, from Franz K. Stanzel, *Theorie des Erzählens*, 7th edn, Göttingen, 2001, 71.

external perspective" is self-evident; "mode" for the opposition "narrating-character/reflector-character" is comprehensible; "person" for the opposition "identity/non-identity of the narrator's and characters' realms of existence" is perhaps not such a happy choice). Now that the basic structure is in place we can come to the finer points, which are the really interesting bit: what possibilities are open to each of the narrative situations just sketched, what they allow us to do and what they assist with, but also which specific problem areas, resistances, and aporias they throw up. Or better: what *narrative* problems authors face when deciding for this or that form of narrative and presentation. For it could well be that every attempt to fabricate narrative authenticity at some point or other carries – as the stamp of its genuine fakeness – the watermark of its "impossible" constructedness, its fabrication and its mediacy.

3   Splitting the In-dividual: The First-Person Narrative Situation

The first-person narrative situation seems at first to be the most "natural" of the three basic narrative situations. What could be more normal than that an individual (as distinctive and unique as possible – that's what many readers expect, anyway) should narrate a story, a story in which s/he did something or something was done to him or her, or at least s/he observed something? The great advantage of a first-person narration is – so we're often told – that it enables the closest degree of identification with a particular character, i.e., with the first-person narrator. "Identification" here doesn't mean "I'd like to be like her or him," but has a purely technical sense: in the fictional world the reader takes up roughly the same position as that from which the first-person narrator experiences and narrates (rather like in *Rückenfigur* paintings, where the viewer himself seems to be copied into the picture). The epic preterite's tendency to make everything seem present surely reinforces this impression.

Yet the phrase "experiences and narrates" obfuscates a problem that can without exaggeration be called *the* basic problem of this narrative situation, which is that in the first-person narrative situation the "I" makes a *double* appearance: as narrator of the story "now" and as a character in the story "then." To conceptualize this splitting of the I, the terms "narrating self" and "experiencing self" have been established. Thus when a naïve reader says: "I'm taking on the position of the first-person narrator," one could reply: "Interesting. So which one? The position of the narrating self or the experiencing self?" And the answers would have to be very different depending on the novel – depending even on the particular passage within one novel, since texts can in this respect produce diverse accentuations; and this or that accentuation can amount to something entirely different.

Let's start by stating that as a rule (present-tense narration excepted – see chapter 4), there is an important temporal distance between the narrating self and the experiencing self: what is being narrated now is something that happened in the past. To be sure, that creates difficulties. These are not due particularly to the fact that after a long time has elapsed we no longer remember so precisely (or correctly). That's a practical problem of life, a psychological problem that the novel brings with it only insofar as it attempts to simulate the memories of a *real* person. (That the first-person narrative situation usually presents the memories more detailed and more accurately than could be the case in real life is purely an artistic convention, which, being admittedly "unrealistic," might or might not bother us; but of course the narrating self also has the re-creative freedom, say, to reproduce word-for-word dialogues that took place decades ago and could not be remembered exactly. Strictly speaking, this is faking – but for the time being let's lay aside this particular mistrust of the first-person narration's claim to authenticity.)

Much more serious are the consequences with regard to *narrative logic* that result from the distance between narrating self and experiencing self. The former always knows more than the latter: for the narrating self always knows what happened *next* and how it turned out (provided s/he can say "now that's over and done with"). But the narrating self *can't* make full use of this knowledge, for two different but equally important reasons. First, every narrative consists in the very fact that it imparts its knowledge only successively – the life-blood of narrative is *postponement, delay*. The effect of every narrative lies in carefully applied doses of postponement – like a delayed-action medicine. What sort of impossible non-narrative would try to tell us *everything* at once? Second, to bring in the extra knowledge of the narrating self on a big scale would confound the first-person narrative's claim to authenticity. It wouldn't just disturb in the sense of being a continual interference, that is, but would destroy the very thing that constituted the situation of the experiencing self *then*, viz. the *not knowing* all that, the *inevitable ignorance* of all that.

So this is the dilemma of first-person narrators. They can either lay their cards on the table all at once, and so fatally disrupt the impression of reality given by their narration of the past – since it surely *wasn't* like *that* at the time!; or they can present themselves throughout and for very good reasons as less informed than they actually are, in an attempt to veil the position from which the narration is made – to make it practically invisible and not thematize it, in the hope that no one will notice it. Leaving aside all the shades and levels in between, we are therefore left with two rather different types of first-person narration. In the first type, the focus is on the narrating self in the "present": on the act of narrating and the work of remembering and expressing. In the second type, the focus is on the experiencing self, on what is being narrated and remembered. *Tristram Shandy* and Siegfried Lenz's *Deutschstunde* [*The German Lesson*] (1968) are examples of the first type, *Robinson Crusoe* and Thomas Mann's *Confessions of Felix Krull, Confidence Man* (1954) examples of the second type.

If you lean back and think about it, it's a rather curious performance: in order to function at all, the "most natural" of all narrative situations must first split the indivisible individual; then either present its narrating half as more stupid than it really is or else narrate its story in a way that it certainly did *not* experience; and the narrative usually ends when the story of the experiencing self approaches temporally so close to the position of the narrating self that both can merge into one again. First-person narration occurs between splitting and fusion: a fully paradoxical undertaking. What's most astonishing about it is that it works at all, and in most cases even quite persuasively. (That may have something to do with the fact that this paradoxical figure corresponds to the equally paradoxical form that is human consciousness. Consciousness can make itself the object of its own observation. But if it does so, it is no longer what it was before it made itself the object of its observation. Thus the focus is either on the contents of consciousness or else self-reflexively on the forms and processes of consciousness. The fact that it can do *both* defines consciousness as consciousness. Yet still it can't observe itself in the same way that it observes other things. To do that it must divide itself temporally and then permanently cross over a dividing line.)

The basic aporia of first-person narrative just sketched can't be removed, but its consequences can be alleviated by considerably reducing the temporal distance between the narrating and the experiencing selves. The epistolary novel is the most successful form of the novel when it comes to such reduction of temporal distance. This form keeps the gap between experiencing and narrating extremely tight, which also means that the moment of narration is always moving forward in step with the action, thus creating a *series*: it is not, as can appear to be the case with a larger temporal distance between experience and narration, a kind of fixed point from which the past is surveyed.

> November 8
> She has reproached me for my excesses! Ah, with such amiability! My excesses, that I sometimes let myself be induced by a glass of wine to drink a whole bottle. – Don't! she said. Think of Lotte! – Think, I said, do you need to tell me to do that? I think! – I don't think! You are always before my soul. Today I was sitting at the spot where you recently got down from the coach – She changed the subject to keep me from going on any further. Dear friend! I am lost! She can do with me what she will.[8]

---

[8] Johann Wolfgang von Goethe, *The Sorrows of Young Werther*, trans. Burton Pike, New York, 2005, 102.

That was obviously written on the very same day: the impression is still very fresh, and Werther's excitement vibrates through it. The epistolary novel is the *al fresco* technique of first-person narration. Its advantages are evident: there is no credibility gap due to the long period of time between occurrence and fixation, but rather there is the possibility of fixing thoughts and feelings as precisely as possible "just afterwards," or of portraying them in flux. Justice is done to outward action and inner resonance in equal measure. It's understandable why this form of the novel was once so popular. Yet the fewer elaborate letters are written in reality, the more unrealistic the epistolary novel comes to seem: it's a dying art. Perhaps email novels or chatroom novels will replace them – an exciting thought.

But from the very beginning, and in its high period in the eighteenth century, the epistolary novel's relationship to "reality" was strange and far from unproblematic. In the cult novels *Pamela, or Virtue Rewarded* and *Clarissa*, Samuel Richardson, the undisputed master of this form, produced works that completely exhausted the possibilities of the genre. Here is the start of the contents list of *Pamela*, which he developed from the idea of a letter-writing manual, just the kind of thing we nowadays find in the "self-help" sections of bookshops or supermarkets (*One Hundred Letters of Application for Every Occasion*, etc.), but with the difference that an ongoing, exciting plot about a chambermaid pursued by the son of her dead mistress obviously spices up the reading:

I.   *To her Parents*. Recounting her lady's death. – Her master's kindness to her. Sends them money.

II.   *From her Parents*. Are much concerned for her lady's death: caution her against having *too* grateful a sense of her master's favour to her. Further cautions and instructions.

III. *To her Father*. She resolves to prefer her Virtue to life itself. Apprehends no danger at present from her master's favour.

IV.   *To her Mother*. Lady Davers praises her beauty, and gives her advice to keep the men at a distance. Intends to take her to wait upon her own person.

V.   *To her Parents*. Mrs. Jervis's the housekeeper's worthy conduct in the family, and friendship to her. She is quite fearless of danger; and why.

VI.   *To the same*. Farther instances of her master's goodness to her. Her joyful gratitude upon it. He praises her person to Mrs. Jervis.

VII. *To her Father*. Inforcing his former cautions and instructions. Is easier, since he knows she has Mrs. Jervis to advise with.

VIII. *From her Father*. Inforcing his former cautions and instructions. Is easier, since he knows she has Mrs Jervis to advise her.

IX.   *To her Parents*. Her master refuses to let her go to Lady Davers. His pretended reason for it. Lady Davers seemingly apprehensive for her. Still hopes the best, and will give them notice of all that happens.

X.   *To her Mother*. Acquaints her, that now her master's designs against her are apparent. That she had written down the particulars of all; but that somebody had stolen her letter. Will write at the first opportunity another, revealing all: but is watched and blamed by her master, for spending so much time in writing.

Indeed. The more voluminous Richardson's novels became (in one large-format paperback edition *Clarissa* clocks in at 1,500 pages), the more people asked themselves when the characters are actually supposed to have found the time to write their letters, and disrespectful literary critics have calculated that no time remained for them to actually experience what they report. Henry Fielding's priceless parody of *Pamela*, entitled *Shamela*, shows that up deliciously – the characters write *in situ*:

Thursday Night, Twelve o'Clock.
Mrs. Jervis and I are just in bed, and the door unlocked; if my master should come – Odsbobs! I hear him just coming in at the door. You see I write in the present tense, as Parson Williams says. Well, he is in bed between us, we both shamming a sleep; he steals his hand into my bosom, which I, as if in my sleep, press close to me with mine, and then pretend to awake. – I no sooner see him, but I scream out to Mrs. Jervis, she feigns likewise but just to come to herself; we both begin, she to becall, and I to bescratch very liberally. After having made a pretty free use of my fingers, without any great regard to the parts I attack'd, I counterfeit a swoon. Mrs. Jervis then cries out, O sir, what have you done? you have murthered poor Pamela: she is gone, she is gone. –
O what a difficulty it is to keep one's countenance, when a violent laugh desires to burst forth!

This is a phenomenon of dialectical tipping over that we've seen before and will meet again: in the attempt to develop narrative techniques that create the illusion of being as close as possible to reality, the whole project capsizes and the totally unrealistic *constructedness* of the text is exposed.

But to return to the contents list in *Pamela*: in this epistolary novel about persecuted innocence something is established that, to an even greater extent, can be found in *Clarissa* and that right from the outset enables the work to operate on a different, higher level from *Werther* – viz., there are *different* addressees and *different* correspondents. That immensely broadens the possibilities for the fictional world's unfolding. When someone writes to different addressees, she doesn't write the same to everyone (also a nice method to fan out the characterization!), neither in content, nor in style or tone – the writing, subjective in any case, now becomes addressee-specific. And if different people write about "the same" event, it becomes clear that one event can be perceived and presented completely differently. So we unwittingly find ourselves plunged into the not so modern (albeit certainly post-1700) phenomenon of *multiperspectivity*. Reality no longer offers itself as an objective given, but as something subjectively mediated, whose intersubjectivity is ascertained through discourse with an equal partner (the reader, the reasonable or enlightened person): in this way the form of this type of novel imitates the discursive commerce of the public sphere of bourgeois society.[9]

It was on purpose that I wrote "perceived *and presented* completely differently," for the fact that letters are written to addressees opens up the possibility of deception, which the reader – who has also come across other, possibly more credible presentations – can see through. Since epistolary novels often portray victim–aggressor or victim–exploiter relationships (Clarissa is kidnapped by the rogue Lovelace, put in a brothel, drugged, raped, and eventually dies insane), this aspect is quite important: the apparent evidence of the letter always contains at the same time the possibility of its opposite (fakes, lies). So every epistolary novel always implicitly thematizes the condition of its own genre: that it is a transparent faking of reality.

Things are different with the other type of novel that also works by shortening the temporal distance, the diary novel. For people don't deceive themselves intentionally (however much they may do so unintentionally) – the lie is always directed *to* someone. Here, discrepancies arise between presentations of one and the same person, and that often has a comic, though sometimes only a sobering effect. The way Bridget Jones lives up to or fails to live up to her lengthy list of New Year's Resolutions (lose weight, smoke and drink less, learn to cope with being single, learn how to program the video recorder, etc.) is amusing in itself, and also speaks for a fair amount of self-irony on the part of the readership of that bestseller. In addition, the fact that this novel, *Shamela*-like, highlights the "impossible" situation of writing (see under "Monday, 12 June") and that it varies Jane Austen's *Pride and Prejudice* in an ingenious intertextual way indicates that its clever author, Helen Fielding, knew exactly what she was doing in writing the book.

In another diary novel, William Golding's *Rites of Passage* (1980), matters are gloomier. The young Mr. Talbot, who keeps a diary during his passage to Australia, doesn't just prove himself quickly to be an arrogant upstart (e.g., at last I was invited to the first officer's table, about time too. – Next entry (X): the invitation "had been extended to every passenger in this part of the vessel"), but his lack of self-knowledge and experience also have tragic, deadly consequences for others on board. The diarist's self-exposure unfolds as a process – until it dawns on both himself and the reader what has meanwhile occurred outside his blinkered field of vision.

A diary can also have a tremendous effect as a part incorporated in a first-person novel. John Fowles' *The Collector* (1963) is the first-person narration of a perverted psychopath, Fred Clegg, who abducts a talented

---

[9]   Cf. Jürgen Habermas, *The Structural Transformation of the Public Sphere: An Enquiry into a Category of Bourgeois Society*, trans. Thomas Burger and Frederick Lawrence, Cambridge, 1989 [1962].

young female art student and keeps her prisoner in his cellar, under the delusion that he could win her affection or even her love. The second part of the novel consists of the extremely upsetting diary entries that Miranda (the abducted woman) writes secretly in her dungeon, to maintain her sanity or to leave something behind for posterity. I won't give away what happens in the third part, which is once again narrated by her kidnapper. The (incorporated) diary often functions as the last residuum of a self that's in danger of breaking apart under the pressure of the outside world – as the last bastion of self-communion, the place where identity and individuality find their final refuge (think of George Orwell's *Nineteen Eighty-Four*).

Since we've already discussed present-tense narration, we can examine a further possibility to shorten the distance between narrating self and experiencing self: interior monologue. Interior monologue is written as though we were following an individual's thoughts in real time – following her unstructured stream of consciousness, with all its momentary associations, recollections, volatile jumps. This technique was first used in Edouard Dujardin's *Les Lauriers sont coupés* (1888), while in German literature one thinks first of Arthur Schnitzler's *Leutnant Gustl* (1901) and *Fräulein Else* (1924), as well as of passages from Alfred Döblin's *Berlin Alexanderplatz* (1930) or Hermann Broch's *Der Tod des Vergil* [*The Death of Virgil*] (1945). But the most famous interior monologue in all of world literature is surely the monologue of Molly Bloom in the crucial chapter "Penelope" in James Joyce's *Ulysses*, which stretches over about 35 pages without full-stops or commas.[10] Molly Bloom is lying in bed, long after midnight, and this is what we read:

> Yes because he never did a thing like that before as ask to get his breakfast in bed with a couple of eggs since the City Arms hotel when he used to be pretending to be laid up with a sick voice doing his highness to make himself interesting for that old faggot Mrs. Riordan that he thought he had a great leg of and she never left us a farthing all for masses for herself and her soul greatest miser ever was actually afraid to lay out 4d for her methylated spirit telling me all her ailments she had too much old chat in her about politics and earthquakes and the end of the world let us have a bit of fun first God help the world if all the women were her sort down on bathingsuits and lownecks of course nobody wanted her to wear them I suppose she was pious because no man would look at her twice I hope Ill never be like her a wonder she didn't want us to cover our faces but she was a welleducated woman certainly and her gabby talk about Mr. Riordan here and Mr. Riordan there I suppose he was glad to get shut of her and her dog smelling my fur and always edging to get up under my petticoats especially then still I like that in him polite to old women like that and waiters and beggars too

[10]   Dorrit Cohn uses the term "quoted monologue" instead of interior monologue, and calls Molly Bloom's monologue an "autonomous monologue": cf. Dorrit Cohn, *Transparent Minds: Narrative Modes for Presenting Consciousness in Fiction*, Princeton, NJ, 1978, 58–98, 217–232. However, neither term has caught on.

We see that although an "I" is speaking, there is no longer any *narration* taking place (assuming narration means selecting, processing, mediating). Rather, this is a *copy*, a *representation* – and that's why in Stanzel's typological circle, "Penelope" is to the left of the boundary line separating s/he and I and below the boundary line separating the teller-character from the reflector-character in a segment of the circle lying exactly between the "pure" first-person narrative situation and the "pure" figural narrative situation. Thus Stanzel's scheme can precisely capture the particularity of a key text of m.

The narrative forms we have just mentioned attempt to approach the experiencing self as closely as possible. On the other hand there are also, as we noted, narrative forms that focus instead on the narrating self (the extreme example of this is surely *Tristram Shandy* again, in which just about the sole topic seems to be narration by a self – a singularly distinctive and amusing kind of self-referentiality). If the focus is on the narrating self, however, the time that has passed meanwhile must somehow be thematized, the intervening period must somehow be covered – *these* first-person narrators can't behave as though nothing had happened in the meantime. They must present and disclose their *relation* to what is gone by, not just at the concluding point, when narrating self and experiencing self conventionally merge, but actually during the narration itself.

One of the most persuasive examples of a successful mediation of a narrative past and a narrative present is Kazuo Ishiguro's novel *The Remains of the Day*. It's the story of the butler Stevens, who in July 1956 takes a six-day tour of the English West Country in order to visit a Miss Kenton. She had once worked, as Stevens still does, at a country seat called Darlington Hall. Stevens is totally wrapped up in his work as a butler, identifies himself with it, and has never allowed himself any opinions of his own. The journey becomes for him a partly painful journey into his own past when he is forced to admit, following a painstakingly meticulous reconstruction of decisive events and situations in his life, that things perhaps happened differently, that such-and-such didn't happen on that evening but on another, that these words maybe weren't spoken exactly like that or not at all. It's probably most painful when he is forced to admit to himself that his conception of the duty and honor of a butler, namely following his superiors unconditionally in everything and never stepping out of his role, had actually led to a devastating moral failure – is even, strictly speaking, *identical* with moral failure. "I can't even say I made my own mistakes." Thus it's actually the process of narration and "present-ing" the past, of bringing the past to present consciousness, that has led to partial self-understanding. It's a triumph of contemporary English novel-writing that the character of Stevens comes to light no less through the manner of his narration than through what he tells, and that the reader can recognize beyond the political and moral failure a further personal sin of omission, a private blindness, about which we don't know precisely how long it will still continue. Such first-person narratives demonstrate something in their narration: in this case the (minimal) possibility of revising one's self-image through narration, at the end of the day, and the difficulty of learning to walk tall after a life of stooping. It's therefore more than doubtful whether the reviewer for a major German newspaper had really understood the point of the book when he wrote that the German reading public couldn't take that much interest in British butlers.

Although the virtues of the first-person narrative situation are often extolled, because it eases the reader's identification with the narrating character and allows a fresh and subjective viewpoint and presentation of the material, it is also conceded that in this situation the narration is always necessarily limited, due to the internal perspective. That needn't necessarily exclude the possibility that this narrative situation can lay out *a whole world*: that an exemplary relationship to the world can certainly be shown using *one* "I," we can easily see in *Robinson Crusoe* and the middle-class world picture it exemplifies. But if a novelist is aiming to unroll a great *panorama* of a society and culture, to write an illustrated broadsheet of history, then the subjective perspective of a single character is clearly not the ideal means.

So how about an alternation between points of view, several first-person narrators in a row? Such multiperspectivity can certainly offer a gain in breadth and depth, but the two principal narrators in Jeanette Winterson's *Sexing the Cherry* (1989) (one a monstrous masculine woman, the other her nice, well-behaved adopted son – their sections of the text are marked with a banana and a pineapple, respectively, to highlight the gender-crossover), or the seven female narrators in Pat Barker's *Union Street* (1982), or the multiperspectival novels *The Moonstone* (1868) and *The Woman in White* (1860) by Wilkie Collins, all remind me of Bertrand Russell's remark that a pile of chocolate bars always amounts to a pile of chocolate bars and not something else. In other words: mere addition cannot produce a leap out of the internal perspective. The addition of subjectively limited perspectives always amounts to just a higher number of subjectively limited perspectives. Instead, though, such an addition provides something different and possibly even more important, viz. a questioning of the supposition that objective reality is something like the intersubjective intersection of subjective perspectives.

Even in the multiperspectival epistolary novel the introduction of further letter-writers doesn't necessarily lead to mutual confirmation, but it is equally (or more) likely to give rise to conflicts between the reports and mutual questioning of them. (And this always implicitly calls into question the very attempt to fake reality in *that* way.) The problems appear similar in the case of multiperspectival narration (outside the epistolary novel), and so multiperspectival narration – which we'll come to in detail later – is employed not primarily to confirm "reality," but to take it apart, to deconstruct it. The aim is not a great panorama, but a reflection of the way experience is parceled up, proof of the incommensurability of different reports.

Lawrence Durrell's series of novels *The Alexandria Quartett* presents a grandiose scene: Alexandria on the eve of World War II. In the first three parts of the trilogy "the same" event is remembered and narrated from three different perspectives. In *Justine* (1957) the teacher and writer Darley narrates his affair with the attractive, married nymphomaniac Justine. Darley finds many relationships between other characters puzzling and hard to get to the bottom of – he embarks on the effortful task of remembering, and in his narration he produces *his* truth. *Balthazar* (1958) is the interlinear version of *Justine*, by Darley's friend Balthazar, commenting on and correcting the former's narrative. Now it emerges that Justine was never really in love with Darley and had just used him to hide another affair that was more important to her. *Mountolive* (likewise 1958) brings in the third perspective, and now it seems as though all Justine's affairs served only as a smokescreen to conceal a plot to overthrow the Egyptian royal family. Finally, *Clea* (1960) is the one of the four novels that's set a bit later, and it leaves the riddles remaining from the first three works unsolved – to some critics' disappointment. But the multiplication of perspectives is only that: it presents subjective truths which don't have to "amount" to anything, and certainly not to "the Truth." Nor do they "solve" anything. Such is life.

In time, one may gain perspective and see some things in a different way (just as other people had already seen things in a different way and are now seeing things differently again from how they saw them then). We'll never experience how it "really" was, because there's no such thing as how it "really" was. At least not in the first-person narrative situation, which nevertheless invites such trust and confidence, parading as it does the idea that *I'm* telling you, because *I* was there – and then splits that narrating self, the indivisible individual, in order to weave its paradoxical spell.

4   The Impossibility of the Familiar: The Authorial Narrative Situation

It's fruitless to argue about whether the first-person narrative situation or the authorial narrative situation strikes us as more "normal" or "natural." First, the two are about equally common. Second, both possibilities – that of narrating *from* a fictional world or *about* a fictional world – seem logically equally plausible, the key feature of both techniques being the evocation of a world. And third, since they are so heavily conventionalized, both narrative situations are easily "readable" and familiar to us.

Unless we question these conventions for a moment – if the text of the novel doesn't do that already. If we look a bit closer, we see that the novel does this surprisingly often. Even if it doesn't directly thematize its conventions, it exhibits them now and then in such a conspicuous way that we're invited to think them over carefully. Although some novels also attempt with radical consistency to cover up their own practice, that attempt is doomed to failure every time, because a text's own narrative practice inevitably lies open to view (successfully to hide how they tick, texts would have to cancel themselves altogether). But one such paradoxical attempt completely to cover up the novel's own practice, to put a taboo on its own foundations, is (alongside the first-person narrative situation) the most familiar type of all: the authorial narrative situation in its pure form.

The authorial narrative situation *par excellence* is characterized, as we noted above, by an omniscient narrator standing outside the fictional world s/he narrates, a world over which s/he can exercise absolute control. Omniscience and absolute power are just two sides of the same coin: if the narrator jumps one moment back into the past, the next forward into the future, looks now into this character and now into that, then conducts an Olympian panoramic survey of the whole, then this free, totally unlimited dealing as s/he sees fit is both proof and exercise of unrestricted authorial narration.

And we enjoy it. For this absolute sovereignty is *in principle* not subject to the mean, nagging doubt that assails every first-person narrative: how this narrative relates to the "truth" of the story, which first-person narrative can "only" construct subjectively (and so perhaps wrongly). By contrast, the authorial narrative situation blazes forth the full glory of infallibility. The authorial narrator says: it was so. And so it was. After all, s/he must know: s/he created this whole world in its totality (without being of this world).

Undoubtedly, we enjoy it because this godlike perspective seems to make everything possible: the extreme close-up and the long shot, the most sophisticated psychological dissection of a character, pursued into the finest ramifications of consciousness (but why only *one* character? *every* character!), as well as great panoramas of society with dozens, or even hundreds of characters, who industriously play their part in the great social machine, do their work and go about various kinds of business.

No wonder then that the great panoptic social panoramas of the nineteenth century – from Charles Dickens' melodramatic novels demanding a reconciliation of opposites (e.g., *Hard Times*, 1854, or *Oliver Twist*); through Honoré de Balzac's monumental portrait of manners in the cycle *Comédie humaine*, originally planned to span 130 volumes (e.g., *Père Goriot*, 1834); to Emile Zola's naturalistic 20-volume cycle of novels *Les Rougon-Macquarts* (e.g., *Germinal*, 1885); as well as singular monuments like George Eliot's *Middlemarch* (1871/72), Victor Hugo's *Les Misérables* (1862), or Stendhal's *Le Rouge et le noir* (1830) – are every one of them written with predominantly authorial narration. The large format seems to require the external perspective.

The advantages of this narrative situation leap off the page – and not only in retrospect. An author who wants to define the place of the individual within the whole, to fathom the sense or non-sense of this totality, to examine a community's humanity, could hardly make a better choice – or so it would seem. But if you take refuge in the security of an almighty being, if you place your confidence in absolute reliability and omniscience, you're also in for bitter disappointments from time to time: almighty beings can tend to arbitrariness or to disconcerting, cold, and cynical indifference.

That's for example how the chapter titles of the first book of Henry Fielding's novel *The History of Tom Jones, a Foundling*, read:

Book I

Containing as much of the birth of the foundling as is necessary or proper to acquaint the reader with the beginning of this history

Chapter

1   The introduction to the work, or bill of fare to the feast
2   A short description of Squire Allworthy and a fuller account of Miss Bridget Allworthy, his sister
3   An odd accident which befell Mr. Allworthy at his return home
    The decent behaviour of Mrs. Deborah Wilkins, with some proper animadversions on bastards
4   The reader's neck brought into danger by a description; his escape, and the great condescension of Miss Bridget Allworthy
5   Containing a few common matters, with a very uncommon observation upon them
6   Mrs. Deborah is introduced into the parish with a simile. A short account of Jenny Jones, with the difficulties and discouragements which may attend young women in pursuit of learning
7   Containing such grave matter that the reader cannot laugh once through the whole chapter, unless peradventure he should laugh at the author
8   A dialogue between Mesdames Bridget and Deborah, containing more amusement but less instruction than the former
9   Containing matters which will surprise the reader
10 The hospitality of Allworthy with a short sketch of the characters of two brothers, a doctor and a captain, who were entertained by that gentleman
11 Containing many rules, and some examples, concerning falling in love; descriptions of beauty, and other more prudential inducements to matrimony
12 Containing what the reader may, perhaps, expect to find in it
13 Which concludes the first book; with an instance of ingratitude which, we hope, will appear unnatural

Whether through such enigmatic announcements as "The reader's neck brought into danger by a description" or such apodictic predictions as "Containing such grave matter that the reader cannot laugh once throughout the whole chapter," the authorial narrator parades his absolute power and exercises it. It's entirely up to him whether he makes a description short or long, or gives or withholds information. The title of the whole first book has already said it all: how much *must* the reader know? How much is appropriate? The authorial narrator alone decides – it's his privilege, and he doesn't only exercise it in matters of little import: the most important piece of information, which he withholds from us until the very end of the novel, is the fact that the foundling Tom Jones is in fact the child of Bridget Allworthy and not of Jenny, who has been wrongly blamed. Had this information been given right at the beginning, *Tom Jones* would have been a very different kind of novel indeed. It's not only in crime novels that the authorial narrator must be allowed to keep something back: that's not just a rule of the game, but a basic precondition on which such narrative texts operate.

The authorial narrator of *Tom Jones* does that in a very playful, amusing, ingenious, and witty way. That's why we tolerate his teasing play with his knowledge and our own ignorance – the manipulation is blatant and necessary. Nevertheless, it's impossible to overlook the unlimited and illimitable arbitrariness of the narrator and our complete dependence on this arbitrariness (because of the omniscience and omnipotence of the authorial narrator this possibility is here infinitely greater than with a first-person narrator). And this absolute arbitrariness casts a shadow even when it is temporarily not exercised. The possibility looms.

The Driver's Seat by Muriel Spark, mentioned above, is about a psychologically disturbed young woman who systematically (and at last successfully) provokes and stages her own murder. An authorial narrator tells the story in the present tense, but with foreshadowings and flashbacks. The events unfold as though with clockwork inevitability, and the narrator tracks them with so little participation that many readers get the sense of the cold eye of God following a tragic sequence with absolute indifference, a sequence that surely (these readers feel) should at least have aroused some sort of emotion or empathy. That would seem to be the human reaction. And precisely that is the decisive point – a category mistake. The lurking question we could ask the sovereign juggler of *Tom Jones*, who coquettishly flaunts the power and art of his narrative, as well as the cold chronicler of *The Driver's Seat*, is "How could you possibly?!" But that question always misses its target. For the authorial narrator (it cannot be emphasized enough) is neither a human being nor a character, but an aspect of the text that we – usually without foundation – anthropomorphize, because when we encounter a "voice," we automatically imagine someone speaking, a person. Some critics consider that we could prevent this category mistake if instead of using "authorial narrator" we'd refer to this textual phenomenon as *Erzählinstanz*, which can be translated as either narrating instance or, better still, narrative authority; these non-anthropomorphic terms would forestall any confusion of categories: an authorial narrator is not a person. But I wonder whether this would really help. As long as people prefer to read novels rather than monographs on narratology, they will continue to infer a speaking person from the narrating voice – it's not as though they read "narrator" and are misled by the term. And all the others are saved already, of course.

"How could you possibly?!" is the first question – a legitimate one but at the same time dead wrong. A second question often follows it like a twin arrow, and it is equally off the mark, though it has far more fatal consequences. "How do you know all that?" Never shall you ask me. That's the one question that we are *never* allowed to ask the authorial narrator. *The trouble-free working of the whole narrative situation depends on that question not being asked.* As soon as it is asked, it's already too late: all innocence is lost, for whoever enquires of the Absolute the basis of its omnipotence and omniscience will soon hit on the fact that it is – obviously – an illusionary construct. A construct that functions pretty well, as long as we don't see through its "impossible" construction. But even after it has been seen through (in another connection, Freud's formulation was "the future of an illusion") it's still good for something: it shows how something like that *generally* functions – the illusion of an inhuman or rather superhuman narrative machine, a sense-and-meaning-making machine from beyond. Let's scrutinize the trick, now that the spell is broken and the magic is gone.

With regard to the great social panoramas of the nineteenth century we noted that the large format demands an external perspective (how can a totality be presented from *within*?), demands in fact the omniscience of a narrator that is ontologically set apart: such a project could not be undertaken by an individual "like us." But this external perspective on the fictional world – which in these "large loose baggy monsters" (as Henry James called these nineteenth-century tomes – though his own volumes weren't exactly slimline!)[11] carries the traits of the author's contemporary society and of the author's understanding of it – is indeed barely more than the *internal* perspective of the author on his society, shot into space, as it were – and now consecrated with the greater glory of a perspective that is no longer humanly limited, but occupies a truly transcendental standpoint. As a rule, novelists make their authorial narrators in their own image.

Novels narrated exclusively by an authorial narrator are about one thing above all: *this* way of seeing the world. Mario Vargas Llosa comments on the situation in Victor Hugo's monumental work *Les Misérables*:

> One of the most ambitious narrative creations of the nineteenth century – the golden age of the novel – *Les Misérables* is steeped in all the great social, cultural, and political events of its time and in all of Victor Hugo's personal experiences over the nearly thirty years he spent writing it (he returned to the manuscript several times after abandoning it for long intervals). It is no exaggeration to say that the novel includes a formidable display of exhibitionism and egomania on

---

[11] Henry James, "Preface," *The Tragic Muse* (New York Edition 7), New York, 1908, x.

the part of its narrator. The narrator is omniscient, technically separate from the world of the narrative, observing from outside the space where the lives of Jean Valjean, Monseigneur Bienvenu, Gavroche, Marius, Cosette, and the other abundant human fauna of the novel intersect. But in truth, the narrator is more present in the tale than the characters themselves: possessed of a proud and overbearing nature and seized by an irresistible megalomania, he can't keep from constantly revealing himself as he presents the story to us. Often he interrupts the action, shifts into the first-person singular from the third to weigh in on whatever he likes, pontificates on philosophy, history, morality, and religion, and judges his characters, mercilessly condemning them or praising them to the heavens for their civic-minded and spiritual inclinations. This narrator-God (and the epithet was never better employed) not only gives us constant proof of his existence and of the lesser and dependent status of the narrative world but also reveals to us – besides his convictions and theories – his phobias and sympathies, proceeding without the slightest discretion or precaution or scruple, convinced of the truth and justice of everything he thinks, says, or does in the name of his cause. [... it is] the story of the narrator, whose embellishments, exclamations, reflections, judgments, whims, and sermons constitute the intellectual context, an ideological–philosophical–moral backdrop to the text.[12]

This might also be the root of the third common misunderstanding of the authorial narrative situation (we've already discussed the first two), namely the idea that the narrator is – "somehow" – to be identified with the *author* of the novel. *Contra* certain vigorous attempts to reintroduce the author or even authorial intention as crucial categories of textual analysis and interpretation,[13] it's necessary to state unequivocally that an identification of the narrator of a story with its author is impossible. No matter what you may think of authors and their opinions and intentions, the authorial narrator is *never* identical with the author, and never *can* be: the author is a *human being* of flesh and blood, and usually dead (one can say this without having to be an adherent of Roland Barthes), whereas the narrator is an *aspect of the text*, therefore not a living being, therefore immortal. This confusion – which is by no means confined to beginners in literary interpretation – points to a suspicious trace at the scene of the crime: the reader has, as it were, stumbled over the rocket-launcher of the "external perspective" and now, like Mr. Truman in *The Truman Show*, has doubts about the reality of his reality. The only difference is that the reader now, in a knee-jerk reaction, tends to deny all art and contrivance and lump everything together as "life," instead of gaining the reverse insight: that *all* this is art, a construct pure and simple.

[12]   Mario Vargas Llosa, *Letters to a Young Novelist*, trans. Natasha Wimmer, New York, 2002, 52–53.
[13]   Cf. Fotis Jannidis et al. (eds.), *Rückkehr des Autors: Zur Erneuerung eines umstrittenen Begriffs*, Tübingen, 1999; and Fotis Jannidis et al. (eds.), *Texte zur Theorie der Autorschaft*, Stuttgart, 2000.

So this is how it works: an extrapolated subjective standpoint is passed off as a transcendental standpoint, and when the latter projects itself back onto the text, it appears as a totalizing view "from outside" the narrated world. There must be no misunderstanding: this is perfectly legitimate, because in art anything is legitimate, as long as it works. It isn't even logically problematic, since the narrator's omniscience relates to the narrated, fictional world, not to our own world. This narrative situation is only paradoxical because it uses a *human* standpoint (what else?) to create or suggest the impression of a superhuman perspective, whose claim to have access to the *whole* of the narrated world (a claim the first-person narrative situation would never venture) is based precisely on the premise that it is impossible for human beings to attain such a perspective. To put it more pointedly: *the heightened claim to truth highlighted or assumed in the authorial narrative situation is founded on the fact that its perspective is impossible.*

Of course, it's possible in the sense that novels do in fact continue to construct it – this is done; but it's "impossible" in the sense that this narrative situation must constantly – by definition – pass itself off as something it is not. The authorial narrative situation is mimicry, deception, fabrication. We shouldn't feel scandalized by this, since we meet with it in *literature*, where we always have to be ready for such things. But this narrative situation (familiar though it is – incidentally in terms of "content" it has achieved the greatest triumphs of realism notwithstanding the most unrealistic narrative technique imaginable) brings with it an even more fundamental paradox. The great paradox of a text that largely operates with the authorial narrative situation is as follows: exactly at moments when it completely forgoes thematizing its own narrative legitimacy – *exactly* at those moments when it appears not to ask the question "anything wrong with this?" – it reveals itself as an "impossible" construct. To the extent to which an authorially narrated novel unswervingly exercises its prerogative to narrate in a humanly *impossible* way, it emerges that this can only be the working of illusion, the deceptive effect of a construction. This narrative situation is never more clearly "just art" than when it tries to be more than that – when it tries instead to simulate a superhuman authority communicating human sense and meaning.

It's possible to descend from the pedestal of omniscience in two directions – and Stanzel's typological circle illustrates this, too. Either you go in the direction of the first-person narrative situation via a "personalization"[14] of the authorial narrator, or in the direction of the figural narrative situation via a

[14]   This is the first and last time I use this term, even though it seems to me quite an appropriate one. It's appropriate for the phenomenon whereby the narrative authority is increasingly endowed with "human" traits and characteristics; but alas! Stanzel (consistently for his own system) already uses "personalization" to denote the movement of the authorial narrator towards the figural narrative situation, i.e., exactly to denote the reverse. To avoid misunderstandings, then, I must resort to ugly phrases like "humanizing the narrative authority."

gradual fading out of the authorial narrator. By the way, neither of these options by any means resolves the paradox of the authorial narrative situation – as we'll see shortly. Let's take the anticlockwise movement around the typological circle first, in the direction of the first-person narrative situation.

As I pointed out earlier, it's not fair to charge the authorial narrator in Spark's *The Driver's Seat* with cold indifference, since you can't accuse an *impersonal entity* of something that is a matter of reproach only in a *person*. However, a fascinating passage in chapter 3 of Thomas Mann's *Lotte in Weimar* (1939), which actually discusses the "divine author" Goethe, claims a fundamental link between omniscience, omnipotence, and omnipresence on the one hand and cold indifference on the other – a link that's worth pausing over:

> Can you imagine the Lord God inspired? No, you can't. He is the object of our enthusiasm; but to Him it is necessarily foreign. One ascribes to him a peculiar coldness, an annihilating equanimity. For what should He feel enthusiasm, on whose side should He stand? For he is the whole, he is his own side, he stands on his own side, and his attitude is one of all-embracing irony [...] If God is all, then he is also the devil; and one cannot approach the godlike without at the same time approaching to the diabolic – so that, in a manner of speaking, heaven looks at you out of one eye, and the hell of the iciest negation and most destructive neutrality out of the other. But whether they lie close together or far apart, it is two eyes, my dearest lady, that make up one gaze. So now I ask you: what sort of gaze is that wherein the horrifying contradiction of the two eyes is united? I will tell you, tell you and myself: it is the gaze of absolute art, which is at once absolute love and absolute nihilism and indifference and implies that horrifying approach to the godlike-diabolic which we call greatness.[15]

You don't have to sweepingly generalize this insight into the argument that, in Mann's words, "comprehensive irony," the ambiguity of the detached–aesthetic viewpoint, is actually the proper and characteristic stance of the novel as the dominant "artform of our time"[16] – in a phase in which the pure poetry of literature was supposed to be utterly separate from conscious, reflexive criticism – in order to admit that this cool irony, which distances itself from the (narrated) "actual facts," has a very strong affinity with the authorial narrative pose. This narrative pose imitates a very particular relationship to the world, for irony – ironic distance – can always be read as a sign of *seeing through* something; and seeing through comes more naturally to the authorial narrative situation than to any other.

If, however, this "curious coldness," "annihilating equanimity," and "comprehensive irony" are not just inevitable accompaniments of a super-

---

[15]   Translation based on that by H. T. Lowe-Porter, Berkeley, 1940.
[16]   Thomas Mann, "Die Kunst des Romans" (1940), in *Romantheorie: Texte vom Barock bis zur Gegenwart*, ed. Hartmut Steinecke and Fritz Wahrenburg, Stuttgart, 1999, 443.

human, non-committal view – if irony is, rather, really foregrounded, then we have to reckon with a special kind of shift:

> It is a truth universally acknowledged, that a single man in possession of a good fortune must be in want of a wife.
>   However little known the feelings or views of such a man may be on his first entering a neighbourhood, this truth is so well fixed in the minds of the surrounding families that he is considered as the rightful property of some one or other of their daughters.

This opening of Jane Austen's *Pride and Prejudice*, which was quoted briefly once before, shows us – as the further course of the novel will bear out – an authorial narrator who is equipped with clearly recognizable *human* traits. It's obvious what effect is intended here: humanizing the authorial narrative voice is meant to close a credibility gap which has opened up because of the epistemological impossibility of the authorial narrative situation. The authorial narrator – actually not a human being at all – now strikes the reader as human. This happens quite often: an authorial narrator who, on the one hand, is imaginable as a person, as a human being owing to the manner of his or her narration, choice of words, commentaries, and value judgments, and who, on the other hand, has given up few authorial privileges, if any. This is an authorial narrator fitted out as a person, a "totally human" incarnation of a superhuman idea – come to think of it, an absurdity.

This hybrid form allows the novelist to combine two advantages: the perspective is not as subjectively limited as in the first-person narrative situation, yet the humanized narrator involves the reader through his judgments and remarks, through a *particular* personal way of telling things, much more easily and more strongly than is possible for a strictly neutral, "inhuman" mediator. The authorial narrator equipped with human traits is the attempt to have the cake and eat it, too. The indisputable narrative gain (for this model does function successfully, as early as *Tom Jones*) is, however, bought at a high price: the impossibility of the authorial situation. For although, as far as the authorial situation in its pure form is concerned, one could still counter the criticism that (as we discussed above) this omniscience is that of an impersonal authority that is "in fact" nothing more than a constructed illusion, in the case of the humanized authorial narrator this argument for the defense is no longer valid. This narrator is in vital ways *supposed* to be like a person – and at the same time, in equally vital ways, entirely unlike any real person. This narrator is the friendly face of the impersonal authority, the porter of the Hotel Authorial.

Novels that employ this narrative situation want the one aspect without sacrificing the other. They mix the divine with childish caprice, and there's no one to deny the author this privilege – no one except the reader. But if readers *share* the attitude and judgments of the humanized authorial narrator, they won't find the illegitimacy of the narrative logic much of a stumbling block. Only when you feel that the narrator shouldn't ironize something that you consider important, or shouldn't make derogatory comments about something you hold dear, are you likely to enquire about the basis of those judgments, or having recognized that they are subjectively limited, to ask about the source of that privileged knowledge that *cannot* be subjectively limited – that knowledge (so the train of thought might continue) that we might happily accept from a higher judge, but less happily from someone who is so obviously prejudiced. The authorial narrative situation cannot resolve this inherent contradiction, but can only augment it and make it appear more blatant.

Anthony Trollope's *Barchester Towers* (1857), the second in his series of Barsetshire novels, is a case in point. The six novels provide a social panorama of mid-Victorian society in the provinces (comparable in this respect with George Eliot's *Middlemarch* or Elizabeth Gaskell's *Cranford*, 1851–1853). *Barchester Towers* humorously but mercilessly critiques the Anglican Church as one of the main pillars of the Victorian establishment. The authorial narrator, however, is not just obviously jovial and garrulous, but also has a firm opinion about the central conflict between the partisans of High Church and Low Church. (This opinion comes to light not only when the two Low Church representatives, Proudie and Slope – the one an opportunist, the other a hypocrite – are eventually hounded out of the city.) Further, this authorial narrator is so entirely a child of his time and community, and thus *part of his readership and their world*, that he can refrain from spelling out what is common knowledge (opening of chapter 2):

> It is hardly necessary that I should here give to the public any lengthened biography of Mr. Harding, up to the period of the commencement of this tale. The public cannot have forgotten how ill that sensitive gentleman bore the attack that was made on him in the columns of the Jupiter, with reference to the income which he received as warden of Hiram's Hospital, in the city of Barchester. Nor can it yet be forgotten that a lawsuit was instituted against him on the matter of that charity by Mr. John Bold, who afterwards married his, Mr. Harding's, younger and then only unmarried daughter.

The last sentence here does after all give information that is *necessary*, because no reader can possibly have it unless it's given to him (Barchester doesn't "really exist"). There's no need to labor that point – but it does serve to underline the fact that this narrator is so strongly humanized, so much a part of the world he narrates, that *Barchester Towers* cannot, *pace* its position on Stanzel's typological circle, belong to the central sector of the authorial narrative situation. It's true that this narrator lives outside the world of his characters, *insofar as* (but *only* insofar as) he doesn't interact or communicate with them, but he is clearly marked out as a witness and a contemporary. On Stanzel's circle, *Barchester Towers* should therefore be moved a good 60° to the left.

So Stanzel has made a mistake in categorization, despite the fact that the narrator in Trollope's novel even (for example, at the beginning of chapter 3) admits his own ignorance (albeit regarding a peripheral matter) and denies having privileged access to any information whatsoever. But how could so exact a reader and analyst as Franz K. Stanzel fall into this error? (Beware: the book you hold in your hands might not be completely error-free in that respect either!) There is an easy explanation. The narrator's declarations do not affect the flow of his story at all – *of course* he's showing us Barchester "as it really is," *of course* he's exercising his privilege: that's the ineluctable impression. But *at the same time* the humanization of the authorial narrator means that we can't really attribute an external perspective to him in the sense that there would be an unmistakable ontological difference between the narrator and his characters. Sometimes he is not of this world, sometimes he is very obtrusively so – and readers with Low Church sympathies might be quicker than others to note instances of the latter.

Stanzel himself, in his *Theory of Narrative*, notes a more serious case of a narratological rupture. The narrator of Thackeray's *Vanity Fair* – in any case a model example of authorial narration, especially if we recall the above-quoted metaphor of the puppet-master! – makes the following surprising declaration in chapter 62:

> It was on this very tour that I, the present writer of a history of which every word is true, had the pleasure to see them first, and to make their acquaintance.
>
> It was at the little comfortable Ducal town of Pumpernickel (that very place where Sir Pitt Crawley had been so distinguished as an *attaché*; but that was in early early days, and before the news of the battle of Austerlitz sent all the English diplomatists in Germany to the right about) that I first saw Colonel Dobbin and his party.

What's happening is that the puppet-master joins the company of his characters and enters the stage himself – true, still rather as an observer than as an agent among others, but also in such a way that no ontological difference can be discerned between him and his characters. But how can that be? Stanzel comments:

> With this transfer of his narrator into the world of Amelia, Becky, Jos Sedley and Dobin, Thackeray invites criticism for inconsistency in the conception of his narrator, since the narrator introduced himself in the preface to the novel ("Before the Curtain") as "manager of the Performance" and had also fully assumed the traditional privileges of omniscience and the right of disposition over the characters as authorial narrator. The narrator's appearance as a young contemporary and fellow visitor in Pumpernickel would seem to require that he renounce these privileges as Olympian narrator. Thackeray actually makes a gesture in this direction. In Chapter LXXVI the narrator hints that Tapeworm, the British chargé d'affaires at the court of Pumpernickel, is the direct source of his detailed knowledge of Becky's story. The perspective of the presentation

is in no way influenced by this suggestion, however. No restriction of the horizon of knowledge of the teller-character corresponding to the reference of his source takes place. We must, therefore, look elsewhere for the reason for this shift of the authorial narrative situation in the direction of the first-person narrative situation.[17]

Stanzel suggests that the reason may lie "in the need of the authorial narrator to furnish his personality with a physical existence, to transform himself from an abstract functional role into a figure of flesh and blood, a person with an individual history."[18] With all due respect for Stanzel, that reminds me of the moment in Thomas Mann's *Buddenbrooks* (1901) when the cause of poverty is ingeniously attributed, by one of the characters, to *la pauvreté*. It is uncontroversial that Thackeray's authorial narrator himself is here provided with the seed of a story of personal development, although as a rule an authorial narrator "tells the story of his character from a fixed point in time with a fixed personality, that is, often without personal recollection of his own past."[19]

This paradox is not explained and certainly not resolved. Its effect and the circumstances of its appearance at precisely this point in the novel nevertheless seem to be clear: at this point the authorially mediated illusion of the reality of this materialistic society without heroes is so unshakably established that the reader can only be reminded of the fiction of this reality by means of this "impossible" ruse. The appearance of the authorial narrator among his characters – by the twentieth century no longer a scandalous topos – serves to foreground the novel's technique: it thematizes the principles of narrative by breaking the very conventions of narrative (in a way that can't be glossed over). If that is so, however, this metaphysical move from the board can't be represented on Stanzel's circle of narrative situations. On the one hand, the narrator is an authorial narrator, and on the other, since he takes part in the world of his characters, he is actually a (closet) first-person narrator. We can't blame the circle for not being able to show *something that is intended to break narrative logic*. Nevertheless it's worth bearing in mind that Stanzel's scheme does not have any systematic place for forms of metafictional self-thematization and self-interrogation in narrative. (Just to be clear – Génette's system doesn't provide for this either.)[20]

[17]   Stanzel, *Theory of Narrative*, 204.

[18]   Stanzel, *Theory of Narrative*, 204.

[19]   Stanzel, *Theory of Narrative*, 205.

[20]   Another interesting kind of narrative that neither Stanzel's nor Genette's schemes can represent is the narration that consistently uses the second-person form of address – "you." The most famous examples are Italo Calvino's novel about reading, *If on a Winter's Night a Traveler* (first published in Italian in 1979, translated by Wiliam Weaver in 1981), Michel Butors's *La Modification* (1957), and Jay McInerney's *Bright Lights, Big City* (1984); but one might also think of Zoran Drvenkar's *Cengiz & Locke* (2002). The effect is extremely unrealistic (cf. Monika Fludernik, "Introduction: Second-Person Narrative and Related Issues," *Style* 28/3

As we round off our consideration of the "I"-admixtures within the essentially authorial narrative situation, it might be useful to make a further critical point: perhaps the phenomenon "I as editor" is also placed misleadingly on Stanzel's circle. Whether we think of Thomas Carlyle's *Sartor Resartus* (1833–1834, 1836), or of Jonathan Swift's *Gulliver's Travels* (1726), even though the worlds of Professor Teufelsdröckh or Lemuel Gulliver may be foreign and strange to their respective editors, their worlds do nevertheless present a possible continuum with their own. They are bound to each other by a link of ontological contiguity, because they touch each other: and so it's not easy to see why novels with an "I as editor" should lie beyond the "internal-perspective/external-perspective" boundary line, assuming we understand that boundary line as ontological and not merely as geographical or historical (that is, not like the boundary that is evoked by the editor of the story in Nathaniel Hawthorne's *The Scarlet Letter* [1850], for example). As far as the novels that Stanzel takes as examples are concerned, the boundary line separating "I" from "s/he" is absolute; but it seems to me that the same cannot be said with such certainty about the "internal-perspective/external-perspective" boundary line.

The second possible path of descent from the Olympus of authorial omniscience is for the narrator gradually to retreat and make ever-decreasing use of narrative privileges. However, that also means that such a narrator makes ever-decreasing use of the possibilities of narrative *mediation per se*, and ultimately resorts to a scenic presentation. This procedure alleviates the main suspicion about the knowledge possessed by a non-first-person narrator, because it only displays what would have been observable – or better,

---

[1994]: 281–311, here 290, as well as the whole issue of this journal edited by Fludernik and dedicated to this topic). This is not so much because we can't deduce the narrator's standpoint from the second person (as Mario Vargas Llosa argues in *Letters to a Young Novelist*, 44), as because the situation of the "you" – at least at the beginning ("You are about to begin reading Italo Calvino's new novel, *If on a Winter's Night a Traveler*. Relax. Concentrate. Dispel every other thought. Let the world around you fade. Best to close the door; the TV is always on in the next room"), and by chance also at the end ("[She] closes her book, turns off her light, puts her head back against the pillow, and says, 'Turn off your light, too. Aren't you tired of reading?' And you say, 'Just a moment, I've almost finished *If on a Winter's Night a Traveler* by Italo Calvino.'") – coincides with the actual reader's, yet everywhere else diverges from it and *must* diverge from it to such an extent that realistically speaking we can only perceive one of two things: (1) a process of someone becoming conscious during a long-drawn period of talking to himself (this is the impression we get from Butor), or (2) a discourse directed at someone plagued by radical amnesia and delivered by some sort of eternal companion who, in turn, must be suffering from logorrhea. Calvino's *If on a Winter's Night a Traveler* is proof that the effect can be amusing in a highly intelligent and ambitious way. Cf., in general, Monika Fludernik, "Second Person Fiction: Narrative You as Addressee and/or Protagonist," *Arbeiten aus Anglistik und Amerikanistik* 18/2 (1993): 217–247; Ursula Wiest-Kellner, *Messages from the Threshold: Die You-Erzählform als Ausdruck liminaler Wesen und Welten*, Bielefeld, 1999.

hearable – for anyone: the text notes only that someone said this, then someone else said that.

This is far from banal and boring, as Henry James' *The Awkward Age* (1899) clearly demonstrates – a novel characterized by the dominance of dialogue. The reader has to face the difficult task of fathoming what lurks beneath the polished surface of high society conversation, what sort of abysses are opening up there. Scenic representation is thus by no means a simple reproduction of the actual, when the community's manners conceal reality and when the character's speeches thus serve the purpose of dissimulation. The reproduction of this concealment leaves unsaid what is essential.

I've already explained a scenic presentation of this kind in connection with the manipulation of the dimension of time in novels (as an example of a pure 1 : 1 relationship between narrated time and narrative time). It also played a part in the section "Character portrayal," however, and it may be relevant to recall once again the difference (mentioned there) between Plato and Aristotle's accounts of *mimesis* and *diegesis* (see pp. 105–106). The question is whether, if the narrator's role is ever more strongly reduced, something like a self-dissolution of the narrative somehow occurs (that is, assuming we define narration primarily as the *adaptation* of speech, not just a mere [re-]production of it); or whether narrative can by definition never give up narration because it after all still continues to create an illusion *through narrative*: the illusion of immediacy. In contrast to a stage drama, the characters in a dialogue scene in a novel don't really speak; rather, there are words *written* on the page that tell us that they said this or that – the conversation is therefore mediated.

In his *Theory of Narrative*, Stanzel recalls Plato when he claims that there is a form of mimesis that creates the impression that narration is no longer taking place.[21] By contrast, Genette (this can be taken either as a reminder or a prolepsis) maintains that, in narrative, narration is evidently *always* taking place, even when an illusion of mimesis is produced. This debate is anything but futile and pointless, for Stanzel makes the basic opposition between narrative and non-narrative (mode) into the third and last constituent of his typological circle: non-narrative becomes the constitutive characteristic of the third narrative situation, the figural, which should have its own subsection, like the other two. In contrast to the respective paradoxes of the other situations, the figural narrative situation's paradox lies open to view: if it "exists," then in nearly half the circle of typical *narrative* situations there is no *narration* at all. Surely, one needs quite a bit of time to assimilate that piece of news.

---

[21] Stanzel, *Theory of Narrative*, 143: "the [illusion of the] immediacy of the mediate."

5   Abolishing Narrative in Narrative – the Illusion of Immediacy: The Figural Narrative Situation

If it were only a question of *identifying* the figural narrative situation as – still, after all this time – the most difficult for readers to understand, we could, as mentioned earlier, do this very simply: for by a process of elimination, if what's in front of us is neither a first-person narrative situation nor an authorial narrative situation, it can only be a figural narrative situation. But in order to fully grasp the aesthetic possibilities of the narrative logic peculiar to this narrative situation, it's of course not sufficient merely to identify it – we need to have traced how it works.

A key distinguishing characteristic of the figural narrative situation is the appearance of a reflector-character, which Stanzel defines as follows:

> [A] reflector-character reflects, that is, he mirrors events of the outer world in his consciousness, perceives, feels, registers, but always silently, because he never "narrates," that is, he does not verbalize his perceptions, thoughts and feelings in an attempt to communicate them. The reader seems to find out directly, by direct insight into the consciousness of the reflector-character, about the events and reactions which are mirrored in his consciousness.[22]

To illustrate this, I'll quote and then comment on a fairly long passage from the first chapter of Franz Kafka's *The Castle* (1926). To set the scene: K. arrives in a village late one evening and wants to stay the night in the inn. The innkeeper gives him a sack of straw and a blanket: he's to sleep in the lounge. Shortly after he has fallen asleep, K. is woken again by a young man, who asks him whether he has the permission of the Count to stay there. K., suspected of being a tramp, says that he is the Land Surveyor "whom the Count has engaged." The young man wants to check up on this story by telephoning – right now, in the middle of the night:

> "I'll ring up and inquire." So there was a telephone in this village inn? They had everything up to the mark. The particular instance surprised K., but on the whole he had really expected it. It appeared that the telephone was placed almost over his head and in his drowsy condition he had overlooked it. If the young man must needs telephone he could not, even with the best intentions, avoid disturbing K., the only question was whether K. would let him do so; he decided to allow it. In that case, however, there was no sense in pretending to sleep, and so he turned on his back again. He could see the peasants putting their heads together; the arrival of a Land Surveyor was no small event. The

---

[22] Stanzel, *Theory of Narrative*, 144.

door into the kitchen had been opened, and blocking the whole doorway stood the imposing figure of the landlady, to whom the landlord was advancing on tiptoe in order to tell her what was happening. And now the conversation began on the telephone. The Castellan was asleep, but an under-castellan, one of the under-castellans, a certain Herr Fritz, was available. The young man, announcing himself as Schwarzer, reported that he had found K., a disreputable-looking man in his thirties, sleeping calmly on a sack of straw with a minute rucksack for pillow and a knotty stick within reach. He had naturally suspected the fellow, and as the landlord had obviously neglected his duty he, Schwarzer, had felt bound to investigate the matter. He had roused the man, questioned him, and duly warned him off the Count's territory, all of which K. had taken with an ill grace, perhaps with some justification, as it eventually turned out, for he claimed to be a Land Surveyor engaged by the Count. Of course, to say the least of it, that was a statement which required official confirmation, and so Schwarzer begged Herr Fritz to inquire in the Central Bureau if a Land Surveyor were really expected, and to telephone the answer at once.

Then there was silence while Fritz was making inquiries up there and the young man was waiting for the answer. K. did not change his position, did not even once turn round, seemed not remotely curious and stared into space. Schwarzer's report, in its combination of malice and prudence, gave him an idea of the measure of diplomacy in which even underlings in the Castle like Schwarzer were versed. Nor were they remiss in industry, the Central Office had a night service. And apparently answered questions quickly, too, for Fritz was already ringing. His reply seemed brief enough, for Schwarzer hung up the receiver immediately, crying angrily: "Just what I said! Not a trace of a Land Surveyor. A common, lying tramp, and probably worse." For a moment K. thought that all of them, Schwarzer, the peasants, the landlord and the landlady, were going to fall upon him in a body, and to escape at least the first shock of their assault he crawled right underneath the blanket. But the telephone rang again, and with a special insistence, it seemed to K. Slowly he put out his head. Although it was improbable that this message also concerned K., they all stopped short and Schwarzer took up the receiver once more. He listened to a fairly long statement, and then said in a low voice: "A mistake, is it? I'm sorry to hear that. The head of the department himself said so? Very queer, very queer. How am I to explain it all to the Land Surveyor?"

K. pricked up his ears. So the Castle had appointed him as the Land Surveyor.[23]

Right from the start, the reader is (as it were) inside the consciousness of K., whose thoughts are reproduced in a form in which, were they isolated, would be called "free indirect discourse" ("So there was a telephone in this

---

[23]   Translation based on Franz Kafka, *The Castle*, trans. Willa and Edwin Muir, London, 1957 [1930], 11–12.

village inn?").[24] But the "location" of the reader *remains* in the character's consciousness, and the character thus functions over a prolonged period as a reflector-character. This in turn means that everything that at first eludes his view is also "spotted" by the reader only when the reflector-character eventually registers it ("It appeared that the telephone was placed almost over his head and in his drowsy condition he had overlooked it"). A narrator – a first-person narrator or an authorial narrator, it doesn't matter – would have been able to eliminate or thematize or explain such an "only now did he ...": his narratorial distance gives him the space to do so, if he wants to. The figural narrative situation, which despite the grammatical past tense always stays very close to the present experience of the reflector-character, doesn't offer that possibility, or offers it at most in a sort of atrophied form ("in his drowsy condition") – just as when we become aware of an oversight in the fraction of a second ("oh, I see!") but *without actually elaborating this oversight in narrative form*. The sentence that follows ("If the young man ...") could be understood as the musing of an authorial narrator, were it not that the expression "he decided" makes clear, in retrospect, that these considerations, too, are those of K. as he is lying under the telephone; and the same goes for the next sentence ("In that case, however, there was no sense ..."). It is through K.'s eyes that the reader sees what is going on in the external scene ("He could see ..."), and so the reader sees only what K. can see, and from K.'s perspective, too: "blocking the whole doorway was the imposing figure of the landlady" signifies that she filled the door from the perspective of K., who is still lying there.

In the figural narrative situation, it's not essential that the telephone conversation should be represented in recorded speech (sometimes known as indirect speech). As other extensive passages in *The Castle* confirm, the most precise direct representation of conversations is actually very conducive to the higher purpose of achieving an illusion of immediacy. This direct reproduction is scenic presentation, pure and simple. So why does the passage we've just read use recorded speech to represent this conversation? What is the special effect of this? What's striking is the step-by-step, highly detailed way in which the recorded speech proceeds ("The young man ... reported that he had found K., a disreputable-looking man in his thirties, sleeping calmly on a sack of straw with a minute rucksack for a pillow and a knotty stick within reach"). This is curious because the technique of recorded speech is "usually" used to compress and summarize, while the most "important" passages are narrated in the 1 : 1 reproduction of *direct* speech. But if,

---

[24] Stanzel, *Theory of Narrative*, 197–198: "If the extent of free indirect style in a narrative increases to the point that it largely replaces authorial utterances, a figural narrative situation results. Figural narrative situation can also be understood as the extended use of free indirect style ... throughout a narrative text."

as in this case, 1 : 1 reproduction is combined with the *indirect* mode, I suppose the aim can only be to represent and highlight the medial refraction of what is heard in K.'s consciousness (it isn't his ears that hear, but rather his brain, which, making a medial difference, adds things that couldn't possibly have been heard – a sure sign of medial difference: "he, *Schwarzer*, had felt bound to investigate" [italics added]). Together with this brilliant highlighting of the reflection of what is heard, the step-by-step, detailed reproduction in recorded speech also demonstrates the other defining characteristic of this narrative situation: lack of selection.[25] To narrate means to differentiate, prioritize, compress, summarize, omit, over- and under-emphasize, etc. We've already encountered this in connection with present-tense narration: probably the easiest way to achieve the impression of non-narrative, of mere registration, in other words, of immediacy, is by (apparently) refraining from any selection. To narrate means to filter. (To *seemingly* refrain from selection – because it is a matter of course that the author, in order to achieve this effect, must select – or, to preclude yet again the absurd misapprehension that in a novel *something* was already there before the text was written, let's say that the author *posits* something that gives the impression of not having been selected.)

Very occasionally, there are authorial interpolations in this predominantly figural text – that's after all the author's privilege, and Stanzel's typological circle is a fine instrument with which to detect such odd moments of intrusion. He "did not seem remotely curious" – that can't possibly come from K.'s consciousness (if this phrase were figurally narrated, it could only be something like "he wasn't remotely curious" or "he tried hard not to seem curious"). Yet since the sentences that follow are, once again, figurally presented through and through, the question arises: why this striking exception to the rule? The answer to this lies in a puzzle (which at the same time constitutes the heart of the novel), the puzzle of the last sentence in the long quotation above: "So the Castle had appointed him as the Land Surveyor." Not, say, "So the castle had confirmed..." or "So the castle had, in some grotesque way, believing his fabrication...," but simply "appointed," as though the act of confirmation had actually created the fact. Actually, the whole novel is basically about the question of K.'s relationship to the castle. The figural narrative situation fully permits that this *primum mobile* of the narrative text remain concealed, that it need not be dis-covered at all – for the fact that the reflector-character's consciousness *does not communicate*

[25]   Stanzel, *Theory of Narrative*, 153–154: "The narrative mode of a teller-character (telling) tends toward the conceptual summarizing of the concrete event in the form of a compressed report supplemented by a commentary which explains or evaluates it. In the presentation by a reflector-character individual and concrete details which have not been reduced or abstracted dominate, just as they are experienced and perceived by that character."

means that it is not necessary to fill up these gaps in *this* or *that* particular way (either he knows that he *is* the commissioned Land Surveyor, or he knows that he is *not* a commissioned Land Surveyor). It isn't necessary for the narrative to explain this in such or such a way – except in this situation here, in which everyone, the outsiders as well as K. himself, are waiting expectantly for the return phone call that is to bring the decision. In the whole of the above-quoted passage, it's here and only here that the perspective changes to an external one ("he did not seem remotely curious"): for a brief moment we leave K.'s consciousness, in order that we should not witness something within his consciousness that must – or ought to – be *there*, if we're thinking in terms of realism: a conspicuous absence.

This hypothesis, it seems to me, is confirmed by the systematic and continued undercutting of the "true" circumstances – circumstances which, as we immediately discover, are very imperfectly defined through the tag "Land Surveyor":

> So the Castle had appointed him as the Land Surveyor. That was unpropitious for him, on the one hand, for it meant that the Castle was well informed about him, had estimated all the probable chances, and was taking up the challenge with a smile. On the other hand, however, it was quite propitious, for if his interpretation were right they had underestimated his strength, and he would have more freedom of action than he had dared to hope. And if they expected to cow him by their lofty superiority in appointing him as Land Surveyor, they were mistaken; it made his skin prickle a little, that was all.

The figural narrative situation is thus better suited than the others for presenting circumstances which are as yet not transparent or distinctly conceived – circumstances which, for the time being are just (immediately) registered and reflected, and which the reader follows within the fictive medium of a consciousness. Owing to the lack of narrative processing, readers are forced into a position similar to that of the reflector-character: we, too, must first of all try to make sense of what is being registered or reflected – and must then try to make sense of the attempts at interpretation offered by the reflector-character.

Finding oneself in the sort of position that Kafka evokes in *The Castle*, or indeed in *The Trial* (1925), one can easily feel cramped and oppressed,[26] and there can be something highly claustrophobic about the reading experience, since without any narrative distance, we lose the knowledge of what "all this" actually means. The figural narrative situation is the one in which that is not yet defined, because everything is still in flux; it's the one in which that is not yet settled, because something new is constantly happening,

---

[26] Or in German *ängstlich* (anxious), a word that derives from *Enge* (narrowness, confinement).

and the consciousness of the reflector-character is still occupied with working through all these impressions and whatever else is going on in his mind (like memories, associations, etc.). (That again brings the figural narrative situation close to present-tense narration.) Let's compare the nightmarish effect that Kafka achieves with figural "narrative" in *The Castle* and *The Trial* to the authorial opening of his novel-fragment *America* (1927) (or *Presumed Dead*, as it is sometimes also called). Kafka himself compared *America*, a text composed prior to *The Castle*, to a Dickens novel:

> As the sixteen-year-old Karl Rossmann, who had been sent to America by his unfortunate parents because a maid had seduced him and had a child by him, sailed slowly into New York harbor, he suddenly saw the Statue of Liberty, which had already been in view for some time, as though in an intenser sunlight. The sword in her hand seemed only just to have been raised aloft [so much for literary realism, CB], and the unchained winds blew about her form.
>
>   "So high," he said to himself, and quite forgetting to disembark, he found himself gradually pushed up against the railing by the massing throng of porters.[27]

To be sure, only the first half of the first sentence is unequivocally authorial; but what a different, new world it lets the reader into (for the time being)!

If we think of the fact that Kafka initially drafted the first chapter of *The Castle* as a first-person narrative, it becomes clear what a *constitutive* effect his decision to alter it had on the "kafkaesque" text that we read today: "As a reflector, K. is released from the reader's demand for an explanation of the countless inexplicable and mysterious circumstances which surround the hero here as in Kafka's other novels."[28] But the example of Kafka's *The Trial*, too, in the course of which authorial interventions diminish gradually, parallel to "the increase of the hero's 'perspective solipsism',"[29] also explains why the above-noted singular change to an authorial voice in *The Castle* ("he did not seem remotely curious") occurs so early and in such isolation: later, the world as it has emerged from reflected sequences attains such density that it already feels threateningly familiar to the reader. At the beginning we may still wonder why K. has come to this place at all (if you wish, that's also a problem of the "how to begin a novel" type); but soon we are reduced to wondering how we are supposed to imagine and figure out his relationship to the castle. The text is in a sense the investigation of this relationship, and interpretations differ widely with respect to this central question. There is no natural limit to misreadings: there's now a computer game called *The*

---

[27]   Translation based on that by Willa and Edwin Muir (1938).

[28]   Stanzel, *Theory of Narrative*, 155.

[29]   Stanzel, *Theory of Narrative*, 69.

Castle, based on Kafka's novel, in which the players have to try to reach and then enter the castle. Is it an unfair speculation to say that the world of this computer game is likely to be unequivocally authorial? And is it too harsh a judgment to say that the makers of this game have completely failed to understand the novel?

Novels in which the figural narrative situation dominates don't necessarily have to be in any way "kafkaesque." Christine Brooke-Rose's experimental novel *Between* (1968) is a good counter-example. We're inside the mind of a middle-aged woman (i.e., someone *between* two phases of life), who works as a simultaneous interpreter (i.e., she mediates *between* languages and interprets *between* positions), a job which means that she often finds herself *between* different conference venues. The novel is written in the present tense and contains many scenic presentations (direct reproductions of dialogue). But of course the woman's own past remains present as far as and as soon as it enters her current consciousness; seen in this way she lives, like everyone else, *between* past and future, in the present. What is more, she is also *between* different relationships, and *between* two home countries, France and Germany. As befits this character, the mind in which we find ourselves is polyglot. Here is a typical passage taken from the beginning of the novel (the woman is in a state *between* waking and sleeping in an airplane, "between the enormous wings" – but of course her consciousness contains vestigial recollections of other situations):

> At any minute now some bright or elderly sour no young and buxom chambermaid in black and white will come in with a breakfast-tray, put it down on the table in the dark and draw back the curtains unless open the shutters and say buenos días, Morgen or kalimera who knows, it all depends where the sleeping has occurred out of what dream shaken up with non merci nein danke no thank you in a long-lost terror of someone offering etwas anderes, not ordered.
>
> Or a smooth floor-steward in white.
>
> The stewardess in pale grey-blue and high pale orange hair puts down the plastic tray covered with various foods in little plastic troughs.
>
> – Mineralwasser bitte.
>
> – Mineralwasser? Leider haben wir keins. Nur Sodawasser.
>
> – Also dann Sodawasser.
>
> Which bears no label. Leider nicht.

Evidently, the combination of the figural narrative situation with the use of the present tense and scenic presentation can also produce an *al fresco* effect – quite the opposite of anything we might want to call "kafkaesque" – in which the meaning must emerge *between* the impressions and the signs; or, as the novel tells us at one point (quoting de Saussure), *between* an absence and a presence, so that actually both the theme *and* the form of the novel are one and the same: the process by which the identity of an "unconscious" person is produced – a process of identity-production and of a generation of meaning that never reaches an end (characteristically, the final sentence of the novel corresponds to the first sentence). The fact that the author of this lipogram-novel has systematically avoided the verb *to be* (in all its forms) is more than merely an experimental gimmick: the verb *to be* is replaced by the mimesis of the process of *being*. We could say that the novel explores *being between* as a central metaphor for modern existence – a metaphor that is readily embodied in a translator ("metaphor" derives from the Greek *meta-pherein* = transfer, in German *über-setzen* = literally "to carry over," i.e., translate).

The figural narrative situation is the paradigmatic narrative situation of literary modernism, because it takes account of an insight that defines an epochal juncture, and transfers it into narrative. This insight is that for human beings there can be no reality "as such": reality can only ever be experienced and interpreted in specific ways. This is how Virginia Woolf programmatically formulated the point against the older novelists H. G. Wells, Arnold Bennett, and John Galsworthy, in her essay "Modern Fiction":

> Is life like this? Must novels be like this?
>   Look within and life, it seems, is very far from being "like this." Examine for a moment an ordinary mind on an ordinary day. The mind receives a myriad impressions – trivial, fantastic, evanescent, or engraved with the sharpness of steel. From all sides they come, an incessant shower of innumerable atoms; and as they fall, as they shape themselves into the life of Monday or Tuesday, the accent falls differently from of old; the moment of importance came not here but there; so that, if a writer were a free man and not a slave, if he could write what he chose, not what he must, if he could base his work upon his own feeling and not upon convention, there would be no plot, no comedy, no tragedy, no love interest or catastrophe in the accepted style, and perhaps not a single button sewn on as the Bond Street tailors would have it. Life is not a series of gig-lamps symmetrically arranged; life is a luminous halo, a semi-transparent envelope surrounding us from the beginning of consciousness to the end. Is it not the task of the novelist to convey this varying, this unknown and uncircumscribed spirit, whatever aberration or complexity it may display, with as little mixture of the alien and external as possible? We are not pleading merely for courage and sincerity; we are suggesting that the proper stuff of fiction is a little other than custom would have us believe it.[30]

It was in *Mrs. Dalloway* that Virginia Woolf for the first time stringently carried out this program. Of course, even this novel still contains isolated passages of authorial narration, but the majority of the text consists of figural passages, of internal monologues, of recorded speech, of directly represented

---

[30]   Virginia Woolf, "Modern Fiction," in *The Norton Anthology of English Literature: Fifth Edition*, Vol. 2, ed. M. H. Abrams, New York, 1993–1999 [1986], here 1996.

speech – all of which are narrative techniques that Stanzel assigns to the lower half of his typological circle. Importantly, the author – unlike Kafka or Brooke-Rose – doesn't let the reader remain within one single consciousness only, but, as it were, jumps from consciousness to consciousness. The frequency of change is particularly high once Clarissa Dalloway has been established as the central reflector-character, roughly in the scene (relatively early on) in which first of all a royal limousine drives down St. James's Street towards Buckingham Palace, and then an aircraft writes letters of the alphabet in the sky. In succession, we find ourselves inside the consciousness of (to give a partial list) several men in White's Club, then Sarah Bletchley, Emily Coates, Mr. Bowley, Rezia, Septimus Warren Smith, Maisie Johnson and, finally, in the consciousness of Carrie Dempster. (Incidentally, most of these characters don't reappear later.) The novel isn't particularly difficult to read, however, for Virginia Woolf almost always takes care to provide a small "anchor" in "objective" reality, whenever the jump is made from one reflector-character to another – an object or event perceived or experienced by various people (a car backfiring, the tolling of Big Ben, an ambulance siren, the plane's writing in the sky, etc.). These anchors enable us to recognize the perspective change promptly, or – to put it more precisely – they are like pontoons that enable the reader to cross over to another subjective consciousness. Sometimes, though, information that signals that a shift in perspective has just taken place is provided only later, for example at the famous opening of the novel:

> Mrs. Dalloway said she would buy the flowers herself.
> For Lucy had her work cut out for her. The doors would be taken off their hinges; Rumpelmayer's men were coming. And then, thought Clarissa Dalloway, what a morning – fresh as if issued to children on a beach.

"And then, *thought Clarissa Dalloway*" (emphasis added) allows us to recognize that the previous thoughts were hers, too. That isn't some capricious way of deceiving the reader; rather, since it happens only within small textual units, right where it's at, at the very core of the novel's theme song, this device imitates in miniature a suggestion communicated by the novel as a whole: that it is always only in retrospect that meaning becomes apparent or recognizable, even if the delay is only minimal. The meaning of anything is never immediately "there."

And that recognition provides the answer to a possible objection: doesn't Virginia Woolf's insertion of "anchor points" in the text – sudden glimpses of "objective" reality – contradict her own program? No, far from it. For the pure data of external reality are absolutely trivial (to repeat – a car backfiring, bells tolling, sky-writing), but what they *mean* differs for every character. As if to underline that fact, Virginia Woolf has every character read something different in the sky-writing. If not even the signifier is fixed and certain, what can you expect ...? The only certainty is: there *are* signs there. What they mean is different for each individual, sometimes extremely so: the bang of the backfire transports Septimus Warren Smith, traumatized by the war, back to the front, whereas of course Clarissa Dalloway, who heard the same sound, has no such recollection.

The aesthetic advantage of such a mode of writing is evident: *in one move* an event, a world, and a particular way of experiencing that world and that event are developed. To be sure, this increases the demand on the reader enormously: everything that a narrator normally does in the way of processing, interpreting, explaining, is now left to the reader alone. Seen like this, it's a paradoxical triumph of realism: the novel written in this seemingly artificial mode actually proves to be hyperrealistic, because it demands of us exactly what we need to be able to *live* at all (assuming we don't just want to vegetate): we have to be able to "read" what's "out there," what's occurring right now, to discover what it could mean; but we must also maintain a *sense of possibility* that avoids too quickly rejecting conceivable alternatives, since jumping rashly to conclusions unnecessarily closes off access to the full meaning of existence. Closure may be essential for survival – but openness is no less so: for if the deadline for conclusions is too early, we reduce the number of interpretative options up to a point when we sink into utter conventionality: "There is no alternative!" Such openness, which increases the intensity of life and its possible continuations, can be rehearsed at leisure in the sanction-free space of literary reading, especially when we read the genre that in some way always thematizes the production of sense and meaning: the novel. It becomes possible to have that experience exactly if and when we have the courage to use our own imagination independently and *without direction from another*, from a narrator, say – just as Kant defined the essence of enlightenment as the free exercise of reason without direction from another.

Identification with a character in this way is normal, even inevitable, if we find ourselves (as it were) inside the reflector-character's consciousness. But that doesn't necessarily mean that we have to be able to "identify" with the reflector-character in terms of behavior or value-judgments. Given that no one willingly inhabits a consciousness that they view critically or downright detest, disambiguating misreadings tend to arise, which refuse to admit – or see at all – the author's self-distancing from her reflector-character. Such readings crudely simplify exactly what the text is evidently problematizing. The character of Mrs. Dalloway is a good example. Not only does Virginia Woolf make Peter Walsh, the outsider who mercilessly dissects the refined British postwar society, describe Mrs. Dalloway with devastating disparagement as "the perfect hostess" (whereupon she retreats wailing to her room, and still hasn't forgotten the incident years later); the liberal left-wing and politically engaged author also makes the eponymous heroine totally apolitical. Shortly after the Turks' genocidal attack on the Armenians,

Mrs. Dalloway confuses the one nationality with the other – or were they, after all, actually Albanians?

> Anyhow, it was her gift. Nothing else had she of the slightest importance; could not think, write, even play the piano. She muddled Armenians and Turks; loved success; hated discomfort; must be liked; talked oceans of non-sense; and to this day, ask her what the Equator was, and she did not know.

Is this an endearing admission of her own weaknesses? Or is it a savage criticism of a mere wife ("Mrs. Richard Dalloway") and society lady, who spends half her time (as she herself prefers to see it) doing things only to please others, who doesn't know the difference between victims and perpetrators in a recent genocidal massacre and goes off to buy flowers instead? It's both: really *both at the same time*. The figurally "narrated" novel thrives on such internal tensions and ambiguities – thrives, too, on the fact that the reader is not expressly *told* this.

If the "reading" of a character thus depends entirely on whether we regard particular statements as authorial directives and assertions or "merely" as the character's own thoughts, in other words as unprivileged statements, then every word and phrase requires constant attention, in order to avoid (in the worst-case scenario) chalking things up as objectively documented which are in fact offered as a character's own self-betraying characterization or idiosyncratic, highly subjective view of himself or herself.

To illustrate that, let's read another passage from a novel by Virginia Woolf. *To the Lighthouse* (1927) – in Virginia Woolf's own opinion "the best novel I have ever written" – maintains figural narration even more consistently than *Mrs. Dalloway*. The context of the following passage is this: Prof. Ramsey and his wife spend their summer holiday together with their eight children and various guests, not to mention servants, on the Scottish Isle of Skye. Right at the beginning there's a discussion about an excursion to the lighthouse, which they're planning to make tomorrow; but Mr. Ramsey dampens everyone's anticipation with his coolly reasonable observation that the weather is going to be too bad for this. Although he will prove to be right about this, he delivers his judgment so coldly, without the least empathy, that little James hates his father for it and would really like to kill him – and another marital row is inevitable. At the end of the first part (also the end of the first day, which fills the whole of the first part of the novel) we encounter the two Ramsey parents in a moment of silence:

> And what then? For she felt that he was still looking at her, but that his look had changed. He wanted something – wanted the thing she always found it so difficult to give him; wanted her to tell him that she loved him. And that, no, she could not do. He found talking so much easier than she did. He could say things – she never could. So naturally it was always he that said the things, and

then for some reason he would mind this suddenly, and would reproach her. A heartless woman he called her; she never told him that she loved him. But it was not so – it was not so. It was only that she never could say what she felt.

So it's Mrs. Ramsey who supposes that her husband wants to hear her say something in particular – something that she can't say. She knows full well that she's tongue-tied – and why. Now, what happens next?

Was there no crumb on his coat? Nothing she could do for him? Getting up she stood at the window with the reddish-brown stocking in her hands, partly to turn away from him, partly because she did not mind looking now, with him watching, at the Lighthouse. For she knew that he had turned his head as she turned; he was watching her. She knew that he was thinking, You are more beautiful than ever. And she felt herself very beautiful. Will you not tell me just for once that you love me? He was thinking that, for he was roused, what with Minta and his book, and its being the end of the day and their having quarrelled about going to the Lighthouse. But she could not do it; she could not say it. Then, knowing that he was watching her, instead of saying anything she turned, holding her stocking, and looked at him. And as she looked at him she began to smile, for though she had not said a word, he knew, of course he knew, that she loved him. He could not deny it. And smiling she looked out of the window and said (thinking to herself, Nothing on earth can equal this happiness) – "Yes, you were right. It's going to be wet tomorrow." She had not said it, but he knew it. And she looked at him smiling. For she had triumphed again.

The key question is whether we ever leave Mrs. Ramsey's consciousness here. If not, then we must be careful, for her suppositions don't necessarily *have* to be correct. (At dinner the previous evening, too, remarks about her enviable beauty were relativized by the unobtrusive interpolation "she could not help knowing it.") In this case, both her assumption about what her husband wanted to hear and the estimate that she had given him to understand this without speaking ("he knew, of course he knew that she loved him"), would be no more than that: *her* assumption, *her* estimate. To admit the obvious ("Yes, you were right") and to regard this admission as a sufficient, implicit statement of love (which she refuses to make *explicitly*) – that would only be *her* way of reading, which she, smiling, understands as her triumph. Indeed, the markers that these thoughts are *hers* are very discreet ("he knew, *of course he knew*," "He could not deny it" [emphasis added] – that's decidedly Mrs. Ramsey's style of thought and language). Nor is it possible to prove conclusively that the later phrase, "but he knew it," is the voice of an authorial narrator that now shares her assessment; but we can't rule out this possibility either. That is why the interpretation of this end of part one – and we're not going to see Mrs. Ramsey alive again – becomes a psychological Rorschach test for the reader: tell me how you read this, and I'll tell you what makes you tick. The trick of that sort of narrative is, of course, that it must really be undecidable on the basis of the text and that there is not one single element in the text, left undetected by the writer, that decidedly tips the balance in this or that way.

By contrast, the clear authorial guiding hand in William Golding's *Pincher Martin* (1956) is impossible to miss, and indisputable when, at the end of the novel – typically for Golding – a radical change in the narrative situation takes place, which suddenly puts everything we've read so far in a completely different light. One night, the marine lieutenant Christopher Hadley Martin, known as "Pincher" Martin, is thrown overboard in the middle of the Atlantic when his destroyer is hit by an enemy torpedo. After a terrible struggle in the rough sea – in which Martin manages through contortions to kick off his heavy seaboots to give himself some sort of survival chance – he's washed up on a completely uninhabited, rocky island. He's injured, half-drowned, totally exhausted. He gains a firm grasp of the rocks, and crawls up at an agonizingly slow pace, possessed by just one thought: survival. All this has been "told" in almost entirely figural narration, and so is the continuation of his desperate struggle, in which we not only learn more and more about his past and his rather unpleasant character, but also witness the increasing confusion of his consciousness – hallucinations and delusions seem to haunt and plague the starving and exhausted man, until by the end there remains only a consciousness of clinching claws and a nameless fear.

But in the last chapter, which is authorially narrated, we're back in the "real" world again. The body of Christopher Martin has been washed up on a shore. His death, remarks an officer who should know, must have come quickly: "He didn't even have the time to kick off his seaboots." We recall: the very same seaboots that Pincher Martin had with great effort kicked off on page four of the novel, and whose loss he continually complains of! The paradox can only be explained in this way: Pincher Martin drowned during the first pages of the novel, and it wasn't his struggle for survival that we witnessed, but the refusal of his stubborn and unrepentant soul to merge into the boundless mercy of God. Figurally narrated, *Pincher Martin* is a novel that is mostly set in the hereafter and aims to reveal the attitude of grabbing and grasping, gripping, clinging and clinching (even beyond death), the inability to let go. The consequence is that the reader is ultimately expected to condemn as morally reprehensible an attitude which he may well before have admired as heroic. In other words: the reader is expected to let go of an interpretation that he would love to hold onto. Not every reader, as the early reception of the novel shows, is prepared to submit to this kind of authorial directive. But what can you do? The author exercises absolute power, even if we feel this more directly with an authorial narrator than in the potentially subtler mode of figural narration.

Not every authorial intervention has to send such a shockwave through the narrative: in Kafka's *The Castle*, for instance, we encountered a more homeopathic dosage, and in *To the Lighthouse* no more than traces of *possible* interventions. Reflecting on this difference, let's recapitulate the relative shares or proportions of authorial and personal in any "mix" of narrative situations that we can imagine and that can be represented on Stanzel's typological circle.

Starting from the point of highest authoriality, the unbounded omniscience of the narrator, the narrator's presence can be gradually reduced, in an infinitely variable way, smoothly on a sliding scale. The typological circle illustrates this excellently, because this model avoids categorical either–or decisions; rather, it allows for the possibility of each basic situation mixing with each of the others. More than that: the very aim of the circle is to represent precisely what kind of mixture we have. Different forms of mixture are discernible not only between different narrative texts within a particular group (the titles of the novels are then assigned to the segment of the circle they belong to): as we've seen, changes in the mixture can also occur within one single text, in temporal differentiation and succession, "resulting from the succession of various narrative situations or from various modulations of a specific narrative situation."[31] Stanzel calls this the "dynamization of the narrative situation."[32]

We perceive the gradual retreat of the authorial narrator as successive renunciation of "superhuman" privileges. The authorial narrator may keep in the background and allow the characters to act, speak, and think on front stage, providing only certain essential connections, but no longer in such a decidedly authoritarian way as (say) the narrator of *Tom Jones*. An amusing phenomenon in the deprivileging of the authorial narrator is what Stanzel calls "the 'contamination' of the narrator's language by the language of the fictional characters":[33] "Mr. and Mrs. Dursley, of number four, Privet Drive, were proud to say that they were perfectly normal, thank you very much." In the first sentence of J. K. Rowling's *Harry Potter and the Philosopher's Stone* (1997), the ironization of the two Muggles is unmistakable.[34]

Sometimes it is open to debate to what extent the authorial narrator of a particular novel has actually retreated – especially if this varies greatly

---

[31]   Stanzel, *Theory of Narrative*, 63.
[32]   Stanzel, *Theory of Narrative*, 63ff.
[33]   Stanzel, *Theory of Narrative*, 192.
[34]   Incidentally, a first-person narrator can also be "contaminated" by the language of one of his characters. Per Olov Enquist's *The Book of Blanche and Marie* (2005) is a good example. In attempting to reconstruct the life story of Blanche Wittman, favorite patient of the famous neurologist Charcot and subsequently assistant to Marie Curie, the male first-person narrator allows himself to be affected by the language of the notebooks that Blanche Wittman left behind, reproducing her "manic repetitions." Since the novel is also a story about contamination and infection with radium, as well as the infectious illness known as love, this narrative arrangement is also conspicuously thematic.

within one and the same novel. Take E. M. Forster's *A Passage to India* (1924), which unquestionably opens with authorial narration, and after that the authorial presence is palpable whenever the narrative voice comments ironically or sarcastically on the behavior and values of the English colonials. But then so many scenic passages are scattered through the book, and Fielding, Dr. Aziz, Angela Quested, and others are introduced as reflector-characters, and interior monologues and free indirect discourse are used as well, that we may wonder whether the novel should not be nudged much further round the typological circle in the direction of the figural narrative situation. Here, too, the language of some of the characters proves contagious and the authorial narrator catches it, which kind of de-privileges his position. Let's carefully read the following passage on Mr. Fielding's "scandalous" remark in the English colonials' club, that the white races are actually "pinko-grey":

> He had no racial feeling – not because he was superior to his brother civilians, but because he had matured in a different atmosphere, where the herd-instinct does not flourish. The remark that did him most harm at the Club was a silly aside to the effect that the so-called white races are really pinko-grey. He only said this to be cheery, he did not realize that "white" has no more to do with a colour than "God save the King" with a god, and that it is the height of impropriety to consider what it does connote. The pinko-grey male whom he addressed was subtly scandalized; his sense of insecurity was awoken, and he communicated it to the rest of the herd.

The fact that the narrator takes up the expression "pinko-grey" and makes it his own indicates that he shares Fielding's opinion; further, this is a discreetly ironic disclosure of the narrator's solidarity (so to speak) with one of his characters. Here, there's no longer an Olympian distance: the narrator has climbed down.

This (according to our analysis, no longer quite authorial) narrative situation does justice to the novel's theme: although the novel shows a fundamental relativization of different individual and cultural standpoints, what follows from this is not a multicultural reconciliation, but rather a resigned insight into the remaining, recalcitrant incommensurability of Orient and Occident, for the time being. The final sentence of Forster's last novel is " 'No, not yet,' and the sky said, 'No, not there.' " – a striking contrast to the optimistic motto of his earlier work *Howard's End* (1910), "Only connect." Therefore, the narrative form of *A Passage to India*, which is more strongly figural than readers tend to notice, is also deeply thematic – anything else would be a performative contradiction. However, a difference of opinion over the placement of a narrative text on the circle by no means puts the model itself in question. On the contrary, the model even helps to illustrate and clarify the difference of views.

We can think of free indirect discourse – a narrative mode already mentioned several times above – as a successful mixture of authorial narrative and the figural reflector-mode. Free indirect discourse is a "dual-voice" phenomenon.[35] The very term "free indirect discourse" (in French, *style indirect libre*) reflects exactly what is involved grammatically: indirect (recorded) speech without any explanatory introduction. "He wondered: 'So is she flirting with me?'" That is obviously direct speech; in free indirect discourse it would be something like: "So was she flirting with him?"

There were certainly embryonic forms of free indirect discourse before Jane Austen and Gustave Flaubert, and non-fictional texts can use them, too.[36] However, the particular attraction of free indirect discourse in literary texts (for in aesthetic and other depragmatized contexts, ambiguities have a considerable potential to excite and attract) consists in the fact that in an isolated sentence it's simply not possible to decide from the grammar whether this is supposed to be the content of a character's mind or a commentary by the narrator.[37] According to context, we incline to read it either one way or the other – or else it just has to remain open and undecidable.

Gérard Genette once declared that complete undecidability in this respect is very rare, noting: "Banfield makes clear that such ambiguities refer us less to an identity of thought between characters and narrator than to an impossible choice between two interpretations that are *nevertheless incompatible*, as in the famous trick drawings analyzed by Gombrich."[38] Even if one were to agree with Genette on this point, it remains true that after we have resolved a passage in this or that way, we remain conscious of having experienced a moment of hesitation, of pausing, during which our attention was directed to the discourse and the context of the passage under scrutiny. Skillfully inserted passages of free indirect discourse are always an excellent index for the increasing self-referentiality of a literary text. The problem of how to read this encouraged us to decelerate, to take a closer look. In the *Kippbilder* that Genette mentions for comparison, at any moment one can only see either one thing or the other – duck or rabbit, a vase or two profiles facing each other – but despite only being able to actualize one at a time, we know that both

[35]　Cf. Roy Pascal, *The Dual Voice: Free Indirect Speech and its Functioning in the 19th-Century European Novel*, Manchester, 1977.

[36]　Cf. Monika Fludernik, *The Fictions of Language and the Languages of Fiction: The Linguistic Representation of Speech and Consciousness*, London, 1993.

[37]　Cf. Ann Banfield, *Unspeakable Sentences: Narration and Representation in the Language of Fiction*, Boston, London, Melbourne, and Henley, 1982, as well as the earlier work by Cohn, *Transparent Minds*. For a different perspective, see Fludernik, *Fictions*, and *Towards a "Natural" Narratology*, London, 1996. Franz K. Stanzel provides a good overview of the controversy surrounding conceptions of free indirect discourse, in "Erlebte Rede: Prolegomena zu einer Wirkungsgeschichte des Begriffs," *Unterwegs: Erzähltheorie für Leser*, Göttingen, 2002, 292–306.

[38]　Gérard Genette, *Narrative Discourse Revisited*, trans. Jane E. Lewin, Ithaca, NY, 1988, 55.

views, though mutually exclusive, are possible. Free indirect discourse is thus a model in miniature for the reading of ambiguous, literary texts, because the traces of rejected possibilities always linger. The realization of one possibility does not disguise the situation from which this realization emerged.

To repeat an idea I introduced earlier on: the longer the free indirect discourse continues, the more likely we are to regard the narrative situation as figural and ascribe the speech to the thoughts of a reflector-character. If, however, the free indirect discourse is only scattered at intervals through the narrative, we hear the narrator's voice through it (so to speak) and interpret this as external "guidance." When, in *A Passage to India*, Adela Quested makes a trip to the Marabar Caves and there realizes for the first time that she and her fiancé Ronny don't truly love each other at all, this is mediated in free indirect discourse:

> But as she toiled over a rock that resembled an inverted saucer she thought, "What about love?" The rock was nicked by a double row of footholds, and somehow the question was suggested by them. Where had she seen footholds before? Oh yes, they were the pattern traced in the dust by the wheels of the Nawab Bahadur's car. She and Ronny – no, they did not love each other.
>
> "Do I take you too fast?" inquired Aziz, for she had paused, a doubtful expression on her face. The discovery had come so suddenly that she felt like a mountaineer whose rope has broken. Not to love the man one's going to marry! Not to find it out till this moment! Not even to have asked oneself the question until now!

To be sure, that's inside her head. But after the traumatic end to the trip, when she is practically held in quarantine, this devastating insight is taken up again:

> No one, except Ronny, had any idea of what passed in her mind, and he only dimly, for where there is officialism every human relationship suffers. In her sadness she said to him, "I bring you nothing but trouble; I was right on the Maidan, we had better just be friends," but he protested, for the more she suffered the more highly he valued her. *Did she love him? This question was somehow draggled up with the Marabar, it had been in her mind as she entered the fatal cave.* Was she capable of loving anyone? [Emphasis added]

It seems to me the italicized parts could also be résumés by the narrator, whereas the concluding question again comes from the character herself.

In fact, the area of distribution possible for free indirect discourse is much greater than its placement on Stanzel's typological circle would suggest (though the text of Stanzel's *Theory* points us in the right direction). It encroaches deeply into the territory of the authorial narrative situation. Indeed, looking at the range of mixes between the authorial and figural narrative situations, free indirect discourse should in my view appear *above*, not underneath, scenic presentation: for in free indirect discourse portions of authorial speech can be evident (even if they can't be differentiated *grammatically*; come to think of it, how *could* they be differentiated when free indirect discourse is by definition grammatically undecidable?), whereas scenic presentation is defined by the (illusion of the) *absence* of a narrator.

Let's now look at the sector that designates the transition between the figural narrative situation and the first-person narrative situation. Here things seem simpler (in the sense of being less varied) and at the same time more complicated, since the phenomenon of the interior monologue (mentioned several times above) that dominates this sector brings with it something that could actually undermine the logic of the circle. This is something that we couldn't have said about the paradoxes we examined previously (i.e., the paradoxes of the first-person narrative situation and of the authorial narrative situation), or that we could only have claimed by insisting rather willfully on it (in relation to the basic paradox of the figural narrative situation, in which supposedly no narration takes place at all).

So what is this undermining factor? The interior monologue, which we have already discussed in relation to the first-person narrative situation, is the premium narrative device of the stream of consciousness novel. In a discourse that is grammatically that of a first-person singular, the thought processes of that person are reproduced: disorderly, chaotic, associative, with gaps and breaks and non sequiturs, "wrong" or inappropriate use of language. This has the effect of unedited immediacy. Because of this effect of immediacy, it's completely correct to place narrative texts that rely on this technique in the bottom-left-hand sector: *at the bottom*, because no narration is taking place, bottom *left* because the speaking voice is an "I," not a he or a she. This particular mode provides wonderful possibilities: examples already mentioned are Arthur Schnitzler's *Fräulein Else* and *Leutnant Gustl* (which indicates the fact that in literary history, this technique was first tried out in shorter texts). Or think of William Faulkner's great experiments in this field: in *The Sound and the Fury*, Faulkner first presents three interior monologues from three different characters, before transferring to the authorial situation. This is led off by a mentally handicapped young man (which follows logically from the title, taken from Shakespeare's *Macbeth* – "[Life's] a tale / Told by an idiot, full of sound and fury, / Signifying nothing"), and the chronology of the four parts is altered (April 7, 1928; June 2, 1910; April 6, 1928; April 8, 1928). But this is not as confusing as one might fear: even though the date of the reflections varies, the consciousnesses mostly "share" a (subjectively discontinuous) past (as long as it's kept present in these consciousnesses). *As I Lay Dying* (whose theme and form Graham Swift borrowed in his prizewinning novel *Last Orders*, without anyone much noticing this at the time) consists of no less than 59 interior monologues, albeit not assigned to as many characters. That's the easy part: we find ourselves inside the mind of an "I," and this "I" does not narrate (obviously, it doesn't *communicate* – we just eavesdrop). And here's the rub: how is it that exactly the same procedure, when carried out by a s/he, constitutes one of the three basic "typical narrative situations" (whose exclusive feature is the presence of a reflector-figure!); whereas if an "I" is reflecting, this is "merely" a hybrid form between the figural narrative situation and the first-person narrative situation?

Stanzel's whole model is designed to systematize certain specific combinations and correlations of narrative characteristics that occur more frequently – in other words, he identifies patterns and clusters of characteristics. Now, with regard to the narrator–reflector opposition, Stanzel remarks, "There evidently exists a close correspondence between internal perspective and the mode dominated by a reflector-character, on the one hand, and between external perspective and the mode dominated by a teller-character, on the other."[39] However, when Stanzel – with full justification as narrative texts are concerned – admits that an "I" can, of course, be a reflector-character, too, the circle's internal logic goes haywire:

> The two lists of illustrative examples indicate that the function of the teller-character is common to authorial narrators of almost all kinds, as well as to the first-person narrators in whom the narrating self is clearly discernible. On the other hand, first-person narrators who are actualized only as an experiencing self, and who therefore restrict themselves to the reflection of experiences not overtly communicated, are reflector-characters. To these we must add all figural media, who represent the largest proportion of reflector-characters. While the concepts reflector-character and teller-character comprise phenomena of the first as well as of the third person, the concept "figural narrative situation" is applicable only to the third-person form.[40]

Actually, why? To be sure, Stanzel *does* define it like that – but why? The expression "largest proportion" suggests empirical, probably quantitative grounds. But wasn't Stanzel's *Theory* all about the elegance of a conclusive system? Why, then, is the reflector-mode something totally distinct as soon as the third person comes into operation and as long as it remains so (the third person is defined as the purest condition of the figural narrative situation – mind: one of the three basic narrative situations), but not when the first person is in operation? In both cases, I should say, we are dealing with a reflector-character, and while we read, the grammatical difference probably fades out anyway, just as in this mode of non-narrative the reader silently and automatically translates the exclusive s/he into an identificatory "I." Yet the "unnatural," arbitrary "first-person/third-person" boundary painfully slices the terrain in two – with the usual consequence of binary

---

[39]   Stanzel, *Theory of Narrative*, 141.
[40]   Stanzel, *Theory of Narrative*, 145.

demarcation: privilege here, discrimination there; invariably, one side is placed above the other. Stanzel, who is always careful to stress the *heuristic* character of his theory and his circle,[41] is far too intelligent not to have seen that. In a passage of *A Theory of Narrative* that is perhaps one of the most brilliant, because one of the freest and most self-relativizing, he writes: "It is conceivable that interior monologue could attain the rank of an important narrative situation in the next decades. Such a narrative situation would have to be located at the internal perspective pole of the perspective axis."[42] Indeed, that is eminently conceivable. But as things stand, it can't be represented in this scheme. Through the triple boundary lines and triple specification of internal vs. external, s/he vs. I, reflector vs. narrator, the figural narrative situation is *unambiguously stipulated* as one of the three basic situations. Even the hierarchical exclusion of first-person reflector-characters occurs thanks to an inappropriately rigid schematism that (if only in this one point, as it seems to me) has become master rather than servant. It is a victory of geometry over judgment. If Stanzel notes with regard to longer passages in *Ulysses* devoted to the rendition of consciousness and "in which the reference to the bearer of consciousness alternates between "I" and "he"," "This change indicates that the opposition person has become unmarked in the zone of transition between first-person narrative and figural narrative situation on the typological circle"[43] – an assertion that Dorrit Cohn has criticized strongly[44] – it's all the more astonishing that, on the other hand, he grants the third person as reflector-character a higher position in the system than the first person.

Stanzel's thought-experiment about the interior monologue as a future narrative situation in its own right is a gesture of respect to the literary–historical and narratological reality beyond his scheme. The scheme itself would be torn apart by the attempt to incorporate something like that – the boundary lines just don't allow it. The symmetry of axes, boundaries, situations, would be over and done with and stand in ruin. The figural narrative situation itself, as it is defined here, thus appears as the *result* of a geometrical construction – a result, it is true, with considerable explanatory power, since it indicates a certain status and a proper systematic place for non-narrative within the realm of narrative, for the illusion of immediacy created through mediacy. But possibly the "center" of this narrative situation is not to be found in the place to which a geometrically constructed boundary line has consigned it: maybe it is, rather, *on* this boundary, which in that case –

---

[41]   In *Unterwegs*, underlining this predominantly heuristic character of his theory and terminology, Stanzel constantly talks in terms of "discovery tools."

[42]   Stanzel, *Theory of Narrative*, 61.

[43]   Stanzel, *Theory of Narrative*, 227.

[44]   Cf. Dorrit Cohn, "The Encirclement of Narrative: On F. Stanzel's *Theorie des Erzählens*," *Poetics Today* 2/2 (1981): 157–182, here 166–169.

to play out this thought-experiment – does *not* have to be constitutive for this narrative situation. "Internal" and "non-narratorial": these two criteria would define the (newly reunited) reflector-situation. But that would be the end of the beauty of the rosette.

6 Genette's Narrative Theory: The Basics

Gérard Genette's narrative theory is fundamentally different from that of Franz K. Stanzel in at least two respects. First, Genette thoroughly discusses several aspects of narrative texts that play little role – or at least no systematic role – in Stanzel's work. Examples are the possibilities of temporal organization in narratives (which we discussed in chapter 4) or the relationship between different levels of narrative (to which we'll come below).

Second, a characteristic trait of Genette's theoretical design is that he splits textual aspects into binary or ternary oppositions. This means that narratologists who follow Genette in their analyses often tend to note the presence (or absence) of mutually exclusive characteristics, and in this way to build up a kind of profile of a text's distinguishing features.[45] Moreover, since Genette is not concerned with identifying particular clusters of textual characteristics that appear more frequently together, there is no strict, inherent logic to the enumeration of the relevant aspects of a text that require analysis. The initial result of this is only a list, and then – if the analysis of textual characteristics is taken further – a tree-diagram. Now, because Genette is really not trying to force particular clusters of characteristics into a geometrical figure (such as a circle), but rather just wants to demonstrate the different ways in which it is in principle possible to organize a narrative text, the visual end-product of his formalization is at most a table representing a classification or possibilities of combination. Assuming he hasn't overlooked anything, this table should cover everything that can be logically deduced as possible.

At first glance – and especially when certain objections to the arrangements in the bottom half of Stanzel's circle are fresh in our minds[46] – this procedure has the advantage of working with fewer premises and is therefore less restricted and potentially more flexible. As we'll see, however, even

[45] Surprisingly, Genette himself expresses astonishment that anyone should link such a schematic procedure with him and his theory: "Here, as elsewhere, the choice is purely operational. This looseness will undoubtedly shock some people, but I see no reason for requiring narratology to become a catechism with a yes-or-no answer to check off for each question, when often the proper answer would be that it depends on the day, the context, and the way the wind is blowing" (Genette, *Narrative Discourse Revisited*, 74). A great many readers must have misunderstood him.

[46] Cf. esp. Cohn, "Encirclement."

this apparently unbiased assessment of the purely virtual possibilities open to narrative does not escape the pressure of a system. But this much should be obvious: with reference to the establishment of the three basic situations, Stanzel is geared to dynamic mixtures and transitions, and to rendering in visual form those types of narrative that in actual fact proliferate in literary history. Genette, on the other hand, works – regardless of the speed the wind is blowing – with strict, exclusive oppositions between characteristics ("A or not A"). These oppositions clearly establish analytical differences, and Genette aims to catalogue completely (in an ahistorical, non-empirical way) every single possibility open to narrative.

Two preliminary remarks before I present and discuss some aspects of Genette's method of narrative analysis. First, the fact that I present Genette's theory more concisely than Stanzel's does not *per se* reflect my personal bias: it's perfectly conceivable that the more persuasive account simply requires fewer words, isn't it? Further, my procedure of thematizing potentially unclear aspects at the outset and noting conceivable objections as early as possible should not be misunderstood as a disturbance of the normal order: both of these, on the contrary, serve to sort out problems of understanding over which even professional narratologists still sometimes stumble.

As early as 1972, in his *Discours du récit*, Genette explained his view that works of literary theory dealing with narrative perspective suffer considerably from a confusion between "what I call here *mood* and *voice*, a confusion between the question *who is the character whose point of view orients the narrative perspective?* and the very different question *who is the narrator?* – or, more simply, the question *who sees?* and the question *who speaks?*"[47] Later, in *Nouveau discours du récit* (1983) – essentially a reworking, refinement, and partly a revision of his previous book in the light of criticism – Genette expanded the question *who sees?* to *who perceives?* and perhaps too categorically denied that a character can be the source of a focalization (that denial seems unnecessarily harsh because Genette himself had, as we've just seen, spoken of a character who "[orients] the narrative perspective"). In any case, eleven years later he writes:

> For me there is no focalizing or focalized character: *focalized* can be applied only to the narrative itself, and if *focalizer* applied to anyone, it could only be the person who *focalizes the narrative* – that is, the narrator, or, if one wanted to go outside the conventions of fiction, the *author* himself, who delegates (or does not delegate) to the narrator his power of focalizing or not focalizing.[48]

---

[47]   Gérard Genette, *Narrative Discourse: An Essay in Method*, trans. Jane E. Lewin, Ithaca, NY, 1994 [1980], 186.
[48]   Genette, *Narrative Discourse Revisited*, 73.

In contrast to the "voice" of the narrator, which, according to Genette, is always delivered as the voice of a person, the focal position can't always be pinned to a person. But apart from that, Genette left the basic opposition expressed by the questions *who speaks?* and *who perceives?* essentially unmodified.

7 Who Speaks? – Voice

Genette differentiates, first of all, between two types of narrative: "one with the narrator absent from the story he tells [...], the other with the narrator present as a character in the story he tells [...]. I call the first type, for obvious reasons, *heterodiegetic*, and the second type *homodiegetic*."[49] One of the "obvious reasons" for the new terminology is that the older designations, "first-person narrative" (= homodiegetic narrative) and "third-person narrative" (= heterodiegetic narrative), can be misleading – we discussed this above, quite early on – in that the authorial narrator of a third-person narrative can, of course, also say "I," without that in any way changing the essential nature of the narrative situation as an authorial one. (Though "first-" and "third-person narrative" were never meant to be *grammatical* indicators in the first place.) Genette's "homo-/heterodiegetic" opposition thus corresponds roughly to Stanzel's "opposition 1" (person).

Although in the earlier *Discours* Genette insisted fairly rigidly that "[d]efined in this way, the narrator's relationship to the story is *in principle invariable* [italics added]: even when Gil Blas and Watson momentarily disappear as characters, we know that they belong to the diegetic universe of their narrative and that they will reappear sooner or later,"[50] a terse addition did make clear that Genette knew pretty well that his fundamental distinction was under-complex and not refined enough. Thus, for those narratives in which the narrator himself is the "star" (such as *Gil Blas* or *Robinson Crusoe*), i.e., those in which the narrator's own story is central, Genette suggested the term "autodiegetic," "which to some degree represents the strong degree of the homodiegetic."[51] However, Genette introduces this distinction, too, with the either–or rigor typical of his thought: "It is as if the narrator cannot be an ordinary walk-on in his [homodiegetic] narration: he can be the only star, or else a mere bystander."[52]

---

[49] Genette, *Narrative Discourse*, 244–245. Diegesis refers to the sequence of narrated actions and events.
[50] Genette, *Narrative Discourse*, 245.
[51] Genette, *Narrative Discourse*, 245.
[52] Genette, *Narrative Discourse*, 245.

If we reflect that in the corresponding part of his typological circle, Stanzel inserts all possible mixed modes (e.g., I as witness or contemporary, I as editor, but the "mixed" narrator of *Barchester Towers* should be placed here, too), Genette's binary taxonomy does indeed seem rather lacking in nuance – in his system all these cases would be lumped together as "homodiegetic." But whether a narrator speaks from the sidelines of his narrated world (and *how far out* on the sidelines?) or whether the narrative centrally concerns him (centrally *in the past*?, centrally *today*? *Both alternately*?), and also whether he does not appear in his narrative because it's not about him, or whether he does not appear in it because he *cannot* appear in it at all, since he is ontologically different from this narrated world (both cases would be indifferently "heterodiegetic" for Genette) – these are, one should think, important differences that can quite fundamentally alter the flavor of a story. A system that cannot assimilate these differences or the transitions and shadings in between seems insufficiently complex: on the one hand it is too rigid in its fundamental opposition, on the other hand it lacks internal differentiation.

Genette himself admitted this when he conceded in 1983:

> I am not sure whether I would adhere today to the idea of an impassable boundary between the two types, hetero- and homodiegetic. Franz Stanzel, on the contrary and in a way I often find convincing, insists on allowing for the possibility of a progressive gradation – either with respect to "figural" (focalized) narrating (in which certain authors, like the Thackeray of *Henry Esmond*, alternate the *I* and the *he*) or with respect to the "authorial" type (in which texts like *Madame Bovary*, *Vanity Fair*, and *Karamazov*, with their fellow-townsman–contemporary-narrator, flirt very obviously with the homodiegetic type that has a witness-narrator).[53]

Following a discussion of the extent to which an epilogue in the present tense already "unequivocally indicates a narrator's relationship to his story, which is a relationship of contemporaneity,"[54] thus making what follows homodiegetic, he even remarked: "On the basis of that, one would justifiably hesitate between diagnosing homodiegesis or heterodiegesis – depending on the definitions of these terms, which in themselves, after all, *have nothing absolute about them*."[55] Perhaps this makes us rub our eyes, but we might discreetly decline to dig deeper. Clearly, the presence or absence of a narrator in his own story is now no longer an absolute antithesis, no longer the basic difference that enables us to fundamentally distinguish two types of narrative, the homo- and heterodiegetic. Rather – as Stanzel would note

---

[53]   Genette, *Narrative Discourse Revisited*, 103.
[54]   Genette, *Narrative Discourse Revisited*, 104.
[55]   Genette, *Narrative Discourse Revisited*, 104. Italics added.

with glee – the narrator's absence and presence now has different *gradations*.[56] It's just a pity that Genette's terminology cannot reflect those gradations.

The question whether the narrator appears in his own story *as a character* must, though, be distinguished from the question of what relationship he has, in his capacity as narrator, to the story. In the standard case (Genette: "by definition"),[57] the narrator has an *extradiegetic* relationship to the story he narrates – provided, it seems to me, that the object of his story is not exclusively the very fact of his telling it (a hypothetical extreme case). An extradiegetic narrator is thus any first-order narrator – someone who narrates something, irrespective of whether he appears in the story as a character or not. If, within this story, a character turns up who for his part, too, narrates a story (a second-order narrator), Genette then speaks of an *intradiegetic* narrator ("intra" in relation to the higher-level story, but "extradiegetic" in relation to his own story). This indicates that "extradiegetic" and "intradiegetic" are not terms that denote in which relation the "person" of the narrator stands to the narrated world (as "homodiegetic" and "heterodiegetic" do); rather, they denote the *relation of the levels* to each other, a relation that can vary with how we look at it. "Extradiegetic" and "intradiegetic" are *relational* qualities, which a carrier may or may not have, but also may or may not have according to our perspective.

For example, the extradiegetic narrator in Walter Moers's *Die dreizehneinhalb Leben des Käpt'n Blaubär* [*The thirteen-and-a-half lives of Cap'n Bluebear*] (1999) is Cap'n Bluebear. However, when he relates how, in his twelfth life, he fought in public as a gladiator liar in Atlantis, in a contest lasting 99 rounds against the one and only Nussram Fhakir, cooking up ever more fantastic tall stories in which he himself sometimes pops up again as a character (for instance in the story in which he falls into the hands of the Yhôllisian cannibals), he thus becomes in this respect (in relation to the *whole* story) an intradiegetic narrator. But at the same time, as the character who tells stories at the lying-contest, he is of course the extradiegetic narrator of these "interpolated" stories. On top of everything, he is also a homodiegetic narrator throughout, because he appears *in* his own story – and he's even an autodiegetic narrator, since he is obviously the story's star. Another apt example: Scheherazade, who narrates for her life in the *Arabian Nights*, is an intradiegetic narrator with respect to the first-order narration or frame narration; but in relation to the stories she tells, she is an extradiegetic narrator. Since, in contrast to Cap'n Bluebear in his stories, she does not (if I remember correctly) appear in any of her own stories as a character, she is (on top of all that) a heterodiegetic teller-character throughout.

---

[56]   Genette, *Narrative Discourse*, 244; *Narrative Discourse Revisited*, 107.
[57]   Genette, *Narrative Discourse*, 229.

Genette himself concedes that "it seems paradoxical to attribute [the prefix "*extra*diegetic"] to a narrator who, like Gil Blas, is indeed present (as a character) in the story he recounts (as narrator, of course). But what matters here is that *as narrator* he is "off-diegesis," is situated outside of the diegesis, and that is all the prefix means.[58]

And what's this difference good for? It has two uses. First, it clarifies the *directedness* of a narrative. The voice of a narrative *addresses* someone: it is, whether implicitly or explicitly, a form of address. The voice of an intradiegetic narrative is doubly addressed: to the intradiegetic listeners as the primary recipients, and to the reader as *cc*, as a concealed co-correspondent (of which the intradiegetic listeners can know nothing – they usually inhabit a completely different world and have no idea that they are being "read," except in those stories in which that's precisely the trick: a character becomes conscious of being read). And that's the second advantage of this terminological distinction: it allows us to articulate the different levels and layers of a narrative.

In these last few sections I have spoken of "first-" and "second-order narrative," of "frame narrative" (which may also be called "overarching narrative"), which is the opposite of "interpolated," "inlaid," "inset," or "embedded narrative" (and if this occurs repeatedly in the form of a hierarchy, the preferred English expression is "Chinese boxes," while one can also speak of the "Russian doll principle" or, with John Mullan, "narratives nested one inside another").[59] None of this, however, is Genette's terminology, and he wouldn't really be happy with "primary" and "secondary" narrative either. For Genette, an inset narrative is instead *metadiegetic narrative*, and a narrative embedded into this is a meta-meta-diegetic narrative.[60] Hardly any other of Genette's choices of vocabulary has attracted as much criticism as this. Indeed, most people seem to associate with an embedded narrative the idea of a descent to a deeper level, which is why Mieke Bal suggested to Genette that he rebaptize "metadiegetic narrative" as *hypo*narrative (*hypo* = under, below), in order to clarify the hierarchical *sub*ordination (second-order narrative *depends* on first-order narrative).[61] Genette did not merely remain stubborn, but even seemed to gain from this criticism the insight as to which spatial image he had actually been trying to express when he spoke in terms of "meta-" (after, behind, beyond):

[58]   Genette, *Narrative Discourse Revisited*, 85.
[59]   John Mullan, *How Novels Work*, Oxford, 2008 [2006], 107. On the phenomenon of Chinese-box worlds, especially in postmodernism, cf. Brian McHale, *Postmodernist Fiction*, London, 1987, 112–130.
[60]   Cf. Genette, *Narrative Discourse*, 228.
[61]   Mieke Bal made this suggestion in her French monograph *Narratologie*, Paris, 1977, 24, 35f. Cf. also her "Notes on Narrative Embedding," *Poetics Today* 2/2 (1981): 41–60.

[T]he way the prefix functions here is opposite to the way it functions in logic and linguistics, where a metalanguage is a language in which one speaks of a (second) language; in my lexicon, a metanarrative is one recounted within a narrative. [...] My objection [to Bal's suggestion] is that it marks it too much, and with an inaccurate spatial image, for if it is true that the second narrative *depends* on the first narrative, it does so, rather, in the sense of *resting on it*, as the second story of a building or the second stage of a rocket depends on the first, and so on. For me, the "hierarchy" (a word I don't much care for) of first, second, etc., levels is progressive, and I say on page 228 that every narrative is at a level "higher" than the level of the narrative on which it depends and which supports it. If I were to abandon *meta-*, therefore, it would not be in favor of *hypo-* but, quite obviously and as one might expect, in favor of *hyper-*.[62]

Apart from Genette, I haven't come across too many people in my life who spontaneously imagine that we *climb up* to an inset narrative (even certain Genettists will admit under their breath, as the evening draws on, that they see things differently from the master) – but maybe we just move in very different circles. As soon as we grasp what's intended, it no longer makes any difference anyway; although perhaps "third-order narrative" (regardless of whether we're moving up or down)[63] is after all terminologically handier than "meta-meta-diegetic narrative."

The identification of different narrative levels, which has no systematic place in Stanzel's theory, is of course extremely important, not just in order to be able to clearly separate out Chinese boxes and to observe transitions from one step to another (which is the indispensable requirement for defining the function of embedded narrative), but also in order to be able to pinpoint analytically conspicuous breaks and discontinuities – in other words, to explain the effect that occurs when a narrative does not keep its levels distinct from each other. Every transition that is not prepared by the narrative, every mixing up of levels, represents a "transgression" or *narrative metalepsis* ("that deliberate transgression of the threshold of embedding").[64] An instance would be when the narrator Tristram Shandy yet again, in book 2 chapter 8, mixes up narrative time and narrated time: he tells the reader that it is now an hour and a half of reading time since the servant Obadiah was sent out to fetch Dr. Slop, and he could well be back by now.[65] Or think of occasions in which characters leave their narration and enter the extradiegetic existence of

---

[62] Genette, *Narrative Discourse Revisited*, p. 91.
[63] Immediately afterwards, Genette proposes an inclusionary scheme displaying speech bubbles within speech bubbles. The *word* "hierarchy" he may have got rid of – but also the *idea*?
[64] Genette, *Narrative Discourse Revisited*, 88.
[65] "It is about an hour and a half's tolerable good reading since my uncle Toby rung the bell, when Obadiah was ordered to saddle a horse, and go for Dr. Slop, the man-midwife;---so that no one can say, with reason, that I have not allowed Obadiah time enough, poetically speaking,

the narrator (i.e., occasions in which they move *out of their narrated present* into the present of the narrative – I'm not thinking of cases when a character from the second-order narrative appears years later in the frame narration; indeed, that's not an infringement of logic). Or when an obviously heterodiegetic ("authorial") narrator quite suddenly appears among his characters, as in chapter 62 of *Vanity Fair*. All these phenomena, which Genette's theory is well capable of describing, participate in the realm of metafictionality, since each such rule infringement thematizes and problematizes the rule, and in this way establishes a reinforced autoreferentiality. In chapter 9, the final chapter of this book, we'll briefly come back to this again.

8   Who Perceives? – Focalization

Under the rubric of "focalization," Genette treats phenomena that traditionally, or in other narratologists' accounts, come under "narrative perspective" or "point of view." But *"narrative* perspective" is here conceivably open to misinterpretation, since it might erroneously lead to the question *who speaks?*; and "point of view" (like "sight," "field," etc.) is, as Genette claims even in the earlier *Discours* (i.e., before he replaced *voir* with *percevoir*), too strongly bound to the visual.[66]

In contrast to his treatment of "voice," in discussing "focalization" Genette begins from a ternary, triple-layered typology. He writes:

> The first term corresponds to what English-language criticism calls the narrative with omniscient narrator and Pouillon calls "vision from behind," and which Todorov symbolizes by the formula *Narrator > Character* (where the narrator knows more than the character, or more exactly *says* more than any of the characters knows). In the second term, *Narrator = Character* (the narrator says only what a given character knows; this is the narrative with "point of view" after Lubbock, or with "restricted field" after Blin; Pouillon calls it "vision with"). In the third term, *Narrator < Character* (the narrator

---

and considering the emergency too, both to go and come;----though, morally, and truly speaking, the man, perhaps, has scarce had time to get on his boots.

If the hypercritic will go upon this; and is resolved after all to take a pendulum, and measure the true distance betwixt the ringing of the bell, and the rap at the door;–and, after finding it to be no more than two minutes, thirteen seconds, and three fifths,----should take upon him to insult over me for such a breach in the unity, or rather probability, of time,—I would remind him, that the idea of duration and of its simple modes, is got merely from the train and succession of our ideas,---and is the true scholastic pendulum,----and by which, as a scholar, I will be tried in this matter,----abjuring and detesting the jurisdiction of all other pendulums whatever."

[66]   Genette, *Narrative Discourse*, 189.

says less than the character knows); this is the "objective" or "behaviorist" narrative, what Pouillon calls "vision from without."[67]

Since Genette then immediately explains his new terminology and offers paradigmatic, well-known examples for each of his three types of focalization, the introduction to this part of his narratology needn't take long:

> So we will rechristen the first type (in general represented by the classical narrative) as *nonfocalized* narrative, or narrative with *zero focalization*. The second type will be narrative with *internal focalization*, whether that be (a) *fixed* – canonical example: *The Ambassadors*, where everything passes through Strether; or, even better, *What Maisie Knew*, where we almost never leave the point of view of the little girl, whose "restriction of field" is particularly dramatic in this story of adults, a story whose significance escapes her; (b) *variable* – as in *Madame Bovary*, where the focal character is first Charles, then Emma, then again Charles; or, in a much more rapid and elusive way, as with Stendhal; or (c) *multiple* – as in epistolary novels, where the same event may be evoked several times according to the point of view of several letter-writing characters; we know that Robert Browning's narrative poem *The Ring and the Book* (which relates a criminal case as perceived successively by the murdered, the victims, the defense, the prosecution, etc.) was for several years the canonical example of this type of narrative, before being supplanted for us by the film *Rashomon*. Our third type will be the narrative with *external focalization*, popularized between the two world wars by Dashiell Hammett's novels, in which the hero performs in front of us without our ever being allowed to know his thoughts or feelings, and also by some of Hemingway's novellas, like "The Killers" or, even more, "Hills Like White Elephants," which carries circumspection so far as to become a riddle.[68]

That's fairly clear, but nevertheless it raises a whole series of questions – for instance the question of whether the terminology is always happily chosen. Does "focalization" really have a less visual connotation than "point of view?" Or: is it really fortunate to say that one of the most important forms of focalization is "nonfocalization," the absence of focalization? Wouldn't it have been better to choose a terminological differentiation between the generic term and subordinate concepts, in order to avoid such a contradiction in terms?

But the logic, too, seems not entirely beyond reproach: what does the answer to the question *who perceives?* have to do with the question of

---

[67] Genette, *Narrative Discourse*, 188–189. Cf. Tzvetan Todorov, "Les catégories du récit littéraire," *Communications* 8 (1966): 125–151. Genette writes in the same place that his term "focalization" corresponds to the term "focus of narration" as used by Brooks und Warren: cf. Cleanth Brooks and Robert Penn Warren, *Understanding Fiction*, New York, 1943.
[68] Genette, *Narrative Discourse*, 189–190.

whether the narrator *knows* more or less than "the" or "some" person, or with the question of whether he *says* more than "the" or "some" person knows? Knowledge isn't the same thing as sight or perception, and speech isn't the same thing as knowledge, and in fact we're not concerned here with reckoning up the deficits in knowledge on one side or the other, but rather with defining and identifying different *forms of presentation* in narratology.[69] Or: doesn't multiple focalization in Genette's definition actually denote a mere subcategory of variable focalization (just as autodiegetic narrative is a particular subcategory of homodiegetic narrative), whereas the fact that he juxtaposes the three types of internal focalization suggests that these three are quite distinct and logically equal in status?

Finally: whereas nonfocalization and internal focalization relate to the question of the *subject* of perception, the definition of external focalization seems rather to turn on the *object* of perception: if, that is, the feeling and thoughts of the "hero" are not *objects* of perception, the narrative must by definition be externally focalized. But even in the case of a "classic" unfocalized narrative, the inner life of a character does not necessarily have to be the object of perception – and the same goes for an internally focalized narration. And now we are asked to believe that this absence is even constitutive for external focalization? It isn't a *differentia specifica*, so it's no use for a definition. That's confusing. The suspicion thus arises that, just as Genette came to lose the concept of focalization in "nonfocalization," so he comes to lose the subject of perception when considering the question *who perceives?* in external focalization. And instead of speaking of the subject, he speaks – inconsistently – of the object-realm of perception.

Some of these questions and some of this confusion may arise from the fact that Genette is not entirely clear about what "focalization" is and what it is not supposed to cover; and evidently this concept does not by any means leave the optical and visual realm behind. In English and in German (*der Brennpunkt*, literally "the burning point"), *focus* is the center (though not in French: *le foyer*). *To focus* means "to unite/bring together in one point," or to "orient," or, say, in the case of a microscope lens, "to adjust." Thus, *to bring something into focus* means to adjust it in order to make it sharply visible; if something is *out of focus*, it's not sharp; if something comes into view, we say *it comes into focus*; *to keep something in focus* is "to keep something that has already been adjusted to sharp visibility in our field of

---

[69]   Cf. Andreas Kablitz, "Erzählperspektive – point of view – focalization: Überlegungen zu einem Konzept der Erzähltheorie," *Zeitschrift für französische Sprache und Literatur* 98 (1988): 239–255. Later in the same article, Kablitz regrettably confuses the terminological pairs "extra-/intradiegetic" and "homo-/heterodiegetic" (254).

vision," or, more metaphorically, "to maintain something in view" – and so on and so forth.

What's problematic about this terminology is that in one field of perception there are always *two* focal points (as Manfred Jahn, with exceptional clarity, was the first to point out).[70] One is in the eye of the beholder (focus 1), the other somewhere in his field of vision or field of view: the latter is the limited area to which the eye is specifically directed (focus 2, or area in focus). Since the eye has a variable, accommodative lens, focus 2 is also the area of greatest *visual acuity*. The field of vision is thus perceived from a particular standpoint, which is identical with the point of view, and which, as the *foyer* of the perceiving eye, can also be called a "focus." But it's within the field of vision – whose defining features consist of being limited to a sector, being tied to a standpoint, and being bounded by a horizon, together with other limitations (subjective and objective hindrances to perception) – that this second focus lies, the area of acutest perception, the area towards which our interest is directed. Are these two foci always clearly distinguished in Genette's account?

Genette's very opening formulation of his key question about mood, *"who is the character whose point of view orients the narrative perspective?"*[71] is deeply ambiguous, for "orients the narrative perspective" is so imprecise that it can relate both to focus 1 and to focus 2. When, in *Nouveau discours*, he revises and refines this as follows: "So perhaps it would be better to ask, in a more neutral way, *where is the focus of perception?*,"[72] the ambiguity of the genitive makes it unclear whether he means focus 1 or focus 2 ("the center of perception lies in the person X" seems to be an answer to this question that's just as possible as "the focus of perception lies in the conversation of polite society"). When soon afterwards he adds that this focus may be "embodied" in a character, or not, as the case may be, only to maintain nine pages later (cf. the discussion of this above) that *a character can never focalize* or be focalized – only a *narrative* can focalize, only a narrator or author can be focalizers[73] – this seems to offer a clarification at least with regard to internal focalization. Here, Genette can in fact only mean focus 1 (in the sense of "point of view"), for it's only this type of focalization that cannot be taken up or put down by a character at random – "in his or her own world" it cannot be discarded

---

[70] Cf. Manfred Jahn, "Windows of Focalization: Deconstructing and Reconstructing a Narratological Concept," *Style* 30 (1996): 241–267; cf. also his "More Aspects of Focalization: Refinements and Applications," *GRAAT* 21 (1999): 85–110.

[71] Genette, *Narrative Discourse*, 186. I regard the translation of French *mode* with English *mood* as most unfortunate, not only because it suggests an emotional anthropomorphism, but also because we have in English a perfectly accurate equivalent in the word *mode*.

[72] Genette, *Narrative Discourse Revisited*, 64.

[73] Genette, *Narrative Discourse Revisited*, 73.

and is "always already" given (whether it's realized in the narrative depends on the narrator). An internally focalized narrative would thus be defined as a narrative in which the center of perception lies *in* a described character, in contrast to external focalization, where the center of perception lies *outside* the described character.

And further, Genette's manner is conciliatory when he deals with the objection that nonfocalization could, *according to his definition* (the narrator knows more than the character or says more than one or other of his characters knows), also occur when there is a sequence of variable focalizations, yet that he (Genette) at the same time regards variable focalization as a different type from nonfocalization (i.e., in his view, variable focalization is a particular form of internal focalization). This non-confrontational attitude, too, tends to suggest that focalization actually means point of view (focus 1):

> That obviously means that the analysis of a "nonfocalized" narrative must always be reducible to a mosaic of variously focalized segments and, therefore, that *"zero focalization" = variable focalization*. That formula would not bother me in the least, but it seems to me that classical narrative sometimes places its "focus" at a point so indefinite, or so remote, with so panoramic a field (the well-known "viewpoint of God," or of Sirius, about which people periodically wonder whether it is indeed a point of view) that it cannot coincide with any character and that the term nonfocalization, or zero focalization, is rather more appropriate for it. Unlike the director of a movie, the novelist is not compelled to put his camera somewhere; he has no camera. Instead, therefore, the right formula would be: *zero focalization = variable, and sometimes zero, focalization.*[74]

For (disregarding the logical nuisance that here an *x* is only "sometimes" an *x* and at other times a subset of its opposite) Genette's assertions about the "place" of the focus imply, after all, that he was not thinking primarily of a zone within the field of perception (such as the roaming focus of a camera), but rather of the *standpoint* of a conceivable observer: a standpoint which, since it's impossible in the (formerly) authorial narrative situation, is referred to as the non-standpoint of nonfocalization. So if one wished to accuse Genette of making an absurd suggestion, owing to his special terminology, the suggestion that, of all "classical" narrative situations, it is this one (which can show *everything, really everything,* with absolute sharpness and in the finest detail) that is unfocalized, i.e. (in everyday usage), unfocused, fuzzy, not properly adjusted – then it would at least not be possible to substantiate such an accusation from the passage just quoted.

[74] Genette, *Narrative Discourse Revisited*, 73–74.

However, that's different with the sentences immediately following:

> So by focalization I certainly mean a restriction of "field" – actually, that is, a selection of narrative information with respect to what was traditionally called *omniscience*. In pure fiction that term is, literally, absurd (the author has nothing to "know," since he invents everything), and we would be better off replacing it with *completeness of information* – which, when supplied by a reader, makes him "omniscient." The instrument of this possible selection is a *situated focus*, a sort of information-conveying pipe that allows passage only of information that is authorized by the situation [...].[75]

That is not unproblematic either, for the formulations "restriction of 'field',", "selection of narrative information," "completeness of information," etc., at least hint at the inclusion of phenomena that are essential for the constitution of focus 2.

And that brings us to a question that's perhaps not entirely uninteresting: whether it's possible at all to create a credible internal focalization through a character without at the same time describing (implicitly or explicitly) the specific way in which that character achieves uninterrupted focalization in his story world. That hardly seems possible to me. But that, in turn, would mean that with this type of narrative text we'd always and inevitably be dealing with embedded focalization (which isn't mentioned in either volume of *Narrative Discourse*), as Jahn has sketched (figure 6.2).[76]

Jahn explains figure 6.2 as follows:

> [T]he outer field of vision (N) is the narrator's, and the embedded field of vision (C) is the reflector's. The narrator [in Jahn's example] not only sees what the character sees and how the character sees it but surveys the whole story world (W). The narrator's focus-2 may light on the reflector's field of vision or on the reflector's focus-2 or on a peripheral area or on something beyond the character's conscious awareness.[77]

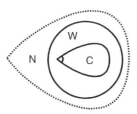

Figure 6.2

[75] Genette, *Narrative Discourse Revisited*, 74.
[76] Jahn, "Windows," 261.
[77] Jahn, "Windows," 261. In my view, this article offers the most concise summary and criticism of Genette's focalization to have appeared so far.

Yet this diagram is at the same time a pretty fair representation of Stanzel's figural narrative situation, with a foregrounded reflector-character and an unobtrusive narrator background (hence the dotted line around the outside). And this finally raises the question of what Genette's approach is capable of achieving with the aspect of "focalization," irrespective of all the matters of terminology and internal logic just discussed; and it raises the further question to what extent his basic distinction *who speaks?* and *who perceives?* is productive and helpful.

There's no longer any need, in this context, to say much about nonfocalization. Since Genette also admits (amazingly early on)[78] alternations or floating transitions between nonfocalization and variable internal focalization, his theory is certainly not less useful in this regard than Stanzel's – even though, since Genette's analytical method relies systematically on binary oppositions, it always manages to impart to transitions, shades, gradations, and alternations the suspicion that they are somehow deviant or illegitimate.[79] When it comes to identifying external focalization, Genette's theory even has certain advantages, since it gives one particular, idiosyncratic narrative situation its due – a situation that Stanzel had identified early on, but had then unfortunately relegated, to the extent at least that he had presented it not as a basic situation, but only as a sub-phenomenon within the figural narrative situation, even adding a question mark to it: "Camera eye?"

9   Internal – External: Advantage Genette?

In his article "Is there such a thing as a 'neutral narrative situation',"[80] Ulrich Broich has explained with exemplary clarity how the narrative technique aptly called *camera eye* works. Broich begins with a passage from Dashiell Hammett's detective novel *The Maltese Falcon* (1930):

> A telephone-bell rang in darkness. When it had rung three times bedsprings creaked, fingers fumbled on wood, something small and hard thudded on a carpeted floor, the springs creaked again, and a man's voice said:
> "Hello ... Yes, speaking ... Dead? ... Yes ... Fifteen minutes. Thanks."
> A switch clicked and a white bowl hung on three gilded chains from the ceiling's center filled the room with light. Spade, barefooted in green and white checked pyjamas, sat on the side of his bed. He scowled at the telephone on

---

[78]   Cf. Genette, *Narrative Discourse*, 189–190.

[79]   Cf. Cohn, "Encirclement," 160–161.

[80]   Ulrich Broich, "Gibt es eine 'neutrale Erzählsituation'? F. K. Stanzel zum 60. Geburtstag," *Germanisch-romanische Monatsschrift* 33 (1983): 129–145. Cf. also Susan S. Lanser's critique of Stanzel's stepmotherly and unsystematic treatment of the neutral narrative situation in *The Narrative Act: Point of View in Prose Fiction*, Princeton, NJ, 1981, 35. But cf., too, Stanzel's response, "Die 'neutrale Erzählsituation': Ein Fall von Kindsweglegung?" in *Unterwegs*, 37–40.

his table while his hands took from beside it a packet of brown papers and a
sack of Bull Durham tobacco.

Broich then explains:

> This passage is typical of the whole novel. This narrative technique registers
> everything that occurs within immediate range of the protagonist, the detec-
> tive Sam Spade. All information is thus withheld from the reader that a cine-
> matic presentation of this scene would also not give him. As long as it remains
> dark, only acoustic phenomena are related; the reader is not told what the
> object is that falls on the carpet in the dark, nor is he told at first that the man
> here calling on the telephone is the man already introduced in the previous
> chapter, Sam Spade. Likewise, the reader does not hear what Spade's inter-
> locutor says on the telephone, so that he learns much later than Spade himself
> that the interlocutor's business partner has just been murdered.
>
> This narrative technique, then, clearly differs from the technique that is char-
> acterized by "the presence of a figural narrator who provides information while
> getting involved with and commenting on what he is narrating." If we can speak
> at all of the presence of a narrator here, then it must be a narrator who has
> relinquished all privileges of "authoriality." Just as this is not an authorial nar-
> rative situation, so it is not a figural narrative situation in Stanzel's sense: like a
> camera, the narrator records everything that occurs within immediate range of
> the protagonist. The "camera" even registers the latter's physiognomic reaction
> to the nocturnal telephone call ("he scowled"), but we don't obtain any access
> at all to Spade's consciousness. Spade thus does not become "a *persona*, a mask
> that the reader puts on," or a "reflector," as Stanzel in *A Theory of Narrative*
> labels the typical narrative medium in the figural narrative situation. Finally, it
> is really not possible to speak of a first-person narrative situation either.[81]

It is surely no coincidence that this wholly "external" description coincides
with the triumphal entry of another great narrative medium: film. These texts,
indeed, deliver only what could be captured on a (sound-film) camera, without any additional narrative mediation. So the poker face of a Humphrey
Bogart represents the successful reimportation of a literary technique which
has discovered the charm and thrill of the impenetrable, pure surface. But its
genuinely *literary* mode of operation is incontestable and anything but derivative. This is not just because this narrative mode generates the "gaps of indeterminacy" essential for the detective novel, and because the impenetrability
of the urban jungle of signs that cannot be read unambiguously and reliably
is here staged as a kind of new *conditio humana*, inspiring and provoking
mistrust. It is not just because this technique enables the dramatic introduction of perspective-shifts relevant to human evolution, as in William Golding's
Neanderthal-novel *The Inheritors* (1955) (in this case the change of focalization

---

[81]   Broich, "Gibt es?," 132–133.

is from internal to "cold" external focalization). It is also because the tunnel-vision of a compulsive, repetitive registering of suspicious clues can be impressively evoked: for precisely that reason, Alain Robbe-Grillet's *La Jalousie* is both a culmination and a borderline case of this technique, since the external focalization that this novel consistently pursues – the orientation towards surfaces and constellations of objects – appears so idiosyncratic that sooner or later one can believe in the possibility, indeed in the necessity, of an internal focalization. In other words, the invisible spectator becomes imaginable through the conspicuously unique and idiosyncratic way of perceiving. Anyway, in "external focalization" Genette has come up with an excellent terminological match for a phenomenon that has no place on Stanzel's typological circle – a phenomenon that Genette is then able to trace back to premodern texts (Walter Scott, Jules Verne, Alexandre Dumas, Balzac, passages from Flaubert's *Madame Bovary*), and whose "cinematic" possibilities seem by no means exhausted even today.

But if we look at how Gérard Genette analytically classifies Robbe-Grillet's *La Jalousie* under "focalization," we hit yet another problem: for Genette, this novel (alongside interior monologue) is the one and only example of a thoroughly realized *internal* focalization![82] The reason why Genette presents it in this way is obvious: his line of argument corresponds to the one we've just sketched, in that he notes *La Jalousie* is a narrative "where the central character is limited absolutely to – and strictly inferred *from* – his focal position alone."[83] But the *fact* that he categorizes *La Jalousie* in this way nevertheless raises doubts about the clarity of his basic distinctions. He had already thought of nonfocalization as *"zero focalization = variable, and sometimes zero, focalization"*[84] (although normally variable focalization is only possible within *internal* focalization), and now he even dissolves the other distinction he started with: external focalization can *also* be conceived of as the extreme case of thoroughly realized internal focalization! Since Genette is usually criticized for maintaining too rigid a taxonomy, it certainly wouldn't be fair to criticize him now for the very opposite; yet especially if one takes a functionalist–nominalist approach to conceptual questions, i.e., not claiming the real existence of ideas, but calculating both the utility of concepts to the *end* that they serve and the *clarity* that they create, it's rather a disturbing prospect to have to work with concepts that – "as the wind blows" – can also denote their exact opposite.

But how does Genette actually get to the rather surprising conclusion that internal focalization (the center of perception lies in a character), when thor-

---

[82] Genette, *Narrative Discourse*, 193.
[83] Genette, *Narrative Discourse*, 193.
[84] Genette, *Narrative Discourse Revisited*, 74.

oughly realized, actually occurs only in interior monologue and in particular instances of the *nouveau roman*? His deduction is very informative:

> We must also note that what we call internal focalization is rarely applied in a totally rigorous way. Indeed, the very principle of this narrative mode implies in all strictness that the focal character never be described or even referred to from the outside, and that his thoughts or perceptions never be analyzed objectively by the narrator. We do not, therefore, have internal focalization in the strict sense in a statement like this one, where Stendhal tells us what Fabrice del Dongo does and thinks: "Without hesitation, although ready to yield up his soul with disgust, Fabrizio flung himself from his horse and took the hand of the corpse which he shook vigorously; then he stood still as though paralysed. He felt that he had not the strength to mount again. What horrified him more than anything was that open eye." On the other hand, the focalization is perfect in the following statement, which is content to describe what its hero sees: "A bullet, entering on one side of the nose, had gone out at the opposite temple, and disfigured the corpse in a hideous fashion. It lay with one eye still open."[85]

Without looking more closely at these two passages from Stendhal's *La Chartreuse de Parme* (1839) (I agree that the first of them seems less clearly internally focalized than the second), we can nevertheless say that at the very outset Genette lays down unnecessarily strict criteria for the presence of internal focalization. To be sure, in a strict, pure internal focalization the focal character should not be described from an external perspective (although perceptions of himself in a mirror, or others' comments about his appearance, or recollections of earlier self-perceptions are perfectly acceptable). However, why the narrator should not analyze his own thoughts and perceptions (what Genette means by "objectively" escapes me despite having thought long and hard about it), or why the focal character shouldn't be referred to by name, is totally incomprehensible. It seems to me that, *pace* Genette, all this is perfectly possible in internal focalization, since the aspects Genette here mentions do not come under the heading of *focalization* ("who perceives?") at all, but rather must be filed under *voice* ("who speaks?").

It is characteristic of Genette's approach that it can celebrate its greatest triumph precisely where, in internal focalization, the focal character (other theories would speak – with more or less relevant expansions of the definition – of the "reflector-character," "figural medium," focalizer, or center of consciousness) and the narrator are conspicuously *dissociated*. (The focal character and the narrator can be identical only in homodiegetic, or first-person, narrative; but even here they can separate out from each other markedly, i.e., when the narrating I takes over the focalization of the experiencing I,

---

[85]   Genette, *Narrative Discourse*, 192–193.

so that we experience the narrating I as distinct, as apart – to translate all this into non-Genettean terminology.) This kind of separation, though, doesn't make the internal focalization somehow "impurely realized" – it merely highlights once again the fact that perception and narration are two different activities. Let's apply the explanatory potential of Genette's fundamental distinction *who perceives? who speaks?* – precisely in the realm of *internal* focalization – to two novels by Henry James in which the difference is thematic.

In *The Ambassadors* (1903), the 55-year-old widower Lambert Strether is sent to Paris, to guide Chad Newsome back to the path of middle-class respectability and to take him home to America. Yet Europe changes Strether too, as those who are sent after him, ambassadors of narrow, unimaginative and uncultured American society, are brought to acknowledge. Even if, at the end, Strether also returns to the USA, the novel is, in fact, a story of a late mental emancipation, of a newly achieved attitude to life ("Live all you can; it's a mistake not to"). The novel has only one center of consciousness, Lambert Strether – and Henry James explains in his "Preface" to the New York Edition of *The Ambassadors* that, compared with the significance of this formal decision, everything else was relatively unimportant:

> [Y]et every question of form and pressure, I easily remember, paled in the light of the major propriety, recognised as soon as really weighed; that of employing but one centre and keeping it all within my hero's compass. [...] Other persons in no small number were to people the scene, and each with his or her axe to grind, his or her situation to treat, his or her coherency not to fail of, his or her relation to my leading motive, in a word, to establish and carry on. But Strether's sense of these things, and Strether's only, should avail me for showing them; I should know them but through his more or less groping knowledge of them, since his very gropings would figure among his most interesting motions, and a full observance of the rich rigour I speak of would give me more of the effect I should be most "after" than all other possible observance together. It would give me a large unity, and that in turn would crown me with the grace to which the enlightened story-teller will at any time, for his interest, sacrifice if need be all other graces whatever. I refer of course to the grace of intensity[.]

Yet precisely because Lambert Strether is a mature, subtly observant, reflective man, the question naturally arises: why did James not let him tell the story of his mental emancipation himself, as a classical (autodiegetic) first-person narrative? After all, his "hero" brings with him all the prerequisites to make him a credible "historian" of his own story. What are the advantages of the combination James chooses, of internal focalization + heterodiegetic narrative? What's the difference? James himself mentions two factors that speak against a first-person narrative. For one, first-person narrative stretched over long periods is a form doomed to "looseness." Whether we interpret "looseness" as meaning slackness, long-windedness, carelessness, or bagginess, it has very negative connotations for James. Secondly, says James, first-person narrative must display a compulsion to communicate, and such a compulsion simply doesn't fit the character of Strether (as a psychological and cultural type):

> The "First person" then, so employed, is addressed by the author directly to ourselves, his possible readers, whom he has to reckon with, at the best, by our English tradition, so loosely and vaguely after all, so little respectfully, on so scant a presumption of exposure to criticism. Strether, on the other hand, encaged and provided for as "The Ambassadors" encages and provides, has to keep in view proprieties much stiffer and more salutary than any our straight and credulous gape are likely to bring home to him, has exhibitional conditions to meet, in a word, that forbid the terrible fluidity of self-revelation.

In other words, first-person narration presumes a *garrulity* that is foreign to this hero's character. But in addition to these factors weighing *against* an autodiegetic narrative, there is also a very considerable factor *in favor* of the above-mentioned combination of internal focalization and heterodiegetic narrative: "The thing was to be so much this worthy's [= Strether's] intimate adventure that even the projection of his consciousness upon it from beginning to end without intermission or deviation would probably still leave a part of its value for him, and *a fortiori* for ourselves, unexpressed." Together with the statement we've already quoted above –

> But Strether's sense of these things, and Strether's only, should avail me for showing them; I should know them but through his more or less groping knowledge of them, since his very gropings would figure among his most interesting motions, and a full observance of the rich rigour I speak of would give me more of the effect I should be most "after" than all other possible observance together.

– it now becomes clear what constitutes the particular *aesthetic* appeal of this technique. With internal focalization, yet heterodiegetic narration, a part of the experience remains realistically unexpressed – viz. precisely its value or meaning for the hero. Thus the actual topic of the narrative consists in the hero's tentative, exploratory attempts to make sense of his own experience. Strictly speaking, then, *The Ambassadors* is not about an American's stay in Europe – that in itself could certainly be told in a different way – but rather about the attempt to make something of one's own experience. (That second point presupposes the first, but is not the same thing.) The narrator thus traces possibilities of interpretation in a subjectively limited and subjectively structured perceptual world, and he profits from the intensity and freshness of the focal character's impressions; but in his articulation of interpretative possibilities, the narrator isn't bound by the outlandish condition that the focalizing character would need to have all this formulated for himself in exactly these words. The special aesthetic benefit of this technique is thus that we're dealing with a doubling of the interpretative possibilities: interpretation *and* interpretation of the interpretation – whereupon we, as readers making our own attempt to understand, contribute an interpretation of the interpretation of the interpretation. As Christopher Butler, the editor of a well-known paperback edition of the novel, remarks in his introduction: "[I]t is interpretation, in all its senses, with which Strether and the reader are primarily concerned, even though it leads often enough to his and our bewilderment at the sheer complexity of it all."[86] But that's also what it's all about: writing a text that imitates reality in one of its essential aspects – its inexhaustibility. "Live all you can" is thus a piece of innerdiegetic advice that comes into its own again on the level of reading, as an admonition to respect the complexity of the story-world and to fathom its depths, to remain conscious of how open that world is to interpretation.

The possibilities of this narrative technique become still clearer if the focalizing character and the narrator separate even further, as in Henry James' *What Maisie Knew* (1897). The focal character, "my light vessel of consciousness" (as James says in his foreword), is Maisie, six years old when the narrative begins (by the end she will be thirteen). After her parents' divorce, she becomes a pawn in the ongoing battle of their relationship. Both parents marry again, and separate again from their new partners, whereupon the latter then ironically find each other and ultimately get married. At the end Maisie finds herself living with *two step*-parents – Sir Claude and the former Miss Overmore – and she gives Sir Claude a predictably hopeless ultimatum: she demands that he give up his new wife and instead live together with her and her governess, Mrs. Wix.

Having been told that everything in *What Maisie Knew* is seen through the eyes of a young girl who does not understand the full meaning of what's being played out before her, you'd be quite surprised by the beginning of the novel:

> The litigation had seemed interminable and had in fact been complicated; but by the decision on the appeal the judgement of the divorce-court was confirmed as to the assignment of the child. The father, who, though bespattered from head to foot, had made good his case, was, in pursuance of this triumph, appointed to keep her: it was not so much that the mother's character had

---

[86]   Christopher Butler, "Introduction," *Henry James: The Ambassadors*, Oxford, 1985, vii.

been more absolutely damaged as that the brilliancy of a lady's complexion (and this lady's, in court, was immensely remarked) might be more regarded as showing the spots. Attached, however, to the second pronouncement was a condition that detracted, for Beale Farange, from its sweetness – an order that he should refund to his late wife the twenty-six hundred pounds put down by her, as it was called, some three years before, in the interest of the child's maintenance and precisely on a proved understanding that he would take no proceedings: a sum of which he had had the administration and of which he could render not the least account. The obligation thus attributed to her adversary was no small balm to Ida's resentment; it drew a part of the sting from her defeat and compelled Mr. Farange perceptibly to lower his crest. He was unable to produce the money or to raise it in any way; so that after a squabble scarcely less public and scarcely more decent than the original shock of battle his only issue from his predicament was a compromise by his legal advisers and finally accepted by hers.

No six-year-old speaks like that. Yet exactly that is the point: the development of the story and Maisie's development from naïve six-year-old to demanding thirteen-year-old is presented in a series of key scenes in which Maisie is the "ironic center" (James' phrase in the foreword; "ironic" because of the discrepancy between her understanding and what's "really going on"), but the narrator is unmistakably an adult. He doesn't, though, tell us in a gossipy or zealous way what the child failed to pick up or wrongly understood, but confines his portrayal to representing her perception, without thereby taking on the absurd task of narrowly limiting his vocabulary or syntactical possibilities to those of a child. This would already be enough to overstretch any writer other than Henry James.

Here is the end of the novel:

> "Good-bye," he repeated.
> "Good-bye." And Maisie followed Mrs. Wix.
> They caught the steamer, which was just putting off, and, hustled across the gulf, found themselves on the deck so breathless and so scared that they gave up half the voyage to letting their emotion sink. It sank slowly and imperfectly; but at last, in mid-channel, surrounded by the quiet sea, Mrs. Wix had courage to revert. "I didn't look back, did you?"
> "Yes. He wasn't there," said Maisie.
> "Not on the balcony?"
> Maisie waited a moment; then "He wasn't there" she simply said again.
> Mrs. Wix also was silent a while. "He went to *her*," she finally observed.
> "Oh I know!" the child replied.
> Mrs. Wix gave a sidelong look. She still had room for wonder at what Maisie knew.

How much does Maisie actually *know*? How much has she actually *understood* of the adults' machinations? That remains open – *that is the question,*

"What Maisie knew." For even when the narrator gives her the focus, he respects that zone within her in which she tries to make sense of what she has perceived. The discrepancy between her kind of perception and our conjectures about what "really" happened is *not a discrepancy between interpretations*, but between inexperienced perception on the one hand and our experience-saturated "weighing up" and processing of this naïvely registered data on the other. Precisely because the narrator does *not* say what Maisie actually knows, we have space to work that out, to speculate, to imagine (like Mrs. Wix in the very last sentence of the novel: "She still had room for wonder at what Maisie knew"). And since that is in turn a question of the *pragmatics of reception*, it's anything but surprising that interpretations of this novel are exceptionally diverse (which is a good thing). They range, to mention only the extremes, from the persuasion that Maisie wonderfully preserves her essential innocence through all this immorality and irresponsibility, and so has not, in effect, become a victim; to the assessment that Maisie is just waiting, a passive seductress, for the moment when her adored Sir Claude will ravish her.

In no other case but here, it seems to me, is Genette's approach so much more effective than Stanzel's, for the differentiation into voice and focalization exactly identifies the specific character of this kind of narrative text. Stanzel places *The Ambassadors* close to the figural narrative situation, but to the right of the "internal-perspective/external-perspective" boundary line. That's questionable right away, on three counts: (1) Strether is *unambiguously* a reflector-character – what else? (2) the perspective is internal, not external, and (3) – and this point makes the suitability of Stanzel's terminology for this type of novel fundamentally dubious – *narration* is obviously taking place – and conspicuously so. This latter point is also presumably the reason why Stanzel does not position *The Ambassadors* directly within the "figural narrative situation": his definition of "reflector-character," after all, excludes any mediacy of presentation. But here *mediation is occurring*, and to an extent that is quite unmistakable. And how much more, then, in *What Maisie Knew*! The latter title therefore gets no entry at all on the typological circle, and quite consistently, too. But whichever way you look at it, there can be no compromise of the kind Stanzel attempts – i.e., not classifying *The Ambassadors* as purely figural, yet nevertheless pushing it fairly far from the narrator-reflector boundary line. That completely bypasses what's really going on in this text.

Since Stanzel's system cannot replicate Genette's distinction *who speaks? who perceives?*, what follows is this: if we attempt at all to find a place for texts of the type internal focalization + heterodiegetic narrative, we end up with absurd classifications that imply, say, that there is no "real" reflector-character, or that hardly any narration is occurring. No: the interior perspective is consistently maintained – and there is a narrator who is strikingly different from the central consciousness. It's just that Stanzel's circle can't show it.

On the other hand, with respect to a different area of narrative, Genette's approach of differentiating between focalization and voice has certain drawbacks, or at any rate (it seems to me) no very great advantages. This area, and it's far from an insignificant one, is (as mentioned in passing above) homodiegetic narrative. When the focal character and the narrator coincide – as in a classic *Bildungsroman* like Charles Dickens' *Great Expectations* – it is beside the point to insist on their difference, given that the most important *raison d'être* of such a text is precisely to establish the *identity* in this difference, to produce *continuity* in discontinuity by way of narrative. The established terminology of "experiencing I" and "narrating I" allows us to capture the dynamic and logic of this process in a much more elegant and sophisticated way than the construction "homodiegetic + internally focalized."

Since Genette later referred to his category of "distance" as "superfluous,"[87] and since for the purposes of a didactic exposition I'm not going to discuss other aspects of "mode" (as opposed to "voice"), such as "narrative of events" or "narrative of words," a summary of our findings so far may be in order. In addition to those major differences in the theoretical architecture of Stanzel and Genette that we noted at the outset, there are certain narrative phenomena that Stanzel's typological circle, though an elegant and flexible tool capable of reflecting all kinds of nuances, is unable (or only with grotesque contortions) to represent; whereas Genette's neat, cleanly drawn lines of opposition collapse, phenomena become interpretable as their opposite, or – a logical nuisance – something reemerges as a subcategory of its opposite.

Although Genette has explained –

> For me, what is important [...] is not this or that actual combination but the combinatorial principle itself, whose chief merit is to place the various categories in an open relationship with no *a priori* constraints: neither unilateral *determination* in the Hjelmslevian sense ("such a choice of voice entails such a course as to mode," etc.) nor *interdependence* ("such a choice of voice and such a choice of mode reciprocally govern each other"), but simply *constellations* in which every parameter can *a priori* come into play with every other,[88]

– it's rather interesting – and Genette himself did undertake this task – to display in tabular form what sort of narrative text would result from crossing the three focalizations (nonfocalization, internal, and external focalization)

---

[87] Genette, *Narrative Discourse Revisited*, 44.
[88] Genette, *Narrative Discourse Revisited*, 129.

Table 6.1

Type (Focal.) Narrating (Relation)	Authorial (Zero focal.)	Actorial (Internal focal.)	Neutral (External focal.)
Heterodiegetic	A *Tom Jones*	B *The Ambassadors*	C "The Killers"
Homodiegetic	D *Moby Dick*	E *Hunger*	

with the two types of narration, heterodiegetic and homodiegetic. Classificatory table 6.1 is Genette's own.[89]

Two points stand out – one of which would strike everyone, the other perhaps only lovers of Melville. One box is vacant, and *Moby-Dick* is written wrongly (and perhaps its position here is not entirely unproblematic for other reasons, too). As for the empty box, Genette passes over it nonchalantly: although he doesn't know of a text with this combination of attributes, in terms of pure logic he doesn't want to rule out that such a book may "exist somewhere on the shelves of the library of Babel."[90]

Moby-Dick, though, is not just written wrongly: we must also wonder how its homodiegetic narrator Ishmael can effect a nonfocalization (= the narrator knows more than the character). Does he know more than he knows? Pretty unlikely. All that virtually impenetrable mass of material on cetology that Ishmael spreads out before us is the result of the lone survivor's obsession – it's impressive, but hardly signals a perceptual ability exceeding the normal level of the character. "Co-vision" is the keyword, internal focalization the term that fits. Except perhaps with regard to one point (which Genette, however, doesn't adduce at all): chapters 37 to 39 of *Moby-Dick* feature a series of interior monologues from Ahab, Starbuck, and Stubbs, and chapters 109 and 113 contain scenes at which Ishmael can hardly have been present as a witness, whereas in chapter 108 that is at least not beyond the bounds of possibility. Yet within the novel these mini-chapters function like products of the re-creative imagination of the narrator, i.e., as a sign of internal focalization. As moments in which the logical possibilities of his narration are overstepped, they remind us all the more powerfully of precisely this limitation: they certainly do not define *Moby-Dick* as a novel with nonfocalization.

---

[89] Genette, *Narrative Discourse Revisited*, 121.
[90] Genette, *Narrative Discourse Revisited*, 121.

Table 6.2

Focalization Narration	Zero	Internal	External
Heterodiegetic	*Tom Jones*	*Portrait*	"The Killers"
Homodiegetic	*Moll Flanders*	*Malone Dies*	*L'étranger*

Manfred Jahn and Ansgar Nünning have filled Genette's classificatory table with titles that appear on Stanzel's typological circle, in order to facilitate a comparison between the two theories. So where does this title appear in Stanzel's scheme, where in Genette's? But here too, the same problems crop up (table 6.2).[91]

They've filled the empty box with Albert Camus's *The Outsider* (1942), evidently following a daring mind game played by Genette:

> Although such a narrative would be taken on by the hero, it should obviously adopt toward him, and toward everything, the point of view of an (anonymous) external observer incapable not only of knowing the hero's thoughts but also of taking on his perceptual field. Such a narrative stance is generally, not to say unanimously, considered incompatible with the logical–semantic norms of narrative discourse. [...] But it seems to *me* that these edicts of unacceptability should not be overworked. [...] So it seems to me wise to "anticipate," that is, to outline a box for the type that interests us, even if for the moment *L'étranger* fills it only provisionally and with a question mark. The kind reader is herewith requested to go and write it in himself.[92]

Maybe Genette's wordplay went unnoticed here: if Camus's *L'étranger* were the stranger that will one day surface to reclaim its empty box, the Messiah would already be with us and be known as such. Consider it carefully: someone who tells his own story and yet is shown exclusively from outside. Tricky, tricky. But as Genette says with a wink: "we don't want to discourage anyone."[93] Seriously: you read the first page of *The Outsider* and ask yourself whether the impossible has already incarnated in the form of the narrator Meursault:

> Mother died today. Or maybe yesterday, I don't know. I had a telegram from the home: "Mother passed away. Funeral tomorrow. Yours sincerely." That doesn't mean anything. It may have been yesterday.

---

[91] Manfred Jahn and Ansgar Nünning, "A Survey of Narratological Models," *Literatur in Wissenschaft und Unterricht* 27/4 (1994): 299.
[92] Genette, *Narrative Discourse Revisited*, 125, 127.
[93] Genette, *Narrative Discourse Revisited*, 125.

Table 6.3

Level ⇒ Relationship ⇓	Extradiegetic			Intradiegetic		
Focalization ⇒	0	Internal	External	0	Internal	External
Heterodiegetic	*Tom Jones*	*The Portrait of the Artist*	*The Killers*	*Der törichte Vorwitz*	*L'ambitieux par amour*	
Homodiegetic	*Gil Blas*	*Hunger*	*L'étranger?*		*Manon Lescaut*	

> The old people's home is at Marengo, fifty miles from Algiers. I'll catch the two o'clock bus and get there in the afternoon. Then I can keep vigil and I'll come back tomorrow night. I asked my boss for two days off and he couldn't refuse under the circumstances. But he didn't seem pleased. I even said, "It's not my fault." He didn't answer. Then I thought I maybe shouldn't have said that. After all, it wasn't for me to apologise. It was more up to him to offer his condolences. But he probably will do the day after tomorrow, when he sees me in mourning. For the moment it's almost as if mother were still alive. After the funeral, though, the death will be a classified fact and the whole thing will have assumed a more official aura.[94]

No, that doesn't remind us much of Sam Spade. Not at all, in fact. For this is clearly nothing other than a strict internal focalization, and precisely *not* the "impossible" combination homodiegetic + externally focalized. With the combination of homodiegetic narrative + nonfocalization, the cetological question pops up again: whether, by her conversion, the repentant sinner Moll Flanders is really catapulted to the same Olympian heights that, say, the narrator of *Tom Jones* occupies with respect to his characters – an ontological difference that allows her to survey both her previous, sinful self and the vanity of the fair earth as though from a different sphere. Even in Genette's final table, this position remains highly dubious (table 6.3). But what does a recent introduction to narrative analysis have to say?

> In a narrative with nonfocalization, then, the narrator by definition knows more than a real person can know. Real people are confined to a single interior

---

[94]   Albert Camus, *The Outsider*, trans. Joseph Laredo, Harmondsworth, 1982.

sight (i.e., their own), and a godlike standpoint is completely unavailable to them. In view of this fact, it is interesting to note that we are readier to forgive this implausibility in heterodiegetic narrators than in homodiegetic narrators. We usually experience genuine omniscience in a homodiegetic narrator as a gross breach of convention. Such a violation is only tolerable if the narrator relates his story with a temporal distance to it and if, furthermore, he at least hints at how he is later going to learn the extra information.[95]

Yet neither Ishmael nor Moll Flanders nor Gil Blas ever even approach such omniscience. There is no such thing, at least in the realm of reliable narration. But there *could* be, Genette would cunningly reply, since his table indicates the logical possibility – and: "what is important [...] is not this or that actual combination but the combinatorial principle itself."[96]

10   Coda

In the afterword to *Discours du récit*, Genette has already admitted mildly and in a spirit of self-relativization[97] that "the proliferation of concepts and terms will doubtless have annoyed more than one reader." He did not expect "posterity" to adhere to very many of these suggestions.[98] Indeed, he even expressed the hope that his offense against Ockham's razor – the principle of scientific economy attributed to William of Ockham, which states that in scientific and philosophical investigation the number of concepts should not be unnecessarily multiplied – will be corrected in the course of time:

> Therefore I think, and hope, that all this technical terminology – prolepses, analepses, the iterative, focalizations, paralipses, the metadiegetic, etc. – surely barbaric to the lovers of belles letters, tomorrow will seem positively rustic, and will go to join other packaging, the detritus of Poetics; let us only hope that it will not be abandoned without having had some transitory usefulness. [...] This arsenal, like any other, will inevitably be out of date before many years have passed, and all the more quickly the more seriously it is taken, that is, debated, tested, and revised with time.[99]

[95]   Peter Wenzel (ed.), *Einführung in die Erzähltextanalyse: Kategorien, Modelle, Probleme*, Trier, 2004, 121.

[96]   Genette, *Narrative Discourse Revisited*, 129.

[97]   Genette's self-styling at the end of the *Nouveau discours* as the Karl Marx of narratology also seems to me a pleasant piece of self-irony: "Until now, critics have done no more than interpret literature. Transforming it is now the task at hand." Genette, *Narrative Discourse Revisited*, 157.

[98]   Genette, *Narrative Discourse*, 263.

[99]   Genette, *Narrative Discourse*, 263.

Genette participated vigorously in these discussions (the *Nouveau discours* is indeed the outcome of this ongoing debate with, among others, Franz K. Stanzel, Mieke Bal, and Dorrit Cohn) – even if he was not always quite so ready to peacefully give ground as the above quotation might lead us to expect.[100]

By the way, F. K. Stanzel, no less than Genette, has emphasized the *heuristic*, instrumental character of his theory. Most recently, Stanzel does so time and again in his (self-)critical retrospective *Unterwegs: Erzähltheorie für Leser [On the Way: Narrative Theory for Readers]*: "Today it is clear to me that the real goal of narratological research must be to provide terms and theories that prove their worth as discovery tools for a specific work, in such a way that they lead the reader to insights that would not have been accessible without these theoretical instruments."[101] The quality of a theory is to be measured by its practical use, by the heuristic yield. The "three cardinal sins of narrative theory"[102] – academic hubris, terminological vanity, canonization of the theorist's own choice of paradigms – share the common trait, or even ultimate cause, that they tend to misunderstand theory as an end in itself, rather than a means to an end. That leads not just to purposive under-readings, which reduce the complexity and the nuances of a literary text, but also to futile and pointless arguments about pseudo-problems – arguments in which one's own theoretically informed construct is usually confused with the actual text.

Genette would surely agree with Stanzel on all these points, and such deescalation always helps to bring things back into true proportion. With so much conciliation and agreement as to fundamentals, perhaps I may be allowed in this coda to add, in passing, a personal and therefore non-authoritative *obiter dictum* to the contrasting characterization I have so far drawn of these two approaches to narrative theory. The following observation has always struck me as a wonderfully ironic reversal of the national stereotypes and prejudices of the international scholarly community: imagine a narratologist who, to an excessive degree, keeps coining ever new terms that sound incredibly formidable and exude an air of hardcore *Wissenschaft* – terms that are at times completely counter-intuitive or diametrically opposed to common parlance, and are defined, or so it seems, quite voluntaristically; a professor who abstractly charts the pure possibilities of narrative and then constructs a kind of periodic table on the drawing-board of theory; who deduces the theoretical possibility of the existence of a phenomenon from his system, without reference to reality – "so much the

[100]   Cf. Dorrit Cohn, Gérard Genette, "A Narratological Exchange," *Neverending Stories: Towards a Critical Narratology*, eds. Ann Fehn, Ingeborg Hoesterey, Maria Tatar, Princeton, NJ, 1992, 258–266.
[101]   Stanzel, *Unterwegs*, 19–20.
[102]   Stanzel, *Unterwegs*, 19–22.

worse for reality" (Hegel) if it hasn't yet realized the possibility thus deduced. Wouldn't such an academic be the very incarnation of the most curious traits in the popular caricature of a *Teutonic* professor – mental inflexibility and inertia, scholarly and ivory-towered solipsism, rigidity of systematic thought – whose terms and ideas, while he is floating in higher spheres, eventually create a confusing chaos of mutual sabotage and contradiction, to the puzzled amusement of the onlookers? In view of such self-destructive overkill, you'd hardly dare to ask whether these ideas would have survived an encounter with reality in the first place.

On the other hand, imagine a narratologist who has invented a continuously and smoothly adjustable automatic gearbox and seductively veils it in a design that – like that of the Citroën DS at one time – can only be understood as a declaration of love: as a declaration of the love for literature, for life, with all its mixtures and transitions that we are allowed to trace, as with our fingertips, an object of desire whose surprises and secrets we can discover and explore, sensitively and open-minded – a trip with minimal baggage and in an open-topped vehicle, feeling the speed of our own motion from the airstream. Would not a scholar of this kind, for whom change and flux is everything, be the very incarnation of those traits readily associated with French cosmopolitanism, lightness, finesse, elegance of design, and a successful synthesis of *savoir faire* and *savoir vivre*? Isn't it just marvelous that this story of Franz and Gérard, of François and Gerhard – in which any resemblance to real persons alive or dead is of course purely coincidental – runs so wonderfully counter to our stereotypical expectations? All good stories should do that. Why else read them?

Other narrative theories have long since joined those of Stanzel and Genette: the most important of these are linked with the names of Dorrit Cohn, Mieke Bal, Seymour Chatman, Michael Toolan, Monika Fludernik, and David Herman. Here I just refer to them by way of summary and recommendation: the more firmly you've grasped the questions discussed by Stanzel and Genette, the easier it will be to achieve an independent, consolidated understanding of this later material and its internal complexity. As I hope will become clear, the same goes for those aspects of narrative that have made themselves felt with a vengeance in the last twenty-five years or so: the aspects of multiperspectival narration, of unreliable narration, and of narratology in the field of feminist or gender studies, whose importance requires a new chapter.

11   The Novel as Atonement

The choice of narrative situation is not a trivial matter and inconsequential. "The same" story told in different narrative situations is no longer the same story. Form is anything but innocent – it cannot be separated from what it's all about. That explains, too, why it's so annoying when a handbook or reference work only offers the "story" of a novel, without even mentioning which narrative situation it employs.

If the choice of narrative situation isn't a trivial matter and inconsequential, however, then the radical alteration of the narrative situation within a novel is even less so. We've already encountered examples of this: *Pincher Martin, The Inheritors*, a passage from *Vanity Fair*, etc. But let's look one last time at how fundamentally the alteration of the narrative situation changes the story – at how, indeed, the alteration changes the subject matter altogether. We'll then consider whether such fundamental transpositions can be better grasped with Stanzel's approach or with Genette's. My example is Ian McEwan's novel *Atonement* (2001). Here's an outline sketch:

It's the hot summer of 1935, and in the country house of the Tallis family, the youngest member of the family, Briony (13), together with her cousins Jackson, Pierrot (both 9) and Lola (15), rehearses a play she's written herself, *The Trials of Arabella*. Briony is fairly precocious, regards herself as a budding dramatist, and enjoys bossing others around, while her mother convalesces and controls the household from her bed – the father is a great absence. Also in the house is Briony's eldest sister Cecilia, who is basically hanging around following the modest success of her studies at Cambridge. Their brother, Leon (aged between Briony and Cecilia), is expected too, and he's bringing his friend from university, the future millionaire in the chocolate business, Paul Marshall. Also important is the presence of Robbie Turner (23), the cleaning lady's son. Supported by Mr. Tallis, he has managed to take a degree at Cambridge, and a brilliant career as a medical practitioner awaits him. The relationship between Cecilia and Robbie, who have been friends from childhood, has cooled off from time to time, but is now unnaturally tense.

All this is mediated mainly via figural narration, and each chapter has a different reflector-character (in succession: Briony, Cecilia, their mother Emily, Robbie). However, it is apparent that each character's perceptions and thoughts are palpably adjusted, ordered, edited. So we're dealing each time with a central consciousness, but never with a stream of consciousness: everything is always already – from outside, one feels – reflected, ordered, brought into relation with past experiences, very explicitly, in a way that would never occur with a pure reflector-character.

The fact that these perceptions and experiences are all partial, limited, and subjective now becomes thematic: Briony observes a meeting between Cecilia and Robbie at the fountain, during which her sister undresses very rapidly and jumps into the water to fish out part of a broken vase. Briony can't make sense of what she sees, and comes to a spontaneous realization: instead of plays, the thing to write are *stories*, in which the radical subjectivity of every experience and perspective would become clear. No more drama – from now on, multiperspectival fiction would be her field!

Later that same day, Robbie, who has realized that he's in love with Cecilia, will give Briony a letter to take with her – a letter meant for Cecilia. Unhappily, however, this is a drastic, very explicit version of the rather more roundabout declaration of love that he actually wanted to send. Briony opens the letter, which is not meant for her at all, and is shocked by its sexual explicitness: she thinks Robbie a sex-monster – and feels compelled to tell her cousin Lola about it at once. This same explicit version of the letter, however, makes Cecilia realize her true feelings for Robbie, and on the spur of the moment, before the family dinner to which he has been invited that night, the two make love in the library. They are surprised by the naïve Briony, who can interpret what she sees in only one way: as a rape. The same scene, initially presented with Briony as the focal character, will later be offered once again from the perspectives of Cecilia and Robbie – which (and this is a skillful technique to indicate that their union is not only physical) are not always distinguished from each other very clearly.

During dinner, the twins Jackson and Pierro disappear, and a search party is sent out. Lola, who takes part in the search, is indecently assaulted in the darkness by an unknown man. Afterwards, she allows Briony to persuade her that the attacker could only have been the sex-mad Robbie, which then becomes the official version. When Robbie returns in the gray light of dawn, bringing the missing twins, he is arrested for his alleged sexual assault of Lola – his intimate letter to Cecilia has meanwhile been read aloud to the family and the police. He is taken away, convicted, and sentenced to five years in prison. Cecilia breaks off all contact with her own family. Briony does not go on to study, but becomes a trainee nurse.

The second part of the novel portrays the retreat of the British army from Dunkirk in May 1940. Robbie, now a soldier and the reflector-character in this part, was released from prison – a broken man. Because of his previous conviction he can't be promoted to the rank of officer, and a medical career is closed to him, too. Cecilia's love was a great support to him in prison. He'd seen her again in 1939, three and a half years after his arrest, and then he went to the front. Even after all this time he cannot understand why Briony (using Lola as an instrument) had, with such momentous consequences, falsely accused him.

In parallel to her work as a nurse, Briony continues to pursue her literary ambitions. A first short story, much indebted to the literary aesthetic of Virginia Woolf, is a (transparent) treatment of the events depicted in the first part of the novel. The publisher rejects it. Briony incidentally displays some consciousness of her guilt, a guilt not substantially alleviated by the fact that those around her had been all too ready to believe her or take up her suggestions. But only when Lola announces her engagement to

Paul Marshall, who was presumably the real attacker that fatal night, does Briony decide (in the third part of the novel) to make a clean breast of things. She seeks Cecilia out, admits everything – and Robbie appears from the next room. She promises to confess everything in writing, to make amends for it all – the possibility of making amends, of atonement, does still seem to remain. And then we read that this part is signed "BT London 1999." "BT" must stand for Briony Tallis.

Then the last part of the novel is entitled "London 1999": we learn from a first-person narrative that, at the end of her life and after several attempts, the successful novelist Briony Tallis has at last completed that novel on which she had worked for practically her whole career – but which for legal reasons cannot be published as long as her cousin Lola and Lola's husband Paul Marshall, who is of high standing in society, are still alive. Briony suffers from progressive vascular dementia, which means that the version of the story we have here will most likely remain the last one. Her 77th birthday is celebrated in her parents' house, which has long since become a hotel. In her honor, 64 years on and in the room that was then the library, *The Trials of Arabella* is eventually staged for the first time.

What we have read in parts one to three is this very novel, completed at last; the concluding part, as a metanarrative, is set in "reality," one level above (for Genette: below) the text of parts one to three. Briony now confesses – outside her novel – what earlier, "ruthless" versions did not pretend to gloss over either: that the meeting with Cecilia and Robbie after Dunkirk never happened, that Robbie died in the war without ever seeing Cecilia again. Cecilia herself died later in the same year, 1940, in a bombing raid on London. Both their lives were therefore finally and irredeemably ruined by the accusations of a thirteen-year-old, who'd herself had a crush on Robbie three years previously – at that time Robbie had, in a friendly but firm way, rejected her. The novel of her life stands as a great atonement for her terrible deed. The sobering thing is that in this final atonement – the only one ever published – she does not show the strength and courage to portray the full extent of the catastrophe, to look it in the eye. Before sinking into dementia, Briony Tallis composed, for herself, a *reconciliatory* conclusion to the novel (the fictitious meeting between the three during the war), which makes everything seem less awful because it was purportedly still possible to make some kind of amends. The first-person metanarrative admits that this was not in fact possible. After Briony has acknowledged the deaths in 1940 and the fact that the meeting between the three of them never took place, the elderly narrator saves herself on the penultimate page by an appeal to the truth of art: "But what *really* happened? The answer is simple: the lovers survive and flourish. As long as there is a single copy, a solitary typescript of my final draft, then my spontaneous, fortuitous sister and her medical prince survive to love."

Shakespeare's "So long lives this…" (Sonnet 18) is travestied to become: the only thing that survives is my self-exculpatory lie.

In this way the final part of the novel forces the reader into a radical perceptual change of the figure–ground kind. The reader recognizes that this is not simply a figural narrative situation with a palpable authorial presence, but rather a concealed first-person narrative. In Genette's terminology, Briony's homodiegetic narration is preceded by a metadiegesis that necessarily has a heterodiegetic effect, although at the end it is unmasked as a homodiegetic narration. Retrospectively, its internal focalizations are to be understood as deliberate, calculated fictions of the extradiegetic narrator Briony, and emphatically not as the disinterested, basically "objective" constructions of a neutral narrative authority. Briony is not just a character in the narration of someone or other: it's her own story. We have been deceived. So the novel isn't about – as we might assume after reading parts one to three – becoming burdened with guilt in puberty and the possibility to make amends opening up, even many years later. Rather, the novel is about the extent to which art, the writing of literature, can constitute atonement for real guilt, and whether the truth of art emerges only in the wake of self-lacerating sincerity. *Atonement* does not provide a clear answer to these questions: in fact, it incessantly nags us with a paradox. Our rejection of Briony (the narrator) has to do with her obstinate dishonesty, which persists even in the face of death: it is based on a critique of a writer's sincerity, which does mercilessly reveal the thirteen-year-old in all her affectation, her pomposity, her egocentricity, yet which stops short of revealing the continuity of these very same qualities in old age. Our reservation about Briony Tallis, the narrator, relates to the lie of her life, and it is morally motivated. *Aesthetically* – and this is the problem – she's spotless. Just as she did as a teenager, she continues with spectacular success to make other people believe things that aren't true: this talent is the source of her greatest moral failure and at the same time the source of her success as a writer. She makes things up and gets others to believe these "truths." She didn't do that only then, in the summer of 1935 – she did it again at this very moment as we read her novel and, fascinated, believed her.

To offer this story as atonement seems dubious and insincere – but as a work of art this story stands irreproachable. What is more, one of the strongest, most impressive passages of the novel is surely the whole central part containing the description of the Battle of Dunkirk – a piece of pure fantasy on Briony's part (and McEwan's too, of course). If this description persuasively evokes the true conditions of the war, what does that say about the necessity of real experience in order to bring out truth in literature? Hadn't *Atonement* explicitly warned us of what fatal misinterpretations inexperience can bring in its wake? And now it demonstrates that gripping art is not at all contingent upon real experience. In a highly unsettling way,

Atonement thematizes why art lies, why we prefer lies to truth (I've found in many seminars that the participants wanted Cecilia and Robbie to have definitely seen each other one more time – oh, one more time, at least!), and why the lie about reality is the reality of art.

Could Stanzel or Genette have helped the reader to see that coming? Yes. Not specifically the twist at the end, to be sure. Yet they would have helped us to grasp and classify the impression of the perceptible presence of a narrative authority exercising control alongside the reflector-character in the first parts of the book. An analysis according to Stanzel's theory would come up with something like "figural narrative situation with the perceptible, sometimes even obtrusive presence of an authorial narrator"; and according to Genette's: "variable internal focalization with a heterodiegetic narrator." Both theories are able to reflect the characteristic aspect of "mixture" in *Atonement,* to elucidate the sudden change to first-person (or homodiegetic) narration, and even (although Genette would surely want nothing to do with such psychologizing) to read the narrative situation of the first part as the telltale trace of the narratorial control freak Briony Tallis. As an author, Briony herself – *contra* the aesthetic of Virginia Woolf – isn't really interested in reconstructing *these* people's truths, to let them speak for themselves and to respect them as individuals. Instead, she wants to have the last word – and she does have it. Like every narrator. As long as no other narrator comes along. If it's a central point of *Atonement* that this maintenance of control is a reason for the incompleteness of an act of atonement, evidently this could only be thematized through such a change in the narrative situation. If (and I don't think there can be any question about this) the novel also thematizes the truth of an experience like that of Dunkirk, then it could convey another remarkable message: that we may expect the greatest truth exactly where narrator and author are in no way involved themselves.[103]

Theories can help us to pinpoint and systematize our impressions, to arrange them in a certain order, to put them in words. They also have the potential to turn us into attentive readers. They're a good thing.

And *Atonement,* incidentally, shows (among other things) that the really important, fundamental questions about "life, the universe and everything" open up when we encounter someone whom we discover (usually afterwards) to have been less than absolutely trustworthy. Or when we realize: Truth is something we believe in as long as we only know one version. But that deserves a new chapter.

---

[103] A reading that Ian McEwan would probably reject: as he explains in public readings, his father was present at Dunkirk and often told him stories about this experience.

7

Multiperspectivity, Unreliability, and the Impossibility of Editing Out the Gender Aspect

This chapter discusses some narrative phenomena that have at least one thing in common: to an even greater degree than elsewhere, the *pragmatics of reception* must join in the work of defining and analyzing them. That doesn't make these phenomena somehow "soft" topics of analysis that elude an objectifying investigation and whose importance would thus be minimized. On the contrary, these phenomena are prominent junctures of narrative texts, points that concrete realizations tend to dock onto or relate themselves to, because it's here that the textual parameters open up (or don't open up, as the case may be) very specific spaces of possibility, allow something (or prescribe something). But our discussion of these spaces of possible realization can be just as "objective" and definite (or just as lacking in objectivity and definition) as our discussion of other textual characteristics. The fact that effects, responses, and realizations tend to diverge does not mean that we can't say anything focused about the (textual, literary–historical, cultural, social) conditions of this divergence.

1 Multiperspectivity

We have already discussed multi- or polyperspectival narration in connection with the first-person narrative situation, specifically with the epistolary novel (chapter 6). Multiperspectival narration occurs as soon as two or more narrators appear in a novel, who – as one recent definition puts it – "describe the same event in different ways from each of their respective

The Novel: An Introduction. By Christoph Bode. Translated by James Vigus. English translation © 2011 James Vigus. Published by John Wiley & Sons, Ltd.
Original German text © 2005 Narr Francke Attempto Verlag GmbH + Co. KG.

standpoints."[1] The particular attraction of a multiperspectivally narrated novel is this: readers have to correlate the different perspectives, to compare the different versions with each other, in order to come up with their own picture of what happened. That's a fairly boring task if the different perspectives barely differ from each other – in that case we can say that the novel has failed to properly utilize the possibilities afforded by this kind of narrative. On the other hand, it can be a fairly irritating and nerve-wracking task – but still a very exciting one at the same time – if the perspectives diverge to such an extent that it's practically impossible for the reader to synthesize and integrate them. So there needs to be *some* sort of discrepancy – otherwise why narrate multiperspectivally rather than just narrate monoperspectivally in the first place? – yet the extreme case of a multiperspectival narration that can no longer be integrated would cause (at that point at the latest) a thematic shift: it would no longer be a question about how to reconstruct what happened in this concrete instance, but rather about the basic possibility of reconstructing events in general. The reader would begin to ask: on the basis of what data and which techniques do we normally deduce a correlation, a comparison, between different narratives, and why doesn't it work in this case? That, too, is a perfectly legitimate objective of the novel considered as an *epistemological* literary genre, which raises questions about the conditions of our knowledge and the construction plans of "world." Such instances would thus inevitably raise questions that in less radical instances just accompany the novel subliminally.

The above-quoted definition of multiperspectival narrative contains two potential stumbling-blocks, which should be cleared away at once. Must a text really describe "the same event" or (as another critic has emphatically formulated it) "one and the same event"[2] from different standpoints before we can speak of multiperspectival narration? That would only fit the case that Genette calls "repetitive narrative" (*"Narrating n times what happened once"*).[3] In my view that's an unnecessarily narrow interpretation. Rather, the reader already perceives different narrative perspectives even if they relate in general to a common fictional world, and not only if one and the same event is recorded as

[1]   Vera and Ansgar Nünning, "Von der Erzählperspektive zur Perspektivenstruktur narrativer Texte: Überlegungen zur Definition, Konzeptualisierung und Untersuchbarkeit von Mulitperspektivität," in *Multiperspektivisches Erzählen: Zur Theorie und Geschichte der Perspektivenstruktur im englischen Roman des 18. bis 20. Jahrhunderts*, ed. Vera and Ansgar Nünning, Trier, 2000, 3–38, here 18.
[2]   Uwe Lindemann, "Die Ungleichzeitigkeit des Gleichzeitigen: Polyperspektivismus, Spannung und der iterative Modus der Narration bei Samuel Richardson, Choderlos de Laclos, Ludwig Tieck, Wilkie Collins und Robert Browning," in *Perspektive in Literatur und bildender Kunst*, ed. Kurt Röttgers and Monika Schmitz-Emans, Essen, 1999, 48–81, here 48, n. 2.
[3]   Gérard Genette, *Narrative Discourse: An Essay in Method*, trans. Jane E. Lewin, Ithaca, NY, 1994 [1980], 115.

though by differently positioned cameras in a stadium and then repeatedly replayed from these different points of view. A too narrow interpretation of "the same event" would, through its very definition, unnecessarily exclude precisely those cases that are the most exciting ones in literary and aesthetic terms: those in which the reader quite properly wonders in what sense the "same" event *is* actually being described, whether there is still any common ground at all between the different narratives (as in, say, Samuel Beckett's *Trilogy*). But it can't be the task of literary theory to exclude precisely the most interesting cases through limiting definitions. The question is, rather, whether our definitions are really wide enough to grasp what's really going on in novels.

But the same goes – in the opposite direction – for the other stipulation in the above-quoted definition, "describe in different ways." That's certainly desirable – whether authors always successfully practice it is another matter altogether. But I don't see why one should wish – without becoming normative or prescriptive – to deny multiperspectivity in a novel with two or more narrators only on the ground that it does not satisfyingly develop the different perspectives (i.e., that it claims rather than really provides them), or because the versions don't diverge from each other in their essentials. Even poorly realized multiperspectivity is still multiperspectivity – an instance of regrettable failure, true, but these things happen.

Multiperspectivity occurs in the modern European novel right from the outset: I'm thinking of Aphra Behn's *Love Letters Between a Nobleman and His Sister* (1684–1687), Choderlos de Laclos's *Les Liaisons dangereuses* (1782), the epistolary novels of Samuel Richardson, etc. It is most certainly not an innovation of modernist and postmodernist literature. But that raises the question whether "one and the same" method of narration may not fulfill very different functions in different periods. If this is indeed the case, it's necessary to ask whether that catch-all term "multiperspectivity" does not in fact summarize very different phenomena in a dangerously sweeping way. That would at any rate explain the striking circumstance that, despite its wide dissemination and great importance, barely more than first steps to a general theory of multiperspectival narration have been made until recently.[4] Arguably with some justification, the phenomena gathered under the generalizing umbrella term of "multiperspectivity" were simply discussed and analyzed in different compartments, under different headings (such as "epistolary novel," "levels of narrative," "framing narrative and embedded narrative," "invented editor," "portrayal and constellation of characters"), because the common ground between these phenomena remained unrecognized or, if recognized, was considered to be too abstract and too general.

---

[4]   This is the starting point for the book – as relevant as it is excellent – edited by Nünning and Nünning, *Multiperspektivisches Erzählen*.

One parameter that enables us to recognize the most diverse, and in literary–historical terms most sophisticated, functions of multiperspectivity is surely that of the hierarchization of narratives and perspectives. Another parameter, related to that first one, is the closure or openness of the worldview mediated through the different narrating characters. Werner Wolf has shown both in a theoretically persuasive way and with a series of instructive examples how literary framing devices may be understood as phenomena of multiperspectivity.[5] As a rule, he points out, the hierarchically higher level of the text (whether this is a framing narration, a fictitious foreword by an invented editor, or whatever) fulfills a certain ordering or classifying function in relation to the subordinate perspectives (i.e., it really "frames" them). Yet again, in an aesthetic context, every stimulating violation of the rules promises some gain, and that's why there are novels in which this second-layer perspective does stray beyond its frame or in some other way shows up the inadequacy of the frame: perhaps, to give an illustration, because the editor or commentator is no match for his material, or demonstrably "undersells" it. The fictitious editor of the memoirs of Professor Teufelsdröckh in Thomas Carlyle's *Sartor Resartus* would be one such instance; another is surely the psychiatrist and editor John Ray, Jr., PhD, in Vladimir Nabokov's *Lolita*; or there's the "editorial" narrator of Nathaniel Hawthorne's *The Scarlet Letter*, not to mention the complex situation in James Hogg's *The Private Memoirs and Confessions of a Justified Sinner* (1824).

In general, it's certainly fair to say that the multiplication of narrative perspectives increases the demand on the reader and on the activity of reading – *provided that* the individual perspectives are sufficiently dissonant or discrepant and *provided that* an integrative conclusion from a higher perspective remains withheld, or no discernible hierarchization or privileging emerges from such a perspective. For if such explicit links or hierarchical integrations (*Aufhebungen*) of other perspectives are lacking, then the proliferation of perspectives will inevitably lead to an increase in the so-called "gaps of indeterminacy" or "blank spaces" in the text and thus to an increase of necessary activity on the reader's part:[6] in this way, the reader is provoked into bringing together and integrating material that does not assemble of its own accord. Without necessarily wishing to speak in terms of a literary–historical teleology, we can say that Iser's hypothesis that the number of gaps of indeterminacy has significantly increased during the past three hundred years of European narrative art isn't refuted by the recognition that

[5]   Werner Wolf, "Multiperspektivität: Das Konzept und seine Applikationsmöglichkeit auf Rahmungen in Erzählwerken," in *Multiperspektivisches Erzählen*, ed. Nünning and Nünning, 79–109.

[6]   Cf. Wolfgang Iser, *The Implied Reader: Patterns of Communication from Bunyan to Beckett*, Baltimore, 1990 [1974]; *The Act of Reading: A Theory of Aesthetic Response*, Baltimore, 1978.

multiperspectivity also occurs in earlier texts. Multiperspectivity *per se* does not yet *automatically* imply radical interrogation of our concepts of reality, of truth, and the accessibility of the world to our knowledge: everything depends on the concrete way in which this multiperspectivity is played out, on how consistently it is developed, and on whether the particular narrative text integrates and synthesizes the different perspectives itself, whether it suggests such an integration, merely leaves it open, or questions or excludes it. That's evidently a sliding scale.

Every reader of this book who has understood even just a little bit of Genette is bound to bump up sharply against the fact that I've so far referred constantly to narrators or narrative authorities in connection with "perspective," as though the distinction between point-of-view theories into *who speaks?* and *who perceives?* had never been made. This objection would be fair. For, obviously, if multiperspectivity is the issue, then the perspectivization of different narrators' standpoints must absolutely be supplemented in equal measure by the perspectivization of different focal characters or focalizers. That I have so far only considered one side of this situation (and, what is worse, the side that actually shouldn't be brought into connection with perspectivization any more) is for didactic and literary–historical reasons: true narrative multiperspectivity manifests itself in the modern European novel earliest and most clearly in the epistolary novel, in which, as we know, the perspectives of the narrator and characters coincide (the fact that the temporal distance between events and their description is minimal contributes considerably to this impression). But the definition of multiperspectivity I quoted in part above is continued with absolute consistency: "narratives in which the same event is represented from the view or standpoint of two or more focalizing characters or reflector-characters, alternately or in sequence."[7] There's no need for any more comment on the phrase "the same event"; while "alternately or in series" is perhaps an overdetermined distinction in view of the sequential nature of all narrative (even when a text is organized to evoke simultaneity, as in, say, B. S. Johnson's *Albert Angelo* [1964], we have to read it sequentially), as is "view or standpoint." Finally, "focalizing characters or reflector-characters" surely constitutes a concession to the fact that there's a genuine terminological schism here.[8]

The analysis of multiperspectivity actually takes off and becomes truly exciting when the perspectives of characters who are not narrators come into play. For it's clear that the different degrees of "control" over individual

---

[7] Nünning and Nünning (eds.), *Multiperspektivisches Erzählen*, 18.

[8] Since it has no particular relevance to the general considerations that follow, I won't discuss the third part of the definition: "narratives with a montage or collage narrative structure, in which figural perspectivizations of the same event from the viewpoints of different narrative and/or focalizing characters are supplemented or replaced in other places in the text." Nünning and Nünning (eds.), *Multiperspektivisches Erzählen*, 18.

perspectives briefly sketched above – is the integration of different perspectives performed by the text itself, suggested by it, left open, questioned, or excluded? – are even more palpable with regard to the relationships narrator/reflector-character or narrating character/focalizing character. Here, too, all shadings of the instrumentalization of the character's perspective are again conceivable, from a transparent doubling-up and reinforcement of the narrator's perspective, through a partial autonomy, to an independently realized and respected individual perspective that is in no way subsumed under a relentlessly integrative super-perspective.

To denote this relationship between the different narratorial and figural perspectives considered as a whole, Vera and Ansgar Nünning have coined the term *perspective structure*.[9] In my view, this term represents an analytical breakthrough, the full importance of which has by no means been recognized yet. For it's only via an analysis of the specific perspective structure, understood as the dynamic, interactive ensemble of the viewpoints offered in a narrative text, that we can make a promising approach to questions about identifying particular viewpoints, about the potential for subversion, about relations of contrast and correspondence, about the openness or closure of the textual cosmos of a particular novel. For example, it's been plausibly argued that nineteenth-century literary realism depended on a "formal consensus," according to which nothing other than the combination of a single-point perspective, authorial narration, and an imagined "neutral" space could produce the narrative effect of an equivalently "neutral" historical time.[10] Nevertheless, the idea of a perspective structure in a novel enables us to investigate more closely why it is that *within* an indisputably "authorially narrated" novel, such as George Eliot's *Middlemarch*, the different intradiegetic perspectives are arranged exactly so that the impression of multiperspectivity arises in spite of that – a multiperspectivity which is not annihilated by the authorial perspective but actually preserved; and preserved in such a way that the explanations and assessments of this narrative can just as well be read as a thematization and a problematizing of the

---

[9]   *Perspektivenstruktur*. Cf. Nünning and Nünning (eds.), *Multiperspektivisches Erzählen*, 51: "The concept of perspective structure in narrative texts takes into account the fact that the whole is more than the sum of its parts. The attributes of the individual perspectives do not determine the characteristics of the overarching structural organization. Rather, the perspective structure corresponds to a network created through the relations between the component parts. The concept of the perspective structure of narrative texts thus captures the structural relationships between all narratorial and figural perspectives as in a model. It is therefore a relational and structural category that denotes both the formal relationships between the individual perspectives and a central aspect of the holistic structure of a narrative text as well."

[10]   Cf. Elizabeth Deeds Ermarth, *Realism and Consensus in the English Novel*, Princeton, NJ, 1983, ix–xiii, 3–37, 65–92, 222–256; and *The English Novel in History 1840–1895*, London, 1997, 66–115.

integration of different perspectives in general.[11] Or, a second example, the concept of perspective structure enables us to define more closely a phenomenon encountered in the above discussion of the authorial narrative situation: the more or less palpable irony of the narrator's attitude to the narrated world and its individual perspectives. Or, to give a final example: it enables us to investigate the potential for identification between readers and characters, and what bandwidth of reception is granted, say, to the equally passionate and vengeful Heathcliff in Emily Brontë's *Wuthering Heights*, through the Russian doll-like integration of perspectives so characteristic of this novel. The concept of perspective structure can achieve this because it unites aspects of narration and aspects of focalization, purely formal structural aspects and semantic aspects, which critics tend (understandably, yet not quite justifiably) to assign to "discourse," but which are vitally important for *every* concrete historical realization and might therefore be regarded as an aspect of "story" as well.[12]

The perspective structure of a novel reveals above all – as a model, something in process, not laid down or fixed – how the novel envisages its handling of divergent viewpoints, of different subjectivities. And since that is at the same time the way in which the novel itself is organized, it's only in this way that the reader, too, can trace and reenact this kind of treatment of divergent viewpoints, of different subjectivities: that is, in the spaces of possibility that the novel opens up or blocks off, via the connections that it has made available without prescribing them, or which it lays down so that *only* these may be followed. What the perspective structure of a text allows us to do can be *fundamentally different* depending on the *sort* of text it is (even if it's surely once again the transitions that are aesthetically and analytically most intriguing) – to borrow a metaphor from Umberto Eco: Playmobil or (old-fashioned) Lego. In other words, do I get a box of different items that I can meaningfully assemble only into one particular thing, or a box of different items that can meaningfully be assembled into different things? Puzzle or paintbox? As Eco asks: "is it [the text] only a box containing the pieces of a puzzle whose end result can only be the *Mona Lisa* over and over again, or is it a pastel-color kit, pure and simple?"[13]

However, precisely that last point – the connection between the specific perspective structure of a novel and the free and open spaces the novel

[11] Cf. Ansgar Nünning, *Grundzüge eines kommunikationstheoretischen Modells der erzählerischen Vermittlung: Die Funktionen der Erzählinstanz in den Romanen George Eliots*, Trier, 1989.

[12] Cf. Carola Surkamp, "Die Perspektivenstruktur narrativer Texte aus Sicht der *possible-worlds theory*: Zur literarischen Inszenierung der Pluralität subjektiver Wirklichkeitsmodelle," in *Multiperspektivisches Erzählen*, ed. Nünning and Nünning, 111–132.

[13] Umberto Eco, *Lector in fabula: Die Mitarbeit der Interpretation in erzählenden Texten*, Munich, 1987 [first published in Italian, 1979], 69.

thereby opens up or denies to the reader's reception – highlights two final problems, or rather one real problem and one pseudo-problem. Since the pseudo-problem really is specious, we can quickly get it out of the way first. In 1996 Matthias Buschmann insisted firmly that multiperspectivity does not necessarily mean an automatic "release" of the reader's reception: "This is indeed a kind of narrative that inclines, as a literary genre, to the recipient's participation in constituting meaning, but it does not necessarily summon that participation."[14] Let's leave aside the fact that it's hard to imagine a form of narrative worthy of the name that does *not* lend itself to an extensive participation from the reader in the process of constituting sense and meaning (well, the endless procession of stereotypes in mass fiction, perhaps? The telenovela?), so that in any case we speak about different *degrees* of participation. It seems to me that Buschmann is theatrically conjuring up a bogeyman (one that Eco helped to produce with his unfortunately chosen metaphor of the paintbox). To be sure, the enhanced self-referentiality of aesthetic structures in the modernist novel results in a greatly increased and irreducible ambiguity of signs[15] – in which the multiplication of perspectives is *one* means of accomplishing such a foregrounding of form (cf. especially the novels of Gustave Flaubert, James Joyce, Dorothy Richardson, Virginia Woolf, William Faulkner, and in postmodernism Thomas Pynchon, Umberto Eco, or David Foster Wallace). Yet that does not mean (and indeed this is never claimed seriously, but only as a hyperbolic exaggeration) that such novels may now have "all possible" meanings.[16] To "prove" this is really futile because the charge being refuted is so obviously absurd.

The second problem, though, is a real one, and it's a fundamental problem for literary criticism that only becomes impossible to ignore in the case of multiperspectivity and the perspective structure of the novel. It's the fundamental question whether it is *possible* to reconstruct historical perspective structures at all. In principle, there are two ways for criticism to engage with literary texts from the past. Either we try to reconstruct their meaning and their potential effect against the situation in which they were conceived, written, and published, i.e., we situate them historically through contextualization; or we try to ascertain their meaning and their potential effect

[14]   Matthias Buschmann, "Multiperspektivität – Alle Macht dem Leser?" *Wirkendes Wort* 46/2 (1996): 259–275, here 271.

[15]   Cf. Christoph Bode, *Ästhetik der Ambiguität: Zu Funktion und Bedeutung von Mehrdeutigkeit in der Literatur der Moderne*, Tübingen, 1988, 381: "The increased ambiguity in modernist literature must be understood as the effect – absolutely unavoidable, because specific to the material – of an overarching evolutionary tendency to self-referentiality in aesthetic structures, which emerged as 'absolute music' and 'post-tonal composition,' and in modern painting as non-objectivity."

[16]   Cf. Bode, *Ästhetik der Ambiguität*, esp. 1–24, 74–170, 242–378.

today, as a stage in the process by which the work has unfolded so far. The latter procedure understands the work's meaning as not tied to its origin, in other words it decontextualizes. (A pertinent example: the meanings of *Hamlet*, the meanings the drama has received in the theatre and from interpreters, considerably exceed their Elizabethan meaning – and that's a good thing, too: the meaning of a literary text is equivalent to the sum of the realizations it has historically accumulated.) Both approaches are legitimate and equally valid: they represent different critical objectives and interests. We should just be clear about which of the two we practice, in order to avoid anachronistic mixtures. For example, it's without doubt completely legitimate to interpret *Hamlet* psychoanalytically, but absurdly anachronistic to claim that, in *Hamlet*, Shakespeare intended to dramatize a psychoanalytic insight; then again, it's legitimate to claim that in *Hamlet*, Shakespeare dramatized a psychosexual constellation that, centuries later, Freud was to conceptualize psychoanalytically (a task in which he was famously assisted by both *Oedipus* and *Hamlet*).

The problem with the historical reconstruction of literary meanings and perspective structures is that we can't be sure whether the perspective structure we have reconstructed was already there *at that time* (in the sense not just of being implied in the artifact, but of having been realized in the historical reception *then*) or whether *we* alone realize it in the novel's text *today*. That would also be fine, but it doesn't yet give us the right to make assertions about the supposed subversiveness of a particular novel *in its time*. To put this in more concrete terms: if it could be proved, from the viewpoint of a feminist literary critical perspective, that in nineteenth-century women's fiction, which otherwise stands for a single-point perspective system, we can actually find subversive, anti-synthesizing strategies of multiperspectival narration, then it would still have to be explained (only, that is, if we're really attempting a *historical* reconstruction – otherwise we are freed from this obligation) what evidence there is that "the potential feminist effect of Austen's novels" was *already at that time* "accentuated" through "ironic generalizations of the female narrator" and the "relativization of Catherine's misjudgments."[17] It would be necessary to ask whether this is an anachronistic retrojection, which obscures its present-day

---

[17] Gaby Allrath, "Multiperspektivisches Erzählen und synthesestörende Strategien im englischen Frauenroman des 19. Jahrhunderts aus der Sicht einer feministischen Literaturwissenschaft: Subversive Variationen des *single-point perspective system* bei Jane Austen, Emily Brontë und George Eliot," in *Multiperspektivisches Erzählen*, ed. Nünning and Nünning, 175–198, here 182. Specifically on the ambivalence of "gender-based discourse" in Jane Austen, and the difficulty of reading it unambiguously either as social criticism or on the other hand as an affirmation of the status quo, see Christine Roulston, "Discourse, Gender, and Gossip: Some Reflections on Bakhtin and *Emma*," in *Ambiguous Discourse: Feminist Narratology and British Women Writers*, ed. Kathy Mezei, Chapel Hill, NC, 1996, 40–65.

standpoint: "However, such a novel-ending [that ultimately brings all perspectives together in one common vanishing-point] cannot allow its recipients fully to forget that alongside the single authoritative viewpoint of the narrated world, other approaches are possible too, even if these are stigmatized as 'immature' and presented in the context of the novel as inadmissible possibilities for interpreting the world."[18] Recipients then? Or recipients now? And if every single type of (finally integrated) departure from the norm constitutes subversiveness, what would a novel have to look like that was totally *free* from such subversiveness? But if, viewed in this way, all novels are subversive, what does it mean to say about one novel in particular that it evinces subversive strategies?

But regardless of how important we consider the "relativization of Catherine's misjudgments," which are, after all, continually exposed as comic, absurd, and quixotic misreadings, stemming from inexperience and a ridiculously know-all attitude, perhaps the novel *Northanger Abbey* (1818) contains a central paradox, if we identify its message as follows: *novels don't teach us anything about life.* Whether this paradoxical reading, too, constitutes a retrojection (that is, a present-day *pro*jection that is targeted at the past), or, quite on the contrary, the outrageous insinuation that this would not yet have occurred to readers at that time, is a question for historical reception studies – or a question about what we deem possible and probable. To be sure, not being able to *prove* the historical actualization of potential subversiveness does *not* mean that no such realization took place at the time, and definitely doesn't mean that it's not "there." Critical appropriation of a literary inheritance, however it may have come down to us, does not just permit but positively *demands* that we think about how canonized texts relate to *us, now*, without having to assure ourselves of a historical legitimation of whatever kind. It may be – may it not? – that we are the first to discover the message in the bottle that reveals subversive strategies – well, then at long last it would have found its addressee. That's always cause for celebration.

2   Unreliable Narration

It seldom happens in literary criticism that one intervention in the process of identifying and discussing a prominent literary phenomenon should obstruct and hold back progress for decades – as is the case with Wayne C. Booth's reflections on unreliable narrators in his seminal standard work *The Rhetoric of Fiction*, which was first published in 1961 and ran to a second edition in 1983.[19]

---

18   Allrath, "Synthesestörende Strategien," 182.
19   Wayne C. Booth, *The Rhetoric of Fiction*, 2nd edn, Chicago, 1983.

It's usual to speak of an unreliable narration when the reader has justifiable reason to distrust a narrative, to doubt its "correctness" or truth. A series of factors need to coincide before the reader abandons the default setting of initially accepting everything the narrator of a novel says, and instead begins to doubt the latter's credibility. However, the following very rough characterization should suffice for the time being: unreliable narration is narration that triggers reasonable doubts and in which credibility gaps become apparent.

If that's approximately correct, it's surely astonishing that until just a few years ago virtually every discussion of unreliable narration began with Wayne C. Booth's definition of 1961 (as I'm doing too, but in order to highlight a fundamental difference, and to express my amazement), which reads as follows: "For lack of better terms, I have called a narrator *reliable* when he speaks for or acts in accordance with the norms of the work (which is to say, the implied author's norms), *unreliable* when he does not."[20]

This statement seems disputable in more than one respect. For clarification of the question "*Reliable* or *unreliable?*" Booth introduces the concept, central to his theory, of an *implied author*. Yet ever fewer critics now regard this supposition of an implied author in narrative texts as necessary or even helpful. Some doubt for reasons of method (Ockham's razor) whether the term "implied author" covers any aspect of narrative texts that could not be described more elegantly and economically in some other way; for others, there is the problem of the ideological implications of this term, which perhaps not everyone who uses it is aware of. To sketch the context of Booth's position: the central thesis of *The Rhetoric of Fiction* is that the author is irreducibly present in the text. Opposing a dogmatic demand for "objectivity" and self-effacement on the part of the author, as well as the idea that the author withdraws or even disappears in narrative literature after Flaubert, Booth responds that in the narrative text there is *always* – as the embodiment of the norms and value judgments held by the real author – a "superior version" of himself implicit, i.e., the implied author, the author's second self.[21] Since a narrative text does not just *contain* rhetorical devices, but *is a rhetorical act* throughout, there can be no such thing as pure narrative art in the sense of narrative texts free from rhetoric. But if a fictional text employs rhetorical devices in pursuit of a particular objective, these rhetorical devices should be judged from the point of view of their effectiveness, and not condemned *a priori*. Booth therefore defends the much-despised expedient of

---

[20]   Booth, *Rhetoric*, 158–159.
[21]   Booth, *Rhetoric*, 151: "*The implied author (the author's 'second self').* – Even the novel in which no narrator is dramatized creates an implicit picture of an author who stands behind the scenes, whether as stage manager, as puppeteer, or as an indifferent God, silently paring his fingernails. This implied author is always distinct from the 'real man' – whatever we may take him to be – who creates a superior version of himself, a 'second self,' as he creates his work."

authorial intervention as basically valid, in fact even desirable (Booth welcomes everything that serves to clarify the text's message – thus his discussion gives the strange impression that authors should intervene to remove ambiguities that had previously crept into the text against their will); but he also regards dramatized narrators and reflector-characters as functions of the author's voice.

And it's exactly at this central point that Booth's analysis and critique of "impersonal" and unreliable narration comes into operation. Since he assumes an inseparable connection between art and morality, as well as the unity of form, moral content, and rhetorical means,[22] he can admittedly provide a fine analysis of the technique and peculiarities of "impersonal" narration and also acknowledge certain advantages of this form of narrative; but he ultimately cannot approve of this kind of modernist literature, because it raises problems of judgment for the reader. Given Booth's conviction that it's an author's duty to present his moral standpoint as clearly as possible,[23] the irresolvable ambiguities that result from the systematic deployment of reflector-characters and unreliable narrators cannot but seem to him dubious or, in extreme cases, objectionable. That's the crux of Booth's *The Rhetoric of Fiction*: narrative texts use rhetorical means to pursue a moral objective; if the moral objective is not recognizable or is at least open to misunderstanding, then the text is, as literature, unsatisfactory. Booth has a firm political and moral agenda: he wants to warn readers in his own age that they are being stealthily corrupted and poisoned by systematic uncertainty and ambiguities. The moral of a novel and its norms are thus of overriding importance – everything else must retreat before them:

> Her [=Jane Austen's, as implied author] "omniscience" is thus a much more remarkable thing than is ordinarily implied by the term. All good novelists know all about their characters – all that they need to know. And the question of how their narrators are to find out all that *they* need to know, the question of "authority," is a relatively simple one. The real choice is much more profound than this would imply. It is a choice of *the moral*, not merely the technical, *angle of vision* from which the story is told.[24]

It's rather paradoxical that, of all people, such a card-carrying *opponent* of equivocation, ambiguity, and unreliable narration as Booth became *the* progenitor of the theory of narrative unreliability.

It's been remarked quite rightly that the implied author is a specious concept whose only function is to lend the greater glory of authorial status to whatever a particular critic has decided is *the* meaning and *the* system of

---

22 Cf. Booth, *Rhetoric*, 397.
23 Cf. Booth, *Rhetoric*, 385ff.
24 Booth, *Rhetoric*, 265, emphases added.

values and norms in a text. Ansgar Nünning speaks of a "literary critical phantom" that functions as the anachronistic guarantor of a "correct" interpretation (of whatever kind).[25] As far as his role in critical debate is concerned, the implied author would thus resemble the so-called "authorial intention," to which critics usually appeal in order to prevent their interpretation from having to take its place as one of many, singling it out as especially "authorized": you call your big brother, who (of course) looks at things just as you do and completely shares your opinion. Due to this self-privileging tendency, both the "implied author" and the "authorial intention" might be labeled narratological bedfellows of the doctrine of divine right in the political sphere.

If the concept of the implied author is highly disputable and controversial, why then should it be used to settle the question of the reliability or unreliability of the narrator? For Booth, that doesn't seem to be much of a problem – he *knows* his implied authors, and if real authors write texts that are open to misunderstanding, that are ambiguous or contradictory, then these texts and these authors are to be rejected, for aesthetic, but above all for moral reasons. The rest of us, however, are left with the disquieting question, "how the recipient of a fictional text can determine the norms and values of an implied author; exactly that would be a necessary precondition for an investigation of the different normative systems, if one were to define the implied author as the measure of unreliability."[26] Nor would this problem be solved by noting (quite properly) that the implied author is defined from the outset as an embodiment of the author's norms and value-judgments.

Even this last objection, however, still leaves untouched what is actually the most amazing thing about Booth's definition of the unreliable narrator – and this is something that can perhaps only be understood as historically contingent, arising from the era of the Cold War and Booth's fundamentalist religious persuasion:[27] *an unreliable person is someone who does not share my value-judgments and normative systems.* That's sufficient. There's no

[25] Ansgar Nünning, "Renaissance eines anthropomorphisierten Passepartouts oder Nachruf auf ein literaturkritisches Phantom? Überlegungen und Alternativen zum Konzept des '*implied author*,'" *Deutsche Vierteljahrsschrift für Literaturwissenschaft und Geistesgeschichte* 67/1 (1993): 1–25. Cf. also Ansgar Nünning's essay in *A Companion to Narrative Theory*, ed. James Phelan and Peter J. Rabinowitz, Oxford, 2008 [2005]. Cf., for an opposed position, Seymour Chatman, "In Defense of the Implied Author," *Coming to Terms: The Rhetoric of Narrative in Fiction and Film*, Ithaca, NY, 1993 [1990], 74–89.

[26] Gaby Allrath, "'But why will you say that I am mad?': Textuelle Signale für die Ermittlung von *unreliable narration*," in *Unreliable Narration: Studien zur Theorie und Praxis unglaubwürdigen Erzählens in der englischsprachigen Erzählliteratur*, ed. Ansgar Nünning, Trier, 1998, 59–79, here 59.

[27] On this, see Tom Kindt and Hans-Harald Müller, "Der 'implizite Autor': Zur Explikation und Verwendung eines umstrittenen Begriffs," in *Rückkehr des Autors: Zur Erneuerung eines umstrittenen Begriffs*, ed. Fotis Jannidis et al., Tübingen, 1999, 273–288.

mention of any need to establish the presence of contradictions, or gather clues. Evidence of a *wayward or non-conformist attitude*, a dissident disposition, is enough to immediately brand the narrator as "unreliable."[28] For Booth, the unreliable narrator is the Other *per se*, and every Other is an unreliable narrator. Committees for unauthorial activities can do the rest. How much ideological baggage is dragged along unawares when critics still continue to relate unreliability to somehow divergent systems of values and norms,[29] rather than to conflicting evidence and other such indications.

Possibly, we are always mistaken when we assume that narrative unreliability is an objective quality of the text, a quality that can be inferred and "proved" from the relationship between particular *internal* dimensions of text (e.g., the narrator's values: the implied author's values). Sometimes words (like "unreliability") mislead us into naïvely thinking of *inherent* attributes, when it's perhaps more appropriate to speak of *relational* qualities.[30] The working definition I gave above, "It's usual to speak of an unreliable narration when the reader has justifiable reason to distrust a narrative, to doubt its 'correctness' or truth," posits text and reader as two elements in a *relationship*, a particular association with each other. According to this view, "unreliable" is a label based on *pragmatic* grounds, which a particular reader applies to a specific narrative if his relationship to that narrative has turned into one of *mistrust*. "Unreliability" thus wouldn't be an objective quality like being 6 foot 4 tall or weighing 160 pounds. It would be a *relational attribute* that stands for the quality of a relationship between at least two elements: the narrative and the reader, with all that reader's assumptions about probability, plausibility, freedom from contradiction, normality, etc. "Unreliable narration" would be a pragmatic quality rather than a purely textual one – an identification that the reader makes in response to a particular textual provocation. As early as 1981, Tamar Yacobi recognized this in a groundbreaking essay in which he suggested thinking of unreliability as the "resolution of textual tensions,"[31] as an interpretative strategy on the reader's part "which serves to resolve inconsistencies or apparent con-

---

[28]   Cf., for instance, William Riggan, *Picaros, Madmen, Naifs, and Clowns: The Unreliable First-Person Narrator*, Norman, OK, 1981, who writes of "the unacceptability of that philosophy [the narrator's moral philosophy] in terms of normal moral standards or of basic common sense and human decency" (36).

[29]   Including, in places, in Nünning's collection *Unreliable Narration*, e.g., 17, 55.

[30]   Cf. Christoph Bode, "Literary Value and Evalution: The Case for Relational Concepts," in *Anglistentag 1988 Göttingen: Vorträge*, ed. Heinz-Joachim Müllenbrock and Renate Noll-Wiemann, Tübingen, 1989, 309–324.

[31]   Tamar Yacobi, "Fictional Reliability as a Communicative Problem," *Poetics Today* 2/2 (1981): 113–126, here 113. Cf. also Yacobi's essay in Phelan and Rabinowitz (eds.), *A Companion to Narrative Theory*.

tradictions in a text, and to integrate components of the text that cannot be made to perform a referential function."[32]

In other words, if the narrative is not consistent, I resolve my interpretative dilemma by assuming that the narrator is unable or unwilling to present a consistent narrative. This happens step by step: if I have the impression that the narrator is exploiting my credulity or is for any other reasons untrustworthy as a witness, I withdraw the presumption of credibility that I have maintained so far – and from then on I will look out all the more carefully for "clues" in the text.

So if that's right – that "unreliability" is a category of *reception*, which nevertheless the reader does not bring into play without previous textual *provocation* – would it not be possible to compile a list of textual signals which, whether singly or in conjunction, cause the narrator's credibility to be doubted? Ansgar Nünning has offered such a list in his excellent essay collection on unreliable narration:

- Explicit contradictions of the narrator and other internal dissonances within the narrative discourse.
- Discrepancies between the statements and the behavior of a narrator.
- Differences between the narrator's self-portrayal and other characters' portrayal of him.
- Dissonances between the narrator's explicit comments on others and his implicit self-portrayal or unintentional self-exposure.
- Discrepancies between the narrator's representation of events and his explanations and interpretations of what happened, as well as further incongruities between story and discourse.
- Verbal utterances and body language of other characters as a corrective.
- Multiperspectival diversification in accounts of events, and contrasting of different versions of the same event.
- Accumulation of utterances centered on the speaker, as well as linguistic signs of intense expressiveness and subjectivity.
- Accumulation of narratorial addresses to the reader and conscious attempts to direct the reception.
- Syntactical indications of a high level of emotional involvement (e.g., exclamations, ellipses, repetitions).
- Explicit, self-referential metanarratorial thematization of the narrator's own credibility (e.g., emphatic assurances).

---

[32] Ansgar Nünning, "*Unreliable Narration* zur Einführung: Grundzüge einer kognitiv-narratologischen Theorie und Analyse unglaubwürdigen Erzählens," in *Unreliable Narration*, ed. Nünning, 3–39, here 21. Cf. Yacobi, "Reliability," 118: "the coherent organization of the narrative is made possible once the reader recognizes the character's interference with the facts or their significance."

- Avowed lack of credibility, gaps in memory, and remarks about cognitive limitations.
- Avowed bias, or bias in particular situations.
- Paratextual signals (e.g., title, subtitle, foreword).[33]

Yet even a cursory glance through the list reveals the key problem: all these signals, at least from the third item onwards, could also be perfectly innocent. Differences between self-image and others' views, for instance, are one of the oldest resources of the comic or humoristic novel – this doesn't necessarily reflect lack of credibility in a narrator. On the contrary, as a sign of an attractive willingness to ironize himself, it could well be interpreted rather as an indication of his relatively high level of reliability. Discrepancies between the narrator's presentation and characters' statements constitute a very exciting means of unfolding the perspective structure of a novel – are they *suspicious*? Furthermore, the linguistic signals just listed can without exception be considered completely legitimate stylistic techniques, whose reliability no one would dream of doubting. The narrators in Thomas Bernhard's *Der Keller* [*The Cellar*] (1976) or *Die Ursache* [*The Cause*] (1975), who actually speak in nothing but tirades, fulfill at least three or four points on the list, yet most readers actually regard their language, the exclusive focus on the speaker, the high level of emotional involvement, etc., as proof that they are paragons of authenticity. Even the "hard" propositions – the first two in the list – aren't compelling indicators: "explicit contradictions of the narrator and other internal inconsistencies within the narrative discourse" could be dismissed as simply mistakes in the author's composition. As for "discrepancies between the statements and the behavior of a narrator" – well, why should an author who is aiming for realism and proximity to reality be denied this, of all methods, to humanize the narrator? This could equally well be presented as a highly trustworthy indicator of outstanding reliability.

Now, Ansgar Nünning himself has made unambiguously clear that "innertextual dissonances [...] by themselves are not sufficient"[34] – they can only work as pointers, and it's ultimately up to the recipient how to deal with them. This kind of "dragnet" problem arises, of course, because here we're at exactly the interface between what the text provides and how the recipient responds. The problem may be stated more emphatically: not one of these signals *has* to indicate unreliability (even if it occurs frequently), not one of them – whether they appear individually or *en masse* – would suffice to arraign the narrator; but each of them *can* in a concrete instance provoke the reader to deliver the verdict of "unreliable." That's a dilemma

---

[33]   *Unreliable Narration*, ed. Nünning, 27–28.
[34]   *Unreliable Narration*, ed. Nünning, 28.

of identification – and a problem of method: is it then impossible to say anything definitive about unreliable narration, understood as a pragmatic, relational phenomenon, except in the context of case studies or empirical surveys of reader responses?

According to the theory I've partially quoted, building on Yacobi and Nünning, "an unreliable narrator must be understood as a projection of the reader, who in this way resolves the contradictions within the text and the contradictions between the fictional world of the text and his own model of reality."[35] It seems possible to be more precise about this, by defining those *conditions* under which the criteria on the above list of unreliability-signals are *activated*; or – to put this more exactly – the conditions under which the reader considers the appearance of these signals to be suspicious. For apart from the text's provocation of the reader through dissonances, something else must also happen if the reader is actually to come up with the projection or assessment: "unreliable narrator." Alongside reasons for *doubt*, the reader must have a second prompt – a prompt to make a new *configuration*: there must be a *diegetic motivation* for unreliability, *internal to the text*, as a core, so to speak, in which the assumption crystallizes that we're dealing with an unreliable narrator here. The narrative itself must suggest a *reason* for its own faultlines.

In principle, there are only two internal textual motivations for unreliable narration. The first case is when the narrator has a *reason* to tell the story differently from how it "really" occurred: he distorts it deliberately, whether perhaps to embellish his own role in it, or to exculpate himself, etc.; and the reader smells a rat because the narrator has entangled himself in contradictions or says implausible things. The unreliable narrator who intentionally leads his reader astray is always the one who can't fabricate or lie quite perfectly enough, who isn't really as astute and convincing as he believes himself to be. On the other hand, the second possibility is that a narration can be presumed unreliable because the narrator is mentally *incapable* of telling his story reliably – for instance, he could be mentally handicapped, unstable, under the influence of drugs, or suffering from memory loss. Even if we differentiate *levels* of unreliability (from "complete unreliability" to "possibly not believable"), or the *extent* of unreliability (an isolated section of the narrative, particular passages or episodes, or the whole narrative), or *types* (Phelan and Martin distinguish "misreporting, misreading, misevaluating"),[36] nevertheless all the mixtures of these relationships and their possible combinations can be classified according to either the one or the other textual

---

[35]   *Unreliable Narration*, ed. Nünning, 5.
[36]   James Phelan and Mary Patricia Martin, "The Lessons of 'Weymouth': Homodiegesis, Unreliability, Ethics, and *The Remains of the Day*," in *Narratologies: New Perspectives on Narrative Analysis*, ed. David Herman, Columbus, OH, 1999, 88–109, here 95.

motivation. Either the narrator deliberately attempts to deceive (he has a motive for doing so), or he simply *cannot* represent reality adequately – his sanity is somehow impaired (he can't help it). For this latter kind of unreliable narrator Greta Olsen has suggested the term "fallible narrator," which I find extremely useful.[37] But in any case, both kinds of narrator give us reason enough for distrust.

Sometimes a narrator will frankly admit his unreliability. After a bombing raid in 1965, Saleem Sinai, the narrator of Salman Rushdie's *Midnight's Children*, loses his memory, which then begins slowly to return. There's no guarantee for the accuracy of his stories about the years up to 1965, quite apart from the fact that they don't always accord with historically objective facts and dates. Right at the beginning of Günter Grass's *The Tin Drum*, we learn that Oskar Matzerath is an inmate of a mental hospital – but we read on anyway. In some novels, there's a revelation of "how things really are" at the end. In Vladimir Nabokov's *Despair* (1936), the first-person narrator and bankrupted chocolate manufacturer Hermann Karlovich murders the tramp Felix, his *Doppelgänger*. Karlovich dresses Felix's body in his own clothes, so that the murderer can disappear and lead a new life. But the plan, which seemed perfect, doesn't work out: for victim and murderer don't look similar at all. That was a projection of Karlovich's madness. Sorry to give that one away.

Other novels indicate the mental instability of their narrators as a possibility without laying it down as the only possibility to account for the tale's warpings. In Leo Perutz's fascinating *The Master of the Day of Judgment* (1923), the editor clearly states his opinion in the "Editor's Postscript" that the first-person narrator Gottfried Adalbert Baron von Yosch and Klettenfeld is nothing other than an insincere scoundrel, who has driven a psychologically fragile person to suicide and is now trying to exculpate himself. However, Yosch's narration, which "from a certain point onwards [...] loses all contact with reality" and enters the realm of fantasy, can also be read as a truly sincere account given by a madman or as a perfectly adequate account of something unbelievably fantastic and supernatural. That serves to highlight the fact that the classification "credible"/"implausible" always remains a question of how the reader realizes the generic conventions and the expectations that he brings to the genre. In the genres of fantasy, science fiction, and pornography, many narrators pass muster who would be judged completely unreliable in a novel operating within a realist paradigm. Incidentally films, too, play with such ambiguous framing possibilities (think of a film such as *The Blair Witch Project*).

---

[37] Greta Olsen, "Reconsidering Unreliability: Fallible and Untrustworthy Narrators," *Narrative* 11/1 (2003): 93–109. Cf. also Chatman's "fallible filter" (*Coming to Terms*, 149), a term which is reserved for figural narrative situations or internal focalization.

Sometimes the narrator's mental instability can even be read as a cipher or objective correlative for the state of mind of a group, a society, or a century. In Kazuo Ishiguro's *When We Were Orphans*, the detective-narrator describes how, in the ruins of Shanghai, overcast with deadly fire from the Japanese, while shots are ringing around him on all sides, he searches, carrying a large magnifying glass, for traces of a crime that may have been committed in a certain house – decades ago, though! It's not too difficult to interpret this scene emblematically: the intellectual explores the roots of his individual, personal catastrophe, while the next, incomparably greater, global tragedy is unfolding around him.

Unreliability isn't always malevolent: Nabokov's *Pnin* (1957) seems for lengthy stretches to have an authorial narrator, but towards the end of the book, indications accumulate that the narrator is a contemporary and acquaintance of Professor Pnin – their paths have fatefully crossed a few times. But that means that substantial and important parts of the narrative lack credibility, for N., the narrator, being a peripheral first-person narrator, didn't have any access at all to Pnin's thoughts and feelings – especially as he was anything but an intimate friend of the Russian exile. Pnin fears and hates N., whom he considers his enemy, and at the end Pnin flees his small college town when N.'s arrival looms. But he was wrong: through N.'s unreliable narrative, readers have learned to love Pnin and hold him in high esteem. Even though N. did not have any information about Pnin's inner life, he did have imagination, empathy, and intuition.

When I said that all types of unreliable narration can be subsumed either under motivation A (deliberately misleading) or under motivation B (impaired grasp of reality), that wasn't completely accurate: sometimes *both* motivations are in play. Humbert Humbert, perhaps the most fascinating and repulsive unreliable narrator in world literature, has both a reason to mislead his readers – his "jury" – and a psychic disturbance for which he has had to undergo residential treatment on four occasions, amounting to a total of several years, long before he was imprisoned for a disgusting crime. It remains unclear whether the crime in question is exclusively the abuse of the under-age Lolita, or also the murder of Quilty. If you work out the chronology of the final days prior to Humbert Humbert's arrest, the murder of Quilty cannot have happened yet – only in his sick mind. One might speculate whether Nabokov, who generally planned and calculated very precisely, simply made a mistake here, or whether he smuggled in a further clue for Humbert Humbert's madness. At any rate, what we read in *Lolita* is the apologia (written in a prison cell) of a man who feels himself obsessively drawn to nymphs, certain girls between childhood and womanhood, and who has every reason to palliate his own behavior and to represent a chain of sexual coercions and infringements – if not rapes – as an intense, loving relationship. The remarks about his own periods in a sanatorium are kept so brief, so uninformatively compressed, that the reader can easily overlook them. But what can't be overlooked is that Humbert Humbert employs a threefold strategy in his defense: (a) he portrays himself as the unfortunate, oversensitive victim of an unscrupulous, demonic nymph, who has terrific power over him; (b) he tries (with longwinded arguments) to demonstrate that it's normal for a relationship to take place between a middle-aged man and a teenager, who is anyway mature for her age – society is hypocritical in condemning as abnormal and immoral what in earlier times and in other places was considered perfectly normal; (c) he presents himself as a penitent pervert, as a bestial monster, who feels extreme abhorrence for his past atrocities. Each of these strategies in isolation would have something in its favor and could perhaps be successful; all three together, as a defense on all fronts, radically undermine his credibility. We get the impression that this guy would claim *anything at all*, if only it was useful to him.

Even so, Nabokov's Humbert Humbert exemplifies a central paradox of unreliable narration, which sends many debates about the level of unreliability in a particular text round in circles. This is the paradox of evidence. Every piece of evidence that can be brought against Humbert Humbert and against the reliability of his version of events comes from Humbert Humbert himself in his capacity as witness, for we have no version other than his and no witnesses other than him.[38] So if one wants to shake the credibility of Humbert Humbert as narrator, one has to present as a credible witness for the prosecution: Humbert Humbert. We take all indications of Lolita's ordeal – her weeping ("every night"), her loathing of him, his terror – from *his* report. But this source also tells us that she was the one who seduced him, that she was no longer a virgin, that it was like paradise, that he – finally cured of his obsession! – really still loved her as a woman and wept bitter tears because he had robbed her of her childhood. Every argument along the lines of "look, that's only what Humbert Humbert says!" is self-undermining, since in the absence of other material, such an argument is obliged at some point or other, sooner or later, to assume the credibility of the very narrative (even if just one element of it) whose reliability it is trying to challenge. In order to make any case at all, we'd have to be radically selective. In such instances we can only say that the narrative is radically and irreducibly unreliable – it's impossible to suggest or "demonstrate" what the real, true story of the relationship between Lolita and her stepfather was. Such texts – and I'll come back to this below – paradoxically thematize our own assessments of probabilities.

So far I've only talked about unreliable narrators in first-person narratives (i.e., homo- or autodiegetic narrators). Does unreliable narration also occur with heterodiegetic narrators and reflector-characters or focalizing

---

[38]   Until Pia Pera published *Lo's Diary* in 1995 – but that lies outside the world of *Lolita*.

characters? Stanzel ("The criterion of reliability, especially if it also means credibility, is irrelevant in regard to reflector-characters")³⁹ and Chatman have denied that there is, on the ground that reflector-characters or filter-characters (Chatman) do not narrate ("She cannot misrepresent it [the story] because she is not attempting to represent it").⁴⁰ However, if we free ourselves somewhat from the idea of *narrative*, and speak about unreliability in general terms, then obviously there can be unreliability with reflector-characters. This always belongs to type B ("fallible"), and betrays itself through idiosyncratic distortions, warped statements, and breaks in continuity. A reflector is not restricted, as Stanzel maintains, to being lucid or torpid: a reflector-character's consciousness can also be a distorting mirror, in which reality is reflected and from whose particular disfigurement we learn (to be sure) nothing about "real reality," but a great deal about this particular consciousness in its distortion (cf., for instance, Benjy in Faulkner's *The Sound and the Fury*, or Edith Hope in Anita Brookner's *Hotel du Lac* [1984] or the reflector-character in Nabokov's *The Magician's Doubts* [1939], the precursor of *Lolita*: he sees a black lettuce eating a green rabbit, he takes a newspaper dated the 32nd, etc. – does that strike us as *reliable?*).

And what about narrative unreliability with heterodiegetic narrators and authorial narrators? Well, there are more things in heaven and earth... But does it make sense? The four examples that Manfred Jahn examines in this regard – Henry Fielding's *Jonathan Wild the Great* (1743), Anthony Trollope's *The Warden* (1855) and *Barchester Towers*, and George Eliot's *The Mill on the Floss* (1860) – all turn out, following Jahn's own analysis, not to qualify.⁴¹ No wonder: his opening gambit, that it's "in no way obvious why authorial narrators in particular should be immune from unreliability,"⁴² could have been answered straight away: because in that case the author wouldn't have chosen an authorial narrative situation. Authorial narrators are not a species with a miraculous immunity to particular weaknesses and diseases – they are narrative options, which an author chooses in order to realize a particular thematic plan. The *portrayal* of guilt and madness, of distortion and limitation *in the narrative itself* – how could that be realized in the godlike external perspective? If an author were to make this inadvisable attempt, the result would surely come across as the discourse of a completely insane *homodiegetic* narrator or reflector-character – both, however,

---

³⁹ Franz K. Stanzel, *A Theory of Narrative*, trans. Charlotte Goedsche, Cambridge, 1986 [1984], 152.

⁴⁰ Chatman, *Coming to Terms*, 92.

⁴¹ Manfred Jahn, "*Package Deals*, Exklusionen, Randzonen: das Phänomen der Unverläßlichkeit in den Erzählsituationen," in *Unreliable Narration*, ed. Nünning, 81–106, here 95–102.

⁴² *Unreliable Narration*, ed. Nünning, 95.

internally focalized. And *that's* the reason why an unreliable authorial narrator has, to this day, yet to be sighted, a fate that the unreliable authorial narrator shares with a squared circle.

Does unreliable narration in fact occur only in the context of realistic–mimetic narrative? Probably, yes. For the impression that we're being deceived by a wayward narrator here, or that we're dealing with a narrator whose sense of reality is significantly impaired, can only arise if the text first intimates a reality that can be understood as continuous with the reader's reality. When the reader then gets to work on this narrative with an arsenal of everyday decoding strategies, and feels prompted to the reconfiguration "unreliable narrator," then he remains within the realistic–mimetic paradigm – unreliable narrators of type A and type B populate realistic narrative worlds. If no appeal is made to the reader's reality, as for instance is possibly the case with the narrator of *The Master of the Day of Judgment* – if, that is, you believe in the reality of the supernatural in this novel – then not only does a *change of genre* occur (it becomes a fantasy novel), but also the narrator automatically ceases to be an unreliable one: he's now reliably reporting something supernatural. Unreliable narration needs realism – at least as a foil, but probably as soil too. For only realism can activate the reader's everyday suppositions about reality. In a nonsense-text by, let's say, Lewis Carroll, a description of a green rabbit eating a black lettuce would not make me doubt the narrator's sanity, any more than would speaking animals, elves, giants, witches, demons, and dragons in a fairy tale. However, in a novel that otherwise fulfilled the parameters of realistic fiction, "the same" description of a green rabbit eating a black lettuce would quickly lead me to suppose that all was not well with the reflector-character. Unreliable narration requires the frame of realism in order to be perceived as unreliable narration at all – and that, according to our pragmatic–relational interpretation, means in order to *be* unreliable narration at all.

Historically speaking, unreliable narration has been available at least since Romanticism as a possibility for dramatizing – in one way or another – deviant or idiosyncratic subjectivity, or as a possibility to explore and question whether and how reality, truth, the past, can be known and reconstructed. Unreliable narrators perhaps constitute the most strongly pronounced antithesis to the position of the authorial narrator in this whole epoch. Yet here it's necessary to warn even more emphatically than with the phenomenon of multiperspectivity: beware anachronistic retrojections! If unreliability is the effect of the clash between a narration and a reader's particular (historically specific and historically variable) assumptions about plausibility and coherence, then we can really start to talk about unreliability in texts distant from us in time only after we have to some extent reconstructed the historical horizon of reception. Thus we are on the hunt for historical differences: was the historical, empirical reader's image of reality such that, when reading this text, he probably pushed the button "reconfiguration: unreliable?" We're working with assumptions about the probability of certain assumptions.

Why is unreliable narration used at all? Because it's a means of activating the reader, a means whose efficiency can hardly be overestimated. As I've shown, narrative unreliability is actually not a purely textual quality, but something that the reader projects onto the text in response to particular problems of configuration. But that means that with narratorial unreliability, to an even greater degree than usual, our whole personality is involved – our opinions, our experiences, our expectations, what we consider probable and credible, what we consider improbable and incredible, plausible or dodgy, our assumptions and assessments. Without all those factors coming fully into play and allowing us to realize a text in such or such a way, it would be impossible to *read* such a text. A novel like *Oliver Twist* you can take on its own terms and then like it or dislike it, interpret it this way or that way – no problem. But you can't say *anything at all* about *Lolita* or *The Master of the Day of Judgment* until you've decided for yourself what's actually going on here. We wonder: what *is* going on here? – and, on the basis of a text that's not entirely to be trusted, we answer our own question: that is, each of us readers gives a different answer, for the responses must *necessarily* diverge, especially the responses to those texts whose goal is to evoke and provoke expectations, cognitive and cultural frames, and decoding practices.

It would be no great exaggeration to say: unreliability thematizes the reader's assumptions about probability and credibility – that is the key theme of these novels. *We are the key theme of these novels.* Or to say: *these books read us.* And that's what we observe in the making: we watch ourselves attempting to create meaning, to make sense. That's actually what reading always is, if it is good reading: an encounter with oneself in an encounter with another.

That's really not difficult. In percentage terms, unreliable narration surely only constitutes a very small (albeit increasing) proportion of novel production. Yet the training field for developing those skills and capacities that make us knowing, discriminating, poised, experienced, alert, shrewd readers of these novels, is huge – in fact, it could not be bigger. It is, after all, life – the world. How could we survive at all as social beings if we were not always already supremely accomplished, wide-awake readers of all the unreliable narratives that we encounter in real, everyday life?

3   The Narration's Gender

In a society shot through with inequalities, the supposedly neutral categories of a major theory that does not systematically reflect these inequalities are not neutral at all – they are partisan and biased, insofar as they systematically edit out and ignore these real inequalities. In a society with racial discrimination, a major theory that does not reflect racism and its consequences is not neutral. In a class society, a major theory that says nothing about class differences is not neutral. In a society that systematically discriminates among people according to their gender or their sexual orientation, a major theory that ignores this situation is not neutral – it is not part of the solution, but probably part of the problem. So, is a narratology based on structuralism or semiotics, inasmuch as it brackets out these inequalities, involved in perpetuating this state of affairs? If so, does it have to be like that?

Which questions an academic discipline asks is always also a question of interests, not just of an interest in gaining knowledge. It's also – and this is very much the case in Social and Cultural Studies – about power, about powerlessness, about changing or cementing certain circumstances and conditions, about access, the allocation of research topics and academic posts, about refusals to tow a party line, and about self-empowerment. All these factors constitute an *object* of critical research, and at the same time these factors are at work in that research's own practice.

Feminist literary criticism is defined less by a particular area of investigation or a unitary method than by a particular way of asking the very questions that have long remained suppressed. In 1986 Susan S. Lanser suggested linking feminist criticism, which was mimetic–realistic oriented, interested in content ("the image of the woman in…"), in the *what* of the story, in contexts and in forgotten female authors, to narratology, which was traditionally formalist–structuralist oriented and interested in the *how* of discourse, text-centered, decontextualizing, ahistorical.[43] This far from uninteresting suggestion, which aimed to unite the strengths of two complementary approaches, was greeted with considerable skepticism, not to say outraged rejection.[44]

Yet it's nevertheless not merely legitimate, but really exciting to ask questions like: what is the gender of a narrative? Or: what is the gender of a narrating authority – exactly if that authority is supposed to be genderless? Such questions are exciting because of what they're driving at: the idea that literature does not just reproduce social–cultural representations of "femininity" and "masculinity," but participates, via these representations,[45] in the *construction* of *gender* (the sociocultural category, as opposed to the biological category, sex). In so doing, though, literature also participates in the perpetuation or interrogation of gender role models,

[43]   Susan S. Lanser, "Toward a Feminist Narratology," *Style* 20 (1986): 341–363; see also Robyn R. Warhol, "Introduction: Why Don't Feminists 'Do' Narratology?" *Gendered Interventions: Narrative Discourse in the Victorian Novel*, New Brunswick, NJ, 1989, 3–24.
[44]   See, for example, Nilli Diengott, "Narratology and Feminism," *Style* 22 (1988): 42–51.
[45]   To be sure, one has to assess the affective power of gender representations in audiovisual media as *at least* equally great.

in closing down or opening up spaces of realization. In short, it can be affirmative or critical and utopian.

This kind of feminist literary criticism, expanded into *gender studies*, investigates the construction of "femininity" and "masculinity" as the manifestation and form of realization of asymmetrical, hierarchical relationships between the genders, in other words, as an expression of a relationship of power. It must therefore always be understood as an intervention that naturally cannot have as its highest aim merely to describe these relationships.

In the attempt to distinguish the presence or absence of gender-markers in narrators, Susan Lanser stated as late as the end of the 1990s

> that the sex of heterodiegetic–extradiegetic narrators is normally unmarked, while the sex of both homodiegetic and intradiegetic narrators is normatively marked. This distinction follows quite simply from the fact that both homodiegetic and intradiegetic narrators are normally also narrated characters, if not in their own narratives then in the narratives that beget them.[46]

Traditional narratologists would not just agree with that, but would explain that it could not be otherwise, since a heterodiegetic narrating authority or an authorial narrator is ultimately not a person at all. Yet Ina Schabert, one of the leading feminist scholars in Germany, had convincingly shown back in 1992 that authorial narrators – just as they can certainly be equipped with human qualities or traits (at least by implication) – can indeed be gendered.[47]

Here, however, it's necessary to distinguish between those cases in which the gender of the authorial narrator is unambiguously clear, because it is explicitly stated (Lanser: "denotation"), and those cases in which we can only deduce it from certain connotations ("inference"). The heterodiegetic narrating authority of Fielding's *Tom Jones* is, as Schabert persuasively shows, undoubtedly male gendered, while that of Ann Radcliffe's *The Mysteries of Udolpho* (1794) is undoubtedly female. With other novels we can only guess case by case, with

---

[46] Susan S. Lanser, "Sexing Narratology: Towards a Gendered Poetics of Narrative Voice," in *Grenzüberschreitungen: Narratologie im Kontext/Transcending Boundaries: Narratology in Context*, ed. Walter Grünzweig and Andreas Solbach, Tübingen, 1999, 167–183, here 173–174; cf. also Lanser, "Sexing the Narrative: Propriety, Desire, and the Engendering of Narratology," *Narrative* 3/1 (1995): 85–94, here 87 – these two articles are to a large extent identical.

[47] Ina Schabert, "The Authorial Mind and the Question of Gender," in *Telling Stories: Studies in Honor of Ulrich Broich on the Occasion of his 60th Birthday*, ed. Elmar Lehmann and Bernd Lenz, Amsterdam, 1992, 312–328. In the very same year – according to Oscar Wilde, life imitates art, not the other way round – Gilbert Adair published his novel *The Death of the Author*, satirizing deconstruction and especially the Paul de Man affair: Adair has the clever, inquisitive student Astrid Hunneker write her dissertation about "The gender of the omniscient author." The fact that she tries to investigate this topic exclusively with reference to Wilkie Collins' *The Woman in White* (1860), though, does not speak entirely in her favor. Cf. also Warhol, "Women's Narrators Who Cross Gender: *Uncle Tom's Cabin* and *Adam Bede*," *Gendered Interventions*, 101–156.

different degrees of certainty (and if the probability is very high, we might wonder again whether we're dealing with a heterodiegetic narrator at all, or if the narrator is not homodiegetic instead; for instance, the supposedly female narrator of Elizabeth Gaskell's *Cranford* has received, as she says immediately on page two of the novel, a specific assessment directly from one of the women of Cranford – doesn't that automatically make her homodiegetic?).

If, as a rule, readers tend to assume that a gender-unmarked authorial narrator has the gender of the author (the production of audio books evidently follows this rule too), then this is *not merely* a category mistake made by people who confuse the narrator with the author. It *also* (this much of dialectics must be allowed) has a certain foundation in that – as we noted above in the discussion of the authorial narrative situation – the "impossible" external perspective often invites identification as "the *internal* perspective of the author on his society, shot into space, as it were." At the heart of this error, then, there lies a truth.

But in the attempt to deduce the gender of the narrator – and thus also that of the narrative (for what wouldn't be gendered in this society?) – from typical gender connotations, caution is required: otherwise we might attribute a process of gender stereotyping to the text which is actually a projection of our own associations. It can be historically verified with great certainty that in modern European societies different types of texts, different genres were, with varying levels of strictness, allocated to the two genders. (The letter and the diary more to women, the epic and the drama more to men. It's possible to specify the reasons for this precisely: the most important is probably the dichotomization of gender relations into "public sphere" and "private sphere.") Also, within the genre of the novel, the male author was, often in duplication of the real spaces of experience reserved for males, allowed other, wider spheres than the female: the experience of the big, wide world results, gender-specifically, in productions different from those of the experience of domesticity. And obviously such dichotomization always forms a hierarchy, too: that is to say, the one is always represented as more valuable than the other.[48]

Yet if we identify a "panoramic," authorial view as "male" and a limited first-person perspective by contrast as "female,"[49] are we really *identifying*

---

[48]   Cf. Hélène Cixous, "Sorties," in *Modern Criticism and Theory: A Reader*, ed. David Lodge, London, 2000 [1988], 287–293. Cf. too the revisionary rereading of established literary history in Nancy Armstrong, *Desire and Domestic Fiction: A Political History of the Novel*, New York, 1989 [1987].

[49]   This hierarchization can be nicely demonstrated with reference to *one* text, Charles Dickens' *Bleak House*: "The text is marked throughout by the contrasting perspectives of an authorial narrative clearly to be attributed to a man because of its range of experience, depth of critical insight and use of male speech registers on the one hand, and of a first-person narration obtrusively in character with Esther, the 'little woman' of the story-world, on the other." Schabert, "Authorial Mind," 319.

historically verifiable ascriptions or are we ourselves reproducing these very stereotypes? If I regard an ironically distanced narrative approach as "male," but an involved and empathetic approach as "female," am I then criticizing such sexist ascriptions or continuing them myself? If an educated, cosmopolitan, and self-conscious narrative tone strikes me as "masculine," as does a dominant, eloquent one, whereas a pointedly modest, introspective, self-relativizing, and self-marginalizing style strikes me as "feminine" – do I, in using such metaphors, discover or do I reproduce the dominant constructions of "femininity" and "masculinity" in our society? Do I ascribe to the text a view from which I cannot free myself? *Who says* that the masculine is acute, gothic, and soaring, whereas the feminine is round, romanesque, and squat? Is it me or is it the text? That's what's fascinating about gender criticism: it requires a permanent self-critique, because its object of investigation – the construction and reproduction of ideas of "gender" in society – is at the same time its own practice.

And why should the gender of the narrator be in any way important for narratology? Because recognizing how gender is narratively constructed clears the ground for us to consider how gender itself can be strategically deployed: "If male writers can create female characters and women authors relate male figures from the inside, they would be liable to practice a similar kind of imaginative cross-dressing with their authorial narrators. The male writer might pose as a female storyteller, the female author invent a male authorial voice to present her narrative."[50]

Cross-gender narration, indeed, is a reference point for studying the strategies of self-authorization and self-empowerment that female authors use in order to raise their voices and gain attention in the asymmetrical gender discourse. More subversive and more profound than merely taking on another's voice, however, is the insight – always presumed in cross-gender narration – that gender is a *construct*, not an essence, and that it can therefore be designed and changed, fabricated and possibly transcended. If the gender of the *narrator* (not just that of a character) can be fabricated from precisely the "props" offered by the patriarchal society, it's also semiotically constructed there, outside the text: and it has become possible in principle to *simulate* the source of the individual discourse, the voice (one's own, or another's). When *such* literature is introduced into *such* a society, that space has opened up in which can occur what Karl Marx had in mind when he wrote that "one can make these petrified social relations dance by singing their own tune!"[51] That female authors (such as

[50] Schabert, "Authorial Mind," 315. Cf., for a general discussion, *Style* 35/2 (2001), "Women as Narrators."

[51] *Writings of the Young Marx on Philosophy and Society*, trans. and ed. Lloyd D. Easton and Kurt H. Guddat, New York, 1967, 253.

the Brontë sisters, and Mary Ann Evans, alias George Eliot) pretended to be male authors and displayed corresponding narratorial attitudes, is only the most striking form of this camouflage, in which self-protection and subversive potential coalesce.

Going beyond a crude dichotomization between "distancing narrative strategies" (= masculine-gendered) and "engaging strategies" (= feminine-gendered),[52] it's worth hanging onto the more nuanced conception of a discourse which, owing to its *internal* ambivalences and *internal* ambiguities (simultaneity of subversive and "traditional" content), must necessarily be seen as a double-voiced discourse, as a counter-discourse; a counter-discourse that, to the extent that it incorporates the dominant discourse, also undermines that discourse (and that's even without yet thematizing the possibility that the potential for subversion may be multiplied through the interplay between the narrator's voice and the characters' perspectives).[53]

No investigation of gender constructions (whether of narrator or character) in the novel can free itself from its own conception of "gender" – and that's a good thing too. But it also explains why evaluations of fictional texts vary so much. Ina Schabert provides a nice example when she quotes Rosalind Miles: "At no point of her work [...] does George Eliot ever address her reader in anything that sounds like a woman's voice. What she strives for, and perfectly accomplishes, is the 'masculine' mode, that of the detached, educated, omniscient outsider. She writes as an honorary male." Schabert continues: "As a reader's testimony, this is set off by other readers' reports to the contrary. Roger Fowler, for example, experiences the authorial narrators in George Eliot's mature novels as unusually sincere projections of a moral and compassionate woman author."[54] This interpretative difference need not be gender specific, for Schabert in fact adds a nuanced endorsement: "A detailed study of the I-figure [= authorial narrator] in George Eliot's novels would show that the – in terms of the Victorian gender system – 'masculine' traits are, as a rule, complemented by 'female' attributions."[55] All that would then need to be done is to win over readers like Rosalind Miles.

The pervasiveness of our conceptions of "gender" – and also of our conceptions about the *meaning* of "gender" – is nowhere more evident than when we're confronted by fictional texts that systematically deny us any clues about the gender of the (homodiegetic) narrator. We are nowhere more

---

[52]   Cf. Warhol, *Gendered Interventions*.

[53]   Cf. Mezei (ed.), *Ambiguous Discourse*; and Lisa Sternlieb, *The Female Narrator in the British Novel: Hidden Agendas*, Basingstoke, 2002.

[54]   Schabert, "Authorial Mind," 323.

[55]   Schabert, "Authorial Mind," 323.

forcefully confronted with our projections of "femininity" and "masculinity" than when the text says absolutely nothing about this – then we're alone with our projections. Since Lanser's essay in 1995, it has become usual to demonstrate this point with the example of Jeanette Winterson's *Written on the Body* (1992). I trust it will be considered an act of literary–historical redress that, instead of the latter text, I choose Maureen Duffy's *Londoners: An Elegy* (1983) – not just because Duffy had the idea nine years before Winterson,[56] but because in my opinion *Londoners* is clearly the more complex and ambitious novel.

The first-person narrator, Al, is a middle-aged writer with working-class roots, who lives in London. He is going through a professional and personal crisis: he is currently without a lover, and encounters obstacles almost everywhere in his various activities as an author. Since Al is a biographer and translator of François Villon, the novel has a distinctly diachronic dimension: Villon accompanies Al as a kind of alter ego on his walks through London – the imaginary conversations between the pair establish Al's consciousness as a decidedly literary one (how could it be otherwise?), and the city of London is thus perceived as a cityscape informed by and charged with literary associations.

Villon could also be understood as a kind of Virgil to Al's Dante as the latter wanders through the inferno of modern London, for the 34 sections of *Londoners* correspond to the 34 cantos of Dante's *Inferno*. That means that we here encounter a structure that transcends the consciousness of the first-person narrator and evinces the intertextual knowledge and constructive ingenuity of the author: from this structure – due to the establishment of the parallel, but still more due to the divergences and variations and transpositions – a wealth of further significations cascades forth.

But what is crucial (in the context of our present discussion) is that we actually can't talk about Al as "he" (as I have done up to this point), for the novel is written in such a way that all evidence about his/her gender is erased. Since, like the characters in Duffy's earlier work *The Microcosm* (1966), Al moves in the gay and lesbian milieu of the capital city, and his (her?) acquaintances have gender-ambiguous first names, Al's gender, too, is impossible to determine. Yet one constantly catches oneself in the act of searching for clues as to whether Al is a woman or a man. The text systematically frustrates this search. Obviously that doesn't mean that Duffy

---

[56] If we also count Duffy's *Love Child* (1971) as a novel which leaves the gender of the first-person narrator unclear, then she beat Winterson to it by as much as 21 years. However, I have my doubts about *Love Child* – as does Monika Fludernik, though her reasons are different. Cf. Monika Fludernik, "The Genderization of Narrative," *GRAAT* 21 (1999): 153–175.

considers the question of gender completely irrelevant – quite the contrary. Through these conspicuous absences the text again and again demonstrates our incorrigible tendency to view others primarily as men or as women, rather than simply as people, as human beings. *Londoners* is a novel whose theme (apart from the elegiac–ironic "où sont les neiges d'antan?") is prejudices, clichéd ideas, and automatic-pilot decodings. The narrative form challenges our mental and imaginative flexibility over and over again, and thus places the question of gender precisely where it belongs: in our mental rigidity and narrowmindedness.

The objective of such novels is not some sort of semiotic game of paper chase – it's *not* about trying to find the one hidden clue that unambiguously proves that Al is a woman (or a man), and then bringing home a big prize for the discovery. The purpose of such novels is that the "answer" cannot be discovered and that we thus become conscious of how much we rely on this kind of orientation, even – perhaps especially – when we want to assure ourselves that it doesn't actually make any essential difference. If the *lack* of markers provokes us to such an extent, then that as good as proves that the presence of these markers is an essential and central category for our assimilation of a text. At the same time, the text of the novel provides a kind of politico-aesthetic *Vorschein* (Ernst Bloch) of what things would be like if gender really didn't make any essential difference any more.

Incidentally, a further turn is built into *Londoners*. At one point, Al meditates on the gender of cities: "Paris is female, so's Vienna; Berlin is masculine, Rome feminine. London is androgynous: all things to all men, and women too. We make our choice, make her in the image we need to love or hate." Further: "Writers should be both, like oysters changing their sex every seven years," and so it dawns on us that apart from *al dente* there is another play on words going on: "Al" is "L," like London – the cityscape of London is at the same time the mental landscape of this consciousness, and vice versa; a mental inscape, if you will, that has an objective correlative in the city of London. In a de-hierarchized form, tenor and vehicle of this metaphorical relationship are brought into full play.

A few years ago, Monika Fludernik usefully carried out an empirical investigation of the following questions: which gender do students attribute to the narrator of texts in which, as in *Written on the Body* or *Love Child* (1971) or *Londoners*, the narrator's gender is systematically concealed; and does it makes a difference if the readers know that the author of the text is a man, or if the readers are themselves male or female (the text Fludernik used was Gabriel Josipovici's "The Bird Cage")? The results of her investigation are highly informative, not only because, interestingly enough, they run counter to her initial hypotheses,[57] but because they underline once again that (and to what extent) we fill up the respective blank spaces of the text by projecting, drawing on our arsenal of cultural knowledge, our norms, ideas, and stereotypes. It's precisely unconventional narrative texts like these that are optimally suited to bring before our eyes, as in a mirror, our own prejudices and stereotypes – likewise our desire for certainty, for unambiguous identification, the inertia and the archaic nature of our ideas. Again, such novels thematize *us*, as recipients, as members of this society, as people who have been conditioned – not to say as trained accomplices in the construction of "masculinity" and "femininity."

But if both such novels as reproduce, represent, and practice the social and cultural construction of gender, and such as deliberately leave the gender of the discourse's source unmarked – if, then, both the thematization and the concealment and systematic withholding of this category in actual fact, i.e., *in the reception*, equally amount to a thematization, so that there is no sphere in which gender is *not* present, then what follows is this: the gender aspect, which we so willingly edit out of our conceptualizations, cannot really (as the title of this chapter emphatically states) be edited out. And those theories that prefer to leave it aside would be confronted with the impossibility of realizing their project – as soon as a reader asks a strikingly different question about differences, frames a question so that it questions the frame of that theory.

---

[57] Fludernik, "Genderization," 155–156: "My hypothesis was that those informants who did not know the author's sex would tend, by default, to read the narrator as belonging to *their own* sex; i.e., women would tend to regard the narrator as female, men would classify the narrator as male. In the case of those informants who knew that "The Bird Cage" was written by *Gabriel* Josipovici I expected the narrator-persona to be read as *male* (and the you-addressee as female), irrespective of the sex of the informant. Since nobody among the informants receiving the anonymous text knew either text or author and nobody in the second set knew any other works by Josipovici, foreseen complications due to familiarity with the author and/or the text did not arise. The results of the test did *not* bear out my hypotheses. Despite a lack of explicit gender markings, the majority of readers classified the narrator as *female* (and the "you" as *male*). This was surprisingly true of even male informants who did *not* know the author's sex; and it was true of male and female readers alike who knew the author was a man."

8

Now You See It,
Now You Don't
Symbolism and Space

"How do I recognize a symbol in a novel? And how I am supposed to know what it means?" Such questions reflect years of schooling in an educational system that primarily trains its pupils and students to get on the trail of something and retrieve it for the instructor to inspect, with a shake of the head or with a nod of approval, at any rate using a logic that remains fundamentally closed to those "sniffing after" knowledge. The questions are thus as sad as they are legitimate. They're sad because they reveal that here something has turned into a baffling exercise, into an arduous duty (the student's resigned response: "He wanted to hear something else") – something which in itself is really highly intriguing, thrilling, fascinating, and which leads directly to the heart of narrative prose, and specifically to the question, "what actually is the special thing that this novel is trying to tell me?" They're legitimate because we should indeed have an initial idea of how to spot a symbol, just in case we come across one, and of where we go on from there.

To the first question, Umberto Eco once gave an answer as succinct as it is apt:

> The symbolic occurs [...] when the author delivers an utterance or a sequence of utterances completely literally, until you notice at some point that this insistence on some aspect or detail is really exaggerated. [...] In view of this waste of narrative energy, this violation of the rules of economy, the reader wonders what the author is *actually* talking about. [You notice that] it's about something else.[1]

[1] Umberto Eco, "Vom offenen Kunstwerk zum Pendel Foucaults," *Lettre International* 5 (1989): 38–42, here 40, 41.

The Novel: An Introduction. By Christoph Bode. Translated by James Vigus. English translation © 2011 James Vigus. Published by John Wiley & Sons, Ltd.
Original German text © 2005 Narr Francke Attempto Verlag GmbH + Co. KG.

So a symbol can always be present when something especially strikes you or catches your eye, whether due to the insistence with which it's mentioned or due to its frequent occurrence. Different things may strike different readers, but that doesn't matter at all: in that case we just swap ideas and mutually profit from our different observations. This is something completely non-compulsory and informal, for no one can *prove* (in the sense of a logical or mathematical proof) that there is a symbol here or that it means this and only this. The utmost one can do is to suggest that another reader could try seeing things in *this* way, "as if"; and then to consider whether it could not also be read in *that* way. It's impossible to force others to see and recognize something that they just don't see and that doesn't speak to them; and it only encourages hypocrisy to encourage or reward others for nevertheless behaving as though they *had* recognized what, in reality, has not disclosed itself to them at all.

To *suggest* to someone else that they try looking at things in such and such a way is, first of all, a fundamental *literary–aesthetic* approach (indeed, every text says that implicitly: "try looking at things like this!"). At the same time, it is a distinctively *philosophical* approach (Ludwig Wittgenstein once defined the work of the philosopher as follows: "the philosopher says 'look at things like *this*!'"),[2] because it aims at considering things and reality differently from the way we're used to, or from the way that's usual, and it thus brings the perspectival nature of truths into the foreground. And finally, it is a decidedly *ethical* procedure, precisely because it acknowledges that no one can successfully force another person to see something that they don't actually see. Whether one discusses a literary text with other people or whether one analyzes it alone, the encounter can only ever be a *persuasive* one – the text *suggests* this or that to me, I *suggest* this or that to another reader. Look at it like this – and then watch and reflect on what happens, how your focus adjusts, whether something meaningful emerges *for you*. Considered in this way, the literary text is always an ethical text, which puts something at your disposal, and does not prescribe anything. This type of wooing persuasion knows only one kind of success: that a new experience really occurs. And for that real thing, there is no substitute whatsoever.

In the quotation above, Eco uses the term "symbol" in a completely non-technical way. It does not mean a particular kind of sign or sign-complex in contrast to, say, allegory, metaphor, metonymy, or anything else of that kind, but simply this: here signs evidently mean, in addition to their literal sense, something more and something different. "It's about something else" (Eco). But in order to be able to answer the question "how am I supposed to know what a symbol means?" it's only necessary to recall once again how

---

[2] Ludwig Wittgenstein, *Bemerkungen über die Farben/Über Gewißheit/Zettel/Vermischte Bemerkungen* (= *Werkausgabe* 8), Frankfurt am Main, 1997 [1984], 537.

a literary text functions, i.e., how it's constructed and how we process it. Having understood the way in which a literary text means more, i.e., what this "more" is based on, we can then get a general sense of how to identify this "extra meaning" – of a novel, say – more closely.

The structuralist Jurij M. Lotman has offered a definition of art and literature beginning from the insights (1) that the amount of information in a message is greater, the more numerous the possible continuations of a sequence are; and (2) that there is a direct correlation between the complexity of the information that I want to communicate and the complexity of the structure that I need in order to communicate it. Now Lotman calls art and literature a "secondary modeling system,"[3] which is considerably more complex than the primary system of natural language, whose material forms the component parts of literature. In other words, the elements of language are the building blocks for these special secondary systems, which are, however, much more complex than even the system of natural language is, because in these secondary modeling systems of art and literature the number of possible continuations is raised enormously, compared to that of the system of natural language. And that, in turn, is because the literary text is allowed to violate the natural language's particular rules of organization and thus adds alternatives to established combinations. In opening up new possibilities, the text makes it harder to predict the further sequence. Reduced predictability, though, means that each further element gives me more information than one that I could have predicted (because I knew the pattern). Thus the artistic text mediates information in an intensified way, owing to a markedly decreased predictability of the sequence of elements.

However, giving up every rule wouldn't mean a maximum of information, but rather total and utter chaos. For that reason, the text must also display new, additional regularities, which structure the material. In poetry, such regularities might consist of, say, a particular meter, a rhyme scheme, general phonetic patterns (or the like). In narrative texts, which adhere much less to the deviation aesthetic just sketched (= the effect of a text is thought to be founded on its deviation from normal language use), what arouse the special attention of the reader are not just the surprising twists and continuations of the narrative, surprising yet convincing transformations of characters, new variations on long-familiar themes, etc., but also quite simply all the factors that (according to Eco's elucidation) constitute a "waste of narrative energy." In a narrative text, which certainly isn't to any great extent *obliged* to violate linguistic rules or other expectations of the reader (although that undoubtedly increases the excitement and the enjoyment), attention soon focuses on striking accumulations, on inner-textual

[3]   Jurij Lotman, *The Structure of the Artistic Text*, trans. Gail Lenhoff and Ronald Vroon, Ann Arbor, 1977 [1971], 9, 21.

regularities, on passages that seem somehow highlighted or foregrounded, because here a multiplicity of elements are coinciding.

When, through cultural convention, texts (whether they are extremely disturbing due to their unconventional coding, or whether they are relatively "tame," yet attractive because of the way they allow us to construct patterns through our own engagement) are "set free" from context, so that we read them not as referentially related to an extra-textual reality (i.e., unlike a timetable or a recipe), but as predominantly self-referential, then with this readjustment of the focus onto the text itself, the possible meanings of an element of the text begin to "flicker."[4] For alongside the literal meaning of a word, which after all can never be entirely erased, there may now appear meanings that go beyond the literal sense, "exaggerated" meanings – and then we say to ourselves: "To be sure, XY normally means such and such, but what does it mean *here*, within this particular set of relations?"

A wise author once compared the functioning of normal linguistic signs in a literary text to the way a snowman is built: there are three snowballs of different sizes, the smallest of which means the head, the middle one the torso, the largest the lower body; a saucepan means a hat, a carrot a nose, two bits of coal to the right and left above the carrot mean the eyes, three bits of coal of the same kind, but placed in a vertical line on the middle snowball, mean buttons – and this, by the way, shows very nicely that the meaning of signs depends on their immediate relations. If you now asked what the carrot means here, and were told "well, it's a carrot," you'd rightly be unsatisfied with this information, since that's what we can obviously see – the question was what it means *here* in this context, and that's something we can only conclude from the surrounding relations: "nose!" Merely repeating the literal sense would just show that the speaker had not understood the concept "snowman." That's exactly how words in a literary text function. It's a piece of cake to decipher them. All you have to do is look at their relationships and play along.

Returning to somewhat more complex sets of sign relations: once a text is "freed up" (decontextualization, i.e., releasing the text from its original situation and suppressing its referentiality, usually implies an *increase* in the possibilities of meaning – whereas contextualization usually implies a *decrease* in the possibilities for meaning), its elements can be read in very different (textually internal) configurations, since each element can be interpreted as the intersection point of a sequence of rules or codes (and that considerably exceeds the meanings a snowman can have):

> In constituting a unified structure on a certain level, this system contains unpredictable intersections, which guarantees that the flow of information will not decrease. That is why the more complex the organization of a text and

---

[4] Lotman, *Structure*, 67.

of each of its levels, the more unexpected will be the points of intersection of individual substructures; the greater the number of substructures in which a given element appears, the more "random" it will seem. Hence the familiar paradox that arises only in an *artistic text*: the more it is structured, the less predictable it becomes.[5]

An artistic text obeys the following law: the greater the number of regular series which intersect at a given structural point, the more individual the text seems.[6]

If "art is the most economical, compact method for storing and transmitting information,"[7] then an artwork, like every extremely complicated system, can be "segmented into signs in different ways when different codes are applied,"[8] just as there is usually more than one correct solution to equations with several variables:

> As a result the text means not only what it means, but something else as well. The new meaning does not supplant the old, but correlates with it. As a result the artistic model reproduces a very important aspect of reality – the fact that there is no exhaustive, finite interpretation.[9]

The artwork, the literary text, is a finite model of the infinite world (and therefore strongly simplifying and reductive, like every model), but it imitates the world in one really essential aspect: the literary text is potentially inexhaustible. The author permits us, as it were, to delight in the abundance of meanings and possible interpretations of the text.

The mechanism of the game effect does not consist in the static, simultaneous coexistence of different meanings, but in the constant recognition that there may be *other* meanings besides those perceived at the moment. The game effect means that different meanings of one element do not statically coexist, but "flicker." Each interpretation forms a separate synchronic slice, but it preserves the memory of previous meanings and recognizes the possibility of future meanings.[10]

The meaning of the literary text, going beyond the literal sense of the signs, is thus something that always remains to be clarified, over and over and again, for "in an artistic text words function as pronouns (in addition to their natural linguistic meaning), signs for designating an as yet unrevealed content. *This content is constructed from their relations.*"[11] The symbolic

[5]   Lotman, *Structure*, 280.
[6]   Lotman, *Structure*, 77.
[7]   Lotman, *Structure*, 23.
[8]   Lotman, *Structure*, 22.
[9]   Lotman, *Structure*, 277.
[10]   Lotman, *Structure*, 67.
[11]   Lotman, *Structure*, 205, emphasis added.

meaning of a sign in a literary text is thus not a secret (or at most it may be an open secret), since everything that one needs in order to decipher or decode it is clear and evident. Let the game begin. In fact it's just like in real life: we wonder what this or that means, then incline to this or that interpretation, but without (hopefully) forgetting that there were still competing interpretations, too; and moreover we can never be certain – in the sense of an irrefutable proof – that our own interpretation was the only correct one.

However, the following point is of the greatest significance: it's *not* that the literary text is on one level thoroughly literal, and then displays particular monuments (like the rock formations in Monument Valley), which alone are symbolically meaningful. The *whole* literary text is always already double-coded (this is actually a pleonasm, for "literary" may be defined as "double-coded" or self-referential). *The literary text is a symbolic text*, because it always already, as a *whole*, means something more and something different from what it says: *Robinson Crusoe* does not merely describe a "real" shipwreck and subsequent survival, *Moby-Dick* is not merely about whaling, *The Magic Mountain* is not merely about a tuberculosis sanatorium. The meaning of *Ulysses* is not that it portrays a day in the life of a Dublin advertising canvasser. Not by a long way.

With regard to the "objects" that crop up in a novel, Italo Calvino has formulated the same idea in the following way:

> I would say that the moment an object appears in a narrative, it is charged with a special force and becomes like the pole of a magnetic field, a knot in the network of invisible relationships. The symbolism of an object may be more or less explicit, but it is always there. We might even say that in a narrative any object is always magic.[12]

Thus a narrative text's mere mention of something is enough to semanticize that thing in a special way: after all, it could just as well have been left unmentioned. This peculiarity of literary texts emerges clearly when a novel is turned into a film, for in a realistic film adaptation a great deal more will always come into view than the original novel explicitly refers to. But that suggests that if a medial translation of this kind aims to highlight particular symbolic meaning, then it has to find a particular medium-specific language in order to make evident that this object isn't simply "there," but additionally stands "for something else," too. For the novel as a linguistic artwork, it's much easier: it can simply choose not to mention anything that it doesn't consider especially meaningful, whereas a film in the realist paradigm can't help showing many things even though they're not supposed to mean anything in particular.

[12]   Italo Calvino, *Six Memos for the Next Millennium: The Charles Eliot Norton Lectures [Harvard] 1985–6*, Cambridge, MA, 1988, 33.

So it's possible to reconstruct what a novel "actually" means. Or, to put this more cautiously, it's possible to follow a novel's traces – through the regularities it builds up, through the recurrences it displays, through the patterns it allows us to construct. Following A. J. Greimas,[13] many literary theorists call the structure that arises through the recurrence of the same semantic unities an *isotope*, and recommend noting such isotopes as a way of identifying the meaning-dimension of texts. That's certainly helpful, provided only we recall that the identification of lexeme-groups in normal language does not automatically have to lead to the identification of the literary meanings of a text, since neither the mere number of repetitions nor their semantic relations within normal language implies perforce a particular symbolic meaning. Such recurrences may undoubtedly provide a first clue, but this method can't achieve the decisive step – it can at most prepare it, because this decisive step on the reader's part has rather the character of a (qualitative) *leap*: it's more like a sudden, creative idea than the account-book summary of an isotope-counting reader. Just as the understanding of an image, a metaphor – or the spontaneous reconfiguration of a figure–ground phenomenon – breaks *all of a sudden* and in the very same moment seems *self-evident* (but also, again, impossible to "prove" to others – we can only suggest it to them), so to (re)cognize the symbolic meaning of a sign or the symbolic dimension of a narrative text is comparable to the experience of switching on a light in a darkened room. While such an experience can retrospectively be traced back to this or that previously recognized configuration, it by no means followed with absolute necessity from that configuration. *It is impossible to conclusively deduce a non-literal meaning of a sign or text from its literal meaning.* Despite Wittgenstein's exclamation mark, "Look at things like *this*" is an invitation, not an order.

To read literary texts means to pay attention to what else they could mean and to which offers they make to generate sense and meaning. That's always assuming we have the curiosity to make that discovery, and that approaching closer to the text's sense and meaning promises us an enjoyable intellectual challenge. Anyone who isn't interested in this symbolic dimension of literature can say straight away that they're not interested in literature at all – and we'd be as taken aback as if someone said that, *as a car*, a Porsche didn't interest them in the slightest.

To want to work out what "that" actually means – so much initial motivation is absolutely essential. Otherwise one is just retrieving things for others to register and inspect, now with a shake of the head, now with a nod of approval. Outside the walls of educational institutions, literary reading is not only a *sanction-free* activity, it is also singularly self-gratifying. Its reward

[13]   Cf. Algirdas Julien Greimas, *Structural Semiotics: An Attempt at Method*, trans. Daniele McDowell, Ronald Schliefer, and Alan Velie, Lincoln, NE, 1983.

consists in the enjoyment, the pleasure we can give ourselves, the satisfaction of having taken up an intellectual and emotional challenge of one's own imagination and reasoning power, and (however much irritated, scandalized, stirred, maturer, wiser, bored, wearied, excited, amused, confirmed, or unstretched) to have passed the test. In this sense, the meaning of a novel is a category that literary criticism has tended to use cautiously: *the meaning is the experience of reading it*. But then that's fine: it's not as though literary criticism has to deal with everything under the sun.

Given what's been said so far about the symbolic dimension of literary texts, it should be clear that exploring this dimension has relatively little to do with identifying socially and culturally *conventionalized* symbols (red cross, red heart, dove of peace, etc.), whose meaning is fixed and which we can therefore look up in reference books. Novels do of course make use of such conventionalized symbols, just as they can in principle use anything at all as raw material, but nevertheless they tend to employ them as mere building blocks for higher structures of meaning. If that's not the case – if, that is, texts are nothing but the sum total of the conventionalized meanings of the ready-made symbols they use – the result is banality and triviality. Non-conventionalized symbolism is harder, because it remains necessary to *work out* what it means; and if it's not simply a question of the (once again regular, conventionalized) symbolism in the *œuvre* of an author or group of authors and a literary movement, then its occurrence is a singularity, a one-off – its meaning is only to be deciphered from its situation in the text *here*, and it's also non-transferable. You might think you've understood what's going on with the letter "A" in Nathaniel Hawthorne's *The Scarlet Letter*, but then nothing whatsoever follows for the meaning of the letter "A" in any other novel (*that*, though, is one of the possible messages of Hawthorne's *The Scarlet Letter*). What is transferable in literary reading is not this sort of identification of the particular content of a specific text, but, at most, the *process of going about* such identification.

As I mentioned in the previous chapter, in Maureen Duffy's *Londoners*, the literarily perceived cityscape of London (L) may be read as the mental landscape of the protagonist Al's consciousness – and vice versa: this London as the externalized objectification of a subjective state (Al = L, cityscape = inscape). In Herman Melville's *Bartleby, the Scrivener*, the desk of the copyist Bartleby is positioned such that it looks out through a window directly onto the wall of the neighboring house, which is barely three feet from the windowpane; at the end, the dead Bartleby will be found lying in a foetal position at the foot of another wall. The story is subtitled "A Story of Wall-Street." In E. M. Forster's *A Room with a View* (1908) the narrative is at first only about the fact that, during her visit to Florence, the young, naïve Lucy Honeychurch has not been given a hotel room with a view, i.e., one overlooking the Arno. Then as the novel goes on, it soon becomes clear – via what Eco would call a considerable waste of narrative energy on the semantic field of views, vision, perspectives, and windows – that it's about free vision and one's own views and opinions, in other words about the (eventually successful) emancipation of Lucy Honeychurch from restrictive conventions and paternalism. When, at the end, back in Florence, she does have a room with a view, we know that she has gained far, far more than just the sight of the Arno.

All three examples are instances of literary symbolism (far from the toughest type, and that's exactly why I chose them), and furthermore they are instances of *semanticized spaces*. These spaces (London, the office, the hotel room), that is, are not simply and straightforwardly what they are; rather, they mean *something else* at the same time, too. One could also say that these spaces are only thematized in the first place because they are supposed to mean something special. It's surely worthwhile to pursue this thought a bit further.

Time and space are not treated even-handedly in narrative texts. Action always and without exception occurs in time, and narrative represents this sequence ("The king died and then the queen died"). It is impossible to narrate without time being involved too, for narrative describes changes that have taken place in time and with time. To narrate means to trace temporal change, to (re)construct the way in which time takes its course in the form of changes. To be sure, it is inconceivable, too, to have action without a space in which to occur (just as everything that we experience and everything that we can imagine necessarily has a spatiotemporal extension). But that doesn't mean that this space has to be mentioned and *specified* (for instance, Forster's mini-story, "The king died and then the queen died," doesn't specify the place where this happened); whereas time in *narrative as the connection of events* is not only always implicitly assumed, but is by definition explicitly "used," narratively realized and laid out in a specific shape. As long as a narrative is only concerned with "somehow" positioning its reader in its discursive space, the simplest deictic markers suffice to establish space, location, and perspective: left, right, above, below, near, far – not only does that position objects in a space, but it also, in turn, constitutes that space through the distribution of objects and opens up the possibility of movement in that space, bound to a shifting perspective (be it internally or externally focalized). Professor Kuckuck in Thomas Mann's *Confessions of Felix Krull, Confidence Man* neatly captures this point during the train journey to Lisbon:

> Being […] had had a beginning and would have an end, and with it space and time; for they existed only through Being and through it were bound to each other. Space, he said, was nothing but the order of material things and their relationship to one another. Without things to occupy it, there would be no space and no time either, for time was only the ordering of events made possible

by the presence of objects; it was the product of motion, of cause and effect, whose sequence gave time its direction and without which there would be no time.[14]

All that can easily be identified by a cognitively inspired narratology, since this works by transferring our daily, lifeworldly cognitive mapping to the fictional world, the fictional space.[15] As a rule, the gentlest textual markers of spatial relations (i.e., markers of the relations of objects to each other) are sufficient to evoke "space"; and perspective may be understood as the continual integration of indexical and iconic signs of space into an image of the relevant space.[16] The abstracted result of this process is the "narrative space" or the imaginary space of the story (for instance the "Florence" of the first part of *A Room with a View*), as distinct from the "discursive space" of the narrative (or space of the plot/discourse), which, despite the fact that it is mentioned only intermittently and spotlighted only sporadically, we nevertheless imagine as continuous, as long as the text displays cohesion and coherence.[17]

If the text does more than merely position a viewpoint in a space, then the reader immediately gets the impression of a *semanticization* of the space, the impression that this explicit specification should now mean something. When, say, in Raymond Chandler's *The Big Sleep* (1939), it's mentioned that the villa of Philip Marlowe's rich client General Sternwood is *up* in the hills over Los Angeles, while *below* stand the old oil pumps with which the foundation of the family fortune had once been laid, in that something was extracted from the earth (and it's at the oil pumps, logically enough, that the puzzle of this detective story is solved, because Marlowe now *unearths* something), then we're already dealing with space implicitly laden with meaning, exactly like when everyday cognitive mapping is deliberately undermined. In Kazuo Ishiguro's *The Unconsoled* (1995), Mr. Ryder's journey in the hotel lift from the ground floor to the first floor takes approximately twenty to thirty minutes. This is not because the lift gets jammed – nothing of the kind: it moves and moves, while the hotel porter Gustav tells Ryder a longwinded story, which someone else in the elevator also butts into – a foretaste of the fact that this world's topography has changed in a dreamlike, even nightmarish way. For example, you leave a building in the

---

[14]   Thomas Mann, *Confessions of Felix Krull, Confidence Man: Memoirs Part I*, trans. Denver Lindley, Harmondsworth, 1977, 290.

[15]   Cf. Daniel Punday, *Narrative Bodies: Toward a Corporeal Narratology*, Basingstoke, 2003, esp. ch. 4, "The Body and Kinetic Space," 117–148.

[16]   Cf. the excellent study by Karin Wenz, *Raum, Raumsprache und Sprachräume: Zur Textsemiotik der Raumbeschreibung*, Tübingen, 1997, esp. 26–56.

[17]   Cf. Wenz, *Raum*, 142ff.

city center and find yourself in open landscape, you go into a country pub and suddenly find yourself in an inner-city café. Here, cognitive narratology can only explain why we feel disoriented: it can't explain what it means.

But if it's true that novels don't necessarily have to thematize space in the novel, and that even the smallest markers suffice to establish space *per se*; and if it's at the same time true that every thematization that goes beyond this necessary minimum can immediately be understood as potentially meaningful, as a semanticization of space – then in one fell swoop this has explained two peculiarities of the critical treatment of space and its representation. It explains, first, the fact that there are – compared to the vast secondary literature on time in the novel, which by now is hardly possible to master even in an outline survey – relatively few studies on space; and second, the fact that these relatively few studies are very far from having developed a standard, systematic approach in terminology or methodology. Putting the point rather starkly, one could say abstract space is not a topic in the novel, and specific space comes under the heading of symbolism.

If you look at Gaston Bachelard's *The Poetics of Space*, you notice just from a glance through the list of contents that Bachelard is obviously concerned with a phenomenology of space:[18]

1   The House. From Cellar to Garret. The Significance of the Hut
2   House and Universe
3   Drawers, Chests and Wardrobes
4   Nests
5   Shells
6   Corners
7   Miniature
8   Intimate Intensity
9   The Dialectics of Outside and Inside
10   The Phenomenology of Roundness

Even though the list is reduced to particular, psychologically grounded archetypal images, it is nevertheless also – like any such list – practically endless and inconclusive. Whether you now think of social and political spaces (the city and the country, homeland and foreign countries, mother country and colonies, etc.) or geographical ones (forest, desert, sea, mountain ranges, the poles, the equator, etc.), whether you think of caves, corridors, rooms, or homes, huts, houses, palaces, cities, civilizations, globes, or galaxies, the novel can incorporate absolutely *anything and everything*: there would be no end to the compilation of lists, yet these lists would, *in summa*, always just reflect the unsystematic nature of their object. Every addition on the same

[18]   Gaston Bachelard, *The Poetics of Space*, trans. Maria Jolas, Boston, 1969, new foreword, 1994.

level just perpetuates a game without limits: the author as almighty interior decorator, the literary critic running along behind with inventory lists.

To be sure, all these spaces are always already somehow laden with meaning,[19] and the effect of some novels is undoubtedly due not least to the fact that they summon up rather than transform this "preloaded" meaning (one thinks of the shire, woods, swamps, and precipices in J. R. R. Tolkien's *The Lord of the Rings*, 1954–1955). Yet making an inventory without identifying the specific ways in which these spaces *function* would be tantamount to an under-reading that clings to the literal sense ("Lucy would like a room with a view." File under: hotel rooms).

If you choose the opposite way, beginning from particular hypotheses – such as "mythical, aesthetic and theoretical space" (Ernst Cassirer),[20] or Elisabeth Ströker's "lived space," which subdivides again into "space of intuition," "space of action," and "attuned space,"[21] or Herman Meyer's mythical, realistic, and symbolic conceptions of space (with a reasonable sliding scale of transitions),[22] or Alexander Ritter's "key concepts […] for research into landscape and space" (" 'feeling for nature' – 'scenic landscapes' – 'experienced space' – 'scene of action' ")[23] – and then classify (deductively, in fact) the presentation and functionalization of space in selected novels within these categories, as Gerhard Hoffmann did in his still very impressive study,[24] then you face a dilemma. Either the texts, despite all their differences, still just stand as examples for the possibilities of the respective types; or they disrupt the system because, standing at cross-purposes to it, they produce their own taxonomy: the strange space, the fantastic and satirical space, the grotesque space, the uncanny space, the hallucinatory and visionary space, the mythical space[25] (and then we'd ironically have returned to an earlier fundamental distinction, that of Cassirer – which shows that such theoretical constructions produce their own hierarchies almost at random).

---

[19] Cf. Simon Schama, *Landscape and Memory*, New York, 1995.

[20] Ernst Cassirer, "Mythischer, ästhetischer und theoretischer Raum," *Beilagenheft zur Zeitschrift für Ästhetik und allgemeine Kunstwissenschaft* 25 (1931): 21–36, also in Alexander Ritter (ed.), *Landschaft und Raum in der Erzählkunst*, Darmstadt, 1975, 17–35.

[21] Cf. Elisabeth Ströker, *Investigations in Philosophy of Space*, Ohio, 1987 [1965].

[22] Herman Meyer, "Raumgestaltung und Raumsymbolik in der Erzählkunst," *Studium Generale* 10 (1957): 620–630; also in Alexander Ritter (ed.), *Landschaft und Raum in der Erzählkunst*, Darmstadt, 1975, 208–231.

[23] Ritter (ed.), *Landschaft und Raum*, 4. In the introduction to his essay collection Ritter continues to maintain that space in literature largely means "landscape" (2).

[24] Cf. Gerhard Hoffmann, *Raum, Situation, erzählte Wirklichkeit: Poetologische und historische Studien zum englischen und amerikanischen Roman*, Stuttgart, 1978.

[25] All in Hoffmann, *Raum*, 109ff. Cf. also Natascha Würzbach, "Erzählter Raum: fiktionaler Baustein, kultureller Sinnträger, Ausdruck der Geschlechterordnung," *Erzählen und Erzähltheorie im 20. Jahrhundert: Festschrift für Wilhelm Füger*, ed. Jörg Helbig, Heidelberg, 2001, 105–130.

Nor does more restrained theorizing[26] banish the fundamental problem that the four categories constitutive of narrative literature – "time, space, character and action"[27] – aren't balanced (just as the known elementary particles that make up matter are a colorfully mixed bunch), and that, due to the *infinite* possibilities of literary symbolism, *semanticized* space eludes the grasp of every would-be comprehensive system: just as there's no such thing as a comprehensive list of all symbols (because anything can become a symbol), so there can be no such thing as a complete list of literary spaces.

On the other hand, if it's right to say (without worrying that the expression refers to an ancient literary form) that "space and time [are] correlative binding forces of epic,"[28] then perhaps it makes sense to approach particular, distinct (in the sense of historically differentiated) *space-time correlations* of the novel as a unitary object of investigation.[29] For such an interrelated space-time continuum, Mikhail Bakhtin coined the term *chronotope*, and, beginning from the ancient novel, pursued the changing configurations of temporal and spatial indications far into the modern era.[30] In Bakhtin's original conception (rather than in Riffaterre's extremely reductive reinterpretation),[31] we're presented with an analytical instrument which would maintain the space in novels as a space that's actualized and summoned in a particular way, and would at the same time locate that

---

[26]   For instance, in her exemplary study of Dorothy Richardson's cycle of novels *Pilgrimage*, Elisabeth Bronfen distinguishes between the "actual, material spaces" presented in the text, the "metaphorical spaces" which offer themselves to the heroine Miriam or which she accepts in the process of her psychological development (the finding of identity as journey and worldmaking – the title *Pilgrimage* is not random), and finally the textual spaces, the text as space. (Elisabeth Bronfen, *Der literarische Raum: Eine Untersuchung am Beispiel von Dorothy M. Richardsons Romanzyklus Pilgrimage*, Tübingen, 1986. Based on this, Bronfen later published a study in English, *Dorothy Richardson's Art of Memory: Space, Identity, Text*, trans. Victoria Appelbe, Manchester, 1999.) Karin Wenz (*Raum*) makes a comparable distinction between "language of space" as the linguistic representation of space in texts, and "spaces of language" as the possibility that texts may themselves develop their own spatiality, by becoming metaphorical spaces in which readers orient themselves in the process of reading.

[27]   Hoffmann, *Raum*, x.

[28]   Herman Meyer quoted in Ritter (ed.), *Landschaft und Raum*, 11.

[29]   Cf. Martin Middeke (ed.), *Zeit und Roman: Zeiterfahrung im historischen Wandel und ästhetischer Paradigmenwechsel vom sechzehnten Jahrhundert bis zur Postmoderne*, Würzburg, 2002.

[30]   Mikhail M. Bakhtin, "Forms of Time and of the Chronotope in the Novel: Notes toward a Historical Poetics," in *The Dialogic Imagination*, ed. Michael Holquist, trans. Caryl Emerson and Michael Holquist, Austin, 1982, 84–258, here 84: "In the literary artistic chronotope, spatial and temporal indicators are fused into one carefully thought-out, concrete whole. Time, as it were, thickens, takes on flesh, becomes artistically visible; likewise, space becomes charged and responsive to the movements of time, plot and history."

[31]   Michael Riffaterre, "Chronotopes in Diegesis," in *Fiction Updated: Theories of Fictionality, Narratology, and Poetics*, ed. Calin-Andrei Mihailescu and Walid Hamarneh, Toronto, 1996, 244–256.

space, in literary–historical terms, in its symbolic functionalization (that means, including the whole range of its possibilities for meaning): *this* kind of space is always a space in which particular ways of acting and meaning seem possible or impossible. Hence, too, the disproportionately significant meaning of *border-crossings* and *threshold-crossings* in the semanticization of space in the novel.[32] *This* kind of space would be an indicator for the evolution of the most successful of all literary genres, which promised right from the very beginning to construct a second space alongside the space of reality – a space deceptively similar or annoyingly dissimilar – in order to fictionally explore how sense and meaning may be generated. At every moment space is present in the novel as the *space of possibility* and the *space of meaning*, and that's true even of the novel in its least challenging vestigial forms: for the space of possible meanings is the novel's province, its ancestral home since its inception.

---

[32] Cf. Lotman, *Structure*, 217ff., esp. 229–230, 240ff.

9

The End of the Novel
and the Future of an Illusion

1 Experience, Storytelling, (Hi)stories

"A man has been through an experience, now he is looking for the story to go with it – you can't live with an experience that remains without a story, and I often used to imagine that someone else had exactly the story to fit my experience."[1] In Max Frisch's *Gantenbein*, different stories, different strands of narrative, different sketches are then tried out and tried on ("I try stories on like clothes!"), such as the imaginative story outline (again and again: "I imagine …") that begins with the opening declaration, "Let my name be Gantenbein" (a declaration which, if you stop to think about it, is no more voluntaristic, nor more upfront about its fictionality than, say, "Call me Ishmael").

Gantenbein, so the narrator imagines, pretends to be blind (he wears dark glasses and a yellow armband and carries a white walking stick), and those around him accept him as such, even though at first he makes many mistakes that threaten to give him away, and later, too, he sometimes falls recklessly out of the role. He's considered to be blind, and then no one looks so attentively any more, whereas he – as the supposedly blind man – looks about him more keenly than ever before.

---

[1] Max Frisch, *A Wilderness of Mirrors: A Novel*, trans. Michael Bullock, London, 1965, 11. The page numbers match those of the work's reprint as *Gantenbein: A Novel* by the same translator and publisher, also 1965.

The Novel: An Introduction. By Christoph Bode. Translated by James Vigus. English translation © 2011 James Vigus. Published by John Wiley & Sons, Ltd.
Original German text © 2005 Narr Francke Attempto Verlag GmbH + Co. KG.

All that is played through as a thought-experiment: what a fantastic career awaits him as an employee who never says what he sees, and can only ever agree with the boss, since any contradiction would reveal that he had the use of his eyes; what a perfect husband, who never gets round to talking about the discrepancies between what he's told and what he sees with his own eyes; how the blind man in his role provokes shameless deception.

Yet this aspect of the imaginative mind-game isn't in the foreground. As the narrator tries out the identities "Enderlin" and "Svoboda" as well as Gantenbein (each time with a number of beginnings to stories), as "he" changes from *I* to *he*, from *he* to *I*, and at one point, in the role of a jealous man, even comes across the love letters that he himself, as lover, wrote to his wife or mistress (so that he's imagined both as the adulterer and the cuckold) – what's foregrounded is the provisionality and tentativeness of all these projections and constructions. All of them, as they're sketched out and then relativized and withdrawn, stand in inverted commas, "as if": "I imagine:" – and there follows a fresh outline of a role, a fresh design for a story. So the actual subject matter of *Gantenbein* is how one conserves, negates, and elevates (the full, threefold Hegelian sense of *Aufhebung*) experience in(to) a story; and the fact that that's a process of invention, of fictionalization: " 'Every story is an invention,' I say after a while, without on that account doubting the horrors of being a prisoner of war in Russia, as a general principle: 'every ego that expresses itself in words is a role –'." [2]

In a historiographical context, Hayden White had maintained that the meaning of a historical event isn't integral to itself, but is attributed to it through its embedding in a story, which in turn may adhere to widely differing (literary) genre conventions – so that the preselected form of the narrative dictates the meaning of the event. (That's also why "one and the same" historical event can take on very different meanings when embedded in different stories.) Analogously, the "greed for stories" professed by the narrator of *Gantenbein* can be understood as the expression of a need to attribute and ascribe a meaning to one's own experiences, since meaning doesn't emerge from experiences of its own accord, but only through a comprehensive and integrated context, which can be generated – somehow or other – by means of a story ("somehow or other" because the events *per se* don't yet comprise a story; rather, a narration can link and process them in very different ways). " '– perhaps a man has two or three experiences,' I say, 'two or three experiences at the outside, that's what a man has had when he tells stories about himself, when he tells stories at all: a pattern of experience – but not a story.' " [3]

2 Frisch, *Gantenbein*, 46.
3 Frisch, *Gantenbein*, 46.

The narrator has a certain idea as to why it is that, rather than being able to fabricate such stories for ourselves, we're dependent on out-sourcing. He reckons it's due to our blindness (not play-acted blindness this time) with respect to ourselves: " 'One can't see oneself, that's the trouble, stories only exist from outside,' I say, 'hence our greed for stories.' "[4] You can only get round this the way he does: by taking on the role of another, by allowing yourself to be someone else ("Let my name be Gantenbein") or several other people ("Enderlin," "Svoboda") and by means of this simultaneous relinquishment and expression to play along and discover where you find yourself again in this space of possibilities unfolded by the narrative: "what I am really doing: – making sketches for an ego!"[5] For: "This is no time for ego stories. And yet human life is fulfilled or goes wrong in the individual ego, nowhere else."[6] The search for the true "I" takes place in the medium of fiction, because it's only in drafting, testing out, and rejecting imagined stories that those relations (i.e., local, internal contexts) may be produced which are capable of bestowing a meaning on experience ("A man has been through an experience, now he is looking for the story to go with it").

Now, for quite a long time it's regularly been questioned whether the term "experience" still designates a valid category at all. If it didn't, that would have far-reaching consequences for the connection that the narrator of *Gantenbein* claims between experience, storytelling, and history. In his essay of 1936, "The Storyteller: Reflections on the Works of Nikolai Leskov," Walter Benjamin claimed that the art of storytelling – as the exchange of experiences – was coming to an end, and the reason for this was "experience has fallen in value. And it looks as if it is continuing to fall into bottomlessness."[7]

As the essay goes on, however, it emerges that Benjamin actually has in mind two different causes for the disappearance of storytelling. Surveying the turning point constituted by World War I, he asks rhetorically (much as he does in his 1933 essay "Experience and Poverty"): "Was it not noticeable at the end of the war that men returned from the battlefield grown silent – not richer, but poorer in communicable experience?"[8] But as the context makes clear, the accent here must lie on "*communicable* experience" – what's at issue is actually not the experience (or lack thereof), but rather the possibility of grasping and communicating it in

---

[4]   Frisch, *Gantenbein*, 46–47.

[5]   Frisch, *Gantenbein*, 115.

[6]   Frisch, *Gantenbein*, 65.

[7]   "The Storyteller: Reflections on the Works of Nikolai Leskov," trans. Harry Zorn, in *Narrative Theory: Critical Concepts in Literary and Cultural Studies*, Vol. 3, *Political Narratology*, ed. Mieke Bal, London, 2004, 88–106, here 88; this translation was first published in Hannah Arendt (ed.), *Illuminations*, New York, 1968, 83–107.

[8]   Benjamin, "The Storyteller," 88.

words. The problem consists not in the disappearance or lack of experiences at all, but rather in their enormity, their incommensurability – these experiences, and even more so some of the experiences that were to follow, break the mold of what is communicable. Storytelling then failed due to the magnitude of the task of continuing to hammer out sense and meaning: not, however, due to any scantiness or scarcity of the raw material "experience."

Benjamin's second proposal, to explain the end of narrative art as due to a supposed disappearance of experiences, is similarly problematic, it seems to me. This suggestion takes up a very much larger part of the essay: "Experience which is passed on from mouth to mouth is the source from which all storytellers have drawn."[9] For Benjamin, narration is defined by orality, by immediate communication of experience within a small circle. The printing press is (as it were) the fall into sin, and so it can't be any wonder that Benjamin pours particular scorn on the one major literary genre that first emerged after printing – the novel:

> The earliest symptom of a process whose end is the decline of storytelling is the rise of the novel at the beginning of modern times. What distinguishes the novel from the story (and from the epic in the narrower sense) is its essential dependence on the book. [...] The storyteller takes what he tells from experience – his own or that reported by others. And he in turn makes it the experience of those who are listening to his tale. The novelist has isolated himself. The birthplace of the novel is the solitary individual, who is no longer able to express himself by giving examples of his most important concerns, is himself uncounselled, and cannot counsel others. To write a novel means to carry the incommensurable to extremes in the representation of human life. In the midst of life's fullness, and through the representation of this fullness, the novel gives evidence of the profound perplexity of the living.[10]

For Benjamin, the isolated novelist corresponds to the isolated novel-reader: "A man listening to a story is in the company of the storyteller; even a man reading one shares this companionship. The reader of a novel, however, is isolated."[11] It's not surprising to find this thought in Benjamin: someone who sees the artwork's "aura" disappear through its mere technical reproducibility will also painfully miss the storytelling of the old sea dog or traveling journeyman in an intimate circle. Rather, what must take us aback is how exclusively Benjamin here binds storytelling to one very particular medium, and then deduces from the disappearance of this medium that

---

[9] Benjamin, "The Storyteller," 89.
[10] Benjamin, "The Storyteller," 91.
[11] Benjamin, "The Storyteller," 100.

storytelling in another medium is not the same thing. A hypostatization of presence (of body, voice, truth) accompanies the cult of orality.

With respect to "experience," Benjamin's argument is still more confused. For he seems on the one hand melancholically to lament that the type of experience that can still be adequately exchanged by word of mouth ("the epic side of truth, wisdom")[12] is in real, historical terms disappearing, yet on the other hand to want to reproach the medium of literature and especially the genre of the novel for no longer participating in the mediation of *such* experiences at all – which, though, according to Benjamin's own argument is absolutely inevitable and fully in keeping with the times.

Yet at another point in the same essay, Walter Benjamin approaches very close to the attitude of the narrator of *Gantenbein*, when he too – rather polemically – tackles the connection between storytelling and the generation of sense and meaning:

> "A man who dies at the age of thirty-five," said Moritz Heimann once, "is at every point of his life a man who dies at the age of thirty-five." Nothing is more dubious than this sentence – but for the sole reason that the tense is wrong. A man – so says the truth that was meant here – who died at thirty-five will appear to *remembrance* at every point in his life as a man who dies at the age of thirty-five. In other words, the statement that makes no sense for real life becomes indisputable for remembered life. The nature of the character in a novel cannot be presented any better than is done in this statement, which says that the "meaning" of his life is revealed only in his death. But the reader of a novel actually does look for human beings from whom he derives the "meaning of life." Therefore he must, no matter what, know in advance that he will share their experience of death: if need be their figurative death – at the end of the novel – but preferably their actual one.[13]

The difference mentioned here between life and the novel resembles the difference asserted in *Gantenbein* between observation of oneself and observation of others: due precisely to the fact that one's own life can only be thought and imagined as ex-pressed, ex-ternalized ("I imagine"), it needs – if the experiences are to be put together into a story – to be channeled through the medium of fiction, in order to test out various configurations of sense and meaning. Benjamin, trapped in resentment towards written narrative and especially towards the novel, is blind to the possibilities offered by this medium and this genre to *thematize storytelling itself*; and with melancholy nostalgia he stakes everything on experiences whose meanings in oral transfer are supposed to be self-evident ("[I]n every case the

---

[12]   Benjamin, "The Storyteller," 91.
[13]   Benjamin, "The Storyteller," 100–101.

storyteller is a man who has counsel for his readers").[14] Benjamin's concept of storytelling is defined in terms of *content*, as the passing on of truths and wisdom (we have to assume: in a world that, in its essentials, does not change). In this essay at least, he can't do anything with the *aesthetically* mediated thematization of types of storytelling and types of experiential processing in narrative. His concept of storytelling and experience is basically pre-modern.

That distinguishes him fundamentally from Theodor W. Adorno, who, in his essay "The Position of the Narrator in the Contemporary Novel," likewise pins the crisis of storytelling to the disappearance of experience and locates its causes in war and alienation:

> [I]t is no longer possible to tell a story, but the form of the novel requires narration. [...] [The narrator who dwelt on material concreteness] would be guilty of a lie: the lie of delivering himself over to the world with a love that presupposes that the world is meaningful[.] [...] The identity of experience in the form of a life that is articulated and possesses internal continuity – and that life was the only thing that made the narrator's stance possible – has disintegrated. One need only note how impossible it would be for someone who participated in the war [by now, World War II] to tell stories about it the way people used to tell stories about their adventures. A narrative that presented itself as though the narrator had mastered this kind of experience would rightly meet with impatience and skepticism on the part of its audience. Notions like "sitting down with a good book" are archaic. The reason for this lies not merely in the reader's loss of concentration but also in the content and its form. For telling a story means having something *special* to say, and that is precisely what is prevented by the administered world, by standardization and eternal sameness.[15]

But in marked contrast to Benjamin, Adorno considers it nothing less than the novel's vocation to thematize these situations: "The reification of all relationships between individuals, which transforms their human qualities into lubricating oil for the smooth running of the machinery, the universal alienation and self-alienation, needs to be called by name, and the novel is qualified to do so as few other art forms are."[16] For: "The novel has long since, and certainly since the eighteenth century and Fielding's *Tom Jones*, had as its true subject matter the conflict between living human beings and rigidified conditions."[17]

A narration after the end of narrative can only be achieved in a self-reflexive medium which permanently reflects the conditions of its possibility, not only

---

[14]　Benjamin, "The Storyteller," 90.
[15]　Theodor W. Adorno, "The Position of the Narrator in the Contemporary Novel," in *Notes to Literature*, ed. Rolf Tiedemann, trans. Sherry Weber Nicholson, 1991, 30–36, here 30, 31.
[16]　Adorno, "The Position," 32.
[17]　Adorno, "The Position," 32.

as an interspersed disclosure of its own poetics, but as a thoroughgoing, onrunning self-thematization (or interrelating and crossing out of its own differences). In Adorno's own words: "The new reflection takes a stand against the lie of representation, actually against the narrator himself, who tries, as an extra-alert commentator on events, to correct his unavoidable way of proceeding. *This destruction of form is inherent in the very meaning of form.*"[18] It's in this sense, too, that Adorno interprets the narrative irony of (say) Thomas Mann:

> Only now can the form-constructing function of Thomas Mann's medium, the enigmatic irony that cannot be reduced to any mockery in the content, be fully understood: with an ironic gesture that undoes his own delivery, the author casts aside the claim that he is creating something real, a claim which, how-ever, no word, not even his words, can escape. Mann does this most obviously, perhaps, in his later period, in the *Holy Sinner* and the *Black Swan* [but surely he already did this constantly in the Joseph-novels as well – CB], where the writer, playing with a romantic motif, acknowledged the peep-show element in the narrative, the unreality of illusion, through his use of language. By doing so, he returns the work of art, as he says, to the status of a sublime joke, a status it had until, with the naïveté of lack of naïveté, it presented illusion as truth in an all too unreflected way.[19]

Thus when we also find the thought in Hans Blumenberg that "over a long period, the concept of experience has undergone a process of emaciation. It is hard to imagine from its endpoint that legibility could have been a meta-phor for experience, or that it could be so today or could be so again in the future,"[20] it's certainly not necessary to infer that storytelling and hence the novel are coming to an end. If storytelling arises from experience not in the sense that something whose worth is already fixed ("a valuable experience") must be communicated, but in the sense that experience requires narration, because experience has no meaning without (hi)story, then even the very lack of individual experience (a point that needn't be contested) becomes the subject matter and occasion of narrative – since if meaning is not the start-ing point but the *result* of narratives, then it's never out of the question that strategies for generating sense and meaning may be tried out on the basis of such a lack. Storytelling doesn't automatically presume that the world *is* meaningful; rather, it requires only the impetus to *make sense of something* (something, not the whole world straight away), *to make something mean-ingful*. It could well be that in this way the narrator is reduced to the condi-tion of the *Gantenbein* narrator, who projects fictions over and over again,

---

18   Adorno, "The Position," 34.
19   Adorno, "The Position," 34.
20   Preface to Hans Blumenberg, *Die Lesbarkeit der Welt*, Frankfurt am Main, 1989 [1987].

always afresh – or to the condition of Sisyphus, who must eternally roll the stone up the hill anew: yet even in this absurd activity we'd still think of and imagine the narrator (and indeed the narrative authority) as a happy and fortunate person, about whom, admittedly, it is also said, "I imagine."

In this situation, the storytelling in Uwe Johnson's *Anniversaries* (1970–1983) is also anything but anachronistic. The chronicle of the news items in the *New York Times* indicates only the absence of a meaning-creating center beyond history (annals and chronicles presume the existence of a transcendental signifier, otherwise it makes no sense merely to list things).[21] Yet Gesine Cresspahl's dialogically organized narrative style (addressed to her daughter Mary, to the dead, and to the *New York Times*, but also correlated with the author in the text: "who's telling this anyway, Gesine. Both of us. You can hear it, can't you, Johnson?") turns the search for truth (in reflecting on the past) and realization (in looking to the future) innerdiegetically and extradiegetically into a dialectical project, which escapes the charge of anachronism precisely through its *flow*: and as readers we're naturally involved in this project too, since nothing here is laid out in front of us – we're not spoon-fed with anything. Precisely because the reader assists with the composition, the impression cannot arise that the narrator was from the outset "capable of such experience" (Adorno).

Even though the Danish writer Peer Hultberg introduces 537 different people in his magnificent *Requiem* (1985), in 537 sections of text that never exceed one and a half printed pages (for the most part figurally, and not, *pace* the Austrian publisher of the German translation and the occasional claims of critics, using interior monologue), sections of text which only ever consist of one single sentence and, taken together, present a depressing psychodrama of dead souls – the living dead of our cities – then, nevertheless, the fabrication of these (otherwise still individually well differentiated) interior worlds has not assisted the façade of realism "in its work of camouflage,"[22] but rather demonstrates and displays – precisely through the failure of a story – the failure of narrative; and so once again, by calling into question the *tellability* of such existence, it also questions the possibility of producing sense and meaning in and against such circumstances.

"We will have lived," wrote Heinrich Detering in his review of the later (1992) Hultberg novel *Byen og Verden* (*The City and the World* – a novel in one hundred texts),

> as we will tell it to ourselves. Only in retrospect can a pattern in experience be discovered (or produced) which makes the single details into a whole. Where

---

[21] Cf. Hayden White, *The Content of the Form: Narrative Discourse and Historical Representation*, Baltimore, 1987, 1–25.
[22] Adorno, "The Position," 32.

from the outset nothing is recognizable but plans and possibilities, conceptions or views, there the material for a future narrative lies in waiting. What was previously just a date will afterwards have been an event. Stories that life writes are in reality life itself, told as (his)story.[23]

If narrative and story possess such importance, where should we place the specific function and the specific achievement of the modern *novel*?

2   Meaning Orientation

As Christoph Reinfandt has shown in his award winning, systems-theoretically oriented work *Der Sinn der fiktionalen Wirklichkeiten* (*The Meaning of Fictional Realities*), against the background of the *function* that the autonomous system of "literature" fulfills for the total system of society, and analogously to the *services* it offers to other social systems and for psychic systems, one can in the first place distinguish two kinds of meaning orientation that the modern novel has to offer:

> Narrative can profess to reproduce or discover a "meaning" objectively existent in the reality it presents. In this way, via the criteria of verisimilitude (fictional narrative) or facticity (historical narrative), the comparability or identity of the reality designed by the text with "empirical" reality is established, and both realities are interpreted as meaningful, using the same interpretative frameworks as in societal communication or reality. The semantic vanishing-point of a narrative model of this kind therefore lies in the ordering patterns of society itself, in and around which the conflicts necessary for the production of narrative coherence, with their respective solutions in the form of a confirmation of the order, are arranged.[24]

This "objective" meaning of reality is above all presented by those narratives

> that conceal the relativity and constructedness of all immanent meaning-creation by referring primarily to those societal constructions of reality that have been most effectively and at the same time most thoroughly conventionalized and

---

[23]   Heinrich Detering, "Hölle auf kleiner Flamme" [review of Peer Hultberg, *Die Stadt und die Welt: Roman in hundert Texten*], *Frankfurter Allgemeine Zeitung*, November 21, 1994.

[24]   Christoph Reinfandt, *Der Sinn der fiktionalen Wirklichkeiten: Ein systemtheoretischer Entwurf zur Ausdifferenzierung des englischen Romans vom 18. Jahrhundert bis zur Gegenwart*, Heidelberg, 1997, 149. *Translator's note*: Reinfandt has presented related work in English: "How German Is It? The Place of Systems-Theoretical Approaches in Literary Studies," *European Journal of English Studies* 5/3 (2001): 275–288; "Integrating Literary Theory: Systems-Theoretical Perspectives of Literature and Literary Theory," *Literatur in Wissenschaft und Unterricht* 28/1 (1995): 55–64.

have therefore become invisible. Such narratives also seek to obfuscate as far as possible their narrative mediation, since only in this way can they allay all suspicion of constructedness with respect to the "objective" meaning of the events presented.[25]

In marked contrast to this meaning orientation are meaning orientations that "turn the individual's subjective worldview into the semantic vanishing-point of narrative meaning":[26]

> Just like the functionalized aspects of social order (power and morality) in the first kind of meaning orientation, so the idea of the subject's identity as the semantic integration-point of the narrative presentation is a product and a part of social "reality" beyond the narrative.
>   Conceptions of this kind are designed in societal communication and become semantically enriched, conventionalized and ultimately invisible, whereupon they form the background for the conflict, necessary for the production of narrative coherence, between desire and law.[27]

The space in which the resolution of the conflict between desire and law ends with a victory for the former can only be the space opened up by the autonomous system of "literature" itself. In other words, the subjective sense of "reality" presented by the narrative obviously satisfies the desire for meaning of psychic systems *in this area* only. Its contribution consists precisely in this "subjective" meaning orientation.

Now, it can hardly be disputed that the success-story of the novel, unique in literary history, must have something pertinently to do with the fact that it formidably couples together two disparate references in a seemingly paradoxical way: a reference to reality and fictionality. Through varying accentuations and different hierarchizations, which are effected through different narrative forms and a primary relationship to either the one or the other system, this coupling produces either the one or the other kind of meaning orientation:

> The coupling of a reference to reality and fictionality may be traced back to this interconnectedness and the accompanying hierarchization of system-references, if one undertakes a correlation between reality-reference and a reference to the social system on the one hand, and between reality-reference and a reference to the psychic system on the other.[28]

---

[25] Reinfandt, *Sinn*, 150.
[26] Reinfandt, *Sinn*, 151.
[27] Reinfandt, *Sinn*, 151.
[28] Reinfandt, *Sinn*, 131.

252   *The End of the Novel*

The crucial thing, however, is that right from the outset of the modern novel a third meaning orientation emerges, which has as its vanishing-point neither "objective" reality nor the subjective view of reality: rather it arises from the autoreferentiality of these texts (Reinfandt's "Meaning Orientation III: From Narrative to Literary Meaning").[29] *This is a meaning orientation that arises from the thematization of the possibilities for generating sense and meaning in narrative.*

In terms of literary history, these three meaning orientations are equivalent *to the extent that* the autoreferential thematizing of the possibilities for generating sense and meaning is (as I emphasized repeatedly in chapter 2) right from the very start inherent in and integral to the modern European novel. But these three meaning orientations are *not* equivalent in literary history *to the extent that* meaning orientations 1 and 2 are increasingly harder to "sell" as solutions adequate to the complexity of the initial problem, which was: how the "subject" can be reconciled with "reality."[30]

According to accounts of the history of the novel that take an evolutionary approach and thus concentrate on the *emergence* of new forms, rather than on recording and tracing life forms that have existed historically for a long while (for which we'd need a sort of "ecological" literary history), there's consequently a striking increase in the number and importance of such novels as play through the *very process* of sense- and meaning-generation in narrative and thus become – in an unmistakable, often annoying, but sometimes also amusing way – *self-referential.* I'm referring, of course, to modernism and postmodernism.

There's also a further reason why the three types of meaning orientation are not, in terms of literary history, equivalent. This reason is that the third type – "the literary meaning" (Reinfandt), the thematization through an extremely intensified autoreferentiality of possibilities for generating sense and meaning in narrative – includes the other two and conserves, negates, and raises them to a new level. As a matter of course, highly autoreferential texts such as, say, Joyce's *Ulysses* or Beckett's *Trilogy* or Frisch's *Gantenbein,* still circle (even if only *ex negativo*) round the possibility of setting subject and world into a relationship that one could dare to call meaningful – even if they do this only by conceiving our insatiable yearning for meaning in the discrepancy between effort and failure.

---

[29]   Reinfandt, *Sinn,* 152ff.

[30]   Cf. Reinfandt, *Sinn,* 207: "The impulse to secularization, initiating in the second half of the nineteenth century and intensified by accelerating development in the fields of business and science, leads to [a situation in which] the systems-referentially mediated integrative-reconciliatory meaning-structures of the realistic novel can no longer be presented as the 'objective' constituents of (represented) reality." Translated into critical theory: the explanatory ability and thus the integrative power of ideology decreases continually in the face of advancing objectivity (*Wirklichkeit*).

To the same extent that "objective" and "subjective" meaning orientations no longer gear into each other – i.e., that on this track, the system "literature" has only reduced efficiency[31] – the importance of such narrative texts as thematize and portray the *objective* failure (i.e., whatever failure can't be traced to individual inadequacy) of the other two approaches must, relatively speaking, increase: it's not just that one can no longer write, "The Marquise went out at 5 o'clock," but that after narration, the narrative exploration of the *possibilities of storytelling*, i.e., *the foregrounding of the contingency of attempts to generate sense and meaning*, is now on the agenda.

It's therefore doubly nonsensical to speak of the "dissolution of the novel" or about the "destruction of the novel's substance."[32] For one thing, something is merely coming into the foreground that has been there all along, for hundreds of years – not just in texts like *Don Quixote* or *Tristram Shandy*, but also, as we saw more than once in chapter 6 in the context of the basic narrative situations, in those texts that you'd at first sight categorize as transmitters of the "objective" sense of reality (because every single narrative, even self-dissimulating ones, leaves ineradicable traces of its constructedness). And the second point is that especially with regard to the novel, more than any other genre, it is misleading to speak of its "dissolution," because there's no such thing as *the* novel (the title of this book notwithstanding), and the genre is anything but finished and washed up. As the genre that has already – up to this very moment – produced an unbelievably abundant, protean variety of forms, and that moreover must still be understood as in a state of becoming (Bakhtin: "The novel is the sole genre that remains in the process of becoming and is still uncompleted"),[33] the novel approaches closer than anything else to what

[31] An "ecological" literary history in the above-mentioned sense would on the other hand show that, viewed in terms of the whole of society, the potential for meaning orientation possessed by these "dated" forms is far from exhausted; and that above all the compensatory function of trivial forms of writing, from fantasy to the soft porn products of glossy and "Romance" magazines aimed at a predominantly female public, guarantees for forms which are in literary and aesthetic terms worn out a life and an affective power well beyond their use-by date. The genre's vitality feeds off this, too. Literary evolution must be understood not just as a self-reproductive process, but as a self-transcending process, which, in order to generate something new, is precisely *not* dependent on the exhaustion of the old, but creates innovation at the forefront of evolution – innovation that would *not* be stimulated and produced *by any significant demand*; rather, it's in response to this literature that its public arises. Cf. Christoph Bode, *Ästhetik der Ambiguität: Zur Funktion und Bedeutung von Mehrdeutigkeit in der Literatur der Moderne*, Tübingen, 1988, 242ff.

[32] Christian Schärf, *Der Roman im 20. Jahrhundert*, Stuttgart, 2001, 69.

[33] Josephine von Zitzewitz's translation from the Russian. Cf. Bakhtin, "Epic and Novel," in *The Dialogic Imagination*, ed. Michael Holquist, trans. Caryl Emerson and Michael Holquist, Austin, 1981, 3.

Friedrich Schlegel called "progressive, universal poetry."[34] Again, this is not only because of its attractive force that's capable of integrating anything and everything: it's also because the novel, with its ability to change form, with its indeterminability, and through its self-referentiality that generates ever new meanings, reflects exactly those factors that produced it – factors that have certainly not diminished since then: change, transformation, becoming, process:

> Only that which is itself in the process of becoming can comprehend this process. The novel became the leading hero of the drama of the literary development of modernity precisely because it best of all reflects the tendency of the modern world *to become*; it is, after all, the only genre born of this modern world and in every respect of a piece with it.[35]

Just as every non-conventional message influences the code (Umberto Eco: "in order to restructure codes, one needs to rewrite messages"),[36] so every truly *novel* novel changes our idea of what a novel is. But if the stimulus and origin of the modern novel consist not just in the "questioning of real life" (according to Vargas Llosa the "secret *raison d'être* of literature"),[37] but also in the desire to wrest meaning from real life through narrative, or to set a meaning against it (a meaning that can no longer be assumed to be simply *given*), then it's also reasonably clear and doesn't require too much wild speculation to outline what the future of this necessary, peril-averting illusion is, precisely in contrast to other media in which narrative occurs as well.

---

[34]   Friedrich Schlegel, "Athenäum Fragments" (no. 116), in *German Aesthetic and Literary Criticism: The Romantic Ironists and Goethe*, ed. Kathleen M. Wheeler, Cambridge, 1984, 46. German: *Kritische-Friedrich Schlegel-Ausgabe*, 35 vols., ed. Ernst Behler, Hans Eichner et al., Munich, 1958–, 2: 182.

[35]   This passage from Bakhtin's essay "Epic and Novel: Toward a Methodology for the Study of the Novel" is taken from Ken Hirschkop's translation in *The Cambridge History of Literary Criticism, Vol. 9, Twentieth-Century Historical, Philosophical and Psychological Perspectives*, ed. Christa Knellwolf and Christopher North, Cambridge, 2001, 145, with an addition by Josephine von Zitzewitz. Cf. Bakhtin, *Dialogic Imagination*, 7.

[36]   Umberto Eco, *The Role of the Reader: Explorations in the Semiotics of Texts*, Bloomington, 1979, 104.

[37]   Mario Vargas Llosa, *Letters to a Young Novelist*, trans. Natasha Wimmer, New York, 2002, 8. Cf. 7: "those who immerse themselves in the lucubration of lives different from their own demonstrate indirectly their rejection and criticism of life as it is, of the real world, and manifest their desire to substitute for it the creations of their imaginations and dreams."

3   Novels: Allegories of Telling

Today, we realize that narrative pervades and informs cultural practices to such a vast extent that it's barely an exaggeration to call it ubiquitous ("Narrative [...] is everywhere")[38] and to regard it as a newly emerging foundational paradigm of cultural studies. For that very reason, when trying to identify the *specific* function of the modern and postmodern novel, it is not sufficient to remark that it offers a variety of different types of narrative. Rather, it would be necessary to identify the dislocation which the novel's place has undergone in the field of all practices that may somehow be called "narrative," in order to deduce, from the changing difference between the novel and other forms, the respects in which the former still retains its particularity. Although more novels are presumably bought and read in western societies today than at any other time in history, nevertheless all major empirical studies suggest that the importance of novel-reading as a leisure activity is on the wane – in parallel to the general decline in significance of the print media – and that it's increasingly superseded by the use of visual and audiovisual electronic media (TV, cinema, video, DVD, audiovisual material on the Internet, etc.).

Although a remarkable number of major electronic media productions are themselves based on textual (in the broadest sense) literary scripts, it would be wrong to underestimate the degree to which they produce their very own material and the *media-specific* complexity they evince. A would-be derogatory term like "MTV aesthetics" only conceals, rather than conceptualizing or spiriting away, how remarkably innovative and effective some music videos, clips, or DVDs are; whereas the possibilities of Net literature are still very far from being fully utilized as long as authors just continue to write the same old texts in a different medium, without converting the specific qualities of the new medium into a vital part of their own poetics.

But if the modern novel is so fundamentally bound to the medium of the printed book (and not just in a *technical* sense, but also in the *historical* sense that the individual, middle-class subject can also – and not least – be understood as a reading subject that re-produces itself through communicating with others about that reading experience in a kind of self-fashioning process), then the question of whether the novel has a future must be answered in a significantly contradictory way. Obviously *not*, since like every historical phenomenon it has a finite lifespan, after which it's exhausted (and with the declining relevance of the print media, its basis in

---

[38]   Carol Jacobs and Henry Sussman (eds.), *Acts of Narrative*, Stanford, CA, 2003, ix. Cf. H. Porter Abbott, *The Cambridge Introduction to Narrative*, Cambridge, 2002, on "the universality of narrative," 1–3; and in general Vera Nünning and Ansgar Nünning (eds.), *Erzähltheorie transgenerisch, intermedial, interdisziplinär*, Trier, 2002.

cultural practice is predictably melting away). All things must pass, and it may happen that something changes to such an extent that we're obliged to address it differently. And yet the novel obviously *does* have a future (for the time being at least), since the modern novel can now (at the most advanced points of its evolution) reflect on its "core business," on what brought it about in the first place. This was not an attempt (say) to conjure up a lost "totality of being,"[39] nor to present some sort of ready-made sense, meaning, viewpoint, or orientation; instead, by designing and dramatizing imagined situations, the novel's core business has always been to offer and display *possibilities of the generation and construction of meaning*. The prediction of someone who, alluding to Lenin, invokes the end of the novel,[40] might miss the mark just as widely as Lenin did with respect to capitalism – and for the same reasons. Such a view, that is, underestimates the persistent vitality of the supposedly deceased (the news of the death of the novel is slightly exaggerated – obituaries are precipitate), because it overlooks its core but also the protean capacity to change that is taken up and accrued by that core: the ability to continue fulfilling the same functions, to perform similar services, through radical self-transcendence and redefinition.

Even a novel trapped in the most conventionalized realism can be regarded as an *allegory of narration*, if we only reflect that it presents in a specific form what must actually be thought abstractly: *a way of making narrative sense, of making sense through narrative*. These allegories of telling, which occur implicitly even in novels dependent on the realistic paradigm, but more emphatically so in the somewhat more capacious paradigm of mimesis, display such amazing scope, depth, and variety that one can think of this genre as like a gigantic, decentralized network of computers, mediating, exploring the field of possibilities for structuring something in a meaningful way, in language. If you conceive the concrete mathematical equation that a given novel calculates out (complete with numbers) as the *instantiation of a formula*, then you've grasped the algorithm attributed above all to poetry, but which surely applies to the novel, too: to see the text at hand as a specific instance of the general principle deduced from that very text, so that the text itself presents a concrete example of the processing and designing of "reality" that it abstractly conveys. It is a concrete illustration of the general thesis it conveys, its own example. This is why I call narrative texts allegories of telling. *The novel can do that because what it "expresses" about ways of constructing and processing world and experience can also be*

---

[39]   Cf. Georg Lukács, *The Theory of the Novel: A Historico-Philosophical Essay on the Forms of Great Epic Literature*, trans. Anna Bostock, London, 1978 [1971, 1920].

[40]   Heinz Schlaffer, "Der Roman, das letzte Stadium der Literatur," *Sinn und Form* 6 (2002): 789–797.

referred to the novel itself. Whether it's *Don Quixote* or *Ulysses*, whether it's Hawthorne's *The Scarlet Letter* or Nabokov's *Pale Fire* (1962), whether it's *Moby-Dick* or Thomas Mann's *Joseph*-tetralogy (1933–1943) – the position that the text ascribes to the reader, the activities that it requires of us, the ways of reading that it suggests to us, are exactly those that the respective novel itself thematizes and unfolds, so that reading these texts emerges as an active, "allegorical" reconstruction and simulation of the never-ending quest for meaning.

Freed from the shackles of any kind of aesthetic of realism, imitation, or mimesis, the postmimetic modernist and postmodernist novel redefines the "exhaustion" (as it appears from the new paradigms' viewpoint) of the possibilities offered by the older paradigms as the overcoming and transcendence of a larval stage whose restrictions are felt as a hindrance to the novel's very own business – just as, to a painter eager to explore the possibilities of freely composing colors and forms, it would certainly seem onerous to stipulate that recognizable "objects" must eventually take shape.

This view, which regards the novel as an allegory of telling and of the possibilities of generating sense and meaning in narrative, necessarily includes the idea that the novel is always already to be regarded as *metafiction*. In saying that I'm not disputing the fact that there are differences in the distribution of explicit and implicit metafictionalization, nor – this is precisely my argument – the fact of an evident increase in metafiction and metanarration (every intensified form of autoreferentiality will bring with it, as a necessary spin-off, reflection on fiction and narration, since autoreflexivity implies nothing less than that: self-reflection – the bending back of reference to the sign-structure itself).

Yet this view of the novel as an allegory of telling, as the self-thematization of methods and possibilities of generating sense and meaning, enables us now to precisely identify the place of the novel today: the aesthetically "released" novel (i.e., the novel that no longer *has to* offer a coherent illusion and that doesn't adhere to any aesthetic program, because it has free, playful – but at the same time aesthetically distancing – access to *all* previous aesthetics; the novel whose vocation consists in the interrelation and erasure of all conceivable codes (Umberto Eco: an aesthetic message is a message that questions the code – compare Adorno's "The destruction of form is inherent in the very meaning of form")[41] is the literary form that, above all others today, radically and compellingly transports narrative into that semiotic condition in which an "aesthetic idea" (as Immanuel Kant defines it in his *Critique of Judgment*) can fully develop and unfold: "by an aesthetic idea," writes Kant, "I mean that

---

[41]   Cf. Umberto Eco, *Einführung in die Semiotik*, Munich, 1972, 139; and Adorno, "The Position," 34.

representation of the imagination which induces much thought, yet without the possibility of any definite thought whatever, i.e., *concept*, being adequate to it, and which language, consequently, can never get quite on level terms with or render completely intelligible."[42] When the "intuition" (*Anschauung*) to which no concept can be adequate (that is, the "aesthetic idea") is offered in the realm of meaning-generating narrative, and when it is offered in "released" form, i.e., self-(re)presenting and thematizing, then what Kant ascribed to "the imagination in its *freedom*" can indeed occur to an increased degree: "furtherance of the cognitive faculties in their free play."[43]

And so that would be the place of the novel today: not merely to be "a machine to think with,"[44] but rather, owing to its *linguistic* constructedness and its *postmimetic freedoms*, to reflect on and revolve in a very much more complex and incomparably more radical (= profounder, deeper) way than the other media in which narration is also possible *how meaning is brought into the world*; that is, ultimately to configure over and over again the paradoxical *tension between contingency and grounding*, to expose the groundlessness of our yearning for a narratively mediated illusion of existential security, at the same time that, through its handling of precisely this human disposition, the novel recognizes and acknowledges such a yearning as fully legitimate.

This is not to dispute, in principle, the possibility of conceiving visually represented narratives, too, as "allegorical" in the above-mentioned sense. But there's the practical objection that something visually displayed is at first taken to be (fictionally) real and doesn't allow the same possibility of doubt as stories evoked through verbal narrative "only": the latter, as a rule (i.e., in non-present-tense narration), are based on the *absence* of what is narrated, and have to do without all sense-related evidence (which is *one* reason why it's difficult to turn a novel like *Lolita* into a film). However, it follows that as far as highlighting its own contingency is concerned, a visual narration has to make do with comparatively crude and relatively unsophisticated (though still potentially attractive) methods (think of *Rashomon*, *The Usual Suspects*), and is perpetually hindered (by the medial conditions) in that it always and by necessity has to show *something concrete that is given to the senses*.

---

[42]   Immanuel Kant, *The Critique of Judgement*, trans. James Creed Meredith, Oxford, 1991 [1928], 175–176 (= §49). German text: *Kritik der Urteilskraft*, Stuttgart, 1981 [1963], 246.

[43]   Kant, *Judgement*, 143 (= §35). In German text, 203.

[44]   I. A. Richards, *Principles of Literary Criticism*, London, 1983 [1967, 1924], 1, referring to books in general; whereas Abbott relates this thought specifically to "narrative": cf. Abbott, *Narrative*, 59.

Considering, too, the incomparably greater sophistication of the linguistic system of signs (discussed above), it can't come as any major surprise that the thematization of possibilities of the generation and construction of meaning through narration will for the foreseeable future occur principally in the medium of the novel. Indeed, even here a "struggle" constantly arises between reader and author,[45] since, as cognitive narratology confirms,[46] the reader's "naturalizing" tendency (the inclination to decode texts *for as long as possible* with codes established, tried, and tested in everyday contexts, i.e., codes that *reduce* complexity) stands diametrically opposed to the tendency of literary texts, which is to *increase* complexity: thus this "naturalization" always tends to reduce and impoverish whatever the text may offer. Lotman's optimistic assessment that the reader "has an interest in mastering the model that the author presents to him," and that therefore the artist's victory is a source of joy to the vanquished reader, clearly doesn't cover those cases in which readers, by "naturalizing" – which is only another word for unliterary reading – haven't remotely grasped the complexity of the text's model in the first place.[47] To the same extent that postmimetic literature functions precisely

[45] Lotman, *The Structure of the Artistic Text*, 288: "The perception of an artistic text is always a struggle between audience and author [...]. The audience takes in part of the text and then 'finishes' or 'constructs' the rest. The author's next 'move' may confirm the guess and make further reading pointless (at least from the point of view of modern aesthetic norms) or it may disprove the guess and require a new construction from the reader. But the next 'move' made by the author once again poses the two possibilities. This continues until the author wins; he outplays the artistic experience, aesthetic norms and prejudices of the reader, and thrusts his model of the world and concept of the structural reality upon him [this formulation suggests once again that a particular view, a particular meaning, is conveyed, which to a considerable extent contradicts Lotman's own aesthetic – CB]. This moment is the end of the work, and it can occur before the end of the text if the author uses a cliché-model whose nature becomes apparent to the reader at the beginning of the work. The reader, of course, is not passive; *he has an interest* in mastering the model that the author presents to him. With its help he hopes to explain and conquer the forces of the outer and inner world. Therefore the artist's victory is a source of joy to the vanquished reader."

[46] Cf., in general, Elrud Ibsch, "The Cognitive Turn in Narratology," *Poetics Today* 11 (1990): 411–418; Manfred Jahn, "Frames, Preferences, and the Reading of Third-Person Narratives: Towards a Cognitive Narratology," *Poetics Today* 18/4 (1997): 441–468; Ray Jackendoff, *Semantics and Cognition*, Cambridge, MA, 1983; Ray Jackendorff, *Consciousness and the Computational Mind*, Cambridge, MA, 1987; Meir Sternberg, "Proteus in Quotation Land: Mimesis and the Forms of Reported Discourse," *Poetics Today* 3 (1982): 107–156.

[47] Cf. Lotman himself, *Structure*, 295–296: "While the author strives to increase the number of code systems and complicate their structure, the reader is inclined to reduce them to a minimum that seems sufficient to him. The tendency to complicate characters is an authorial tendency; a black-and-white contrasting structure is the tendency manifested by the reader."

by hindering, erasing, and undermining everyday processes of cognition, a narratology based purely on cognitive psychology can hardly articulate more (indeed, can only articulate less) than good hermeneutics already could about the frictions and interferences that such postmimetic texts produce.[48] It is to be feared that the reader-as-serial-offender, as modeled by cognitive narratology, is guilty of the crime that was absolute anathema to the seasoned novelist Vladimir Nabokov – *identification*: "Or, and this is the worst thing a reader can do, he identifies himself with a character in the book. This lowly variety is not the kind of imagination I would like readers to use."[49]

It is not so much between vacancy and encyclopedia that the contemporary novel moves[50] – even as early as *Bouvard et Pécuchet* (1881) the author, Flaubert, could conceive the encyclopedia only as a farce[51] – as between two extreme points that perhaps come most graphically to the fore in Thomas Pynchon's *œuvre*: either *nothing* has meaning, i.e., there is no such thing as a sign, because everything stands alone and singly *for itself*, but as a consequence human beings also stand isolated and lost; or, instead, *everything* is a sign – a situation that causes characters and readers alike to fall into the paranoid delusion of seeing meaningful relationships everywhere (as already happened to Charles Kinbote in Nabokov's *Pale Fire*). The freedom to make it like this or like that or in any conceivable mixture of the available possibilities – as long as we don't forget, on pain of suffering the fate of Don Quixote or of a Kinbote, that it is we, as readers, who set this particular mechanism in operation – has been the freedom of the novel-reader right from the very start: the reader who, even here, faced with the possibility of either understanding a story "just" as a story, as what it ostensibly seems to be, or on the contrary of understanding it as a representative of something else (an allegory, in the broadest sense), *meets himself* as the constructor of "such" worlds – just as long as he does not forget this situation of *choice*. So in general terms, one possible end (in the sense of "goal" or "objective") of the novel would be this: to make possible an encounter with oneself in the medium of another – and that's *experience*; which, in

---

[48]   With respect to the possible contributions that a narratology based on Possible Worlds Theory (PWT) could make to our knowledge of the processes of understanding and configuration in reading fictional texts (cf. above all the publications of Marie-Laure Ryan, primarily *Possible Worlds, Artificial Intelligence and Narrative Theory*, Bloomington, 1991), it's also evidently the case that the cognitive flow always proceeds from the level of higher complexity to the level of lower complexity; and therefore it may be that PWT can profit considerably from relevant works of literary theory and criticism on fiction, fictionalization, mimesis, realism, postmimesis, etc. – whereas it seems to me far from certain that this would work the other way round.

[49]   Vladimir Nabokov, *Lectures on Literature*, ed. Fredson Bowers, London, 1980, 4.

[50]   But see Blumenberg, *Lesbarkeit*, ch. 19; Calvino, Harvard Lectures.

[51]   Cf. Blumenberg, *Lesbarkeit*, 308.

order to be understood and be felt as meaningful, would in turn need to be embedded in a narrative.

It was to that end (so one version of the story goes) – to make sense of epochal, new experiences, to thematize the experience of innovation and novelty – that the modern novel arose; but it isn't coming to an end, because *this* still persists: the condition of its beginning.

References

Abbott, H. Porter. *The Cambridge Introduction to Narrative*. Cambridge, 2002.

Abrams, M. H. (ed.). *The Norton Anthology of English Literature: Fifth Edition.* 2 vols. New York, 1986.

Adorno, Theodor W. "The Position of the Narrator in the Contemporary Novel." *Notes to Literature*, ed. Rolf Tiedemann, trans. Sherry Weber Nicholson. New York, 1991, 30–36. German text: "Form und Gehalt des zeitgenössischen Romans." *Akzente* 1 (1954): 410–416.

Allrath, Gaby. "'But why will you say that I am mad?': Textuelle Signale für die Ermittlung von *unreliable narration.*" *Unreliable Narration: Studien zur Theorie und Praxis unglaubwürdigen Erzählens in der englischsprachigen Erzählliteratur,* ed. Ansgar Nünning, Trier, 1998, 59–79.

Allrath, Gaby. "A Survey of the Theory, History, and New Areas of Research of Feminist Narratology." *Literatur in Wissenschaft und Unterricht* 33/4 (2000): 387–410.

Allrath, Gaby. "Multiperspektivisches Erzählen und synthesestörende Strategien im englischen Frauenroman des 19. Jahrhunderts aus der Sicht einer feministischen Literaturwissenschaft: Subversive Variationen des *single-point perspective system* bei Jane Austen, Emily Brontë und George Eliot." *Multiperspektivisches Erzählen: Zur Theorie und Geschichte der Perspektivenstruktur im englischen Roman des 18. bis 20. Jahrhunderts*, ed. Vera and Ansgar Nünning, Trier, 2000, 175–198.

Arendt, Hannah (ed.) *Illuminations.* New York, 1968.

Aristotle. *The "Poetics" of Aristotle*, ed. and trans. Stephen Halliwell. London, 1987.

Armstrong, Nancy. *Desire and Domestic Fiction: A Political History of the Novel.* New York, 1987, 1989.

Arnold, Heinz Ludwig and Heinrich Detering (eds.). *Grundzüge der Literaturwissenschaft*. Munich, 1997.

The Novel: An Introduction. By Christoph Bode. Translated by James Vigus. English translation © 2011 James Vigus. Published by John Wiley & Sons, Ltd.
Original German text © 2005 Narr Francke Attempto Verlag GmbH + Co. KG.

Arnold, Matthew. "The Function of Criticism at the Present Time." In *The Norton Anthology of English Literature: Fifth Edition*, Vol. 1, ed. M. H. Abrams. New York, 1986, 1408–1424.

Assmann, Aleida. "Fiktion als Differenz." *Poetica* 21/3–4 (1989): 239–260.

Auerbach, Erich. *Philologie der Weltliteratur: Sechs Versuche über Stil und Wirklichkeitswahrnehmung*. Frankfurt am Main, 1992.

Auerbach, Erich. *Mimesis: The Representation of Reality in Western Literature*, trans. Willard R. Trask, 50th anniversary edn (first published 1946), Princeton, NJ, 2003.

Axelrod, Mark. *The Poetics of Novels: Fiction and Its Execution*. London, 1999.

Bachelard, Gaston. *The Poetics of Space*, trans. Maria Jolas, new introduction and foreword by John R. Stilgoe. Boston, 1969, new foreword, 1994.

Bachtin, Michail M. *Die Ästhetik des Wortes*, ed. Rainer Grübel. Frankfurt am Main, 1979.

Bachtin, Michail M. *Literatur und Karneval: Zur Romantheorie und Lachkultur*. Frankfurt am Main, 1985.

Bakhtin, Mikhail M. "Epic and Novel." *The Dialogic Imagination*, ed. Michael Holquist, trans. Caryl Emerson and Michael Holquist. Austin, 1981. German text: Michail M. Bachtin, *Formen der Zeit im Roman: Untersuchungen zur historischen Poetik*. Frankfurt am Main, 1989.

Bakhtin, Mikhail M. "Forms of Time and of the Chronotope in the Novel: Notes toward a Historical Poetics." *The Dialogic Imagination*, ed. Michael Holquist, trans. Caryl Emerson and Michael Holquist, Austin, 1982, 84–258.

Bal, Mieke. *Narratologie*. Paris, 1977.

Bal, Mieke. "Notes on Narrative Embedding." *Poetics Today* 2/2 (1981): 41–59.

Bal, Mieke. *Narratology: Introduction to the Theory of Narrative*. Toronto, 1985.

Banfield, Ann. *Unspeakable Sentences: Narration and Representation in the Language of Fiction*. Boston, 1982.

Barthes, Roland. "l'effet de réel." *Communications* 11 (1968): 84–89.

Bauer, Matthias. *Romantheorie*. Stuttgart, 1997.

Benjamin, Walter. "The Storyteller: Reflections on the Works of Nikolai Leskov," trans. Harry Zorn. In *Narrative Theory: Critical Concepts in Literary and Cultural Studies*, Vol. 3, *Political Narratology*, ed. Mieke Bal, London, 2004, 88–106; this translation was first published in Hannah Arendt (ed.), *Illuminations*, New York, 1968, 83–107. German text: "Der Erzähler: Betrachtungen zum Werk Nikolai Lesskows." *Illuminationen: Ausgewählte Schriften 1*. Frankfurt am Main, 1974, 1977, 385–410.

Benjamin, Walter. *Sprache und Geschichte: Philosophische Essays. Ausgew. von Rolf Tiedemann*. Stuttgart, 1992.

Bialostosky, Don. "Dialogic Criticism." In *Contemporary Literary Theory*, ed. G. Douglas Atkins and Laura Morrow. Amherst, MA, 1989, 214–228.

Birch, David. *Language, Literature and Critical Practice: Ways of Analyzing Texts*. London, 1989, 1993.

Blumenberg, Hans. *Die Lesbarkeit der Welt*. Frankfurt am Main, 1987, 1989.

Bode, Christoph. *Ästhetik der Ambiguität: Zu Funktion und Bedeutung von Mehrdeutigkeit in der Literatur der Moderne*. Tübingen, 1988.

Bode, Christoph. Review of Shlomith Rimmon-Kenan. *Narrative Fiction: Contemporary Poetics.* London, 1983, 1986. *Literatur in Wissenschaft und Unterricht* 21 (1988): 157–163.

Bode, Christoph. "Literary Value and Evaluation: The Case for Relational Concepts." *Anglistentag 1988 Göttingen: Vorträge,* ed. Heinz-Joachim Müllenbrock and Renate Noll-Wiemann. Tübingen, 1989, 309–324.

Booker, Christopher. *The Seven Basic Plots: Why We Tell Stories.* London, 2005.

Booth, Wayne C. "The Self-Conscious Narrator in Comic Fiction before *Tristram Shandy.*" *Publications of the Modern Language Association of America* 67 (1952): 163–185.

Booth, Wayne C. *The Rhetoric of Fiction,* 2nd edn. Chicago, 1983.

Booth, Wayne C. "The Struggle to Tell the Story of the Struggle to Get the Story Told." *Narrative* 5/1 (1997): 50–59.

Borchmeyer, Dieter and Viktor Žmegač. *Moderne Literatur in Grundbegriffen.* Tübingen, 1994.

Borges, Jorge Luis. *Eine neue Widerlegung der Zeit und 66 andere Essays.* Frankfurt am Main, 2003.

Bradbury, Malcolm. "A Jaundiced View." *Who Do You Think You Are? Stories and Parodies.* London, 1976, 1986, 165–171.

Bradbury, Malcolm (ed.). *The Novel Today: Contemporary Writers on Fiction.* Glasgow, 1977.

Brenkman, John. "On Voice." *Novel: A Forum on Fiction* 33/3 (2000): 281–306.

Breton, André. "Erstes Manifest des Surrealismus." In *Surrealismus in Paris 1919– 1939: Ein Lesebuch,* ed. Karlheinz Barck. Leipzig, 1990, 82–120.

Brink, André. *The Novel: Language and Narrative from Cervantes to Calvino.* London, 1998.

Broich, Ulrich. "Gibt es eine 'neutrale Erzählsituation'? Franz K. Stanzel zum 60. Geburtstag." *Germanisch-Romanische Monatsschrift* 33 (1983): 129–145.

Broich, Ulrich and Manfred Pfister (eds.). *Intertextualität: Formen, Funktionen, anglistische Falstudien.* Tübingen, 1985.

Bronfen, Elisabeth. *Der literarische Raum: Eine Untersuchung am Beispiel von Dorothy M. Richardsons Romanzyklus Pilgrimage.* Tübingen, 1986.

Bronfen, Elisabeth. *Dorothy Richardson's Art of Memory: Space, Identity, Text,* trans. Victoria Appelbe. Manchester, 1999.

Brooke-Rose, Christine. *A Rhetoric of the Unreal.* Cambridge, 1986.

Brooke-Rose, Christine. "Narrating Without a Narrator." *Times Literary Supplement,* December 31, 1999, 12–13.

Brooks, Cleanth and Robert Penn Warren. *Understanding Fiction.* New York, 1943.

Burckhardt, Jacob. *The Civilization of the Renaissance in Italy,* trans. S. G. Middlemore. Harmondsworth, 1990.

Bürger, Peter. *Prosa der Moderne.* Frankfurt am Main, 1988 [1859].

Burgess, Anthony. *Joysprick: An Introduction to the Language of James Joyce.* London, 1973.

Burwick, Frederick. *Illusion and the Drama: Critical Theory of the Enlightenment and Romantic Era.* University Park, PA, 1991.

Buschmann, Matthias. "Multiperspektivität – Alle Macht dem Leser?" *Wirkendes Wort* 46/2 (1996): 259–275.

Butler, Christopher. "Introduction." *Henry James: The Ambassadors.* Oxford, 1985, vii–xviii.

Butler, Christopher. *Interpretation, Deconstruction, and Ideology: An Introduction to Some Current Issues in Theory.* Oxford, 1998 [1984].

Calvino, Italo. *Six Memos for the Next Millennium: The Charles Eliot Norton Lectures [Harvard] 1985–6.* Cambridge, MA, 1988.

Cassirer, Ernst. "Mythischer, ästhetischer und theoretischer Raum." *Beilagenheft zur Zeitschrift für Ästhetik und allgemeine Kunstwissenschaft* 25 (1931): 21–36.

Chatman, Seymour. "Genette's Analysis of Narrative Time Relations." *L'Esprit Créateur* 14/4 (1974): 353–368.

Chatman, Seymour. *Story and Discourse: Narrative Structure in Fiction and Film.* Ithaca, NY, 1978, 1993.

Chatman, Seymour. *Coming to Terms: The Rhetoric of Narrative in Fiction and Film.* Ithaca, NY, 1990, 1993.

Ci, Jiwei. "An Alternative to Genette's Theory of Order." *Style* 22/1 (1988): 18–38.

Cixous, Hélène. "Sorties." In *Modern Criticism and Theory: A Reader*, ed. David Lodge. London, 1994, 287–293.

Cobley, Paul. *Narrative.* London, 2001.

Cohan, Steven and Linda M. Shires. *Telling Stories: A Theoretical Analysis of Narrative Fiction.* London, 1988, 1991.

Cohn, Dorrit C. *Transparent Minds: Narrative Modes for Presenting Consciousness in Fiction.* Princeton, NJ, 1978, 1983.

Cohn, Dorrit C. "The Encirclement of Narrative: On Franz Stanzel's *Theorie des Erzählens.*" *Poetics Today* 2/2 (1981): 157–182.

Cohn, Dorrit C. "Signposts of Fictionality: A Narratological Perspective." *Poetics Today* 11/4 (1990): 775–804.

Cohn, Dorrit C. *The Distinction of Fiction.* Baltimore, 1999.

Cohn, Dorrit and Gérard Genette. "A Narratological Exchange." In *Neverending Stories: Towards A Critical Narratology*, ed. Ann Fehn, Ingeborg Hoesterey, and Maria Tatar. Princeton, NJ, 1992, 258–266.

Coleridge, Samuel Taylor. "Biographia Literaria." In *The Norton Anthology of English Literature*, Vol. 2, ed. M. H. Abrams. New York, 386–547.

Culler, Jonathan. *The Pursuit of Signs: Semiotics, Literature, Deconstruction.* London, 1981.

Culler, Jonathan. *Literary Theory: A Very Short Introduction.* Oxford, 1997.

Currie, Mark. *Postmodern Narrative Theory.* London, 1998.

Davis, Lennard J. *Factual Fictions: The Origins of the English Novel.* New York, 1983.

Detering, Heinrich. "Hölle auf kleiner Flamme" [Review of Peer Hultberg, *Die Stadt und die Welt: Roman in hundert Texten*]. *Frankfurter Allgemeine Zeitung*, November 21, 1994.

Detering, Heinrich (ed.). *Autorschaft: Positionen und Revisionen.* DFG-Symposion 2001. Stuttgart, 2002.

Diengott, Nilli. "Narrative Level and Participation as Criteria for a Typology of Narrators: A Reconsideration." *Yearbook of Comparative and General Literature* 35 (1986): 51–55.

Diengott, Nilli. "Narratology and Feminism." *Style* 22 (1988): 42–51.

Dilthey, William. "Drafts for a Critique of Historical Reason." *Selected Works, Vol. 3, The Formation of the Historical World in the Human Sciences*, ed. and trans. A. Makkreel and Frithjof Rodi. Princeton, NJ, 2002. German text: Wilhlem Dilthey, "Entwürfe zur Kritik der historischen Vernunft." *Seminar: Philosophische Hermeneutik*, ed. Hans-Georg Gadamer and Gottfried Boehm. Frankfurt am Main, 1976, 1979, 189–220.

Docherty, Thomas. *Reading (Absent) Character: Towards a Theory of Characterization in Fiction*. Oxford, 1983.

Eagleton, Terry. *The English Novel: An Introduction*. Oxford, 2004.

Eco, Umberto. *Einführung in die Semiotik*. Munich, 1972.

Eco, Umberto. *The Role of the Reader: Explorations in the Semiotics of Texts*. Bloomington, 1979.

Eco, Umberto. *Lector in fabula: Die Mitarbeit der Interpretation in erzählenden Texten*. Munich, 1987.

Eco, Umberto. "Vom offenen Kunstwerk zum Pendel Foucaults." *Lettre International* 5 (1989): 38–42.

Eggert, Hartmut et al. (eds.). *Geschichte als Literatur: Formen und Grenzen der Repräsentation von Vergangenheit*. Stuttgart, 1990.

Eliot, George. "The Morality of *Wilhelm Meister*" and "The Natural History of German Life." *Selected Critical Writings*. Oxford, 1992, 129–132, 260–295.

Erlich, Victor. *Russian Formalism*, 3rd edn. New Haven, CT, 1981.

Ermarth, Elizabeth Deeds. *Realism and Consensus in the English Novel*. Princeton, NJ, 1983.

Ermarth, Elizabeth Deeds. *The English Novel in History 1840–1895*. London, 1997.

Fielitz, Sonja. *Roman: Text & Kontext*. Berlin, 2001.

Fish, Stanley. *Is There a Text in This Class? The Authority of Interpretive Communities*. Cambridge, MA, 1995.

Fludernik, Monika. "Narratology in Context." *Poetics Today* 14/4 (1993): 729–761.

Fludernik, Monika. "Second Person Fiction: Narrative *You* as Addressee and/or Protagonist." *Arbeiten aus Anglistik und Amerikanistik* 18/2 (1993): 217–247.

Fludernik, Monika. *The Fictions of Language and the Languages of Fiction: The Linguistic Representation of Speech and Consciousness*. London, 1993.

Fludernik, Monika. "Introduction: Second-Person Narrative and Related Issues." *Style* 28/3 (1994): 281–311.

Fludernik, Monika. *Towards a "Natural" Narratology*. London, 1996.

Fludernik, Monika. "The Genderization of Narrative." *GRAAT* 21 (1999): 153–175.

Fludernik, Monika. "Beyond Structuralism in Narratology: Recent Developments and New Horizons in Narrative Theory." *Anglistik* 11/1 (2000): 83–96.

Fludernik, Monika. "Tempus und Zeitbewußtsein: Erzähltheoretische Überlegungen zur englischen Literatur." In *Zeit und Roman: Zeiterfahrung im historischen*

Wandel und ästhetischer Paradigmenwechsel vom sechzehnten Jahrhundert bis zur Postmoderne, ed. Martin Middeke, Würzburg, 2002, 21–32.

Fludernik, Monika. *An Introduction to Narratology*. London, 2009.

Fokkema, Aleid. *Postmodern Characters: A Study of Characterization in British and American Postmodern Fiction*. Amsterdam, 1991.

Foltinek, Herbert, Wolfgang Richle, and Waldemar Zacharasiewicz (eds.). *Tales and 'their telling difference': Zur Theorie und Geschichte der Narrativik: Festschrift zum 70. Geburtstag von Franz K. Stanzel*. Heidelberg, 1993.

Forster, E. M. *Aspects of the Novel*. Harmondsworth, 1977 [1927].

Foucault, Michel. *Schriften zur Literatur*. Frankfurt am Main, 1988.

Fowler, Alastair. *Kinds of Literature: An Introduction to the Theory of Genres and Modes*. Oxford, 1982, 1997.

Fowler, Roger. *Linguistics and the Novel*. London, 1977, 1983.

Frenk, Joachim (ed.). *Spatial Change in English Literature*. Trier, 2000.

Genette, Gérard. "Fictional Narrative, Factual Narrative." *Poetics Today* 11/4 (1990): 755–774.

Genette, Gérard. *Fiktion und Diktion*. Munich, 1994.

Genette, Gérard. *Narrative Discourse: An Essay in Method*, trans. Jane E. Lewin. Ithaca, NY, 1980, reprinted 1994.

Genette, Gérard. *Narrative Discourse Revisited*, trans. Jane E. Lewin. Ithaca, NY, 1988.

Genette, Gérard. "Vraisemblance and Motivation." *Narrative* 9/3 (2001): 239–258.

Gibson, Andrew. *Towards a Postmodern Theory of Narrative*. Edinburgh, 1996.

Goethe, Johann Wolfgang von. "Maximen und Reflexionen." *Werke (Hamburger Ausgabe)*. Munich, 1982, 12: 365–547.

Goethe, Johann Wolfgang von. "Noten und Abhandlungen zu besserem Verständnis des West-östlichen Divans." *Werke (Hamburger Ausgabe)*. Munich, 1982, 2: 126–264.

Grabes, Herbert. "Fiktion – Realismus – Ästhetik: Woran erkennt der Leser Literatur?" In *Text – Leser – Bedeutung: Untersuchungen zur Interaktion von Text und Leser*, ed. Herbert Grabes. Grossen-Linden, 1977, 61–81.

Grabes, Herbert. "Wie aus Sätzen Personen werden …: Über die Erforschung literarischer Figuren." *Poetica* 10 (1978): 405–428.

Gravil, Richard (ed.). *Master Narratives: Tellers and Telling in the English Novel*. Aldershot, 2001.

Greimas, Algirdas Julien. *Structural Semiotics: An Attempt at Method*, trans. Daniele McDowell, Ronald Schliefer, and Alan Velie. Lincoln, NE, 1983.

Greimas, Algirdas Julien. "Die Struktur der Erzählaktanten. Versuch eines generativen Ansatzes." *Literaturwissenschaft und Linguistik*, Vol. 3, ed. Jens Ihwe. Frankfurt am Main, 1972, 218–238.

Grünzweig, Walter and Andreas Solbach (eds.). *Grenzüberschreitungen: Narratologie im Kontext/Transcending Boundaries: Narratology in Context*. Tübingen, 1999.

Guillén, Claudio. "On the Concept and Metaphor of Perspective." *Literature as System: Essays Towards the Theory of Literary History*. Princeton, NJ, 1971.

Habermas, Jürgen. *Erkenntnis und Interesse.* Frankfurt am Main, 1968, 1979.

Habermas, Jürgen. *The Structural Transformation of the Public Sphere: An Enquiry into a Category of Bourgeois Society*, trans. Thomas Burger and Frederick Lawrence. Cambridge, 1989 [1962].

Hale, Dorothy J. *The Novel: An Anthology of Criticism and Theory 1900–2000.* Oxford, 2005.

Hamburger, Käte. *Die Logik der Dichtung.* Stuttgart, 1980 [1957].

Hamon, Philippe. "Un discours contraint." *Poétique* 16 (1973): 411–445.

Hegel, Georg Wilhelm Friedrich. *Hegel's Aesthetics: Lectures on Fine Art*, trans. T. M. Knox, 2 vols. Oxford, 1975.

Hegel, Georg Wilhelm Friedrich. *Vorlesungen über die Ästhetik, Dritter Teil: Die Poesie*, ed. Rüdiger Bubner. Stuttgart, 1977.

Heine, Heinrich. "Einleitung zur Prachtausgabe des *Don Quijote* (1837)." *Sämtliche Werke in sieben Bänden.* Stuttgart, n.d., 5: 128–142.

Heise, Ursula. *Chronoschisms: Time, Narrative and Postmodernism.* Cambridge, 1997.

Hempfer, Klaus W. *Gattungstheorie: Information und Synthese.* Munich, 1973.

Henrich, Dieter and Wolfgang Iser (eds.). *Funktionen des Fiktiven (Poetik und Hermeneutik X).* Munich, 1983.

Henrich, Dieter and Wolfgang Iser (eds.). "Fiktion im Recht." *Zeitschrift für Semiotik* 12/3 (1990): 175–242.

Herman, David (ed.). *Narratologies: New Perspectives on Narrative Analysis.* Columbus, OH, 1999.

Herman, David (ed.). *The Cambridge Companion to Narrative.* Cambridge, 2007.

Herman, David (ed.). *Basic Elements of Narrative.* Oxford, 2009.

Herman, David, Manfred Jahn, and Marie-Laure Ryan (eds.). *The Routledge Encyclopedia of Narrative Theory.* London, 2005.

Hess-Lüttich, Ernest W. B., Jürgen E. Müller, and Aart van Zoest (eds.). *Signs & Space: Raum & Zeichen: An International Conference on the Semiotics of Space and Culture in Amsterdam.* Tübingen, 1998.

Hochman, Baruch. *Character in Literature.* Ithaca, NY, 1985.

Hoffmann, Gerhard. *Raum, Situation, erzählte Wirklichkeit: Poetologische und historische Studien zum englischen und amerikanischen Roman.* Stuttgart, 1978.

Homans, Margaret. "Feminist Fictions and Feminist Theories of Narrative." *Narrative* 2/1 (1994): 3–16.

Hoops, Wiklef. "Fiktionalität als pragmatische Kategorie." *Poetica* 11 (1979): 281–317.

Hunter, J. Paul. *Before Novels: The Cultural Contexts of Eighteenth-Century English Fiction.* New York, 1990.

Hutcheon, Linda. *Narcissistic Narrative: The Metafictional Paradox.* London, 1980, 1984.

Hutcheon, Linda. *A Poetics of Postmodernism: History, Theory, Fiction.* New York, 1988, 1996.

Hutcheon, Linda. *The Politics of Postmodernism.* London, 1989.

Ibsch, Elrud. "The Cognitive Turn in Narratology." *Poetics Today* 11: 2 (1990), 411–418.

Iser, Wolfgang. *The Implied Reader: Patterns of Communication from Bunyan to Beckett*, Baltimore, 1974, 1990.

Iser, Wolfgang. *The Act of Reading: A Theory of Aesthetic Response*, Baltimore, 1978.

Iser, Wolfgang. "Die Appellstruktur der Texte: Unbestimmtheit als Wirkungsbedingung literarischer Prosa." In *Rezeptionsästhetik: Theorie und Praxis*, 2nd edn, ed. Rainer Warning. Munich, 1979, 228–252.

Iser, Wolfgang. *Prospecting: From Reader Response to Literary Anthropology*. Baltimore, 1989.

Iser, Wolfgang. *The Fictive and the Imaginary: Charting Literary Anthropology*. Baltimore, 1993.

Iser, Wolfgang. "Fiktion/Imagination." In *Fischer Lexikon Literatur*, ed. Ulfert Ricklefs. Frankfurt am Main, 1996, 662–679.

Jackendoff, Ray. *Semantics and Cognition*. Cambridge, MA, 1983.

Jackendoff, Ray. *Consciousness and the Computational Mind*. Cambridge, MA, 1987.

Jacobs, Carol and Henry Sussman (eds.). *Acts of Narrative*. Stanford, CA, 2003.

Jahn, Manfred. *"Package Deals*, Exklusionen, Randzonen: das Phänomen der Unverläßlichkeit in den Erzählsituationen." *Unreliable Narration: Studien zur Theorie und Praxis unglaubwürdigen Erzählens in der englischsprachigen Erzählliteratur*, ed. Ansgar Nünning, Trier, 1998, 81–106.

Jahn, Manfred. "Windows of Focalization: Deconstructing and Reconstructing a Narratological Concept." *Style* 30 (1996): 241–267.

Jahn, Manfred. "Frames, Preferences, and the Reading of Third-Person Narratives: Towards a Cognitive Narratology." *Poetics Today* 18/4 (1997): 441–468.

Jahn, Manfred. "More Aspects of Focalization: Refinements and Applications." *GRAAT* 21 (1999): 85–110.

Jahn, Manfred and Ansgar Nünning. "A Survey of Narratological Models." *Literatur in Wissenschaft und Unterricht* 27/4 (1994): 283–303.

Jakobson, Roman. "Über den Realismus in der Kunst." In *Texte der russischen Formalisten*, ed. Jurij Striedter. Munich, 1969, 373–391.

Jakobson, Roman. *Poetik: Ausgewählte Aufsätze 1921–1971*. Frankfurt am Main, 1979.

James, Henry, "Preface." *The Tragic Muse* (New York Edition 7). New York, 1908.

James, Henry. "Preface." *The Altar of the Dead/The Beast in the Jungle/The Birthplace/And Other Tales* (New York Edition 17). New York, 1909.

Jannidis, Fotis et al. (eds.). *Rückkehr des Autors: Zur Erneuerung eines umstrittenen Begriffs*. Tübingen, 1999.

Jannidis, Fotis, Gerhard Lauer, Matias Martinez, and Simone Winko (eds.). *Texte zur Theorie der Autorschaft*. Stuttgart, 2000.

Jauß, Hans Robert (ed.). *Nachahmung und Illusion (Poetik und Herrmeneutik I)*. Munich, 1969.

Johnson, B. S. "Aren't You Rather Young to be Writing Your Memoirs?" In *The Novel Today: Contemporary Writers on Fiction*, ed. Malcolm Bradbury. Glasgow, 1977, 151–168.

Juhl, Peter D. "Life, Literature, and the Implied Author." *Deutsche Vierteljahrsschrift für Literaturwissenschaft und Geistesgeschichte* 54 (1980): 177–203.

Kablitz, Andreas. "Erzählperspektive – point of view – focalization: Überlegungen zu einem Konzept der Erzähltheorie." *Zeitschrift für französische Sprache und Literatur* 98 (1988): 237–255.

Kant, Immanuel. *The Critique of Judgement*, trans. James Creed Meredith, Oxford, 1928, 1991. German text: *Kritik der Urteilskraft*. Stuttgart, 1963, 1981.

Kearns, Michael. *Rhetorical Narratology*. Lincoln, NE, 1999.

Kienzle, Bertram. "Wissen, Indexikalität und Sozialität." *Zeitschrift für Semiotik* 21/1 (1999): 29–41.

Kindt, Tom and Hans-Harald Müller. "Der 'implizite Autor': Zur Explikation und Verwendung eines umstrittenen Begriffs." In *Rückkehr des Autors: Zur Erneuerung eines umstrittenen Begriffs*, ed. Fotis Jannidis et al. Tübingen, 1999, 273–287.

Knellwolf, Christa and Christopher North (eds.). *The Cambridge History of Literary Criticism, Vol. 9, Twentieth-Century Historical, Philosophical and Psychological Perspectives*. Cambridge, 2001.

Kohl, Stephan. *Realismus: Theorie und Geschichte*. Munich, 1977.

Kristeva, Julia. "Bachtin, das Wort, der Dialog und der Roman." In *Literaturwissenschaft und Linguistik*, Vol. 3, ed. Jens Ihwe. Frankfurt am Main, 1972, 345–375.

Lachmann, Renate (ed.). *Dialogizität*. Munich, 1982.

Lämmert, Eberhard. *Bauformen des Erzählens*. Stuttgart, 1955, 1993.

Lämmert, Eberhard et al. (eds.). *Romantheorie 1620–1880: Dokumentation ihrer Geschichte in Deutschland*. Cologne, 1971.

Lämmert, Eberhard et al. (eds.). *Romantheorie: Dokumentation ihrer Geschichte in Deutschland seit 1880*. Cologne, 1975.

Lanser, Susan S. *The Narrative Act: Point of View in Prose Fiction*. Princeton, NJ, 1981.

Lanser, Susan S. "Toward a Feminist Narratology." *Style* 20 (1986): 341–363.

Lanser, Susan S. "Shifting the Paradigm: Feminism and Narratology." *Style* 22 (1988): 52–60.

Lanser, Susan S. *Fictions of Authority: Women Writers and Narrative Voice*. Ithaca, NY, 1992.

Lanser, Susan S. "Sexing the Narrative: Propriety, Desire, and the Engendering of Narratology." *Narrative* 3/1 (1995): 85–94.

Lawrence, David H. *Studies in Classic American Literature*. Harmondsworth, 1978 [1923].

Lehmann, Elmar and Bernd Lenz (eds.). *Telling Stories: Studies in Honour of Ulrich Broich on the Occasion of His 60th Birthday*. Amsterdam, 1992.

Lentricchia, Frank and Thomas McLaughlin. *Critical Terms for Literary Study*. Chicago, 1995.

Lévi-Strauss, Claude. *Mythologiques: Introduction to a Science of Mythology*, 4 vols., trans. John Weightman and Doreen Weightman. Harmondsworth, 1970–1981.

Lindemann, Uwe. "Die Ungleichzeitigkeit des Gleichzeitigen: Polyperspektivismus, Spannung und der iterative Modus der Narration bei Samuel Richardson, Choderlos de Laclos, Ludwig Tieck, Wilkie Collins und Robert Browning." *Perspektive in Literatur und bildender Kunst*, ed. Kurt Röttgers and Monika Schmitz-Emans, Essen, 1999, 48–81.

Link, Jürgen. "Literaturanalyse als Interdiskursanalyse: Am Beispiel des Ursprungs literarischer Symbolik in der Kollektivsymbolik." *Diskurstheorien und*

Literaturwissenschaft, ed. Jürgen Fohrmann and Harro Müller. Frankfurt am Main, 1992, 284–307.

Link, Jürgen and Ursula Link-Heer. "Diskurs/Interdiskurs und Literaturanalyse." *Zeitschrift für Literaturwissenschaft und Linguistik* 77 (1990): 88–99.

Link, Jürgen and Rolf Parr. "Semiotik und Interdiskursanalyse." In *Neue Literaturtheorien: Eine Einführung*, 2nd rev. edn, ed. Klaus-Michael Bogdal. Opladen, 1997, 108–133.

Lobsien, Eckhard. *Theorie literarischer Illusionsbildung*. Stuttgart, 1975.

Lodge, David. "Milan Kundera, and the Idea of the Author in Modern Criticism." *Critical Quarterly* 26 (1984): 105–121.

Lodge, David. *Consciousness and the Novel: Connected Essays*. Cambridge, MA, 2002.

Lotman, Jurij, *The Structure of the Artistic Text*, trans. Gail Lenhoff and Ronald Vroon. Ann Arbor, 1977 [1971].

Lubbock, Percy. *The Craft of Fiction*. London, 1921.

Ludwig, Hans-Werner (ed.). *Arbeitsbuch Romananalyse*, 6th edn. Tübingen, 1998.

Lugowski, Clemens. *Die Form der Individualität im Roman*. Frankfurt am Main, 1976 [1932].

Luhmann, Niklas. "Das Problem der Epochenbildung und die Evolutionstheorie." In *Epochenschwellen und Epochenstrukturen im Diskurs der Literatur und Sprachhistorie*, ed. Hans Ulrich Gumbrecht and Ursula Link-Heer. Frankfurt am Main, 1985, 11–33.

Lukács, Georg. *The Theory of the Novel: A Historico-Philosophical Essay on the Forms of Great Epic Literature*, trans. Anna Bostock. Cambridge, MA, 1971, 1978 [1920].

McDowell, Linda and Joanne P. Sharp (eds.). *Space, Gender, Knowledge: Feminist Readings*. London, 1997.

McHale, Brian. "Free Indirect Discourse: A Survey of Recent Accounts." *PTL: A Journal for Descriptive Poetics and Theory of Literature* 3 (1978): 249–287.

McHale, Brian. *Postmodernist Fiction*. London, 1987.

McKeon, Michael. *The Origins of the English Novel 1600–1740*. Baltimore, 1987.

McQuillan, Martin (ed.). *The Narrative Reader*. London, 2000.

Makaryk, Irena R. "Narratology." In *Encyclopedia of Contemporary Literary Theory: Approaches, Scholars, Terms*, ed. Irena R. Makaryk. Toronto, 1993.

Margolin, Uri. "The Doer and the Deed: Action as a Basis for Characterization in Narrative." *Poetics Today* 7/2 (1986): 205–225.

Margolin, Uri. "Individuals in Narrative Worlds: An Ontological Perspective." *Poetics Today* 11/4 (1990): 843–871.

Margolin, Uri. "The What, the When, and the How of Being a Character in Literary Narrative." *Style* 24/3 (1990): 453–468.

Martin, Wallace. *Recent Theories of Narrative*. Ithaca, NY, 1986.

Martinez, Matias. "Krise und Innovation des Erzählens in der Literatur der Moderne: Eine Skizze." In *Stories: Erzählstrukturen in der zeitgenössischen Kunst, Katalog der Ausstellung im Haus der Kunst, Munich, 28.3.–23.6.2002*, ed. Stephanie Rosenthal. Cologne, 2002, 78–84.

Marx, Karl. *Writings of the Young Marx on Philosophy and Society*, trans. and ed. Lloyd D. Easton and Kurt H. Guddat. New York, 1967.

Mayoux, J.-J. "Diderot and the Technique of Modern Literature." *Modern Language Review* 31 (1936): 518–531.

Meyer, Herman. "Raumgestaltung und Raumsymbolik in der Erzählkunst." *Studium Generale* 10 (1957): 620–630.

Mezei, Kathy (ed.). *Ambiguous Discourse: Feminist Narratology and British Women Writers.* Chapel Hill, NC, 1996.

Middeke, Martin (ed.). *Zeit und Roman: Zeiterfahrung im historischen Wandel und ästhetischer Paradigmenwechsel vom sechzehnten Jahrhundert bis zur Postmoderne.* Würzburg, 2002.

Mihailescu, Calin-Andrei and Walid Hamarneh (eds.). *Fiction Updated: Theories of Fictionality, Narratology, and Poetics.* Toronto, 1996.

Miller, Norbert (ed.). *Romananfänge: Versuch zu einer Poetik des Romans.* Berlin, 1965.

Mitchell, W. J. T. (ed.). *On Narrative.* Chicago, 1981.

Moretti, Franco (ed.). *The Novel, Vol. 1, History, Geography, and Culture; Vol. 2, Forms and Themes.* Princeton, NJ, 2006.

Morreall, John. "The Myth of the Omniscient Narrator." *Journal of Aesthetics and Art Criticism* 52/4 (1994): 429–436.

Mullan, John. *How Novels Work.* Oxford, 2006, 2008.

Müller, Günther. *Morphologische Poetik.* Darmstadt, 1968.

Nabokov, Vladimir. *Strong Opinions,* London, 1974.

Nabokov, Vladimir. *Lectures on Literature,* ed. Fredson Bowers, introduction by John Updike. London, 1980.

Nabokov, Vladimir. *Lolita.* Harmondsworth, 1980, 1989.

Nelles, William. "Historical and Implied Authors and Readers." *Comparative Literature* 45 (1993): 22–46.

Nünning, Ansgar. *Grundzüge eines kommunikationstheoretischen Modells der erzählerischen Vermittlung: Die Funktionen der Erzählinstanz in den Romanen George Eliots.* Trier, 1989.

Nünning, Ansgar. "Renaissance eines anthropomorphisierten Passepartouts oder Nachruf auf ein literaturkritisches Phantom? Überlegungen und Alternativen zum Konzept des implied author." *Deutsche Vierteljahrsschrift für Literaturwissenschaft und Geistesgeschichte* 67/1 (1993): 1–25.

Nünning, Ansgar. "A Survey of Narratological Models." *Literatur in Wissenschaft und Unterricht* 27/4 (1994): 283–303.

Nünning, Ansgar. " 'But why *will* you say that I am mad?' On the Theory, History and Signals of Unreliable Narration in British Fiction." *Arbeiten aus Anglistik und Amerikanistik* 22/1 (1997): 83–107.

Nünning, Ansgar. "Die Funktionen von Erzählinstanzen: Analysekategorien und Modelle zur Beschreibung des Erzählerverhaltens." *Literatur in Wissenschaft und Unterricht* 30 (1997): 323–349.

Nünning, Ansgar (ed.). *Unreliable Narration: Studien zur Theorie und Praxis unglaubwürdigen Erzählens in der englischsprachigen Erzählliteratur.* Trier, 1998.

Nünning, Ansgar. "Reconceptualizing the Theory and Generic Scope of Unreliable Narration." *GRAAT* 21 (1999): 63–84.

Nünning, Ansgar. "On the Perspective Structure of Narrative Texts: Steps Towards a Constructivist Narratology." In *Cognition and Emotion: New Perspectives on Narrative Perspective*, ed. S. Chatman and Willie van Peer. Albany, 2000, 207–223.

Nünning, Ansgar. "Towards a Cultural and Historical Narratology: A Survey of Diachronic Approaches, Concepts, and Research Projects." In *Anglistentag 1999 Mainz. Proceedings*, ed. Bernhard Reitz and Sigrid Rieuwerts. Trier, 2000, 345–373.

Nünning, Ansgar. " 'Time is variable': Innovative Zeitstrukturen und der Wandel von Zeiterfahrungen in zeitgenössischen englischen 'Zeitromanen'." *Germanisch-romanische Monatsschrift* 51/4 (2001): 447–465.

Nünning, Ansgar (ed.). *Metzler Lexikon Literatur- und Kulturtheorie*, 3rd revd. edn. Stuttgart, 2004.

Nünning, Vera and Ansgar Nünning. " 'Multiperspektivität – Lego oder Playmobil, Malkasten oder Puzzle?' Grundlagen, Kategorien und Modelle zur Analyse der Perspektivenstruktur narrativer Texte." *Literatur in Wissenschaft und Unterricht* 32/4 (1999): 367–388 and 331 (2000): 59–84.

Nünning, Vera and Ansgar Nünning (eds.). *Multiperspektivisches Erzählen: Zur Theorie und Geschichte der Perspektivenstruktur im englischen Roman des 18. bis 20. Jahrhunderts*. Trier, 2000.

Nünning, Vera and Ansgar Nünning (eds.). *Neue Ansätze in der Erzähltheorie*. Trier, 2002.

Nünning, Vera and Ansgar Nünning (eds.). *Erzähltheorie transgenerisch, intermedial, interdisziplinär*. Trier, 2002.

Nünning, Vera und Ansgar Nünning (eds.). *Erzähltextanalyse und Gender Studies*. Stuttgart, 2004.

Oldsey, Bernard. "William Golding." In *Dictionary of Literary Biography*, Vol. 15: 1. Detroit, 1983, 119–134.

Olsen, Greta. "Reconsidering Unreliability: Fallible and Untrustworthy Narrators." *Narrative* 11/1 (2003): 93–109.

Oltean, Stefan. "Fictionality as a Pragmatic and Referential Category." *Journal of Literary Semantics* 28/2 (1999): 92–104.

Onega, Susana (ed.). *Telling Stories: Narrativizing History, Historicizing Literature*. Amsterdam, 1995.

Onega, Susana and José Ángel García Landa (eds.). *Narratology: An Introduction*. London, 1996.

O'Neill, Patrick. *Fictions of Discourse: Reading Narrative Theory*. Toronto, 1994.

Pascal, Roy. *The Dual Voice: Free Indirect Speech and its Functioning in the 19th-Century European Novel*. Manchester, 1977.

Perry, Menakhem. "Literary Dynamics: How the Order of a Text Creates Its Meanings." *Poetics Today* 1/1–2 (1979): 35–64, 311–361.

Petersen, Jürgen H. *Fiktionalität und Ästhetik: Eine Philosophie der Dichtung*. Berlin, 1996.

Pfister, Manfred. *The Theory and Analysis of Drama*, trans. John Halliday. Cambridge, 1991. German text: *Das Drama: Theorie und Analyse*. Munich, 1977.

Phelan, James. *Reading People, Reading Plots: Character, Progression, and the Interpretation of Narrative.* Chicago, 1989.

Phelan, James and Mary Patricia Martin. "The Lessons of 'Weymouth': Homodiegesis, Unreliability, Ethics, and *The Remains of the Day.*" *Narratologies: New Perspectives on Narrative Analysis,* ed. David Herman, Columbus, OH, 1999, 88–109.

Phelan, James and Peter J. Rabinowitz (eds.). *A Companion to Narrative Theory.* Oxford, 2005, 2008.

Plato. *The Republic.* In *The Dialogues of Plato translated into English with Analyses and Introductions by B. Jowett, M.A. in Five Volumes,* Vol. 3, 3rd revd. edn. Oxford, 1892.

Plumpe, Gerhard. *Epochen moderner Literatur: Ein systemtheoretischer Entwurf.* Opladen, 1995.

Polhemus, Robert M. (ed.). *Critical Reconstructions: The Relationship of Fiction and Life.* Stanford, CA, 1994.

Preminger, Alex and Terry V. F. Brogan (eds.). *The New Princeton Encyclopedia of Poetry and Poetics.* Princeton, NJ, 1993.

Prince, Gerald. *A Grammar of Stories: An Introduction.* The Hague, 1973.

Prince, Gerald. *Narratology: The Form and Functioning of Narrative.* Berlin, 1982.

Prince, Gerald. *A Dictionary of Narratology.* Aldershot, 1987, 1988.

Prince, Gerald. *Narrative as Theme: Studies in French Fiction.* Lincoln, NE, 1992.

Propp, Vladimir. *Morphology of the Folktale,* 2nd edn. Austin, 1968 [1928].

Punday, Daniel. *Narrative Bodies: Toward a Corporeal Narratology.* Basingstoke, 2003.

Raible, Wolfgang. "Was sind Gattungen? Eine Antwort aus semiotischer und textlinguistischer Sicht." *Poetica* 12/3–4 (1980): 320–349.

Ray, William. *Literary Meaning: From Phenomenology to Deconstruction.* Oxford, 1984.

Ray, William. *Story and History: Narrative Authority and Social Identity in the Eighteenth-Century French and English Novel.* Cambridge, MA, 1990.

Reichel, Norbert. *Der erzählte Raum: Zur Verflechtung von sozialem und poetischem Raum in erzählender Literatur.* Darmstadt, 1987.

Reinfandt, Christoph. "Integrating Literary Theory: Systems-Theoretical Perspectives of Literature and Literary Theory." *Literatur in Wissenschaft und Unterricht* 28/1 (1995): 55–64.

Reinfandt, Christoph. *Der Sinn der fiktionalen Wirklichkeiten: Ein systemtheoretischer Entwurf zur Ausdifferenzierung des englischen Romans vom 18. Jahrhundert bis zur Gegenwart.* Heidelberg, 1997.

Reinfandt, Christoph. "How German Is It? The Place of Systems-Theoretical Approaches in Literary Studies." *European Journal of English Studies* 5/3 (2001): 275–288.

Reyre, Dominique. *Dictionnaire des noms des personnages du Don Quijote de Cervantès.* Paris, 1980.

Richards, I. A. *Principles of Literary Criticism.* London, 1967, 1983 [1924].

Richardson, Brian. "Remapping the Present: The Master Narrative of Modern Literary Theory and the Lost Forms of Twentieth-Century Fiction." *Twentieth Century Literature* 43/3 (1997): 291–309.

Richardson, Brian. *Unlikely Stories: Causality, Ideology, and Interpretation in Modern Narrative*. Newark, NJ, 1997.

Richardson, Brian. "Linearity and Its Discontents: Rethinking Narrative Form and Ideological Valence." *College English* 62/6 (2000): 685–695.

Richardson, Brian. "Narrative Poetics and Postmodern Transgression: Theorizing the Collapse of Time, Voice, and Frame." *Narrative* 8/1 (2000): 23–42.

Richardson, Brian (ed.). *Narrative Dynamics: Essays on Plot, Time, Closure, and Frames*. Columbus, OH, 2002.

Ricœur, Paul. *Zeit und Erzählung, Bd. 2: Zeit und literarische Erzählung*. Munich, 1989.

Riffaterre, Michael. "Chronotopes in Diegesis." In *Fiction Updated: Theories of Fictionality, Narratology, and Poetics*, ed. Hamarneh Mihailescu. Toronto, 1996, 244–256.

Riggan, William. *Picaros, Madmen, Naifs, and Clowns: The Unreliable First-Person Narrator*. Norman, OK, 1981.

Rimmon-Kenan, Shlomith. *Narrative Fiction: Contemporary Poetics*. London, 1983, 1986.

Ritter, Alexander (ed.). *Landschaft und Raum in der Erzählkunst*. Darmstadt, 1975.

Robbe-Grillet, Alain. *For a New Novel: Essays on Fiction*, trans. Richard Howard. Evanston, IL, 1989.

Ronen, Ruth. "Paradigm Shift in Plot Models: An Outline of the History of Narratology." *Poetics Today* 11/4 (1990): 817–842.

Rosenthal, Stephanie (ed.). *Stories: Erzählstrukturen in der zeitgenössischen Kunst: Eine Ausstellung im Haus der Kunst Munich, 28. März bis 26. Juni 2002*. Cologne, 2002.

Roulston, Christine. "Discourse, Gender, and Gossip: Some Reflections on Bakhtin and *Emma*." *Ambiguous Discourse: Feminist Narratology and British Women Writers*, ed. Kathy Mezei, Chapel Hill, NC, 1996, 40–65.

Roy, Marie-Luise. *Die Poetik Diderots*. Munich, 1966.

Rushdie, Salman. "Is Nothing Sacred?" *Granta* 31 (Spring 1990): 97–111.

Ryan, Marie-Laure. *Possible Worlds, Artificial Intelligence and Narrative Theory*. Bloomington, 1991.

Sarraute, Nathalie. *Tropisms, and The Age of Suspicion*. London, 1963.

Sarraute, Nathalie. *Zeitalter des Mißtrauens: Essays über den Roman*. Frankfurt am Main, 1975.

Schabert Ina, "The Authorial Mind and the Question of Gender." In *Telling Stories: Studies in Honour of Ulrich Broich on the Occasion of his 60th Birthday*, ed. Elmar Lehmann and Bernd Lenz. Amsterdam, 1992, 312–328.

Schabert, Ina. *Englische Literaturgeschichte: Eine neue Darstellung aus der Sicht der Geschlechterforschung*. Stuttgart, 1997.

Schama, Simon. *Landscape and Memory*. New York, 1995.

Schärf, Christian. *Der Roman im 20. Jahrhundert*. Stuttgart, 2001.

Schlaffer, Heinz. "Der Roman, das letzte Stadium der Literatur." *Sinn und Form* 6 (2002): 789–797.

Schlaffer, Heinz. *Die kurze Geschichte der deutschen Literatur*. Munich, 2002.

Schlegel, Friedrich. *Kritische Friedrich Schlegel-Ausgabe*, 35 vols., ed. Ernst Behler, Hans Eichner et al.. Munich, 1958ff. Selected Athenaeum Fragments in English in Kathleen M. Wheeler (ed.), *German Aesthetic and Literary Criticism: The Romantic Ironists and Goethe*. Cambridge, 1984.

Schmid, Wolf. "Die Semantisierung der Form: Zum Inhaltskonzept Jurij Lotmans." *Russian Literature* 5 (1977): 61–80.

Schmidt, Siegfried J. "On Understanding Texts: Some Constructivist Remarks." In *The World, the Image and Aesthetic Experience*, ed. Clemens Murath and Susan Price. Bradford, 1996, 65–84.

Schneider, Ralf. *Grundriß zur kognitiven Theorie der Figurenrezeption am Beispiel des viktorianischen Romans*. Tübingen, 2000.

Scholes, Robert. "Metafiction." *Iowa Review* 1/4 (1970): 100–115.

Scholz, Bernhard F. (ed.). *Mimesis: Studien zur literarischen Repräsentation: Studies on Literary Representation*. Tübingen, 1998.

Schütte, Wolfram. "Die Geburt des Kubismus aus dem Geiste der Anarchie." *Frankfurter Rundschau*, December 9, 1997.

Shakespeare, Nicholas. *Bruce Chatwin*. London, 1999.

Shklovsky, Victor. "A Parodying Novel: Sterne's *Tristram Shandy*" (originally published in *O Teorii Prozy*, Moscow, 1929), trans. W. George Isaak. In *Laurence Sterne: A Collection of Critical Essays*, ed. John Traugott, Englewood Cliffs, NJ, 1968, 66–89.

Shklovskii, Viktor. "The Parody Novel: Sterne's *Tristram Shandy*," trans. Richard Sheldon. *Review of Contemporary Fiction* 1 (1981): 190–211.

Šklovskij, Victor. "Der parodistische Roman: Sternes 'Tristram Shandy'." In *Russischer Formalismus: Texte zur allgemeinen Literaturtheorie und zur Theorie der Prosa*, ed. Jurij Striedter. Munich, 1969, 1971, 245–299.

Stanzel, Franz K. *A Theory of Narrative*, trans. Charlotte Goedsche. Cambridge, 1984, 1986. German text: *Theorie des Erzählens*, 7th edn. Göttingen, 2001.

Stanzel, Franz K. *Unterwegs: Erzähltheorie für Leser*. Göttingen, 2002.

Steinecke, Hartmut and Fritz Wahrenburg (eds.). *Romantheorie: Texte vom Barock bis zur Gegenwart*. Stuttgart, 1999.

Stephan, Inge and Sigrid Weigel (eds.). *Frau: Sechs Beiträge zu einer feministischen Literaturwissenschaft*. Berlin, 1983.

Sternberg, Meir. "Proteus in Quotation Land: Mimesis and the Forms of Reported Discourse." *Poetics Today* 3 (1982): 107–156.

Sternlieb, Lisa. *The Female Narrator in the British Novel: Hidden Agendas*. Basingstoke, 2002.

Stierle, Karlheinz. "Erfahrung und narrative Form: Bemerkungen zu ihrem Zusammenhang in Fiktion und Historiographie." In *Theorie und Erzählung in der Geschichte*, ed. Jürgen Kocka and Thomas Nipperdey. Munich, 1979, 85–118.

Ströker, Elisabeth. *Investigations in Philosophy of Space*. Athens, OH, 1987 [1965].

Sturgess, Philip J. M. *Narrativity: Theory and Practice*. Oxford, 1992.

Style 28/3 (1994). "Second-Person Narrative and Related Issues."

Style 34/2 (2000). "Concepts of Narrative."

Style 35/2 (2001). "Women as Narrators."

Surkamp, Carola. "Die Perspektivenstruktur narrativer Texte aus Sicht der *possible-worlds theory:* Zur literarischen Inszenierung der Pluralität subjektiver Wirklichkeitsmodelle." *Multiperspektivisches Erzählen: Zur Theorie und Geschichte der Perspektivenstruktur im englischen Roman des 18. bis 20. Jahrhunderts*, ed. Vera and Ansgar Nünning, Trier, 2000, 111–132.

Sutherland, John. *So You Think You Know Jane Austen?* Oxford, 2005.

Todorov, Tzvetan. "Les catégories du récit littéraire." *Communications* 8 (1966): 125–151.

Todorov, Tzvetan. "The Origin of Genders." *New Literary History* 8 (1976/77): 159–170.

Toolan, Michael J. *Narrative: A Critical Linguistic Introduction*, 2nd edn. London, 2001.

Trilling, Lionel. *E. M. Forster: A Study*. London, 1944.

Vargas Llosa, Mario. *Letters to a Young Novelist*, trans. Natasha Wimmer. New York, 2002.

Veeder, William and Susan M. Griffin (eds.). *The Art of Criticism: Henry James on the Theory and Practice of Fiction*. Chicago, 1986.

Wall, Kathleen. "*The Remains of the Day* and its Challenges to Theories of Unreliable Narration." *Journal of Narrative Technique* 24 (1994): 18–42.

Warhol, Robyn R. *Gendered Interventions: Narrative Discourse in the Victorian Novel*. New Brunswick, NJ, 1989.

Warhol, Robyn R. "Guilty Cravings: What Feminist Narratology Can Do for Cultural Studies." In *Narratologies: New Perspectives on Narrative Analysis*, ed. David Herman. Columbus, OH, 1999, 340–355.

Warning, Rainer. *Die Phantasie der Realisten*. Munich, 1999.

Watt, Ian. *The Rise of the Novel: Studies in Defoe, Richardson and Fielding*. Harmondsworth, 1957, 1974.

Waugh, Patricia. *Metafiction: The Theory and Practice of Self-Conscious Fiction*. London, 1984.

Weich, Horst. *Cervantes' "Don Quijote."* Munich, 2001.

Weimar, Klaus. "Wo und was ist der Erzähler?" *Modern Language Notes* 109 (1994): 495–506.

Weinrich, Harald. "Fiktionssignale." In *Positionen der Negativität (Poetik und Hermeneutik VI)*, ed. Harald Weinrich. Munich, 1975, 525–526.

Weinrich, Harald. *Tempus: Besprochene und erzählte Welt*, 6th rev. edn. Munich, 2001.

Wellershoff, Dieter. *Von der Moral erwischt: Aufsätze zur Trivialliteratur*. Frankfurt am Main, 1983. In *Werke 4. Essays, Aufsätze, Marginalien*. Cologne, 1997.

Wells, Lynn. *Allegories of Telling: Self-Referential Narrative in Contemporary British Fiction*. Amsterdam, 2003.

Wenz, Karin. *Raum, Raumsprache und Sprachräume: Zur Textsemiotik der Raumbeschreibung*. Tübingen, 1997.

Wenzel, Peter (ed.). *Einführung in die Erzähltextanalyse: Kategorien, Modelle, Probleme*. Trier, 2004.

White, Hayden. *Metahistory: The Historical Imagination in Nineteenth-Century Europe*. Baltimore, 1973.

White, Hayden. *Tropics of Discourse: Essays in Cultural Criticism*. Baltimore, 1978.

White, Hayden. "The Value of Narrativity in the Representation of Reality." *Critical Inquiry* 7/1 (1980): 5–27.

White, Hayden. *The Content of the Form: Narrative Discourse and Historical Representation*. Baltimore, 1987.

Wiest-Kellner, Ursula. *Messages from the Threshold: Die You-Erzählform als Ausdruck liminaler Wesen und Welten*. Bielefeld, 1999.

Wildekamp, Ada et al. "Fictionality and Convention." *Poetics* 9 (1980): 547–567.

Wittgenstein, Ludwig. *Bemerkungen über die Farben/Über Gewißheit/Zettel/ Vermischte Bemerkungen* (= Werkausgabe, 8). Frankfurt am Main, 1984, 1997.

Wittgenstein, Ludwig. *Philosophische Untersuchungen, Werkausgabe Band 1, Tractatus logico-philosophicus, Tagebücher 1914–1916, Philosophische Untersuchungen*, 11th edn. Frankfurt am Main, 1984, 1997.

Wolf, Werner. *Ästhetische Illusion und Illusionsdurchbrechung in der Erzählkunst. Theorie und Geschichte mit Schwerpunkt auf englischem illusionsstörenden Erzählen*. Tübingen, 1993.

Wolf, Werner. "Multiperspektivität: Das Konzept und seine Applikationsmöglichkeit auf Rahmungen in Erzählwerken." *Multiperspektivisches Erzählen: Zur Theorie und Geschichte der Perspektivenstruktur im englischen Roman des 18. bis 20. Jahrhunderts*, ed. Vera Nünning and Ansgar Nünning Trier, 2000, 79–109.

Woolf, Virginia. "Modern Fiction." In *The Norton Anthology of English Literature: Fifth Edition*, Vol. 2, ed. M. H. Abrams. New York, 1986, 1993–1999.

Würzbach, Natascha. "Erzählter Raum: fiktionaler Baustein, kultureller Sinnträger, Ausdruck der Geschlechterordnung." *Erzählen und Erzähltheorie im 20. Jahrhundert: Festschrift für Wilhelm Füger*, ed. Jörg Helbig, Heidelberg, 2001, 105–130.

Yacobi, Tamar. "Fictional Reliability as a Communicative Problem." *Poetics Today* 2/2 (1981): 113–126.

Yacobi, Tamar. "Narrative Structure and Fictional Mediation." *Poetics Today* 8/2 (1987): 335–372.

Further Reading

Just as in any area of study and research, the golden rule applies to the analysis of novels: one hasn't really mastered it and can't pursue it properly as long as that's *all* one masters and *all* one pursues. (What do they know of novels who only novels know?) For that reason the following list also contains titles that discuss narratology in general, or introduce literary criticism in an illuminating way, or offer essential information on literary or cultural theory.

Abbott, H. Porter. *The Cambridge Introduction to Narrative*. Cambridge, 2002, 2008. A very fine introduction that treats narrative "as a human phenomenon that is not restricted to literature, film, and theatre, but is found in all activities that involve the [re-]presentation of events in time." At times, the line of argument is not fully sustained and interrupted by a great number of boxes with explanations or side-topics, but the book is lively, original, and thought-provoking.
Chatman, Seymour. *Story and Discourse: Narrative Structure in Fiction and Film.* Ithaca, NY, 1978, 1993. A classic for beginners.
Fludernik, Monika. *An Introduction to Narratology*. London, 2009. An invaluable guide to narratological theory and its application to literature, with detailed practical examples. Lucid, well informed, up to date: highly recommendable. For readers who prefer their theory presented in a systematic way.
Genette, Gérard. *Narrative Discourse: An Essay in Method*, trans. Jane E. Lewin. Ithaca, NY, 1980, reprinted 1994. Also the sequel, *Narrative Discourse Revisited*, trans. Jane E. Lewin. Ithaca, NY, 1988. Absolutely fundamental for the discussion of time in the novel and of the narrative situations, even for those readers who are uneasy about the terminology and a certain schematism. Long stretches of the work are a stylistic delight.
Gibson, Andrew. *Towards a Postmodern Theory of Narrative*. Edinburgh, 1996. A deconstructive attempt to overcome the structuralist geometry of narratology – useful in provoking independent thought.

The Novel: An Introduction. By Christoph Bode. Translated by James Vigus. English translation © 2011 James Vigus. Published by John Wiley & Sons, Ltd.
Original German text © 2005 Narr Francke Attempto Verlag GmbH + Co. KG.

Hale, Dorothy J. *The Novel: An Anthology of Criticism and Theory 1900–2000*. Oxford, 2005. A recommendable collection of seminal essays or chapters on the theory of the novel in the twentieth century. Excellent introductions to each section.

Herman, David (ed.). *The Cambridge Companion to Narrative*. Cambridge, 2007. Less theoretical than Phelan and Rabinowitz's *Companion to Narrative Theory* (see below), but still quite ambitious, this *Cambridge Companion* offers, first, a "starter-kit" for studying narrative fiction, then a comparatively meager section on narrative outside literature, and finally "Further Contexts for Narrative Study," whose chapter headings read like a shopping list ("Gender," "Rhetoric/ethics," "Ideology," etc.) of items that somehow have to be covered, though it is by no means clear whether these concepts – and if so, how – form contexts for each other. Less coherent than Herman's *Basic Elements* (see immediately below), less useful than the joint effort of the *Encyclopedia of Narrative Theory* (see below), this *Companion* has essays of varying quality and varying ambition, but is still worth a look.

Herman, David (ed.), *Basic Elements of Narrative*. Oxford, 2009. Suggesting that narrative can be viewed under three different aspects – as a cognitive structure, a type of text, and a resource for communicative interaction – Herman here (as in his 2007 *Companion*) identifies stories as "a basic human strategy for coming to terms with time, process, and change." Exploring what different stories have in common and what changes if one and the same story is told in different media, Herman is particularly illuminating on narratives as blueprints for worldmaking (and world disruption).

Herman, David, Manfred Jahn, and Marie-Laure Ryan (eds.). *Routledge Encyclopedia of Narrative Theory*. London, 2005. Using an excellent system of cross-referencing, this handbook aims to be a comprehensive reference resource "that cuts across disciplinary specializations to provide information about the core concepts, categories, distinctions, and technical nomenclatures that have grown up around the study of narrative in all of its guises." Indispensable.

Lanser, Susan S. *Fictions of Authority: Women Writers and Narrative Voice*. Ithaca, NY, 1992. Groundbreaking, influential attempt to fuse feminist criticism and narratology.

McKeon, Michael. *The Origins of the English Novel 1600–1740*. Baltimore, 1987. A good and welcome correction of and supplement to Ian Watt (see below).

Mezei, Kathy (ed.). *Ambiguous Discourse: Feminist Narratology and British Women Writers*. Chapel Hill, NC, 1996. One of the finest collections of feminist narratology: ambitious, demanding, highly sophisticated.

Moretti, Franco (ed.). *The Novel. Vol. 1, History, Geography, and Culture, Vol. 2, Forms and Themes*. Princeton, NJ, 2006. A selection from the original five-volume Italian work *Il romanzo*, published between 2001 and 2003. Global in its aim and scope, the collection has also a number of essays on the pre-modern novel and on the novel outside Europe. Volume 2 contains fine pieces by (among others) Thomas Pavel, Fredric Jameson, Umberto Eco, and A. S. Byatt.

Mullan, John. *How Novels Work*. Oxford, 2006, 2008. Drawing on Mullan's *Guardian* column, this book is addressed to the general reader. Curiously anti-academic and anti-theoretical as well as almost exclusively focused on

English-language novels, it is endearingly unsystematic, non-technical, and in places oddly fuzzy, but it contains some valuable insights. (Has sections on "Weather" and "Meals," too, under "Detail." And one on "Parenthesis," under "Style.")

O'Neill, Patrick. *Fictions of Discourse: Reading Narrative Theory*. Toronto, 1994. Probably one of the most seriously underestimated works of recent years: the argumentation and examples are refreshingly clear and free from any kind of dogmatism.

Phelan, James and Peter J. Rabinowitz (eds.). *A Companion to Narrative Theory*. Oxford, 2005, 2008. A superb collection of essays that covers, among other subjects, the (im)possibility of narrating the history of narrative theory; narrative form and its relationship to history, politics, and ethics; and the future of narrative. Has also essays that treat "stubborn problems" like unreliability or focalization and others that engage in narratologically inspired new readings of fiction. Highly differentiated on narrative outside literature. A must.

Preminger, Alex and Terry V. F. Brogan (eds.). *The New Princeton Encyclopedia of Poetry and Poetics*. Princeton, NJ, 1993. This reference work of literary criticism and literary theory is a very hard act to follow in terms of latitude, rigor, and depth.

Stanzel, Franz K. *A Theory of Narrative*, trans. Charlotte Goedsche, preface by Paul Hernadi. Cambridge, 1984, 1986. An indispensable classic. Not the least of its fine qualities is the flexibility of its approach and its emphasis on the heuristic function of our analytical instruments.

Toolan, Michael J. *Narrative: A Critical Linguistic Introduction*, 2nd edn. London, 2001. A linguistically based, no-nonsense introduction.

Watt, Ian. *The Rise of the Novel*. Harmondsworth, 1957, 1974. Widely disparaged in the last three decades or so, Watt's classic offers a still valid, gripping, and highly informed account of how the modern realist novel came into existence in England in the eighteenth century. The narrative sweep and integrative power of Watt's *grand récit* and of his textual analyses have yet to find their match.

Index of Authors and Critics

Note: This index refers not only to pages on which a particular author is explicitly mentioned by name, but also to pages on which allusions to the respective author's work occur. For instance, a reader who looks up Mark Twain will be directed to page 23, where the first word of Twain's novel *The Adventures of Tom Sawyer* is quoted: "Tom!".

The Novel: An Introduction. By Christoph Bode. Translated by James Vigus. English translation © 2011 James Vigus. Published by John Wiley & Sons, Ltd.
Original German text © 2005 Narr Francke Attempto Verlag GmbH + Co. KG.